LETTERS *from* PRISON

MARQUIS *de* SADE

LETTERS *from* PRISON

Translated and with an
Introduction and Epilogue by Richard Seaver

Arcade Publishing • New York

FIRST EDITION

Letters number 76, 77, 83, 108, and 109 from *Justine, Philosophy in the Bedroom, and Other Writings of the Marquis de Sade,* translated, compiled, and edited by Austryn Wainhouse and Richard Seaver. Copyright © 1965 by Richard Seaver and Austryn Wainhouse. Used by permission of Grove/Atlantic, Inc., and revised for this edition.

A fragment of the Introduction, entitled "An Anniversary Unnoticed," appeared in *Evergreen Review* in 1964, marking the 150th anniversary of Sade's death.

Library of Congress Cataloging-in-Publication Data

Sade, marquis de, 1740–1814.
    [Correspondence. English. Selections.]
    Letters from prison / the Marquis de Sade ; translated from the French and with an introduction by Richard Seaver. — 1st ed.
      p.   cm.
  ISBN 1-55970-411-X
  1. Sade, marquis de, 1740–1814—Correspondence. 2. Authors, French—18th century—Correspondence. I. Seaver, Richard. II. Title.
  PQ2063.S3 A83 1999
  843'.6—dc21   97-43150

Published in the United States by Arcade Publishing, Inc., New York
Distributed by Time Warner Trade Publishing

10 9 8 7 6 5 4 3 2 1

PRINTED IN THE UNITED STATES OF AMERICA

To the memory of
Gilbert Lely
through whose perseverance these letters were recovered

and to
Jean-Jacques Pauvert
whose courage under fire was exemplary

The translator would like to express his gratitude to Professor Robert Darnton for his gracious and generous help in verifying certain facts and characters of Sade's universe.

"My manner of thinking, so you say, cannot be approved. Do you suppose I care? A poor fool indeed is he who adopts a manner of thinking to suit other people! My manner of thinking stems straight from my considered reflections; it holds with my existence, with the way I am made. It is not in my power to alter it; and if it were, I'd not do so."

—*Sade to his wife [November, 1783],*
Letter Number 83

" . . . it is impossible for me to turn my back on my muse; it sweeps me along, forces me to write despite myself and, no matter what people may do to try to stop me, there is no way they will ever succeed."

—*Sade to Abbé Amblet [April, 1784],*
Letter Number 94

G. Corvel inv. et sc.   SADE. TOME I.

Contents

Introduction   1

Note on the Letters   41

Part One: Letters from Vincennes   45

Part Two: Letters from the Bastille   349

Epilogue   381

Frontispiece: Four of Sade's prisons. Clockwise from top: Miolans, the Bastille, Pierre-Encize, and Vincennes. This nineteenth-century engraving served as the frontispiece of Maurice Heine's 1883 anthology of Sade's works. Reprinted from Maurice Heine, *Œuvres Choisies et Pages Magistrales du Marquis de Sade*, volume 1 (Paris: Editions du Trianon, 1883)

Introduction
by
Richard Seaver

In mid-November 1814, the newly appointed student doctor to the insane asylum of Charenton on the outskirts of Paris, L. J. Ramon, age nineteen, noticed as he made his rounds an aged, obese inmate, carelessly dressed, always alone, remote but courteous, gentlemanly of manner, who ambled slowly along the corridor outside his room. The man, he was told, was incurably insane and had been in the institution for more than eleven years. Ramon was struck by the man's imposing air, despite his age and obesity. Roughly two weeks after that first encounter, the old man received a visit from his son, who, finding his father much weakened and no longer able to walk, asked Monsieur Ramon to spend the night with him. During the evening, Ramon helped the man take a few sips of herbal tea to help ease his pulmonary congestion. Shortly before ten, since he noted his patient had increasing difficulty breathing, Ramon got up to fetch him a drink. Surprised by the sudden silence from the bed behind him, Ramon turned back to find that the old man was dead. At the time, the fledgling doctor still had no idea that his charge was the infamous Marquis de Sade. More than fifty years later, writing about his early memories of the inmate, Ramon noted:

> Never once did I catch him talking to anybody. As I passed I would bow and he would respond with that chill courtesy that excludes any thought of entering into conversation. . . . Nothing could have led me to suspect that this was the author of *Justine* and *Juliette;* the only impression he produced on me was that of a haughty, morose, elderly gentleman.

Eight years earlier, Sade had written his last will and testament, specifically setting forth the site and manner of his modest burial, asking that his body be borne to his property at Malmaison near Epernon, and there, "without display or pomp of any sort," a ditch be dug in a copse that he specified, and his body laid therein.

> The ditch once covered over, above it acorns shall be strewn, so that the spot may become green again, and the copse grown back thick over it, the traces of my grave may disappear from the earth as I trust the memory of me shall fade out of the minds of all men. . . .

Despite his express instructions, Sade's wishes were ignored, and he was given what amounted to a pauper's burial in the cemetery of Charenton. As for his desire—surely sincere—that he be forgotten, in that too he was contravened. His works were banned, burned, and destroyed; his descendants, starting with his son Donatien-Claude-Armand, all bearing the cross of his presumed shame, did their best to make sure his memory indeed faded from the minds of men. Yet his name, however maligned, lingered on throughout the nineteenth century, both in the public mind and, later, in the dictionaries and etymologies of the world. That name, in its pure and associated forms—sadism, sadist, sadomasochist—became synonymous with the gratuitous infliction of pain, the pursuit of wanton pleasure, delight in cruelty, especially excessive cruelty, specifically in the context of sexual release. His works—those that survived the censor's sword or the family's pyre—were spoken of (if at all) in hushed tones. Few were available to the public, though copies of some of the early editions of *Justine, The New Justine, Juliette*, and *The Crimes of Love* remained locked up on the top shelves of private libraries.

In the early part of the twentieth century, however, a number of enterprising and daring spirits, not content with the then current legend, began to examine Sade's works more closely and came to the conclusion that there was much more to both the man and the myth than had hitherto been admitted. At the turn of the century, a German, Dr. Iwan Bloch, writing under the name of Eugène Dühren, published a study, *The Marquis de Sade, His Life and Work*, simultaneously in Berlin and Paris in 1901. A few years later, the poet Guillaume Apollinaire wrote his groundbreaking and daring *Work of the Marquis de Sade*, in a collection of classics aptly entitled "The Masters of Love." With that one work Sade was if not resurrected at least a fit subject for drawing room—and sidewalk café—discussion. But it was not until after World War II that the Sadean rehabilitation began in full force, perhaps in part because the world had seen, through the ravages of that monstrous war, the full evil of which man was capable. In any event, the French surrealists, the pioneering biographers Maurice Heine and Gilbert Lely, the Mexican poet Octavio Paz, the writers Simone de Beauvoir and Pierre Klossowski, and perhaps most daringly and courageously, considering the powerful forces of censorship then prevailing in France, the French publisher Jean-Jacques Pauvert, who in the 1960s undertook the gargantuan task of issuing, at great personal risk, the complete works of Sade, all rank among the sturdy pioneers in this phoenixlike endeavor. So successful was the resurrection that in the second half of the twentieth century there were voices proclaiming Sade as one of the seminal thinkers not only of the eighteenth century but of all time, a precursor to Nietzsche, Stirner, Freud, Krafft-Ebing, and the surrealists. Simone de Beauvoir hailed him as a "great writer," adding that he "must be given a place in the great family of those who wish to cut through the banality of everyday life." If today evaluations are less dithyrambic, more measured, the fact remains that Sade still enjoys a measure of respect far greater than he ever could have imagined in his wildest dreams.

Yet, even in this presumably enlightened age, to pronounce the name Sade in polite company (or even impolite) generally draws a skeptical if not disapproving look, a knowing guffaw, a remark that, however seemingly innocuous, is fraught with negative implications: Why is someone like *you* involved with someone like *him?* (Such a question presumes judgments about both parties that are, in all probability, far from the mark.) The fact is, despite all redoubtable efforts to rehabilitate him by contemporary scholars and writers, Sade remains a marked man, as he was during most of his lifetime, and those in any way involved with him and his writings are generally assumed guilty by association. That is doubtless how Sade would have liked it, for however the world might judge him, he was without question one of the great rebels of history. Doubting everything, attacking everything, railing against society, religion, and authority in all its forms, excoriating laws and the courts, bewigged judges, corrupt prosecutors, venal police, decrying hypocritical clergy, he reached the only philosophical conclusion that such an attitude demanded if taken to its extreme: utter anarchy, in which no law or official constraint impeded the freedom of the individual—especially if that individual was the marquis himself.

Sade was different from most men, physically and psychically, as he was the first to recognize. On the one hand, he had insatiable and, putting it mildly, bizarre sexual appetites, and at the same time he suffered from a sexual dysfunction that made it increasingly difficult to satisfy those imperious appetites. In a moving letter to his wife written from the Bastille, probably in late 1784, he expounds candidly on the problem, which, he notes, is becoming increasingly acute, adding that he intends to seek immediate medical advice as soon as he is free. By the time he was in his mid-thirties, if not before, Sade fully recognized his difference—his "separateness," as de Beauvoir terms it—and set about not only justifying it, which he does endlessly both in his work and his extraordinary letters, but analyzing it. What clearly emerges from these letters is the extent of Sade's self-awareness. "Know thyself," said the philosopher, and Sade spent endless hours, thanks in great measure to the thousands of hours of solitude imposed upon him by society, in the introspective search for who and what he was *au fond*. Society's intent, he believed, indeed its mandate, was to skewer separateness by forcing the individual to integrate into the community: thus the uncontrolled rage in his writings against those who would try to inhibit him, control him, make him conform. Yet ironically Sade was in a very real sense a conformist; as a proud aristocrat, from one of the oldest and most distinguished families of Provence, he wanted, and strove to be, a member of the community. He wanted all the rights and privileges of the reigning establishment, but none of its restrictions. Obviously, he could not have both. As de Beauvoir noted in her pioneering essay, "Must We Burn Sade?" written some fifty years ago:

> Sade tried to make of his psycho-physical destiny an ethical choice; and of this act, in which he assumed his separateness, he attempted to make an example and an appeal. It is thus that his adventure assumes a wide human significance. Can we, without renouncing our individuality, satisfy our aspirations to universality? Or is it only by the sacrifice of our individual differences that we can integrate ourselves into the community? This problem concerns us all. In Sade the differences are carried to the point of outrageousness, and the immensity of his literary effort shows how passionately he wished to be accepted by the human community. Thus we find in his work the most extreme form of the conflict from which no individual can escape without self-deception. It is the paradox and, in a sense, the triumph of Sade that his persistent singularity helps us define the human drama in its general aspect.

This volume collects most of the surviving letters that Sade wrote during his more than thirteen-year imprisonment in the dungeons of Vincennes and the Bastille, and the Charenton Asylum, from 1777 to 1790. He was thirty-seven when he went to prison this time (he had been in prison several times before, once in debtor's prison and thrice for offense to the morals of the kingdom), and when he was freed, on Good Friday, 1790, he was fifty, vastly overweight from lack of fresh air and exercise (and also, despite all his grumbling about prison fare, from overeating), his health virtually ruined, his burning appetites banked to embers. Despite the fact that he had been released by the

Revolution, he was an aristocrat and, more dangerously, allied to the royal family by birth and background. A free man at last, he was in this brave new society fully as vulnerable as he had been inside those dank, airless prison walls about which he complains so often and so eloquently in these letters. But what is perhaps most remarkable about this undoubtedly remarkable man is that, for all that he had gone through and suffered—and these letters do attest to the full extent of that suffering, a word that occurs probably more often than any other in his fulminations—his spirit was far from broken. He had read widely and eclectically in prison, had written feverishly in several genres—novels, short stories, philosophy, plays—and had formulated a literary master plan that was wildly ambitious, especially given his age and health. (In addition to his increasing corpulence, he suffered from migraines, serious eye problems, chest pains, and hemorrhoids.)

Whether his motive was revenge or enlightenment, during his prison years and the twenty years that followed, he produced a body of work that is unique. Whatever else he was, Sade was pure—admittedly a surprising term in his connection; he cut through, with a terrible swift sword, the hypocrisies of the day, the cant, the false, the sham, be it sacred or profane. A sybarite beyond compare, endowed with a sexual appetite that was prodigious, hot tempered, arrogant, prone to violence yet capable of great tenderness and acts of kindness, this most contradictory of men can only be understood—if indeed he can be understood at all—in the context of his time. Who, in fact, was this man who wrote four of the most outrageous novels ever penned: *Justine, Juliette, Philosophy in the Bedroom,* and *The Days of Florbelle?*[1]

First, make no mistake: Sade was a libertine, as he was the first to admit. In his self-styled "Grand Letter" written to his wife from the dungeon of Vincennes to mark the anniversary of his fourth year incarcerated there, Sade says:

> Yes, I am a libertine, that I admit. I have conceived everything that can be conceived in that area, but I have certainly not practiced everything I have conceived and never shall. I am a libertine, but I am neither a criminal nor a murderer, and since I am

---

1. Only the first three survive. *Conversations from the Château de Florbelle,* or *The Days of Florbelle* as it came to be known, was seized by the police in 1807. After Sade's death, Sade's son Donatien-Claude-Armand not only gave the order that it be destroyed but personally witnessed the manuscript's burning.

obliged to place my apology next to my justification, I shall therefore say that 'tis quite possible that they who condemn me so unfairly are in no position to offset their infamies by good deeds as patent as those I can raise to compare to my misdeeds. I am a libertine, but three families living in your section of the city lived for five years on my charity, and I rescued them from the depths of poverty. I am a libertine, but I saved a deserter from the military, a man abandoned by his entire regiment and his colonel, from certain death. I am a libertine, but at Evry, with your entire family looking on, I saved at the risk of my own life a child who was about to be crushed beneath the wheels of a cart drawn by runaway horses by throwing myself beneath the cart. I am a libertine, but I have never compromised the health of my wife. . . .

That admission, coupled with a cursory reminder of some of his offsetting good deeds, can be taken literally. The author of *The 120 Days of Sodom* was capable of acts of kindness and charity, of true friendship and deep devotion, as these letters will attest. They are in fact perhaps more revealing of the many sides of Sade than anything more formal he wrote or said. One can also take at face value what he says in that same letter about conceiving of a great deal more in the realm of libertinage than he ever practiced. Condemnation of the man for over a century was based in large part on the presumption that Sade had done everything he described in such excruciating detail, therefore was either a criminal or mad, probably both. As usual, the truth is much more complex and subtle. Sade, who as these letters reveal was much given to introspection and self-analysis, was born with huge appetites and a violent temper. Add to this that he was born into a society where aristocratic privilege in the areas of sex and sensuality were taken for granted, and only rarely admonished, and that he came from one of the oldest and noblest families of France, allied through his mother directly to royal blood, and one sees the possibility of unfettered behavior from the earliest age.

In a letter of April 25, 1759, written when he was not yet nineteen, Sade, who was already a captain in the cavalry, fighting the Prussians during the Seven Years War, wrote to his childhood tutor, Abbé Amblet:

I rose every morning to go in search of pleasure and the thought of it made me oblivious to all else. I believed myself fortunate the moment I found it, but what seemed happiness evaporated as quickly as my desires, leaving me with but regrets. By evening I was desperate and saw my mistake, but that was evening; with a new day there were my desires back again, and back I flew to pleasure.

Though he apparently gave an excellent account of himself as a cavalry officer, his regimental commander in the Burgundy Horse wrote in 1763, shortly before Sade was discharged from the army at the age of twenty-two, "terrible things" about the young man: "He was a gambler, a spendthrift, and a profligate. He spent all his leisure hours lurking backstage at local theaters, looking to pick up some pretty actress, and he frequented the houses of procuresses." Reading the memoirs of the time, however, creates the impression that the gay blades of the latter half of the eighteenth century looked upon amorous conquests as a kind of competitive game. As actresses, demi-mondaines, and courtesans rose to prominence through either their beauty or their sexual prowess (or both), men vied against one another for them, and if a man could not steal that season's pick from her prevailing lover, he would often content himself with the number two or three position in his mistress's heart (and her pocketbook, for lover number one bore the brunt of her expenses, and those lower on the ladder paid incidentals and frivolities). To frequent whores, singly or in group, though not satisfying the same competitive instinct, was still common practice, with no stigma attached and certainly bearing little or no threat of official retaliation on the part of the police vice squad. That is why, in many of his prison letters, Sade rails against being singled out for what so many others, he rightly claimed, were doing with impunity.

How is it, then, that this proud aristocrat, who traced his ancestry back to the thirteenth century, specifically to Laura, the wife of Hugues de Sade, Laura the beloved of Petrarch and object of the poet's love poems, ended up spending some thirty of his seventy-four years behind bars? How could this man, whom the poet Guillaume Apollinaire termed "the freest soul that ever lived," endure roughly half his adult life in jail? Was Sade, as the world would have us believe, a danger to society, a man who, had he been free, might well have acted out the fantasies of his fictions and lived a life of crime, raping and maiming and killing along his fateful path? As suggested, the letters in this volume tend to belie that; the more likely scenario being that it was prison, with all its physical and mental restrictions, that gave rise to his literary scatology and cruelty, his obsessive and gleeful descriptions of sexual encounters and combinations such as the world had never seen. Deprived of freedom, this born rebel, this ardent anarchist, this "freest of men," took revenge against his enemies, both real and imagined, in the only way he knew how: by fantasizing to the extreme. Prison gave him the time to write, which would have largely eluded him had he been living outside, engrossed first in the pursuit of pleasure, then in defending his outrageous acts against the powers that would consort to do him in—be they the police, the judiciary, or his own family—all of whom provided him the grist for his wild, and incredibly fertile, imagination. Throughout the letters, he writes with vitriolic pen of those who he believes are responsible for his being behind bars, who are out to get him. Enemy Number One is his mother-in-law, the présidente de Montreuil,[2] who (to Sade) not only sought but reveled in her endless revenge against him. Revenge for what, one might ask?

The litany of allegations, or what Sade would minimize as "misdeeds" or "errors of youth," is long and complex. One should bear in mind, however, that his misconduct, if that is strong enough a term, took place not only in the context of an extraordinarily permissive society but in a family for whom pleasure, especially sexual pleasure, was a dictate and goal. To know the son, then, one must know the father.

Jean-Baptiste Joseph François de Sade, born in 1702, bore the title Count de Sade[3] and was the first member of the family to turn his back on his native Provence and try his luck in the Paris of Louis XV. Armed with letters of introduction from his father, who vainly tried to dissuade him from leaving the gentle southland for the spite and malice of the court, the handsome, intelligent young Provençal quickly made a place for himself in the courtly whirl. He had a ready wit and "an astonishing talent for composing short pieces in prose or verse" that won him the admiration of the fashionable women of the time and impressed the men. Not surprisingly, the count set out to conquer not just the minds of the women but their hearts as well, and succeeded to an astonishing degree. The number and quality of his mistresses is legendary, even by the libertine standards of the day, and included

---

2. Sade's father-in-law, Claude-René Montreuil, was president of the Court of Taxation. As such, his wife had the right to be called "présidente," and whenever that title is used here, it refers to Madame de Montreuil.
3. The titles "count" and "marquis" were used alternately from generation to generation. When Sade's father died early in 1767, he therefore assumed the title "count," though history has linked him forever under his original title.

several of the fairest and most highly placed ladies of the court of Louis XV (not to mention both sisters of his friend and protector, the Prince de Condé). Thus we can say without exaggeration that the young marquis's propensity for libertinage came naturally to him, *de père en fils*. Today the term "role model" would spring to mind.

Politically, the count's ambitions equaled his amatory skills, and early in his Paris stay he managed to ally himself with the Prince de Condé, scion of the illustrious Bourbon family. Through the Condé connection, Sade *père* made himself both a military and diplomatic career of considerable distinction. He was a colonel in the pope's light cavalry and lieutenant-general for the provinces of Bresse, Bugey, Valromey, and Gex (a title purchased, not earned, but nonetheless one that had to be approved by the king, who awarded them stingily). He was briefly ambassador to the court of Russia, minister plenipotentiary to the Elector of Cologne, and the principal negotiator in concluding the alliance between France and Spain in 1741. During the decades of the 1730s and 1740s the count's reputation as a skilled negotiator grew impressively: indeed, as he approached the age of forty he had to feel that he had, despite his father's warnings, unquestionably made the right decision in forsaking Provence for the glittering capital.

The count had not hastened to marry: there were too many hearts to conquer, if only for a week or a month (or even a day) to think of marriage. But in 1733, the count, at age thirty-one, did marry the lady-in-waiting to the young Princess de Condé. The bride was Marie-Eléonore de Maillé de Carman, a Bourbon by blood but relatively impecunious. It was not a love marriage—in those days few were among aristocrats—but in the context of our Sadean epic the count's methods and motives are especially meaningful. Thirteen years after the death of his first wife, the Prince de Condé had remarried: his choice was a German princess, who was by all accounts utterly ravishing, and who, at fifteen, was almost twenty-five years younger than her new husband. Seeing her, the count made up his mind he must have her. But how, since the prince, insanely (and rightfully) jealous, kept her under close and constant guard? Through her lady-in-waiting, of course. Thus Sade the Father's marriage to Mlle Maillé de Carman was an act of total duplicity, a clever but completely cynical means of hopefully bedding the Princess of Condé, wife of his patron and protector. Morality aside, as libertine behavior, it ranked among the best (or worst).

In his later years, the count constantly accused his son of wanton profligacy and libertinage, venting his disapproval and fears, especially in letters to his younger brother the Abbé de Sade, that Donatien would be the ruin of him. A classic case of memory lapse, because by the time the count had penned these dire concerns about his son, he had already done a rather masterful job of running through the family fortune himself. His tastes were sumptuous, his ambitions large, his financial restraints virtually nil. If one were to compare father and son as profligates, the count would win hands down.

One of the grave charges against the marquis, for which he served long years in prison and for which he was sentenced to death in absentia, was that of sodomy. *Quelle horreur!* But here again, look to the father: police reports of the time show that, however many fair mistresses he seduced, Jean-Baptiste was known to frequent the Tuileries Gardens, to solicit the favors of young men. At one point, in fact, he was arrested for soliciting a male prostitute, who turned out to be a police decoy, but the count's name and exalted position kept him (barely) out of jail. *Tel père tel fils.*

And then there was the count's brother, the Abbé de Sade, a cleric of some distinction—vicar general of Toulouse, later vicar general of Narbonne. This high-ranking man of the cloth was entrusted with the education of his nephew when Sade was only five, largely because Sade's father, finding it hard to deal with the boy's ardor and violent temper, essentially abdicated his paternal responsibilities and turned them over to his brother. From 1745 to 1750 the future marquis's education was entrusted to his uncle, largely at the Château de Saumane in the Vaucluse region of southern France, a castle that still exists today in much the same state it was in when Sade was growing up: Its dark, forbidding air, its remote, austere setting on a craggy promontory overlooking the tiny village of Saumane and, beyond, the lush valley of the Vaucluse, and especially its underground network of dungeons and cells had to have made a deep impression on the boy, impressions that would later find voice in many of his major fictions. So too must his uncle's scarcely concealed amorous exploits have affected young Sade. At one point the abbé kept at the château a mother and daughter, of whom he apparently made frequent and indiscriminate use. He also was the known protector of an infamous local prostitute. In fact, throughout his life the abbé was an active and shameless libertine, and at one point, despite his name and title, was imprisoned for several days on the charge of debauchery, arrested in Paris "in the house of the woman named Peron, given to debauchery, together with the prostitute Leonore." Further, during his years in Paris, the abbé always had as his mistress a certain Madame de la Polelinère, who also happened to be the mistress of the Maréchal de Saxe. Writing later of those years at Saumane, Sade describes his uncle's abode as a veritable seraglio, then corrects himself: "No, it was a bordello." If a man of God could permit himself such license, what restraints could either church or state impose on one as hot-blooded and independent as he? Early on, then, Sade witnessed—and loathed—the hypocrisy of convention, the arbitrary and restrictive laws and customs whose purpose, he became convinced, was to rob the individual of his own special character with which nature had endowed him at birth.

In his novel *Justine*, Sade rightly qualified the eighteenth century as "an age of total corruption." And in *Juliette* he has Saint Fond, clearly modeled after one of Louis XV's ministers, say: "What a fool a statesman would be not to let his country pay for his pleasures. What does the people's misery matter to us if only our passions are satisfied." Leading the dissolute way was Louis XV himself, whose Parc-aux-Cerfs at Versailles, constructed in 1750, was well known by the populace to be a veritable seraglio, which the king's mistress, Madame de Pompadour, constantly restocked with a bevy of young beauties to satisfy the king's desires. The clergy, which might have acted as a brake on the excesses and narrowed the widening gap between people and state, was often as bad as the court itself. Sade's uncle, the Abbé de Sade, was as we have seen no better than his dissolute brother. And the abbé was far from alone: police reports and records of the time, including those of Sade's nemesis Inspector Marais, are filled with reports of the clergy's unfettered debauchery, from one end of France to the other.

Thus as the eighteenth century advanced steadily toward its explosive conclusion, young aristocrats like Sade thought themselves beholden to no one, accountable to nothing save their own pleasures and desires. As Sade would later write in his novel *Aline and Valcour*, in a passage that is surely autobiographical:

> Born in Paris in the lap of luxury, as soon as I could think for myself I came to the conclusion that Nature and fortune had combined to heap their bounties upon me. I thought this because people were stupid enough to tell me so, and that idiotic presumption made me haughty, domineering, and ill-tempered. I thought the world was at my feet, and the entire universe would serve my slightest desire. If I wanted something, all I had to do was take it.

Until he was ten, Sade did not attend any schools. His uncle engaged for his instruction at Saumane a tonsured young priest, Abbé Amblet, with whom Sade would remain friends for most of his life. In the fall of 1750, Sade was sent off to Paris to continue his education at the Louis-le-Grand College on the rue St-Jacques, a Jesuit institution that catered to the children of high aristocrats and was reputedly the most expensive school in Paris. Abbé Amblet came along to provide additional tutoring. "I returned to Paris," wrote Sade, writing of Amblet, "to continue my studies under the guidance of a man who was both strict and intelligent, and who would probably have been a good influence on my youth, but unfortunately I did not keep him long enough." Young Sade and Abbé Amblet took up quarters on the rue Fossés Monsieur-le-Prince, around the corner from the school and a stone's throw away from where his mother was living at the Hotel de Condé. We know little of Sade's years at Louis-le-Grand, but one aspect—unique at the time—of the school's curriculum had to interest him especially: the good fathers stressed the literary, especially drama, and were famous for their theatrical productions. Surely Sade's lifelong interest in the theater stems from that period.

For some inexplicable reason, Sade's father aborted his son's education when the lad was only fourteen, and at the end of the school year in 1754 sent him off to join the army. For the next five years Sade served his king not only honorably but with distinction, acquitting himself well in a number of battles during the Seven Years War. By the time he was nineteen he was captain in the king's cavalry, and he remained in the army till February 1763, when the Treaty of Paris ended the war. But if he was a good soldier he had also devoted much of his time and energy during these nine long years to the dual indulgences of garrison life: gambling and wenching. So ardent were his efforts in both fields that his father, again conveniently forgetting his own youth, lamented to his brother and a number of other friends that his son was—ye gods!—a libertine and, worse yet, a profligate! It was time, the father decided, to find Donatien a wife. Preferably—no, necessarily—a wealthy one. For in his heart of hearts Sade's father knew that he alone, by his overreaching political ambition and lavish spending during his more than forty years in Paris, had managed to accomplish what none of his forebears had: squander the family fortune. Only he knew the extent of the financial debacle, only he knew that his son the marquis, he of the violent temper and scathing tongue, would shower his father with blame when he learned of it. How unduly alarmed he was about the possibility that his son, by 1758 a captain in the cavalry, would make further inroads into his declining if not wholly depleted estate is shown in a letter to his brother the abbé in which he deplored the fact that young Donatien had promised not to gamble more than a louis a day, hardly a princely sum. "As if that scoundrel had a louis a day to lose!" he wrote. "He promised me not to risk more than an ecu."

The way out of his financial morass, the count decided, was to marry off the marquis into a family of high position, he hoped, but in any case, one of impeccable means. After several unsuccessful attempts—Sade's reputation as a rake had preceded him—he settled on a family of lesser nobility, the Cordier de Montreuils. They were only recently ennobled—in the previous century—but they had excellent connections at court and, more important, were solidly wealthy. Through them, the Count de Sade must have figured his own fault of financial recklessness might be redeemed and the family fortune recouped. Sade's early biographer, Gilbert Lely, believes the count was acting out of baser motives: referring several times in letters to his "no-good son," who in his opinion was "a bad buy" for whatever family he married into, the count very simply wanted his son out of his life. Forever. One has to wonder why, for until then the sins of the Sade family had been largely the father's, not the son's. Still, as the count wrote his brother, if he could pull off this marriage, he'd "be rid of the boy." Sade had to have felt his father's dislike, and if filial obedience had had any restraining effect upon him till now, it was certainly now cast aside.

Sade had openly and often declared that he would marry only for love, and putting his words into practice at the same time his father was in deep and delicate marriage negotiations with the Montreuils, Donatien managed to fall madly in love with a young beauty he had met in Paris whose lineage was as long and glorious as his: Laure-Victoire Adeline de Lauris. What was more, she was a Provençal lady of the manor in Vacqueras, a town not far from La Coste, so there was an added geographic affinity. Soon after they met, she yielded to his ardent advances, but unlike his other mistresses, this one Sade truly wanted for his wife. A letter discovered in 1948 in the Bibliothèque Nationale by Sade biographer Gilbert Lely revealed not only the existence but the depth of the affair. Laure's father, the Marquis de Lauris, agreed to the young man's proposal of marriage, but suddenly she herself resisted. The more she did, the more inflamed Sade became. It would be difficult to understand her change of heart—it was clear she and Donatien were passionately in love—without the knowledge that at some point in the spring of 1763 Sade contracted a venereal disease, which he doubtless passed on to his mistress. More to the point, Sade's father learned of his son's illness just as he had finally concluded negotiations with the Montreuils.[4] If ever they were to learn of Donatien's condition, the marriage would be off. Sade, in Provence now, was still courting Laure-Victoire and refusing his father's urgent pleas to come back to Paris. Finally, only two days before the scheduled date for their marriage, Sade showed up, displaying little inclination for this creature he was to marry, this Renée-Pélagie who, he had been told, was neither attractive nor very feminine. But the die was cast: thanks to the count's influence and importuning, the king had agreed personally to sign the marriage contract, an act that so flattered the Montreuil clan, especially Sade's future mother-in-law, Madame la présidente de Montreuil, that all else was forgiven. On May 1 the two families journeyed to Versailles to be officially introduced at the court. The only person lacking was the bridegroom, who had still not renounced his hopeless suit to sway his beloved Laure. In fact, despite his father's and his uncle's cajoling and threats, Sade did not arrive in Paris till the afternoon of May 15, less than 48 hours before the wedding was scheduled to be celebrated.

So, despite all his brave declarations, Sade married not for love but for money. As he had been forewarned, his bride Renée-Pélagie was no beauty. She had been a bit of a tomboy, cared little about fashion or dress, but she was plucky, unpretentious, had a good head on her shoulders, and in her letters, despite the almost childish hand, she shows intelligence and, for the most part, sound judgment. She would need all that and much more to cope with the hand she had been dealt, for though she went into the marriage open-eyed—her mother had warned her about some of the characteristics and shared with her some of the escapades of her husband-to-be—she had no inkling of what she was really getting into. Who could have? Yet she felt grateful to her parents—especially her mother, who ruled the roost with an iron hand—for having secured her not only a handsome husband but one who allied her to royal blood. And, after all the prenuptial Sturm und Drang, the newlyweds seemed to settle into a routine of Paris high society life. Several letters and reports of the time refer to the young marquis as pleasant and seductive, attentive and loving to his wife; the

---

4. Learning of his son's "illness," the Count de Sade immediately assumed it was the lovely Laure who had given his son "the pox." Hardly likely.

most oft-repeated word is "charming." Even his mother-in-law, who had had grave misgivings earlier, was completely taken by her son-in-law. "Your nephew could not be more charming or more desirable as a son-in-law," she wrote the Abbé de Sade the day before the marriage, "with that genial intelligence of his and that tone of good education that your care seems to have instilled in him." Later, she wrote Sade's father that he was sorely mistaken in judging his son so harshly. Her feelings about him are understandable: in many ways the présidente and Donatien were kindred souls: egotistical, authoritarian, ambitious (albeit in different ways), energetic, brutal, unscrupulous. That is doubtless why she was so drawn to him at first; that is also why she turned on him with such vengence when, as time went on, he betrayed—in her eyes—the trust she had placed in him.

In these prison letters, it is interesting to see how Sade can convincingly assume one persona with one correspondent, then almost immediately adopt a second when addressing another. Sade's letters to Madame de Montreuil, for example, are alternately contrite, entreating, endearing, flattering, seductive—he presses all the old buttons that once worked with her, for in the early days of his marriage she had been utterly won over by his undeniable charm, and he still hoped one might do the trick. Now none did: once she had decided Sade had, irrevocably in her opinion, demeaned her, betrayed her personal trust, and besmirched the family honor, no reconciliation was possible. All her many talents were focused on making sure her son-in-law—whom she was convinced was mad—remained behind bars so that he could do no further harm. It was not so much the judgment of society she was worried about, it was her family, the reputations of her children and grandchildren. Her once good name was by the time Sade entered Vincennes for the second time in 1777 compromised almost beyond redemption. From her viewpoint, Sade was, if not mad, certainly a man to try the most patient of souls.

After several months of relative quietude Sade's debauching—and blasphemous—impulses took over. In mid-October 1763, just five months after his marriage, Sade left his wife behind in the country and came to Paris on the pretext of business. On the night of October 18 he took a prostitute, a woman named Jeanne Testard, to his rented room on the rue Mouffetard on Paris's Left Bank. In the eighteenth century, it must be repeated, it was common practice—noblesse oblige—among men of the upper class to practice marital infidelity with a vengeance. Marriage was a business arrangement, and children were part of that pact. But a man's real pleasure had to be sought outside the marriage bed. Women's obligations at the time were to be dutiful spouses, as they had sworn to be before God at His altar, serving their husband faithfully and humbly, and sexually according to their husband's whims or demands but without any thought of providing him pleasure, much less enjoying any on their own. Thus the mere fact of Sade—or anyone else—going with prostitutes bore no stigma and certainly was not considered a crime. But with Jeanne Testard, Sade, who throughout his life loved to provoke trouble if it arrived on its own volition, upped the ante: whether out of true conviction or as a sexual stimulant, Sade spent the night blaspheming God, Christ, and the Virgin Mary and forcing Jeanne to do the same, trampling on crucifixes and reviling the Church and all its works at the top of his lungs. In the morning, when her procuress came to fetch her, Jeanne related her ordeal and went straight to the police. One of those to whom she went was Inspector Louis Marais of the Paris vice squad, who as it happened had been assigned to watch Sade, among other young aristocrats, and who would be involved with Sade's fate for many decades. (Several of the letters in this volume are to Monsieur Le Noir, lieutenant-general of the Paris police, and Marais's superior.) Marais put together a dossier containing Jeanne Testard's deposition and those of other prostitutes Sade had frequented and forwarded it to the king, who, having voraciously read and savored the report (Louis XV reportedly delighted in hearing in full detail the lubricious reports of his subjects' wayward indulgences), ordered Sade's arrest. On October 29, accompanied by Marais, Sade was incarcerated in the dungeon of Vincennes. His crime was not debauchery—half the court would have been imprisoned if that "crime" had been applied—but blasphemy and profanation, which was far more serious in the eyes of the law.

Was Sade an atheist? Some Sadean commentators have taken his private and public stance against God and the Church, and especially the violence thereof, as proof that he really deeply longed for belief, but this argument is extremely difficult to justify. For Sade, who thought in increasingly universal terms as he matured, God was a chimera, and his blasphemies were meant both to provoke and to prove His nonexistence. He viewed religion and all its trappings as a gigantic lie, a hoax used to oppress, tyrannize, and deprive the individual of his freedom and his true nature, which he believed was unique in each of us. That being so, Sade, to be true to himself, needed to desecrate and despoil, to publicly voice his conviction. If you believe something to be true, Sade would say, you must carry it to its extreme, no matter what the consequences.

In jail now for blasphemy, Sade was mainly concerned with keeping the scandal from his wife—who was three months pregnant—and his wife's family. His father soon heard the bad news and hastened to Fontainebleau to beg the king's indulgence, which was granted, and on November 13 Sade was released from Vincennes but confined to his parents-in-law's property, the Château d'Echaffour, under the watchful eye of Inspector Marais. In understanding his letters from his later, thirteen-year incarceration in Vincennes, one can be edified by those he wrote in those early years. In a letter to Monsieur de Sartine, the lieutenant-general of police, Sade—imprisoned for desecrating the Almighty—invokes the name of the deity not once but thrice, and asks for a priest "by whose good guidance and my sincere repentance I may soon be in a position to come to those holy sacraments, the complete neglect of which had become the first cause of my fall." In distress— and much of his life was spent in distress—Sade would stoop to anything, assume any guise, repudiate any stance, to gain his end. He could grovel in mortification if that's what it took, he could cajole, beg, lie, castigate, cheat, charm, flatter. Only in his letters to his wife could he be himself; only to her could he bare his heart. Despite the enormous variations in the tone and tenor of the letters to his wife—in some he is the most loving, the tenderest of men, while others drip in sarcasm tainted with vitriol—one senses that in these alone is a direct line to his real self. Which brings us to the enigma of the true relationship between this "infernal couple." Reading Sade's letters to his wife over this span of thirteen years, one cannot help but be struck—even while deploring the loss of many of her corresponding letters to him, which would have been utterly revealing—by the sheer amount of undisguised affection and love they contain. True, Sade had married beneath himself, for the Montreuils were of new money, the paint of their aristocracy barely dry, whereas the Sades' aristocratic roots ran deep. True, Renée-Pélagie was not the raving beauty he had dreamed of marrying; true, she was a simple woman, with scant taste for elegance in word or dress, so completely unlike the courtesans and coquettes with whom he was so often besotted. Even her own mother, though skirting the word *ugly*, stressed her qualities of "reason" and "gentleness" in describing her to the groom's uncle. But Renée-Pélagie was nobody's fool. She was a woman of great common sense, dedicated beyond belief, resolute, faithful to a fault, and possessed of a native intelligence that more than made up for her lack of formal education. Reading these letters, one senses a bond between them that was inviolable, forged by mutual trust and mutual pain.

As a young woman, the future Madame de Sade was what can fairly be described as a dutiful daughter. When her impending marriage to the young marquis was announced to her, she accepted it not only with good grace but with gratitude. She was made acutely aware of the fine catch the family had made. (Sade's father had already turned on the charm with the présidente, who was so flattered by the match she could barely contain herself, even after she heard more than one disquieting story about her future son-in-law's antics and tastes, even after she learned, weeks before the marriage, that he was suffering from the pox!) Cowed by her overbearing and overweening mother in her youth, Renée-Pélagie found during the fourteen years she had lived with Sade the courage to defy the présidente, to stand up for her husband against all charges and accusations—indeed against all proof that what he deserved in fact was her scorn. She revealed herself to be far more than a dutiful wife. Given as a pawn in a business transaction in which she had had no say, she ended up loving this miscreant, this utter scoundrel who betrayed her physically in more ways than anyone can count. Most Sade biographers and commentators see in Renée-Pélagie a passive, unimaginative creature completely in thrall of her forceful husband, a simple masochist to his ... well ... sadism. True, from prison he sometimes issues orders to her as if he were still a cavalry captain charging the enemy; he insults her when his errands and commissions have not been fulfilled in a timely manner, charging her with indolence and neglect. But beneath and beyond all that is a tenderness, a caring about her health, her well-being, her state of mind. And when in her infamy the présidente, alone or through intermediaries, tries to make Sade believe his wife has taken a lover, his jealously is unfeigned, his fury knows no bounds. This from a man who wrote endlessly of the need for woman's emancipation from the servitude—sexual and otherwise—to which society condemned her. Even for a chameleonlike creature such as Sade, there is an underlying current of care and concern in his letters to his wife (which constitute well over half the letters in this volume) that cannot be denied.

There is no question in my mind that she loved him. Yet we cannot help but wonder why, given that Sade gave her dozens, nay hundreds, of reasons to loathe him. It was not only the nocturnal forays into all of the capital's bordellos that would have him (Inspector Marais had forbidden some madams to allow Sade into their houses, so wild was his reputation), Sade also had had, early in his marriage, the effrontery to parade his mistresses publicly—to concerts, theaters, and receptions. Barely two years after his vows, he took one mistress, the actress and demimonde known as La Beauvoisin, down to La Coste, where he passed her off as Madame de Sade to the villagers. (Since they had never seen the real marquise, he had no trouble doing so; later he would deny on his most solemn word of honor that spiteful charge.) That gratuitous and heedless act was the beginning of the end for Sade, for it alienated Madame de Montreuil, who till then had, despite all his "lapses," supported her son-in-law and continued to believe he would eventually "come around." Now, she noted in a letter to Sade's uncle the abbé in midsummer of 1765, she would no longer take part in the effort to change him. Severity, she says, seems to have had no more success with him than kindness. Still, in 1765 they were twelve years from the major incarceration, and despite her declaration to the abbé, many subsequent acts on her part demonstrate that she had not given up altogether on her charming scoundrel. By his libertinage, she reasoned, he was proving that he was at heart a conformist, for he was doing no more or less than so many of his contemporaries in this jaded world. And if he were at heart a conformist at age twenty-five, then at thirty and forty that same conformism would cause him to change accordingly, as happens in each generation. Just look at his father: he had been an outrageous libertine; he had been a freemason and atheist. Yet now he had turned to philosophy and writing, had refound God and become a true believer. Who was to say the son would not evolve in the same manner?

What a misjudgment! While it was based as much on wishful thinking as anything else, Madame de Montreuil could not have imagined the lengths to which Sade's predilections, impulses, and beliefs would take him. Even the Jeanne Testard affair was a pale precursor of outrages to come. The ubiquitous Inspector Marais—who seemed to have had not only a strange fascination for his job but for Sade in particular, as if he sensed that of all the rakes and reprobates under his scrutiny this one was special—kept close tabs on the marquis, and two years after the Testard scandal, he rightly predicted that the world would doubtless soon hear more of the horrors of "Monsieur le comte de Sade."[5]

Madame la présidente de Montreuil is the person to whom history attributes, or blames, the long and painful incarceration of the

---

5. In referring to the count, Marais of course meant our marquis.

marquis. In addition to what had already transpired to try the good lady's patience, there were four key events in Sade's life that determined her not only to turn her back on him completely but also to bend her every effort to make sure he was put behind bars for, she hoped, the rest of his life. Had it not been for the Revolution, which brought a swift end to her influence and power, she doubtless would have attained her goal. There were other elements, of course, but these four led directly to his doom, not only because of their special nature but because they became, despite Madame de Montreuil's efforts, fodder for the increasingly popular newspapers and broadsheets of the day. As today, scandal was the be-all and end-all of these papers' existence. The first was known as "The Arcueil Affair," the second "The Marseilles Affair," the third (and most important from the viewpoint of Sade's ultimate condemnation), "The Seduction of Lady Anne," and the fourth, "The Young Girls' Scandal." The first occurred in 1768, the second and third hard upon each other four years later, and the fourth during the winter of 1774–1775.

For some time Sade had kept a cottage in the Paris suburb of Arcueil, to which he repaired frequently for his affairs—all of which were duly recorded by the ubiquitous Inspector Marais. On Easter Sunday 1768—and that fact is important—Sade had his valet bring two prostitutes to the house. Sade arrived somewhat before noon accompanied by a woman he had picked up at the Place des Victoires in Paris, promising her the job of housekeeper. The woman, Rose Keller, a widow, was a cotton spinner by trade who had been out of work for a month and reduced to begging in the streets. Inside, Sade ordered her to undress; she refused, but complied when Sade threatened her with a knife. Subsequently he whipped her, then, she claimed, cut her backside with a pen knife and poured sealing wax in the wounds. Later locked in an upstairs room, she managed to escape at about four in the afternoon and report the incident to the local authorities. This was precisely what the authorities had been waiting for: an innocent woman, not a whore, bound and tortured by the evil marquis. While the police and legal authorities of Arcueil proceeded with their investigation, the indomitable Madame de Montreuil sprang into action, motivated less by the desire to save her son-in-law than to preserve the family's good name. She convoked the ever-faithful Abbé Amblet and the trusted attorney Maître Claude-Antoine Sohier and dispatched them to Arcueil to buy off Rose Keller. Simultaneously, she sent her husband to speak to his friends with influence at the court: the only way to nip the incipient scandal in the bud was to have the king issue a *lettre de cachet*[6] sequestering Sade in a royal fortress before the case was brought to the public courts. The plan worked, or so the family thought: Sade, accompanied only by his ex-tutor Abbé Amblet, journeyed to the royal prison at the Château de Saumur, where he was duly incarcerated. From there he wrote a deeply apologetic letter to his uncle begging his forgiveness and adding: "If people get wind of this affair down there, tell them it's all a terrible pack of lies and say that I am with my regiment. . . ." In other words, dear uncle, lie through your teeth. But what Sade was learning to his distress if not edification was that public opinion was having an even greater effect on a population that was increasingly fed up with the so-called misdemeanors of the aristocrats, whose sexual indulgences were rarely punished with any severity. Sade made a perfect scapegoat: not only did he not conceal his predilections and practices, he tended to boast of them. For a man who abhorred hypocrites, to do less would have been to become one himself. But his candor and honesty were only feeding the public's fury. "At this time he is the victim of the public's ferocity," wrote Sade's beloved Madame de Saint-Germain[7] to his uncle on April 18. Be that as it may, from now on Sade would be a marked man, as he began to realize. Did that sure knowledge impel him to reason? Hardly, as events will show.

Paying off Rose Keller was the easy part. Her demands were exorbitant—the price of silence in matters of scandal always comes high—and in this instance it was 2,400 livres, plus seven gold louis for medicines. Once again, Madame de Montreuil had triumphed, or so she thought. But in fact even the king's *letter de cachet* could not save Sade this time. The criminal chamber of Parlement—or high court—in Paris, seized the information gathered by the Arcueil villagers, convened an investigation, and issued a warrant for the arrest of the marquis, who was already in jail under the king's warrant. If Parlement was aware of this situation, it chose to ignore it, perhaps subtly hoping

---

6. A royal warrant bearing the king's seal that took precedence over other legal documents and offered no appeal. It had the added virtue for wayward nobles of taking their case outside the workings of the normal judicial system.
7. One of Sade's two surrogate mothers (and probably a former mistress of Sade's father). When Sade was a student at Louis-le-Grand, he spent part of at least one summer, and perhaps two, at Madame de Saint-Germain's country home. She loved the boy and lavished all sorts of kindnesses upon him. Sade, whose relations with his mother were virtually nil, remained devoted to Madame de Saint-Germain throughout his life.

to thwart the Montreuils' preemptive strike and play on public opinion. Part of the problem, for Sade, was that the head of Parlement was one Charles de Maupeou, long an archenemy of Monsieur de Montreuil, who saw a rare opportunity to discredit the family. In addition, in those days, only two decades before the Revolution, efforts were being made by various members of the judiciary to undercut the king's authority. In all likelihood, first in issuing its warrant, then, when Sade failed to respond (which he could hardly do since he was already in prison), sending the official crier to trumpet in Paris, including under the Montreuils' windows, that "the gentleman Sade" must appear in person for trial, the high court was trying to establish its legal authority over that of the king. Meanwhile, the prisoner, after being transferred from Saumur to the less lax prison of Pierre-Encize—ostensibly an act of sovereign kindness to keep him out of the clutches of the Paris criminal court—was granted a letter of annulment by the king on June 3. In the tug of war between the court and the judiciary, such a royal pardon was final, and essentially expunged the case from the books, much to the chagrin of President de Maupeou. The high court, with de Maupeou presiding, met and approved the king's decision. In all this, once again the long arm of Madame de Montreuil could be seen. Now, purely for form, the prisoner was brought to the Conciergerie in Paris for trial on June 10, where he was nominally fined "alms of one hundred livres to be used for bread for the prisoners of the Conciergerie." After that he was returned to Pierre-Encize to await the king's pleasure for release. On November 16, 1768, the king ordered Sade to be released and sent to his estate at La Coste. Thus Sade's first long-term acquaintance with prison life—by now he had been in jail seven months—was over. The question was, had it proved a sobering experience? The answer came in the form of a resounding no less than four years later.

The second event that sealed his fate with the long-suffering Madame de Montreuil began to unfold in the afternoon of June 23, 1772, when Sade and his valet Latour set off from La Coste for Marseilles, ostensibly to attend to some business there. In fact, he and Latour spent the next five days visiting the city's bordellos. On the fifth day Sade ordered his valet to round up several girls—all prostitutes—and a "meeting" was scheduled for ten o'clock in the morning at the house of one of them, Marie Borelly, on the rue d'Aubagne, for Sade rightly judged that to indulge the fantasies he had in mind he needed privacy. There Sade and Latour proceeded to hold a matinal debauch involving five prostitutes, all of whom whipped the gentlemen and

were whipped by them in turn, with Sade dictating the action and
sometimes reversing roles, calling his valet "Marquis" and referring to
himself as Lafleur, and, in one further strange twist, keeping a concrete count of the beatings he had received.[8] But the heated action,
which went on for at least two hours, was not the cause of Sade's impending downfall: from a little gold-rimmed box he had in his coat, he
took out some aniseed candies, whose sugar coating was soaked with
the extract of what is commonly known as Spanish fly, and tried to
force them on the girls. Only one, Marianne Laverne, ate any, though
another pretended to but spit them out. That same evening he amused
himself—alone this time—with another prostitute, Marguerite Coste,
whom he convinced to down even a greater quantity of the aniseed
candies. The following day, his sexual appetite presumably satiated,
Sade and Latour peacefully returned to La Coste by postal coach. But
the pastilles he had fed the two girls were having an effect that would
cost the marquis dearly. The most severely afflicted was Marguerite
Coste, who fell ill the same night she had been with Sade and whose
condition worsened over the next two days, during which she was
wracked by terrible vomiting. A doctor was summoned, and when he
heard the source of her illness he reported it to the police. Convinced
the man with the pastilles had tried to poison the girls, the police had
the vestiges of the girls' regurgitations—plus two untouched pastilles
found at Marie Borelly's place—analyzed and found absolutely no
trace of poison. Puzzled, the police never thought of Spanish fly, which
can be dangerous if taken in more than moderate doses. Sade's doses
were clearly immoderate, and Marguerite Coste came close to death,
so close in fact that she was administered last rites. The police took depositions from all six girls, and on July 4 a warrant was issued for the arrest of both Sade and Latour. Before it could be carried out, however,
someone came to La Coste to warn the marquis of the impending
danger, adding that one of the "poisoned" girls had died and now
the marquis and his manservant would be arrested for murder. Sade
and Latour beat a hasty retreat. Anne-Prospère de Launay, Renée-
Pélagie's younger sister by eleven years, who had been visiting at La
Coste for some time, also disappeared, and one could only suppose she
had, inexplicably, followed the marquis into hiding. When she resurfaced several days later, she was in a state of great agitation. Thus
Renée-Pélagie was left by herself to face the music and deal with the

---

8. Later, investigators would find notches carved in the mantelpiece, the anal
marquis's recording of the number of beatings he endured.

police, who arrived in large numbers, headed by the bailiff of Apt. Finding neither of the accused, and being told by one and all—the marquise, the notary Fage, the townspeople, the servants—that both men had been "away" for a good week now, the police finally left. As usual, in her despair Renée-Pélagie turned to her mother for help and succor, but the présidente wanted no part of this new development. She had bailed out her son-in-law for the last time, she declared, not because his conduct this time was even worse than the others, but because she had by now learned from good authority what she had feared but refused to believe before, namely that Sade had done the unthinkable, even for him: he had seduced her young daughter, Anne. To his many other crimes against not just society but, far more important, the family, he had now added the unthinkable: incest. To make matters worse, Renée-Pélagie, her formerly docile elder daughter, seemed to accept this quite unacceptable situation. As for Anne-Prospère, Anne-the-Pure, Anne the canoness, she had apparently fallen madly in love with her mad brother-in-law.

The seduction and debasement of Anne-Prospère was the third event, and the one that finally pushed Madame de Montreuil over the edge, that caused her to shift her allegiance and expend all her energies henceforth to isolate and incapacitate her son-in-law, to have him put away where he could do the family no more harm. Henceforth, if she had her way, they would lock him up and throw away the key.

Unlike her mother, however, Renée-Pélagie was far from ready to give up on her husband. That was, and remains, one of the great Sadean mysteries: How, after such conduct, with clearly not the slightest remorse on his part, could she remain so attached to the man? So faithful to him? So in love with him? In any event, in early August she managed to round up four thousand livres and set off for Marseilles where, enlisting the help of a local notary, she managed to buy off Marguerite Coste and Marianne Laverne, both of whom agreed to withdraw their charges. A victory, yes, but after several days in Marseilles she returned to La Coste in shock, for while there she had heard all the gossip, seen the scandal sheets, listened to all the wild rumors about her husband—one of which maintained that the marquis had poisoned his wife because he had fallen in love with her younger sister. The port city seethed with stories about and hatred for her husband, whose latest case seemed to be all anyone was talking about. The story was fast escalating into fantasy, and the magnitude of the marquis's crime exploded with each retelling. Memories of Arcueil resurfaced. Why had he been let off so leniently then? It *was* true that there were two levels of justice, one for the aristocrats, another for common folk; a scapegoat had to be found, if only to appease the popular anger, which was growing day by day.

Later that month Renée-Pélagie's father arrived at La Coste, presumably to visit his two daughters, salvage Anne-Prospère if he could, see what he could do to keep the lid on this latest scandal, and use his personal connections among the judiciary to influence its decision regarding his son-in-law. Monsieur de Montreuil was an excessively passive man—la présidente ruled the roost almost single-handedly—and at sixty he surely did not come all the way from Paris, a journey of several days, on his own. He came at the instigation and demand of his wife, to seal Sade's doom.

On September 2, the royal prosecutor handed down his decision. Sade was found guilty of poisoning and he and Latour were both found guilty of sodomy.[9] Both were required to "expiate their crimes at the cathedral entrance before being taken to the Place Saint Louis, where a scaffold was to be erected, and there Sade was to be beheaded and Latour hanged or strangled until he was dead, after which their bodies were to be burned and their ashes scattered to the wind." On September 11 the Parlement of Provence confirmed the prosecutor's sentence, and the following day both Sade and Latour were burned in effigy on the Place des Prêcheurs in Aix. Though the act was symbolic, for Sade

---

9. In truth, Sade was guilty of neither in the strict sense of the term. When asked if the marquis had sodomized them, all the girls said they would never commit such a horrible act; for them to have said the contrary would have put them in jeopardy, because sodomy, though practiced frequently enough in the whorehouses of the time, was by law punishable by "death by fire" and the victims' ashes scattered to the wind. If sodomy there was, it was between the two men, which was not in question by the prosecution. As for poisoning, two master pharmacists of Marseilles, who examined the unused pills and regurgitations of the two girls, found no traces of arsenic or any other corrosive matter. That he used Spanish fly is unquestioned, but so did hundreds if not thousands of other bordello clients. In fact, pills containing the substance were known in France as Richelieu's pills, for he himself was a known exponent. Used in moderation, Spanish fly had been known since Roman days as an effective aphrodisiac. Sade's crime, obviously, was having given both girls what amounted, in today's parlance, to an overdose.

Years later, in his letters from Vincennes, Sade is still arguing not his innocence but his "right" to use such an aphrodisiac, which, he maintains in one of his letters to his wife, whores are well aware of: "There are, I think, very few who do not know what it is," he writes.

it had grave repercussions, because he was stripped of his civil rights. From a libertine and dissolute, the Marquis de Sade was henceforth a marked man, a fugitive from justice, his name and acts linked in infamy in the press and in the minds of the public. Though he would escape the verdict of the Marseilles court, he would be guilty, fettered even if not behind bars, condemned for the rest of his life. To make sure, Monsieur de Montreuil had set off for Aix-en-Provence on September 7 to confer with the authorities of the appeals court to which the Marseilles sentence had been referred and to try to accomplish a dual and delicate task: make sure the case was handled in such a way as to bring no dishonor to the family name and see to it that his son-in-law was, once and for all, prevented from doing any further damage.

But it was already too late. Sade had decamped, fleeing as fast as the Provençal coaches could take him, to Italy, where he traveled under the name of the Count de Mazan.[10] The damage he was inflicting even more deeply on his wife's family—not to mention his wife herself—was his choice of companion, for Anne-Prospère de Launay had fled with him. They went first to Venice, thence on to several other Italian cities. Then, abruptly, and for reasons still unknown, Anne left her brother-in-law—and all her baggage—and returned to La Coste on October 2, roughly a month after their idyllic flight had begun.

What of this incestuous relationship between Sade and Anne-Prospère? How could a well-brought-up young lady who, barely past twenty and presumably pure not only of heart but of body—she was a canoness when she appeared at La Coste to visit her sister and brother-in-law—engage in such a total act of folly that she must have known would ruin her relations with her sister, her parents, and endanger her own future? Sade's every act was now followed avidly, and this most juicy tidbit could scarcely be kept out of the press.[11] There is no simple answer, but there are some reasonable surmises. At thirty-two, Sade was still attractive, possessed of an undeniable charm, and highly seductive. Anne-Prospère could also see that her sister, once submissive and unassertive, had taken on a new air: despite all her husband's myriad escapades and betrayals, all the scandal surrounding him, it was

10. Sade took the name from one of the ancestral properties he owned in Provence, the Château de Mazan.

11. Though under the law newspapers could say nothing disparaging about aristocrats, the foreign press and broadsheets—a kind of underground press—were under no such restriction and thrived on scandal, especially royal scandal.

obvious that Renée-Pélagie still loved the man and was ready to defend him to the last ounce of her energy, to such a degree in fact that she was fully prepared to stand up even against their tyrannical mother. What manner of man could have wrought such change in her older sister? For the young canoness, the temptation to be seduced, to taste those forbidden pleasures that had had such a tonic effect on Renée-Pélagie, must have been strong, especially there in the confines of La Coste, where the marquis felt completely at ease and could be his most charming, seductive self. From Sade's point of view, the temptation must have been even greater, although he knew—as he surely did—that he was courting trouble. One senses that, if anything, the threat of trouble, of unredeemable scandal, acted on him as an aphrodisiac far more powerful than Spanish fly.

After Anne-Prospère deserted him, Sade left Italy and settled in Chambery, then a part of Piedmont and Sardinia. After roughly a month of secluded existence in an isolated house he had rented outside that city, Sade, who was still traveling incognito under the title the Count de Mazan, was arrested one evening upon a warrant from the king of Sardinia and incarcerated in Fort Miolans, which was known as the Bastille of the Counts of Savoy. How had the marquis's real identity been discovered, and why had a foreign king issued a warrant for his arrest? Very simply, the présidente, to whom Sade had rashly written a letter revealing his whereabouts, immediately set about having him clapped behind bars. For the next four months he remained at Fort Miolans as the most famous, but also the most closely watched, prisoner in the keep. In March, the indomitable Marquise de Sade journeyed to Savoy disguised as a man and made desperate efforts to visit her husband, to no avail. On the night of April 30, by as clever a ruse as the novel or theater has ever invented, Sade, another prisoner, the Baron de l'Allee, and Sade's manservant Latour escaped from the impregnable fortress. Thence Sade and Latour made their way back to La Coste.

For the better part of the next four years Sade remained in and around La Coste, with occasional discreet forays to other French cities, as well as venturing abroad on another extended trip to Italy. Early in 1774, Madame de Montreuil made an abortive effort to have Sade arrested at La Coste, but the marquis had his loyal local informants, who forewarned him in time to go into hiding until the arrest party had given up and departed. Though master of his domain, Sade was still very much a fugitive. He and his wife made efforts to have the Marseilles sentence quashed, and to that end she made several trips to

Paris, though with scant success. Sade's name was too hot, and the Montreuil influence and money too powerful, for any minister or magistrate to rule in his favor. In fact, after the death of Louis XV on May 10, 1774, one of the présidente's first acts was to request that the *lettre de cachet* issued by the late king, which was no longer valid, be reinstated by the new regime. In the fall of that year a new *lettre de cachet*, ordering Sade's arrest and incarceration in the prison of Pierre-Encize, was duly issued by the court of Louis XVI.

Despite that, it is possible—not probable but possible—that if Sade had behaved reasonably at this point in his life—and each would have to define for him- or herself the precise meaning of that term— further prison might never have been his lot. The présidente's secret attempt to have him arrested in January had cost her a small fortune— over eight thousand livres—and she may not have been of a mind to mount another such expensive expedition in the near future. Still, feeling himself constantly menaced in France, Sade decided in March to emigrate to Italy, leaving Renée-Pélagie behind to handle his affairs and pursue his legal appeals. After several months there, however, plagued by a shortage of money and bored for lack of language and "activity," he returned to France in late September, meeting his wife in Lyons. There he—or perhaps they together—sowed the seeds of the fourth scandal, which would irrevocably seal both their fates. In that city and despite their groaning finances, the Sades engaged several servant girls, plus a young male secretary for the marquis, for their needs at La Coste. One of the girls, Anne Sablonnière, also known as Nanon, was twenty-four; the others were probably no more than fifteen or sixteen. Given their age, her husband's known predilections, and the fact that she had just pawned the family silver to raise money, one has to wonder why Renée-Pélagie ever allowed herself to be involved in their hire, for she had to know that nothing but trouble lay ahead. All we can assume is that by now, stripped of any illusions about her husband she might ever have harbored, she had become his full and willing accomplice.

Precisely what went on at La Coste during the winter months of 1774–1775 is not known, for little evidence remains. Much of what we know stems from Sade's "Grand Letter" to his wife, but since this letter is largely self-justification, it can hardly pass for fact. In it Sade does maintain, and is probably right, that Nanon was a well-known procuress in Lyons, and that since the other servants were in turn either hired or approved by her, they all had to be aware of what they were getting into. In other words, despite their tender age he looked upon all six as prostitutes and felt he could treat them as such. We do know that during that several-week period in December and January Sade and his little menagerie rarely left the château. Darkness fell early, and few if any locals were invited inside, probably to keep prying eyes and wagging tongues distanced. In a letter to his attorney Gaufridy, in the late fall of 1774, inviting him to dinner—which was to take place at three o'clock sharp—Sade painted a saintly picture of himself, totally immersed in his work, which consisted of research and writing, and of domestic tranquillity on the part of Madame de Sade and her staff. In all likelihood, however, Sade was really spending the greater part of his time in those dark months indulging in two of his favorite pastimes: the theater and erotic play. His libertinage far from stilled, his status as fugitive very much in his mind, he literally closed the château doors to the outside world and created within the close confines of La Coste his own fantasy drama, with himself as director and leading man. In all probability, Renée-Pélagie was also involved, but in what role and to what extent it is hard to say. She had been married to the man for more than eleven years now and knew him as no other did: his insatiable appetites, his uncontrollable willfulness, his obsessions, his profligacy (demonstrated anew by his hiring so many servants without any notion how they would be paid), his arrogance, his pride, his egocentricity, his seductive charm, his tireless energy. However much he tried her patience, however much he abused her, betrayed her, took advantage of her, she loved him unconditionally. If her role was to be long-suffering, so be it. If it was to pick up the pieces after him, she would stoop to that, too. If his heedless propensity for getting into trouble led him to the precipice, she would pull him back. At least, she must have thought as winter closed in around La Coste, no matter what he dreams up as fantasy entertainment, he is here with me, I know the cast of characters we are involved with, which is better than not knowing where he is or what new mischief he is up to.

That cast included, in addition to the new hires from Lyons, a couple of servants already in place: Sade's valet Carteron, also known as La Jeunesse, and his mistress, a Swiss chambermaid, Gothon Duffé, whom Sade describes in one of his letters from prison as being possessed of "the most beautiful a—— that ever managed to escape from the mountains of Switzerland in over a century." Rounding out the troupe were a Mademoiselle Du Plan, a former ballet dancer from Marseilles, who bore the title of governess (though there were no children to govern, unless one includes the new teenage recruits); a young lady from Montpellier named Rosette; and Nanon's niece. Plus a number of cooks and scullery maids who had not necessarily been chosen for their culinary talents. A considerable and varied cast, and it is natural to conclude, both by imagining and from the known repercussions, that Sade put virtually everyone to good exotic use, their exact roles in the winter orgies depending less on their age or experience than on their presumed position. There is no doubt the five Lyons girls were flagellated, as there is clear evidence they were not returned to their parents until their wounds had healed. For those horrified by such an admission, it must be noted that in those days flagellation—often referred to as "the English vice"—was fairly common practice among libertines, as police reports attest. But Sade, like most of his peers, did not employ that erotic stimulus indiscriminately. As far as we know, Sade never subjected his wife or any of his mistresses to any form of flagellation. That rite was reserved for whores, with whom anything went. If one was paying, one could choose whatever one wished, and if the poor girl complained to the authorities, the examining magistrate would ask her if she had received money; if her answer was yes, she was sent packing. And in Sade's view, since he had hired the Lyons servants through a "well-known procuress" there, they were fair, unrestricted game, no matter their age. Nonetheless, once again Sade's rampant sexuality and provocative personality was dragging him ineluctably into the snares of the law.

However restricted the La Coste château, too many people were involved in Sade's theatrical shenanigans—probably as many as twenty—for word not to leak out. Several of the underage servant girls somehow managed to contact their parents in Lyons, who immediately filed charges of kidnapping and seduction. With Gothon in tow, the ever-faithful Renée-Pélagie set off for Lyons to placate the parents, assuring them their girls (and boy) were fine and would soon be home. Meanwhile, three were sequestered in various nearby nunneries, one was kept under close watch at La Coste, while the last, judged the most dangerous by the looseness of her tongue and the seriousness of her wounds, was dispatched to Saumane, where the Abbé de Sade was asked to look out for her—and make sure she didn't escape. Even the jaded abbé was shocked by what his new charge revealed to him, and went on record as not wanting ever to have any dealings with either the marquis or his wife again. Strong words, coming from an old debaucher such as he. Given the abbé's position, it is almost shocking to find that about now, apprised of the gravity of the affair, the présidente waded in and again took charge, issuing orders, generally through Gaufridy, on how to deal with the girls until they were better, how and when to return them to their homes, what to do to obtain written releases, etc. Did this mean Madame de Montreuil had reversed herself, that she was forgiving her son-in-law of this latest aberration? Hardly. All she was doing was, once more, trying to keep a lid on the explosive situation, to save the already badly tarnished family escutcheon. On her basic position of having Sade arrested and put away she was as adamant as ever.

But there were just too many pots boiling in the *vallis clausa* for the présidente to tend them all. During those lurid winter weeks, someone—La Jeunesse? one of the other revelers? Sade himself?— had managed to impregnate Nanon, who gave birth to a baby girl, Anne Elizabeth, on May 11, 1775, but "the paternity was attributed to Nanon's husband, Barthélmy Fayère," and scandal was thereby if not scotched at least muffled.

Moreover, Nanon had too dubious a background herself to do the Sades much harm, or so they thought. But on June 10, 1775, Nanon and the marquise had a violent argument at the château, after which Nanon fled, screaming at the marquise and "showering her with a million imprecations." What was the argument about? It may have had to do with the paternity of her month-old baby; it may have been about money (for Madame de Sade had none with which to pay her); it may have had to do with the young charges she had brought with her for whom she felt (a little late in the day) responsible. Whatever it was, Nanon took refuge in a nearby convent, where she confessed to the prior, Alexandre de Nerclos, all that had been going on at her former place of employ, and since she had often not only played an active role but been the *plat de résistance* at the château revels, she doubtless had a great deal to tell. After hearing her out, the prior wrote immediately to his colleague the Abbé de Sade that his nephew would doubtless "have to be shut up for the rest of his life," adding that he was convinced "Madame de Sade was no better than her husband." Was his opinion based on Nanon's recounting of mad sexual exploits in the dark dungeons of La Coste? No, his complaint was based on the fact that "nobody in that house went to confession on Easter and Lady de Sade allows her young manservants to have dealings with a *Lutheran* woman"![12] Madame de Montreuil pulled some royal strings, managed to have a *lettre de cachet* issued against Nanon, and paid money to have her locked up. But what she was giving with the one hand she was taking away with the other. As noted, with Louis XV's death in May 1774,

---

12. Italics mine.

the *lettre de cachet* concerning Sade's arrest was no longer valid and, legally speaking, he was once again a free man. That also meant his civil rights had been restored, and, theoretically at least, he could regain control of his income and business affairs, now in the hands of the présidente. But Madame de Montreuil was just as aware of this potential development as Sade was and, as we have seen, lost no time in obtaining another royal warrant from the new regime through her friend in court, the duc de la Vrillière.

Had Sade learned anything from the "Young Girls" scandal? Apparently not, for less than a year later he hired another group of young servants, this time from Montpellier and through the good offices of a monk, a Father Durand. The night of their arrival to take up their jobs, they were so upset by the marquis's advances that three of the four left the very next morning. News of the incident reached the father of another girl from Montpellier who had been working as cook at the château since November, Catherine Treillet, affectionately known there as Justine. Fearful for her safety, Treillet, a weaver by trade, set out to fetch her. He arrived at the château and demanded to see his daughter, whom Sade promptly produced. After heated words on both sides, Sade escorted the man toward the main gate, at which point Treillet suddenly turned and fired a pistol point-blank at the marquis's chest. Fortunately (for the marquis), only the primer went off, after which the man turned and fled. Later he returned and fired a second shot into the château courtyard, in the direction of where he thought he heard Sade's voice. Next day the local La Coste judge began hearing witnesses regarding the incident, for the charges were bearing arms illegally and attempted murder. (Commoners in those days were not allowed to bear arms, much less fire them at aristocrats.) Meanwhile Treillet journeyed to Aix where he lodged a complaint against Sade, demanding his daughter back. She in turn signed a document (doubtless drawn up by Sade) saying she was perfectly happy in her work and had no cause for complaint. With all the mounting evidence of former servants telling juicy tales out of school, and the danger that Nanon—who was still in jail under royal warrant—would be released or escape, the only recourse was to send "Justine" back to her father. But when Sade informed Catherine that he was sending her back to Montpellier, Catherine, who like so many others before her seems to have been seduced by the charms of this Provençal Casanova, begged him to let her stay, and he (quickly) relented.

As January faded into February, both the marquis and marquise decided it was time to leave La Coste behind and go to Paris—for two reasons. First, they had received alarming news from Madame de Montreuil that Sade's mother, the dowager Countess de Sade, was failing (in fact, she had died on January 14 and been buried three days later, but word of this had not yet reached them); second, it was only in Paris that they could approach the courts directly and move heaven and earth to get Sade's sentence quashed. All his friends advised him against going. Did he forget, after all, that he was still a fugitive, that a new royal warrant had been issued demanding his immediate imprisonment, that he still had a sentence of death hanging over his head from the Marseilles affair? Since the news about his mother had come from the présidente, did he not suspect a trap? His steward Reinaud, Gaufridy, even Gothon warned him against the trip. But he would hear none of it. Once Sade made up his mind to do something, nothing on the face of the earth could deter him.

He set out accompanied by La Jeunesse, while Madame de Sade had with her Justine, who had asked to come along. After a long, arduous, and fatiguing journey—their coach broke down a number of times and the roads were frightful at that time of year—they arrived in Paris on February 8 and were received warmly by Sade's former tutor, Abbé Amblet, on the rue des Fossés Monsieur-le-Prince. There they learned of the dowager countess's death three weeks earlier, which seemed to affect Sade profoundly, despite the fact that his relations with his mother through the years had been virtually nonexistent.

Madame de Sade went to spend the night at the dowager countess's apartment, and the next day moved into the Hotel de Danemark on the rue Jacob. At nine o'clock in the evening, as Sade was visiting his wife at the Hotel de Danemark, Inspector Marais arrived armed with a *lettre de cachet* and placed Sade under arrest. An hour later he was a prisoner in the fortress of Vincennes. Two days later he was transferred to room 11.

Madame de Sade was beside herself. She blamed the arrest on her mother's machinations, but Madame de Montreuil hotly denied any involvement. "I know nothing about it," she stoutly maintained. Privately, however, she admitted, "Things could not be better or more secure: it was about time."

Thus Sade's thirteen-year calvary as a prisoner began. However upset he was at losing his freedom, he clearly had no idea it would be for long. In fact, Inspector Marais told Sade as they made their way from the Hotel de Danemark to the Vincennes dungeon, the arrest was for his own good—it would speed up the appeals process. The présidente told Renée-Pélagie the same thing.

But in truth the présidente's firm intent was that her son-in-law be kept locked up for as long as possible—hopefully for the rest of his days. She knew how clever and resourceful he could be, how convincing and seductive, but she felt she could more than match him move for move. In the strange symbiosis that joined them, he was now but a pawn and she the queen.

Ostensibly, Sade was incarcerated because his excesses had reached, if not exceeded, the point of madness. Various commentators have tried to argue the pros and cons of Sade's sanity, as it is easiest to dispense with him if he is simply judged insane. But these prison letters seem anything but the product of a demented mind. As Antoine Adam wrote in his preface to the French edition of these letters:

> All these scandals do not prove that Sade's intelligence has been profoundly affected and that he is [at age 37 when he entered prison] living in a state of continued dementia. Without question he is subject to transports of anger that verge on madness. . . . But these are only momentary crises, and once they are over it is probable that he reverts to the basically likable, basically refined person he really is. His intelligence remains generally sound, his behavior is for the most part reasonable. He is even aware of the morbid aspect of his aberrations, though he is not yet at the point of planning to construct a system of morality from them. In an astonishing letter to his wife, written in 1782 [thus five years after his arrest] . . . he says: "In 1777 I was still fairly young; my overwhelming misfortune could have laid the foundation [to reform me]; my soul had not yet become hardened . . ." He dreams of a cure, which, it seems to him, is still possible. . . .
>
> When he enters Vincennes, Sade is not the theorist of evil, the satanic genius that both his devotees and detractors would like us to believe. He is a man far too often invaded by his demons, who lead him into the most shameful follies, and he doubtless makes the most of them and through them satisfies both his sensuality and his pride; but he is also a man who, in his hours of sangfroid and lucidity, realizes the true character of his crises and, far from drawing any philosophy from them, would on the contrary prefer to conceal them.

While prison for Sade, as for most people, is humiliating, infuriating, stifling, maddening—and the letters reflect all this—he has the advantage that, in preparing his revenge, he can channel his boundless energy, his insatiable appetite, his unique experience, and considerable erudition, into a vast, creative act.

Sade is a man of many guises, and like a stag at bay, he will resort to any stratagem, any artifice, to attain his end, which is to regain his freedom. But below the surface of his immediate purpose the essence of the man does emerge in these letters. Both he and Renée-Pélagie know that their every missive will be read by not one but several watchdogs; therefore they constantly have to resort to subterfuge, to pseudonyms and code names, numbers and signals, many of which are often misread and misunderstood, especially by the prisoner. They also write each other at times in invisible ink, inserted either between the visible lines or on a partially blank page at the end of a letter, the purpose being, especially for Madame de Sade, to feed information that the prison censors would not have let pass. Later Sade would reproach his wife for failing to use this subterfuge judiciously, because, he said, her invisible ink jottings were most often nothing but idle banter, whereas if she had used the system properly it could have provided him much needed and much desired information, especially the date of his release, with which he was understandably obsessed.

Doubtless because of that obsession, Sade developed another, which lasted throughout his years in Vincennes and the Bastille and disappeared as soon as he was free, namely a fixation on "signals" in the letters he received from his wife. He would count the number of lines on a page or in an entire letter, the number of times a word or phrase recurred, he would seize on a word that implied or suggested a number or figure, and from these "clues" try to deduce some meaning. In most of these signals he was searching for the date, the month, the year of his release, which he was sure the présidente, and therefore his wife, knew for certain and was refusing to tell him. But he was also searching in these signals for secret information the censors would not allow: when his walks, which were often restricted or eliminated, would be restored; when Renée-Pélagie would be allowed to come and see him; when certain errands and commissions he had requested would be fulfilled. The problem was, his wife maintained—and one has to believe her—that she never sent him any signals, that it was all in his own mind. Sade would for a time believe her and agree to cease combing her letters for these arcane signs, but then he would revert. "You promised not to search my letter for signals," she wrote him two years after his incarceration in Vincennes, "and then you keep going back on your word. Be assured, my dear friend, that if I could tell you what you want to know [the date of his release] I would not use signs. I would state things very clearly."

Concerning these "numbers," these "signals," these "ciphers" Sade again and again refers to in his letters (and in his "Note Concerning My Detention"), Gilbert Lely writes (*L'Aigle, Mademoiselle*, pages 153–54): "In almost all of Sade's letters of this period one meets with allusions to more or less comprehensible numbers which he often calls *signals*. What does this curious arithmetic signify? Imprisoned in Vincennes by *lettre de cachet*, that is, utterly at the mercy of his persecutors' discretion, Sade found himself in tragic ignorance of how long his detention was to last; wherewith he contrived a system of deduction based upon his calculations which, while they may appear ludicrous to us, were in his mind of a nature to reveal the wildly yearned for day of his liberation . . . Actually, the Marquis's troubling arithmetical operations constitute a kind of defense mechanism, a partly unconscious struggle to ward off the despair which, he dreaded, were it to gain the upper hand, would lead to the overthrow of his reason. Absolutely in the dark as to his captors' concrete intentions, Sade is led 'to ferret out the most unexpected points of departure for his calculations,' writes Maurice Heine. 'To his eye everything has the look of a hint of his fate, or perhaps of a mysterious indication that has escaped the censor's notice. His mind fastens desperately upon the number of lines in a letter, upon the number of times such and such a word is repeated, even upon a consonance which, spoken aloud, suggests a figure.' But his efforts are not confined to trying to discover the date of his return to freedom; he also seeks for clues regarding his life while in prison: upon exactly what day will he again be allowed to take exercise? When will Madame de Sade visit him? His wife's letters are the major source from which he mines the elements for his reckonings, and sometimes when the deductions he extracts from them have a baneful or contradictory look, he accuses Madame de Montreuil of having suggested to the Marquise such *signals* as might demoralize or throw him into perplexity."

An example: "This letter has 72 syllables which are the 72 weeks remaining. It has 7 lines plus 7 syllables which makes exactly the 7 months and 7 days from the 17th of April till the 22nd of January, 1780. It has 191 letters and 49 words. Now, 49 words plus 16 lines makes 59 [*sic*], and there are 59 weeks between now and May 30. . . ."

Another: "On March 28 he sent to borrow 6 candles from me; and on April 6, 6 others whereof I lent only 4 . . . Thursday the 6th of January, 9 months after the borrowing of the candles, on exactly the same day 25 were returned to me instead of the 10 I had lent, which seems very plainly to designate another 9 months in prison, making 25 in all?"

And finally: "I know of nothing that better proves the dearth and sterility of your imagination than the unbearable monotony of your insipid signals. What! valets still sick of cleaning boots, workers reduced to idleness? . . . Recently, because you needed a 23, walks reduced by one and restricted to between 2 and 3: there's your 23. Beautiful! Sublime! What a stroke of genius! What verve! . . . But if you must make these signals of yours, at least do so with honest intent, and not so they are forever a source of vexation!"

To date, no one has been able to figure out the exact meaning of Sade's deductions, which, by the way, he never again alluded to once he was free.

These letters, covering thirteen key years—he went into Vincennes a still dashing, still seductive man of thirty-seven and emerged an obese, elderly gentlemen of fifty—in a sense reveal more about this most enigmatic of men than any of his other work. Here he is not putting on a face for the world, he is not posturing or proselytizing, he is not indulging in his outrageous philosophical fantasies of evil, which, as an act of vengeance against "the stupid scoundrels who torture me" (see letter 67), including and indeed starting with the présidente, were his therapy and psychic salvation. In short, in these letters from prison, we are as close to the real Marquis de Sade as we will get. In the letters to his wife, his chief correspondent and confidante, he often expresses his irritation, his frustration, even his hate for her entire clan, but more often it is affection, gratitude, and love that informs them. Renée-Pélagie was the enduring love of his life:[13] his passions were many and varied, but she alone remained true to him, and he both recognized and appreciated that. The terms of endearment he used to her are touching and sincere: *my pet, my turtle dove, miracle of Nature, delight of my eyes, flame of my life.* His frequent concerns about her health and her well-being are heartfelt. One summer when the weather, which had been scorching, turns cold, he hastens to write and order her to take out her warm garments again lest she fall ill. When he learns that on more than one occasion her mother had not provided a carriage when she came to see him, he flies into a rage against the stingy présidente who dared expose his darling wife to the dangers of crossing Paris on foot and unattended.

---

13. In all fairness, after her refusal to see him following his release, Sade took up with a young ex-actress, Marie-Constance Quesnet, whom he also loved.

In his few letters to the présidente, he can be imperious and groveling at the same time, but he understands she wields the power and
controls his fate, and he writes accordingly. In his letters to one of the
few women he loved but never physically conquered, Marie-Dorothée
de Rousset, also known as Milli, Milli Springtime, Fanny, or the Saint,
there is a closeness, a bantering but respectful tone, an intimacy not
found elsewhere. And when, after spending several months in Paris
seconding Madame de Sade's efforts to plead the marquis's cause both
with the présidente and the king's ministers, Milli Springtime writes
him that she is returning to Provence, he writes her a letter of disappointment and disdain that reveals the depths of his feeling for her.
His letters to his attorney, business manager, and boyhood friend
Gaufridy are those of irritated master to recalcitrant employee. While
Sade sorely needs him, increasingly he cannot suffer him, and in his
paranoia—here doubtless justified—taxes him for yielding to the hateful stratagems of la présidente and essentially accuses him of working
for her. His letters to Monsieur Le Noir, the lieutenant-general of police, are generally respectful, both because in the main he had dealt
fairly with the prisoner and had—unlike the Vincennes warden de
Rougemont—treated him as the gentleman he was. As for the latter,
both in the letters to de Rougemont and his references to the man in
his letters to others, Sade's vitriolic pen knows no bounds. As for the
letters to his valet Carteron, a.k.a. La Jeunesse, a.k.a. Martin Quiros
(pseudonyms the marquis made up for his favorite valet), Sade re-
serves a whole other tone, one of teasing and twitting, a complicity that
can only come from those who have been through a lot together (which
they surely had) and whose relationship, even though of master to servant, was one of friendship and intimacy. In his Carteron letters, Sade
displays a rollicking sense of humor completely lacking anywhere else,
with the possible exception of some of his buoyant tales and novellas,
such as the delicious "Mystified Magistrate."

Several years after Sade's death, the need to excavate the Charenton Cemetery caused Sade's grave to be dug up. Dr. L. J. Ramon, now
fully aware of his early patient's fame, attended the exhumation, where
he asked for and received Sade's skull. Phrenology[14] was all the rage
then, and Ramon made a careful examination of the skull. According to
that study, the prominent features of Sade's character were theosophy

---

14. In the nineteenth century, a branch of medicine that maintained that a person's character and mental faculties could be ascertained by measuring the skull.

and benevolence (top of the cranium), lack of combativeness (no exaggerated development behind the ears), no excess in physical love (no exaggerated distance between nostrils). In fact, Sade's skull, Dr. Ramon concluded, "was in all respects similar to that of a Father of the Church."

Later, Ramon yielded to the entreaties of a German phrenologist of some renown, Dr. Spurzheim, and loaned him the skull in connection with a number of lectures Spurzheim was scheduled to give in England and America. Spurzheim died some years later, and no trace of the famous skull was ever found.

Sade would doubtless have highly approved of both Dr. Ramon's extraordinary conclusions about his character and Dr. Spurzheim's supreme carelessness in losing his demon-filled head.

Note on the Letters

It is to Sade's early biographer, Gilbert Lely, that we owe the discovery of the vast majority of Sade's letters from prison, which were "lost" for 150 years. In researching his biography in the late 1940s, Lely came upon the bundle of letters at the Chateau of Condé-en-Brie, the residence of Sade's direct descendant Xavier de Sade, in January 1948. Lely's invaluable find consisted of one hundred seventy-nine letters in all, plus a number of notes, memoranda, and receipts. Lely used them to good effect in his biography—published in two volumes, the first in 1952, the second in 1957—to trace the evolution of Sade's thought and work during that crucial thirteen-year period of his life. During the 1950s Lely also transcribed and published three volumes, consisting of ninety-one of the letters. The three volumes were respectively entitled: *The Eagle, Mademoiselle; The Carillon of Vincennes;* and *Monsieur Six* (the last-named edited with the assistance of Georges Daumas). In 1966 the French publisher Jean-Jacques Pauvert published a thirty-volume edition of Sade's works, the last two volumes of which contained his prison letters. The Pauvert edition added twenty or so letters that had subsequently come to light following Lely's three volumes (the letters in his Condé-en-Brie discovery ended in 1786), and deleted a few of lesser importance from the Lely volumes. To these we have added four important letters written in 1790, immediately following Sade's release, on Good Friday of that year, from the Charenton Asylum to which he had been sent from the Bastille just a few days before that dungeon was stormed on July 14, 1789.

Roughly two-thirds of these prison letters are to his wife, the only person to whom he was allowed to write on a regular basis and also the only person to whom he felt he could open his heart freely. Although they vary greatly in tone and content, and often express exasperation and sometimes drip with disdain, they are, collectively, a tribute to the solidity of the relationship between these two, who have more than once been referred to an "an infernal couple." Lely writes:

> One should never be misled by Sade's biting sarcasms, nor his terrible bouts of anger, whenever his least wishes are thwarted—which are quite understandable in the light of the frightful conditions under which he was being held—about what Madame de Sade's real role was in all this or what her husband's true feelings about her were. Despite all his reproaches and his ever alert suspicions—some of which were perhaps an attempt on his part to spur her on to greater efforts, which he judged too slow or ineffective, given the agony of his state of limbo, he could not be unaware that his wife's entire existence was focused on his liberation, and to achieve that cherished end she would shrink from nothing. For years she bombarded the ministries with her touching pleas. Thus to the extent that he hoped that his letters would escape either the censor's vigil or the indiscretion of Madame de Montreuil, he never hesitated to open his heart to Madame de Sade, and even at times reveal to her his most secret desires, knowing that this woman, who had already offered him so many proofs of her love, would never do anything to harm or hurt him.[1]

Precisely because of this candor, this confidence in his correspondent, we have through these letters insights into the mind and heart of this most scandalous of writers as accurate and truthful as we will doubtless ever have. Lely compares them to "Shakespearan monologues," and Maurice Lever calls them "an epistolary soliloquy unique in world literature," which may be stretching things a bit, but they are indeed of a rare eloquence and honesty, especially those to Renée-Pélagie, and cast a whole new light on the Divine Marquis.

In addition to those correspondents already mentioned, this volume contains letters to the following: Abbé Amblet, his boyhood tutor and longtime friend; his elder son Louis-Marie; the noted Paris oculist Grandjean and his son, both of whom treated Sade for his serious eye

---

1. Gilbert Lely, *Vie du Marquis de Sade*, rev. ed. (Paris: Au Cercle du Livre Précieux, 1966), Book V, p. 236. References to and quotes from Lely refer to this edition.

problems in prison; Commander de Sade, his elderly uncle, who under the influence of la présidente tried to convince the marquis to give him a power of attorney so that he could manage his nephew's affairs (he failed); Chevalier du Puget, the king's lieutenant-general at the Bastille, who befriended Sade; Monsieur de Montreuil, the président, from whom Sade requests a sum of money; Madame Le Faure, a longtime servant of the Sades; Sade's beloved aunt, Gabriella-Eléonore de Sade; and Monsiur Reinaud, one of Sade's stewards. There are in addition a few open letters: an Evening Prayer; a letter to the entire officer corps of the Bastille; a presumed exchange with a Paris columnist relative to a famous prisoner of the Bastille (himself); an affidavit relative to an altercation between him and one of the prison guards; and the aforementioned letter addressed simply "To the Stupid Scoundrels Who Are Tormenting Me."

Most of Sade's letters, as one can see by the samples of the originals in this volume, were written in an excellent and elegant calligraphy, with very few erasures or changes. The longest is sixteen pages, but most cover one or both sides of a single sheet or, in some instances, two sheets. Lely rightly notes that most if not all were written at a single sitting, with no preliminary draft, which makes their power and cogency all the more remarkable.

A few remarks on the translation:

—The ellipses in the letters are Sade's, who tended to use them rather freely and indiscriminately, and unless otherwise noted do not indicate an omission.

—In those few instances where there is a seeming or obvious omission, we have so indicated by the bracketed [*words missing*]. In a few instances—letters 31, 52, 56, 61—parts of the letters are indeed missing, and that too we have noted.

—Sade was enamored of the semicolon, and we have upon occasion, where sense dictates, used full stops to divide some of his longer sentences into logical parts. Otherwise we have kept faithfully to the original punctuation.

—There are times when Sade does not follow a question with a question mark but rather a full stop or exclamation point. In most instances we have followed standard stylistic usage and inserted question marks, unless it seemed logical that an exclamation point should prevail.

—All italics in the text, unless otherwise noted, indicate Sade's own underlining of words and passages.

—For the most part, we have followed Sade's paragraphing, but in a very few instances, where there was an obvious shift in mood or subject, we have begun a new paragraph where Sade does not.

As for the dates, most of the letters are undated, or bear only the day but not the month or year. Lely and others since have, by various references in the letters themselves or by cross references, managed to date them fairly precisely. But to differentiate those with specified dates from those without, the latter have been bracketed.

In his letters, Sade refers to various monies current at the time: ecus, louis, livres, francs, pistoles, sous, and liards. The ecu, a silver coin first struck under the reign of Louis IX, or Saint Louis (1214–1270), was worth three livres, the louis 24 livres. The value of the livre varied considerably, depending on the historical moment, and was replaced by the franc. The livre and franc seem to have been of relatively equal value; before 1789 the term "franc" was used loosely to mean livre. The pistole, an ancient gold coin also of varying value from country to country, was worth ten francs in France. The sou was worth five centimes, or 1/20th of a franc, and the liard, a copper coin, was worth a fourth of a sou.

To give an idea of the cost of living then, in 1789 a semi-skilled worker made 25 or 30 sous a day; a skilled laborer as much as 50 sous. A provincial bourgeois could live comfortably on 3,000 livres a year. Sade in a letter to his wife writes despairingly that it had cost the family a hundred thousand francs to have him incarcerated for ten years, or ten thousand francs per annum for room and board at Vincennes and the Bastille. For her own room and board at the convent of Saint-Aure, Madame de Sade paid half that amount for quarters she described as far from luxurious. Monsieur de Rougemont, warden of Vincennes prison, earned a salary of 18,000 francs a year (which he augmented, according to Sade and other prisoners there, by an additional "illegal" 15,000 francs annually by overcharging his wards for food, wine, and other necessities). After the Revolution, Sade complains to his lawyer Gaufridy about the diminishing value of the paper money issued by the new government. He is referring to the *assignat*, whose value declined between 1792 and 1795 to virtually nothing. Thus Sade's complaint of often going to bed hungry during those years was doubtless not exaggerated.

R. S.

Part One

Letters from Vincennes

The *Château de Vincennes*, a vast structure in the Val de Marne to the east of Paris, was built over a period of more than three decades, from 1337 to 1370. (It was, coincidentally, completed the year construction began on Sade's other prison nemesis, the Bastille.) It long served as a residence for the kings of France, and in the sixteenth century an imposing sainte-chapelle was added to the several imposing buildings within its walls. The dungeon, which stood on a slight promontory, was flanked by four forbidding towers. The cells, which Gilbert Lely, Sade's pioneering biographer, describes as "heartbreakingly grim," were disproportionately high and bathed "in eternal twilight," since their narrow windows with their double bars filtered out most of the daylight. In a letter written roughly two months after his incarceration, Sade describes his situation: "I am in a tower locked up behind nineteen iron doors, my only source of light being two little windows each outfitted with a score of bars. . . ." In his sixty-five days there, he notes, he has been allowed only five hours of fresh air: "When they let the dog [Sade himself] out of his kennel, he trots off to spend one hour *in a kind of cemetery about forty feet square, surrounded by walls more than fifty feet high.*"

In an earlier letter to his wife shortly after his incarceration Sade writes: "My blood is too hot to bear such terrible confinement . . . If I am not released in four days, I shall crack my skull against these walls."

Many subsequent letters raise the threat of suicide if he is not soon set free. But Sade's innate love of life, of pleasure, and his growing conviction that through writing he could find another kind of release and also take revenge on his hated enemies kept him from that fatal step. Still, had he known in those early months that he was to spend the next thirteen years behind bars, he might well have put an end to his agony there and then.

1. To Madame de Montreuil

[End of February 1777]

Of all the possible forms revenge and cruelty could assume, you must agree, Madame, that you have indeed chosen the most horrifying of all. Having come to Paris to bid farewell to my mother, who was breathing her last, with no other thought in mind than to see her and embrace her one last time, if indeed she were still alive, or to mourn her if she were not, 'twas that very moment you chose to make

me your victim once again! Alas! I asked you in my first letter whether
I would find in you a second mother or a tyrant, but you have not left
me in doubt for more than a trice! Is it thus that you repay me for having wiped away your tears when you lost the father you cherished? And
did you not find at that trying time my heart as sensitive to your grief
as it was to my own? It is not as if I had come to Paris only to defy you,
or with purposes in mind that might have made you wish to see me
gone! ... But after the care and attention my mother's situation required, my second goal was only to calm and comfort you, then to
come to an understanding with you, and as far as my affair[1] is concerned, to take whatever measures would have suited you and that you
would have suggested to me. Apart from my letters, Amblet, if he is
candid (which I do not believe), must have told you as much. But the
perfidious friend has been working in concert with you to deceive me,
to undo me, and in this both of you have succeeded admirably. As I
was being taken away [after my arrest] they told me it was only to expedite my case, and for that reason my detention was essential. But in
all good faith, do you believe I can be duped by such talk? And when
in Savoy[2] you resorted to the same measures, what slightest effort on
my behalf was undertaken? Since then did my two year-long absences
produce the slightest initiatives? And is it not exceeding clear that
what you seek is my total undoing, and not my rehabilitation?

I am willing to go along with you for a moment that a *lettre de cachet* has been indispensable, in order to avoid a remonstration, which is
always troublesome, but did it have to be so harsh, so cruel? Would a
letter banishing me from the kingdom not have served the same purpose? And would I not have most scrupulously complied with that order, since I had just, of my own volition, put myself in your hands and
submitted to whatever you might have demanded? When I wrote you
from Bordeaux, asking that you send me the money wherewith to
move to Spain, and you refused it to me, was that not a further proof

---

1. Sade is referring to his sentencing as a result of the Marseilles scandal.
2. After his brief but passionate idyll with his wife's younger sister Anne-
Prospère in Italy, Sade traveled to Savoy, where he lived for several months
incognito. As noted, he wrote a letter to Madame de Montreuil in late November 1772, thus revealing his whereabouts to the one person who most
wanted him behind bars. On December 8, only days after that fateful letter,
he was arrested and incarcerated in Miolans, doubtless at the request of
Madame de Montreuil.

you wanted me not far away but behind bars; and the more I ponder the circumstances the more I am completely convinced that you have never had any other thought in mind. But I am mistaken, Madame: Amblet revealed to me another one of your devices, and that is the one I intend to fulfill. He told me, Madame—at your behest no doubt— that a *death certificate* was the most essential and most appropriate document to bring this unfortunate affair to an end as quickly as possible. You must procure that piece of paper, Madame, and I swear I shall make sure you have it very soon. As I shall not multiply my letters, not only because of the difficulty I have in writing them but also because they seem to have not the slightest effect upon you, the present one shall contain my final sentiments, of that you may be sure. My situation is horrible. Never—and you know it—has either my blood or my brain been able to bear being cooped up. When I was under much less rigorous confinement—that you also know—I risked my life to rid myself of that yoke.[3] Here such means are denied me, but I still have *one* that no one on earth can strip me of, and I shall take full advantage of it. From the depths of her grave my poor mother beckons to me: I seem to see her open her arms to me again and summon me to bury myself in her bosom, into the one haven I still have left. To follow her so closely is to me a satisfaction, and as a last favor I ask you, Madame, to have me laid to rest near her. Only one thing holds me back; 'tis a weakness, I admit, but I must confess it to you. I should have liked to see my children. For I so enjoyed going and holding them in my arms after having seen you. My most recent misfortunes have not stilled this desire, and I shall in all likelihood bear it with me to the grave. I commend them to your care, Madame. Even though you have hated their father, at least do love them. Give them an education which, if that is possible, will preserve them from the misfortunes my neglectful upbringing has vouchsafed to me. If they were aware of my sad fate, their souls, modeled after that of their tender mother's, would hasten to cause them to fall at your knees and their innocent hands, raised in supplication, would doubtless cause you to be swayed. 'Tis from my love for them this consoling image arises, but it can in no wise affect the course of events, and I make haste to destroy it for fear it may soften my heart at a time when what I most need is steadfastness. Adieu, Madame.

---

3. Sade is referring to his imprisonment in the fortress of Miolans, from which he made a daring escape in April, 1773.

2. To Madame de Sade

March 6, 1777

O h, my dear friend! When will my horrible situation cease? When in God's name will I be let out of the tomb where I have been buried alive? There is nothing to equal the horror of my fate! Nothing that can depict everything I am suffering, that can convey the state of anxiety wherewith I am tormented and the sorrows that devour me! Here, all I have as support are my tears and my shouts, but no one hears them . . . Where is the time when my dear friend[1] shared them? Today I no longer have anyone; it seems as if the whole of Nature were dead for me! Who knows whether you even receive my letters? No reply to the last one I wrote you proves to me that they are not being given to you and that 'tis to make sport of my sorrow or to see what is going on in my head that I am allowed to write them to you.[2] Yet another refinement invented no doubt by the rage of her who stalks me as her personal prey![3] What can so much cruelty auger for the future? Judge for a moment in what state my poor mind must be. Till now, a faint hope sustained me, calmed the early moments of my terrible sorrow; but everything concerts to destroy it, and I clearly see from the silence wherein I am left, from the state I am in, that all they want is my undoing. If 'twere for my good, would they proceed in this manner? They must realize full well that the severe measures that are being taken with me can only unhinge my brain, and, consequently, from this naught can result (supposing they mean to keep me alive) save the greatest ill. For I am quite certain I cannot hold out a month here without going mad:[4] which is probably what they want, and that fits in wonderfully with the means they proposed this past winter. Ah! my dear friend, I can see all too well my fate! Remember what I sometimes told you, that they had decided to let me finish out my five years in peace, and then . . . There's the idea that torments me and is driving

---

1. Sade is of course referring to his wife.
2. All of Sade's letters were read and if deemed necessary censored by the prison authorities.
3. That is, Madame de Montreuil.
4. Sade understands that the family's easiest explanation for his unrepentant sexual excesses is simply that he is mad. If by keeping him confined in prison they manage to drive him mad, they will prove to the world they were right.

me to my grave. If 'tis in your power to reassure me on that score, please do so, I beseech you, for my state is frightful in the extreme and if you could only understand it fully for what it is, your heart would most assuredly be filled with pity for me. Nor do I doubt that they are making every effort to separate us: for me that would be the final blow, and I would not survive it, of that you may be sure. I beseech you to oppose this with all the strength at your command, and to understand that the first victims of this effort would be our children: there is no example of children made happy when their mother and father are in disagreement. My dear friend, you are all I have left on earth: father, mother, sister, wife, friend, you are all those to me, I have no one but you: do not abandon me, I beg you, let it not be from you that I receive the final blow of misfortune.

Is it possible, if indeed they have my best interests in mind, that they do not sense they are ruining everything by meting out this punishment? Do they imagine the public will even try to understand? It will simply say: *He certainly must have been guilty, since he has been punished.* When a crime has been proven, you resort to these means either to calm a high judicial court or prevent it from passing sentence, but when 'tis certain no crime has been committed and that the sentence has been the height of madness and of meanness, one must not be punished, because you then undo all the good that could be accomplished if the verdict was annulled, and you clearly prove that influence alone has been operative, that crime has existed, and that one has besought the king to punish to avoid having the court do so.[5] I contend that there could be nothing worse done against me than that, 'twould be to do me in for the rest of my life; and only a few years ago your mother was offered an excellent example of how little the military and the public were taken in by these maneuvers and continued to look askance at whoever took it upon himself to mete out punishment, whether it be at the king's hands or the court's. But that is how she is: whenever it's a question of acting on some matter, she leaps before she thinks, people mislead her, and they end up doing me far more harm than she has often intended. 'Tis the St. Vincent story all over again, tell her I would be greatly obliged if she would bear that in mind; here somebody else is playing the same role, and it's not difficult to figure out who.

---

5. Under the monarchy, while an elaborate judiciary system did exist, the king could take matters into his own hands and condemn—or pardon—as he saw fit.

Finally, my dear friend, all I humbly ask of you is that you get me out of here as soon as possible, no matter what the cost, for I feel I cannot hold out much longer. They tell you I'm fine; it calms you to hear it, so much the better, nothing could make me happier. I am not going to disabuse you, because I'm forbidden to do so: that is all I can say to you. But please remember that I have never endured anything like what I am experiencing today, and that, considering the circumstances I was in, 'twas vile of your mother to have forced me into this present situation. The poor lawyer who said 'tis unnatural to heap sorrow upon sorrow, knew little about your mother when he made that declaration. I beseech you, while awaiting the blessed day when I shall be delivered from the horrible torments into which I am plunged, to arrange to come and see me, to write to me more often than you do, to obtain permission for me to take a little exercise after my meals, something which you know is more essential to me than life itself, and to send me without delay my second pair of sheets. For the past seven nights I haven't slept a wink, and during the night I throw up everything I've eaten during the day. Get me out of here, my good friend, get me out, I beg of you, for I feel I'm dying a little more each day. I don't know why they were so barbaric as to refuse me my camp bed: 'twas a very slight favor to grant, and which would at least have given me the satisfaction of forgetting my misfortunes for a few hours each night. But at least send me my sheets right away, I beg of you. Farewell, my dear friend, love me as much as I suffer, that is all I ask of you, and believe that I am at the height of my despair.

3. To Madame de Montreuil

March 13, 1777

If in a soul capable of having betrayed in one fell stroke all the most sacred sentiments, those of humanity in having a son arrested beside the coffin of his mother, those of hospitality by betraying someone who had just given himself over to your care, those of Nature in not even respecting the refuge of your daughter's embrace; if, I say, in such a person some slight spark of compassion might still exist, I should perhaps try to awaken it by the most accurate and at the same time most frightful description of my horrible plight. But independently of the fact that these complaints are completely useless, I still have enough pride, however brought low it may be, not to embellish your triumph with my tears, and even in the bosom of misfortune I shall still find the courage to refrain from complaining to my tyrant.

A few simple considerations will therefore be the sole point of this letter. You can value them as you like, and then I shall say no more . . . Yes, I shall seal my lips, so that my opinions shall no longer be dinned into your ears, leaving you for a while at least the chance to revel in the knowledge of my unhappiness.

I have long been your victim, Madame, but do not think to make me your dupe. It is sometimes interesting to be the one, always humiliating to be the other, and I credit myself with being blessed with as much insight as you can presume to have of deceit. For pity's sake, Madame, let us never confuse my case and my imprisonment: you will seek to bring my case to a conclusion for the sake of my children; and my imprisonment, which you claim indispensable to that end, and which it is most certainly not, is not, and cannot be, anything but the effect of your own vengeance. The most terrifying of all the legal opinions heard so far is that of M. Siméon of Aix, who said in no uncertain terms that it was quite possible to obtain a judgment whereby *exile would serve as prison to the accused.* Those are Siméon's very own words.[1] Would not a *lettre de cachet*, in fact, which would have banished me from the kingdom, have served the same purpose?—of course it would— but it would not have served your fury nearly as well.

Was it you, then, who concocted and had carried out the plan to have me locked up between four walls? And by what misadventure have the wise magistrates who today govern the State allowed themselves be hoodwinked to the point of believing they were serving the interests of a family when it was clearly a question of slaking a woman's thirst for revenge? Why am I once again behind bars? why is an imprudence being mistaken for a crime? why am I not being allowed to prove to my judges the difference between the two? and why are you the one who is keeping me from doing so? These are the questions to which Madame deigns not to reply, is that not true? Ten or a

---

1. Joseph Jérome Siméon, a lawyer with the high court of Aix-en-Provence, who drafted a petition to be presented to the king and his council in an effort to overturn in absentia the sentence condemning Sade to death.

dozen bolts and locks serve as your answer instead, but this tyrannical argument, to which the laws are formally opposed, is not eternally triumphant. That is what consoles and comforts me.

Focusing upon my case alone, is it to clear my name that you are having me punished? and are you suffering under the illusion that this punishment shall be ignored? Do you for a moment believe that they who, sooner or later, shall hear of it shall surely assume that there has to have been a crime somewhere, since there has been a punishment? Be it meted out by the king, be it meted out by judges, 'tis still a punishment, and will the public—which is neither indulgent nor overly curious to find out the truth of the matter—make this frivolous distinction? And will it not always see crime wherever punishment has been exacted? And what a triumph then for my enemies! What fertile soil you prepare for them in the future! and how tempted they will be to have a further go at me, since the results correspond so nicely to their intentions! All your scandalous acts over the past five years have nicely prepared people's minds and behavior in my regard, and you have been well aware of the cruel situation I have found myself in during this whole period, the constant target of fresh calumnies, which a sordid interest used to build upon the unhappiness of my situation. How do you think people can fail to judge a man guilty when the authorities have come knocking at his door three or four times, and when they then throw him in jail once they have their hands on him? Who do you hope to convince that I have not been in prison when they haven't seen me or even heard from me all this time? After all the means taken to capture me, you can well imagine that the only conclusion people can come to, since I have dropped out of sight, is that I have been arrested. What advantage will derive from this? My reputation lost forever, and new troubles at every turn. That is what I shall owe to the wonderful manner in which you are handling my affairs.

But let us consider matters from another point of view. Is this a personal punishment I'm receiving? and is the thought this will turn me back onto the straight and narrow, as if I were a naughty little boy? A complete waste of time and effort, Madame. If the wretchedness and ignominy to which the Marseilles judges' absurd proceedings have reduced me, by punishing the most commonplace of indiscretions as though it were a crime, have failed to make me mend my ways, your iron bars and your iron doors and your locks will be no more successful. You ought to know my heart well enough by now to be convinced that the mere suspicion of dishonor is capable of withering it completely, and you are smart enough to understand that a misdeed, whose origin lies in hot-bloodedness, is not corrected by making that selfsame blood more bitter, by firing the brain through deprivation and inflaming the imagination through solitude. What I am calling to mind here will be supported by every reasonable being who knows me passing well and who is not infatuated with the idiotic notion that, to correct or punish a man you must shut him up like a wild beast; and I challenge anyone to conclude other than that, from such methods, the only possible result in my case is the most certain perturbation of my organs.

If therefore neither my behavior nor my reputation stand to gain from this latest act of kindness on your part—if, on the contrary, there are nothing but negatives and, what is more, it disturbs my brain— what purpose will it have served, Madame, I ask you? Your vengeance, true? Ah, yes! I know all too well, 'tis always there one must return, and everything I have just written is quite beside the point. But what does all that mean, so long as I play the sacrificial lamb . . . and you are satisfied? On the contrary, you must surely say to yourself, *the greater the damage wrought, the more content I shall be.* But should you not already have been sufficiently contented, Madame, by the six months of prison I served in Savoy *for the same reason?* Am I to believe that five years of afflictions and stigmas were not enough? and was this appalling denouement absolutely necessary, especially after the frightful demonstration I gave you of what lengths this sort of mistreatment could drive me to, by risking my life to escape from it! You must admit that, after that experience, 'tis an act of barbarity on your part to have the same thing inflicted upon me again, and with episodes a thousand times crueler than before and which, having the effect they do on my brain, will at the first possible opportunity have me dashing my head against the bars that presently confine me. Do not reduce me to despair, Madame; I cannot endure this horrible solitude, I feel it. Remember that you will never derive any good from making my soul more savage and my heart immune to feeling, the only possible results of the frightful state in which you have had me put. Give me time to make amends for my errors, and do not make yourself responsible for those into which perhaps I shall again be swept by the dreadful disorder I feel aborning in my mind.

I am respectfully, Madame, your most humble and most obedient servant.

DE SADE

P.S.—If the person from Montpellier[2] returns there, I hope it will not be without the most urgent recommendation for her not to breathe a word about the scandalous scene to which you, with your usual wit, made her a witness, a blunder that, considering the circumstances of what her father has been up to,[3] is assuredly quite inexcusable.

4. To Madame de Sade

April 18, 1777

'*T*is most rightly said, my dear friend, that edifices constructed in a position such as mine are built only on sand, and that all the ideas one forms are naught but illusions, which crumble to dust as soon as they are conceived. Of the six combinations I figured out all by myself, and upon which I based a hope of some enlightenment in the near future, there remains, thanks be to God, not a single one, and your letter of April 14 caused them to disappear the way the sun's rays dissipate the morning dew. 'Tis true that on the other hand I did find in that same letter the comforting sentence telling me that *I could be quite sure that I shall not stay here one minute longer than the time necessary.* I know nothing on earth so reassuring as this expression, so that if 'tis necessary for me to remain here six months, six months I shall remain. That is charming, and verily, those in charge of guiding your style must perforce congratulate themselves upon the progress you are making in their profound art of sprinkling salt on the wounds of the wretched. Indeed, they have succeeded masterfully. I warn you, however, that

---

2. Sade is doubtless referring to Catherine Treillet, known at La Coste as Justine, who had accompanied Madame de Sade to Paris in February but was now planning to go home. Before she left Paris in April, Madame de Montreuil had a "private talk" with her, admonishing not to reveal the specifics of that mad winter at La Coste—an admonishment surely accompanied by money.
3. Catherine's father had tried to kill Sade by firing a pistol at him point-blank at La Coste. After which, he hurried to Aix and lodged a complaint against the marquis with the procureur général—the attorney general—for kidnapping his daughter.

'twill not be long before my head explodes because of the cruel life I am leading. I can see it coming, and I hereby predict that they shall have every reason to repent for having used an excessive dose of severity with me, which is so ill-suited to my character. 'Tis for my own welfare, they maintain. Divine phrase, wherein one recognizes all too clearly the ordinary language of *imbecility triumphant.* 'Tis for a man's own good that you expose him to maddening conditions, for his own good that you wreck his health, for his own good that you feed him on the tears of despair! So far, I must confess, I've not had the pleasure of understanding or experiencing that kind of well-being . . .

You are wrong, the fools gravely declare to you: *this gives you the chance to think things over.* 'Tis true, it does make one think, but would you like to know the one thought this infamous brutality has engendered in me? The thought, deeply engraved in my soul, of fleeing as soon as I am able from a country where a citizen's services count as nothing when it comes to compensating for a momentary lapse, where imprudence is punished as if it were a crime, where a woman, because she is cunning and filled with deceit, finds the secret of enslaving innocence to her caprices, or rather to her commanding and personal interest to bury the veritable crux of the matter; and, far from those whose goal is to harass and annoy, and all their accomplices, of setting off in search of a free country where I can faithfully serve the prince who will provide me with asylum there, and thus may merit from him what I could not obtain in my native land . . . justice and to be left in peace.

Those, my dear friend, are my sole and unique thoughts, and I aspire to naught but the happy moment when I can put them into effect. We have been misled, you say. Not so . . . I assure you that I was not fooled for one minute, and you ought to remember how, just before your room was filled with *a pack of rascals*[1]—who, without producing any order from the king, had come, or so they claimed, to arrest me on the king's behalf—I told you that I did not trust your mother's reassuring letter and that since it was full of tenderness, one could be sure that her soul was feeding on a diet of deceit. No, my dear friend, no, I may have been surprised, but as for mistakes I shall admit to none until the day I see that creature turn honest and truthful, which in all

---

1. Sade is referring to Madame de Montreuil's earlier effort to have him arrested at La Coste on January 6, 1774. In connivance with lieutenant-general of police Sartine, she ordered a veritable assault—consisting of three brigades of Marseilles's deputies plus several constables—made on the château, wreaking havoc there. But the marquis was nowhere to be found.

likelihood is not just around the corner. In coming here I acted like Caesar, who was wont to say that *'twere better to expose oneself once in one's life to the dangers one fears than to live in a constant concern to try to avoid them*. That reasoning led him to the Senate, where he knew full well the conspirators were awaiting him. I did the same, and like him I shall always be greater through my innocence and my frankness than my enemies through their baseness and the secret rancors that motivate them. You ask me how I am. But what's the use of my telling you? If I do, my letter will not reach you. Still, on an off chance, I am going to satisfy you, for I cannot imagine they will be so unfair as to prevent me from replying to something they have allowed you to ask me. I am in a tower locked up behind nineteen iron doors, my only source of light being two little windows each outfitted with a score of bars. For about ten or twelve minutes a day I have the company of a man who brings me food. The rest of the time I spend alone and in weeping ... There's my life ... That is how, in this country, they set a man straight: 'Tis by cutting off all his connections with society, to which on the contrary he needs to be brought closer so that he may be brought back to the path of goodness whence he had the misfortune to stray. Instead of good advice, wise counsel, I have my despair and my tears. Yes, my dear friend, such is my fate. How could anyone fail to cherish virtue when they offer it to you under such divine colors! As for the manner in which I am treated, 'tis in all fairness with civility in all things ... but so much fussing over trifles, so much childishness that, when I arrived here, I thought I had been transported to the Lilliputians' isle, where men being only eight inches tall, their behavior must be in keeping with their stature. At first, I found it funny, finding it difficult to get it into my head that people who otherwise appeared to be fairly sensible could adopt such foolish conduct. Later on I began to lose patience. Finally, I have taken to imagining that I am only twelve years old—'tis more honest than if I were to pretend the others were that age—and this idea of having reverted to childhood somewhat tempers the regret a reasonable person would otherwise feel at seeing himself treated in this manner. But one completely amusing detail I almost forgot is their promptness to spy on you, down to your least facial expression, and to report it on the spot to whomever is in charge. At first I was fooled by this, and my frame of mind, always affected by and attuned to your letters, indiscreetly revealed itself one day when I was especially enjoying a note from you. How quickly your following letters made me realize how foolish I was! From then on I resolved to be as hypocritical as the others, and these days I control myself, so that not even the shrewdest of them can figure out my feelings from my face. Well then, my pet, there's one virtue I've nonetheless acquired! I dare you now to come here and tell me that one gains nothing in prison! As for the walks and the exercise you advised me to take, verily you speak as if I were in some country house where I might do as I please . . . When they let the dog out of his kennel he trots off to spend *one hour* in a kind of cemetery about forty feet square, surrounded by walls more than fifty feet high, and this charming favor is not yet granted him as often as he would like. You can well imagine—or at least you ought to—how many disadvantages would result from leaving a man the same freedom one allows animals; his health might pick up all of a sudden, and then where the devil would their projects be, they whose only goal is to see him dead? During the sixty-five days I have been here, I have consequently breathed fresh air for five hours all told, on five different occasions. Compare that with the exercise you know I am used to taking, which is absolutely essential for me, and then judge for yourself what state I am in! The result is terrible headaches, which refuse to go away and totally exhaust me, dreadful nervous pains, vapors, and a complete inability to sleep, all of which cannot fail to lead to serious illness sooner or later. But what does that matter so long as the présidente is pleased and so long as her dull-witted husband can say: *"That's all to the good, all to the good, 'twill make him mull things over."* Farewell, my heart, be well and love me a little: that idea is the only one capable of easing my sufferings.

As yet they have brought me nothing to sign. There was no need to announce this *petition* to me so far in advance with nothing concrete to show for it. And what is more, the draft you gave me leads me to believe that I am in for all kinds of lengthy delays. I am therefore going to ask permission to appoint someone my power-of-attorney. First this permission must be obtained, then the attorney must be appointed, informed, made to act . . . Just imagine the delays that will ensue, and what an enormous amount of time it will take! Add to all that the meticulous way in which they hasten to have me sign the necessary papers and you will see that the whole thing adds up to an eternity. 'Tis true, however, I have the consolation of knowing *that I shall not stay here one minute longer than the time necessary!*

Once again farewell, my dear good friend. Here's a long letter which may never reach you, since 'tis not written *à la Lilliputienne.* No matter, it will not go unseen, and who knows whether, amongst all those who are obliged to see it, you are the one to whom I most directly address it?

What you tell me of your children pleases me. You surely know how delighted I shall be to embrace them, although I have no illusions about the fact that—despite my affection—'tis upon their account I am suffering at present.

Rereading my letter, I can see all too plainly that they will never pass it on to you, which is proof positive of the injustice and the horror of everything I am being made to suffer, for if there were nothing but justice and simplicity in all I am experiencing, why would they fear your being told or finding it out? In any case, I shall not write to you again until I positively receive a reply to this one, for what is the purpose of writing to you if you do not receive my letters?

5.   To Madame de Sade

REFLECTIONS AND NOTES UPON
THE PETITION IN QUESTION[1]

April 21, 1777

*T*he beginning of the third page is very weak and very poorly done. At least you should have put after the words *had stomach pains and vomiting:* "but does it follow that creatures who eat all sorts of unwholesome food every day of their lives are justified in ascribing the cause of their indisposition to these candied lozenges?[2] However, influenced by the women to whom they related what had taken place between the petitioner and themselves, they did not fail," etc.

On page 7, you state that women of this kind would not, or could not, be familiar with *the etymology, the properties, and the effects of cantharides vesicatoria.*[3] That is wrong; such women are often well ac-

---

1. The petition in question, which has been sent to Sade for information, vetting, and signature, relates to quashing the Marseilles affair. The title of the response is Sade's.
2. Sade's term tries to minimize the fact that they were steeped in Spanish fly.
3. Spanish fly. Sade is trying to make the case that the prostitutes' stomach ills derived not from the cantharide candies he gave them but either from the poor food women of the profession were used to eating or from the royal feast he gave them in the course of their "revels."

quainted with this variety of drug, whose properties have the same virtue as their art, and there are very few among them, I firmly believe, who do not know what it is; and 'tis precisely because they do know what it is that they rushed to take it. It would have been better to say that it were strange indeed that they had not immediately noticed the difference between Spanish fly and poison, and, consequently, if indeed they knew full well the effect of the cantharides, that they pounced upon the poison; but that having found neither the one nor the other, they declared something they were familiar with instead of what they saw very well did not exist at all. Perhaps I may not have expressed my idea clearly enough, but they should have no trouble understanding what I mean. However, at least by adopting the one in the petition rather than claim that these women know neither *its etymology, its property, nor its effects*, I would at least have said that there was a good chance that women of this sort would not be so familiar with this drug as to be able to identify its taste, etc.

At the bottom of the same page, a certain fact that is well known should have been added; namely, that all five of those women sat down together to a culinary feast with the money they had earned from the Marquis de Sade. The fact is known and established beyond any doubt. Hence 'tis most likely that the indisposition all five suffered derives therefrom. To prove that those five women were all sick at the same time and fail to mention this salient fact looks highly suspicious, and without certain knowledge of that fact I would be the first to find it most extraordinary that five women seen one after the other by one man, to all of whom he gave something to eat, could all five suffer from a case of indigestion. If in matters as basic as this they consulted the person most directly interested in vindicating himself, and assuming they did not look upon him as some kind of automaton, such essential anecdotes would not be forgotten and everything would certainly proceed more positively.

By invoking that culinary feast at table, which has been well proven, you destroy your supposition at the beginning of page 8, which still seems dubious. By including it, how much force you add to the first seven lines of page 9: *"vomitings may,"* etc.! 'Twas a grave error not to include this point.

On page 15, at the beginning, I do not like having your assumption that this girl could even have been "sole witness," because she is not nor could she have been, as is constantly attested by the posture which, according to her own deposition, she maintained throughout the alleged consummation of the crime. In the position she claimed to be in, it is impossible that she could have seen what was going on. Therefore, she could not properly serve as a witness, and her opinion here can be founded only on the fact that at this moment the domestic went up to his master to whisper in his ear, recommending that he not have his way with this girl (believing him on the point of wishing to do so) because, said he, *she is surely not in good health.* That single incident could have led that creature to suppose what she has dared maintain as certain.

Note at the bottom of the same page: I do not believe there is any girl who testified in the course of the proceedings that the crime of sodomy had been actively committed with her. So far as I know, I have not read that anywhere or heard it said. In any case, this allegation is perfectly false; no such proposition was ever even made to any of those creatures.[4]

The bottom of page 18 and the top of page 19 are very strong, faultlessly done. That in itself ought to destroy their entire thesis, I should think. But I do not like your terminating your petition with an admission of the defendant's misdeeds; for then, given this admission, the court must perforce find moral delinquency, and the least pronouncement of that sort is, as everybody knows, defamatory. It seems to me it would be preferable to let that be deduced or conjectured, without having the defendant sign this formal admission, which is visibly reprehensible and consequently held against him, and make him loath to sign the said petition.

Furthermore, my dear friend, you must admit that 'tis rather remarkable that they are being so secretive about all this, to the point of not telling me to what high court this case is going to be sent for review. From this petition it looks as though it were to be the one in Paris, that quashing the decision becomes pointless, and that imprisonment, which sets aside contumacy, has served in its stead, and that the question remaining being one of procedure alone, as the petition says, a simple appeal would suffice. That is what comes through from this petition. It remains to be seen whether that is what it boils down to. I have no idea myself, and, thanks be to God, they leave me in complete ignorance, which is without any doubt the most ridiculous thing in the world, for considering where I am to whom could I breathe a word

---

4. Sade is probably lying through his teeth. However, as noted earlier, in all likelihood that punishable act, though proposed, may not have been committed with any of the five. Even if it was, none of the women would have admitted it under oath, knowing the penalty was being burnt at the stake.

about it? Therefore being secretive is pointless, and it is used here simply to vex me all the more. This I find both exceedingly hard and exceedingly stupid, for I am vexed enough as it is; this further touch was useless. And who has a greater interest than I in all this? I beseech you therefore to keep me fully informed on everything, and without making me wait for three weeks, as you did after the other letter, which keeps me in a truly frightful state of anxiety and, of this you may be sure, succeeds only in embittering me and making my blood boil.

In general, I do not find this petition written with the same force as the memorandum your mother presented to us a year ago. The difference between them strikes me as great, and I doubt whether they come from the same hand. In the memorandum there were much more powerful arguments for nullifying the second charge, which apparently are not raised here and yet of the two 'tis that one which, while equally false, would seem the easier to contend with; for in the first we have the girls vomiting: that, if you like, seems probable enough to justify, at least theoretically, the blindness, or rather the malicious obstination, of the so-called Marseilles judges. But what have we in the second? Nothing, absolutely nothing, not even the slightest probability.

Nothing in this petition hints that the sentence was carried out. Is that yet another one of these things about which you say we have been misled? Please let me know what you think anent that.

Be kind enough to communicate my notes to the lawyer. As for the first note, 'tis a stylistic fault urgently in need of correcting, because it leaves a terrible weakness in that area. As for the rest, I shall submit to his greater knowledge, and he will do as he sees fit; but at least he must make an issue of those creatures' culinary orgy at table: that, in my view, is essential to accounting for the stomach trouble all five of them suffered.

The passage in the petition that says, page 10, "But the court which shall weigh the complaints, the records of verification and of decomposition, the report upon the state of the two girls," and so on, suggests major delays, for 'tis clear they are going to start the whole procedure all over again, and in that case, all too clearly set forth by these phrases, I still have ahead of me more furious suffering from a misery that is already beyond my power to endure. For verily, my dear friend, I am truly at the end of my rope, and 'tis all I can do to ward off the impulses of my despair.[5]

---

5. Once again, Sade is using the threat of suicide to urge his wife on.

What is most strange is that in all this there is never a word about my five months of prison in Savoy. It would seem that these were for the pure and simple satisfaction of your most gracious mother. How charming.

What I do like about this petition is the clear field it seems to leave me to take to task all the poor beggars who have brought this ridiculous suit against me and for crushing, or so I hope, Martignan's divine brother-in-law.[6] 'Tis a joy that will surely console me in great measure for all my sufferings, indeed if I am successful, and, verily, justice demands I be given that privilege, for they are great brutes, these people. That appears to me to explain your phrase that *we shall have the wherewithal to confound our enemies in Provence.* Let me know if that is what you meant. In general, the end of the petition is quite good, and I am most satisfied with it; the only fault I find in it is that it is somewhat less forceful than last year's memorandum, as I have just pointed out; and then the few observations duly noted in the first two pages of this letter.

All this, as you see, my dear friend, is written helter-skelter and jotted as ideas occur to me after the two consecutive and careful readings of this petition I have just concluded. But you'll arrange all that, and understand, or so I trust, what I am trying to say despite my incoherent style.

There is however, in the concluding part of this petition, one sentence, I must admit, that I am unable to grasp at all. Here it is, isolated to be sure, but read it in context and you will see that you may understand it no better than I: " . . . and the veritable judges who, in judging, draw no distinction between contumacy and post-trial hearings, pass no other judgment upon the one than they would upon the other. But, through a contrary principle," etc. I do not understand a word of that sentence. If they can clarify it for me, I shall be most obliged. In general, what would have been the drawback in allowing me to chat here with my lawyer? None that I can see.

In a word, having read and reread this petition, I come back to the point that if during the past five years everything has been prepared, as I had every reason to suppose, then this may well be over with

---

6. Probably Monsieur le Mende, the Marseilles procurator who signed the arrest warrant for Sade and Latour on July 4, 1772.

quickly; but if nothing has been, as is also quite possible, it may yet drag on for a long time and keep me cooped up in here all that while. And another much more unpleasant possibility must be foreseen: if this admission of debauchery that I am going to be made to sign were, without regard for my imprisonment, to bring on yet another unfortunate ruling of a court, where would that leave me? New terrors and new anxieties in which they are pleased to leave me to stew, for I am quite right in saying that since I arrived here I have received neither the slightest legal advice nor the slightest comfort, and 'tis impossible to experience a more terrible plight.

I most earnestly pray you, my dear friend, to obtain permission from M. Le Noir to write two notes a week to me instead of the one I am in the habit of receiving. 'Tis not in order to have news about my affairs more frequently: confine yourself to discussing those matters in the letter you customarily write each Monday, as I see from your dates; and I most earnestly beseech you, let the other contain nothing but a word about your health, without any detail regarding any other subject, which, I tell you, is dearer to me than anything else. Ponder what I am asking you here; and if you refuse, or if you fail to obtain it for me, you will hurt me terribly and cause me great anxiety.

I have been meaning to tell you since learning that you are at the Carmelites'[7] to steer clear of a certain room to your right as you enter the drawing room. Bear in mind that 'tis a worthless room, and that more than a decade ago my mother told me she did not dare enter it, because the architect had told her in no uncertain terms that the ceiling was on the verge of collapse. For my sake, please do not set foot in that room.

When you write to them down there,[8] make sure that they take proper care of the park; have instructions given to replace the little row of hazelnut trees; it costs nothing and this is the time of year to do it. Also send orders that the Devaux[9] keep at it, their price being met, and that it be completely done before the first of June when, as you know, they are in the habit of packing up and leaving; otherwise the

---

7. Renée-Pélagie, probably to be free of her mother's influence and proximity, had taken lodgings in the same Carmelite convent on the rue d'Enfer where Sade's mother had lived.
8. That is, La Coste.
9. Workers who are effecting repairs on the château, which is in a state of increasing neglect.

accounts with those people will become so entangled they will never get straightened out. Generally speaking, we departed in such haste and left everything in such disorder that it will cost us a pretty penny if we are not soon allowed to return, to put our affairs in order.

Here is one more favor I might ask, which is hardly worth mentioning, because I am quite sure it will not be granted me: 'twould be to rescue me from the dreadful anxiety in which I find myself by telling me when I might be released. I confess, 'twould be a great favor you did me, almost a charity, in view of all I am suffering in my horrible situation. If you can manage merely to give me some vague idea, 'twill be a mighty service you render me. Why, if this petition must involve delays, did you wait for almost three months of suffering before submitting it for my signature? That is naught but calculated cruelty, and if there are not to be further delays, and if everything is both arranged and formalized, why not say so? What is to be gained from this overzealous severity? Moreover, between the two favors I ask here, remember, my dear friend, that the one relative to the second note I ask from you each week in order to inform me *about your health* is to me the more important, the more precious, and the one I most earnestly request, being full ready to sacrifice everything to the happiness of keeping forever such a friend as you, whose least indisposition would reduce me to utter despair.

Farewell, my dear friend, I embrace you with all my heart.

Supplement to the Notes Relative to the Petition.[10]

Why was it not indicated in this petition, during the discussion of the first charge, that *Marguerite Coste's* vomiting did not occur until after a man, known as an itinerant practitioner of medicine on the streets of Marseilles, had come (sent by lord knows who) and administered strange remedies to this girl for the simple stomachache about which she had complained to her hostess? This fact strikes me of sufficient importance not to be neglected. You must remember it crops up throughout both the proceedings and the memorandum.

---

10. The post scriptum title is Sade's.

6. *To Madame de Sade*

[Between September 7 and 28, 1778]

*A*fter my letter written yesterday, dear friend, I have been granted permission to write you another more detailed one, and I am taking full advantage of the opportunity, as you will see. But let neither you nor anyone else who may read this letter[1] be alarmed; 'tis the first and the last time that I shall indulge in details; all my protests, all my complaints, have always been so useless that in the future I want to spare you the boredom of reading them, and myself the bother of writing them.

What has just been done to me is so absurd, so contrary to all the laws of common sense and fairness, so much the work of an enemy hand bent solely on ruining me—not only me but my children—that most assuredly I do not suspect your mother: perhaps I have never given her her due, and I have perhaps never felt more remorse for not having done so sooner. Letters, opinions, maneuvers discovered, conversations, five weeks of freedom, did, in short, open my eyes regarding the whole mystery. . . . Be that as it may, I no longer accuse her. . . . But how is it possible that she did not do everything in her power to discover and parry this blow,[2] and how could she have been the dupe

---

1. Sade is not referring to anyone in his wife's entourage to whom she might give this letter, but to the prison censor, Monsieur Boucher, whom Sade considered a cross between a dolt and an idiot.
2. The "blow" to which Sade is referring is his rearrest on August 26 at La Coste. On June 14, Sade, whose Marseilles case was on appeal, was released from Vincennes and allowed to travel by coach under the watchful eye of Inspector Marais and three policemen to Aix, where he arrived in late afternoon. The next morning he was incarcerated in the royal prison of Aix, where he spent the next twenty-three days. The appellate court overturned the Marseilles verdict relative to the charge of poisoning, which, it found, was "totally unproved," and ordered a new trial on the further charges of debauchery and sodomy. On July 14, the high court of Aix, after hearing witnesses, including the accused, also overturned the Marseilles court on these latter counts, reducing the charges to those of "debauchery and excessive libertinage" admonishing Sade "to behave more decently in the future," fining him fifty livres, and prohibiting him from living in or visiting Marseilles for a period of three years. In other words, Sade was, after sixteen months in Vincennes prison, a free man. Or was he?

of people who were only too willing to help arrange my affairs for my children's sake and not for mine? What kind of person can settle for this sophism, and who do you suppose can fail to see that the verdict is naught but a work of favoritism? and who is going to believe honor repaired where favor alone shows forth? This matter has reached a point where I do not hesitate to say that after an affront so glaring as that of which I've just been the victim, 'twould have been a thousand times better for me had there been no verdict at all. They were beginning to talk about this affair less and less: it should have been allowed to die of old age. I dare say the effect would have been nothing compared to what this latest bit of slander has just produced . . .

What repercussions, great God! what repercussions! After having received compliments from all my family, solicitations to visit them to receive their embraces and congratulations, after having allowed myself to spread it abroad that everything was over with, that, my verdict delivered, any eventual punishment could only be punishment for a crime and that most assuredly there would be none and could be none, since the crime had just been declared null and void, after all that, I say, to see oneself arrested at home and with a rage, a desperation, a brutality, an insolence not utilized with even the lowest of scoundrels issued from the dregs of society, to see oneself dragged off, bound hand and foot, with the whole of one's province looking on and through the very places where one has just proclaimed one's innocence and the decree verifying it! —Tell me, dear friend, would it not have been a hundred times better had the good folk who render me such important services, who have me tried in order to have the pleasure of subsequently defaming me, simply given instructions to blow my brains out in my own house?[3] . . . Ah! how I'd have preferred that,

---

3. After the Aix verdict, Sade was returned to the royal prison, assuming he would be freed the next day. But at three in the morning on July 15, Marais awakened Sade and announced he was being brought back to Vincennes. Why, Sade wanted to know, didn't the Aix final verdict mean he was a free man? By reply, Marais produced the king's *lettre de cachet*, revalidated only days before, which meant that Sade's return to Vincennes, and all it implied, was inevitable.

The next night, during a stopover near Valence, Sade made a daring escape from his three escorts, and stealthily returned to La Coste via Avignon. There for the next several weeks he rejoiced in his freedom and savored his role of lord of the manor, especially because the local populace, having heard of the Aix verdict, flattered him with its compliments and respectful attention.

But just before dawn on Wednesday, August 26, Inspector Marais,

and how much better 'twould have been for the honor of the entire family! But what am I saying? This behavior is as injurious to my judges as to me: if I were guilty, they were obliged to condemn me, and if they did not condemn me and if according to their conscience I am not guilty, then I should not be punished afterward. Was it from a bed of roses I arose when I went to present myself before them? and sixteen months of the harshest captivity, had that not more than atoned for the one charge of debauchery that could legitimately be brought against me in the proceedings?

What will they say to justify themselves, they who dare abuse all the rights of humanity in order to treat me thus? Will they revive all the calumnies concocted during the five years of contumacy,[4] and use them for their text authorizing the new infamies they are visiting upon me? But in doing so let them at least not turn their backs upon the laws of justice; let them take a closer look at the facts and not condemn me without a hearing. They cannot be unaware of all the enemies I had during that interval. How many there were who did all they could to make sure I never got back on my feet! All those traps set, all those false reports, especially during the sixteen months! But let all that be put aside, let me be interrogated, let me be confronted, in short, let fair means be employed and 'twill soon be seen just what all the alleged sins actually amount to. In a word, I swear and I solemnly declare that for those five years I was guilty of naught save a little too much trust in a trollop who ought to have been strung up and not left at large. But I assert, and whenever you like shall prove beyond all doubt, that I am guilty of nothing serious, and that in all that there is a chain of events that I alone can unravel, and that I shall clarify whenever you like. Strokes of mischance, indiscretions, far too much weakness and confidence in people who deserved none, too sharply written letters, *strong and rash remarks* (you know what I mean) might well, I admit, have succeeded in giving me the appearance of some wrongdoing. My enemies have exploited this, and there is the sole basis of the opinion that prevails and which doubtless is the cause for my being treated the way

---

backed by Paris police and local gendarmes, burst into the château, captured the marquis, bound him hand and foot, and shoved him into a police wagon. After a thirteen-day journey Sade arrived back in Paris on September 7 and was reincarcerated immediately in Vincennes, in cell number 6.

4. Sade's 1772 flight, after the warrant for his arrest and the sentence in absentia following the Marseilles affair, ended only five years later when he was arrested in February 1777.

I am. Enough of that; if they have a shred of humanity, they'll look into the matter and not damn me without a hearing: that is all I ask.

Nothing can doubtless approach the execrations of Gaufridy's conduct.[5] I questioned you about it, but you did not deign to reply, because you and your mother have closed your eyes when it comes to that swindler. Whether through some secret errand or simply out of vain curiosity, he managed to get *what he got*, but did he have to misuse it and voice it abroad throughout the province? And when he was told, "Careful, sir, you're ahead of yourself; you owe greater regard to someone who places his confidence in you," had he to reply: "No, no, no, I know precisely what I am talking about"? "But sir," 'twas responded to him, "but sir, we all saw it . . . 'twas at such and such a place, in plain sight of everybody . . ." Did he then have to answer with a torrent of insults flung at me, with all the relentlessness of the beggar he is; showing how eager he is to have me out of the way in order to be able to manage everything according to his fancy, to distribute leases at a loss of 400 livres per annum, in exchange for 1,800 livres in bribes, as I was to discover? That man is a scoundrel, I declare it to you, and for basic evidence all I need are the statements made by Nanon, who returned to La Coste as soon as she was set free: here they are, word for word as uttered to someone who will swear to it if need be: "Monsieur! . . . I must see Monsieur! . . ." "And why?" "To tell him to beware of Monsieur Gaufridy: he's tried everything to get me to make dreadful charges against him. 'Avenge yourself, avenge yourself,' he keeps telling me, 'he's the one that had you put in jail: just say things happened in such and such a way and we'll have him put away to rot for the rest of his life . . .'" This is how this monster behaved, and this is how he betrayed the trust of my mother-in-law—whom I do not blame for having sought to enlighten herself, but whom I dare assure you is still very much in the dark. As second proof of his readiness to turn his discoveries against me, all I need is a paper, in due form and duly signed, which I have fortunately kept, which is a very circumstantial report of what *la Du Plan*[6] fetched from Marseilles, wherein those alleged discoveries are laid out in full. Therefore, that was their only source of informa-

5. During Sade's short-lived freedom at La Coste, during July and August 1778, rumors that his trusted friend and longtime attorney Gaufridy was actually working against him—and probably for Madame de Montreuil—reached Sade and he immediately assumed the worst. Thus Gaufridy's acts became, in Sade's mind, "execrations."
6. Mademoiselle Du Plan, a dancer from Marseilles whom Sade engaged late

tion . . . Must a third and more eloquent proof be added? I can provide it, I can provide it: my best witnesses reside today exactly where they did two years ago; I had news from them during my five weeks of freedom, and they will appear if called upon, and swearing most solemnly thereto I end what I have to say upon this score.

Now let us talk about the unfortunate mishap which has just overtaken me, but before we do, permit me to offer you a slight word of reproach. The shots were fired from the direction of Paris, and you told me your mind was at ease about Paris; that only Aix was dangerous; and as I felt sure I had nothing to fear from that quarter, and taking my cue from you, my peace of mind was secure. I asked you whether I could go on with my work: you replied "yes," and consequently said you were going to send me the necessary papers. You did not hesitate to fill me with the firm belief I was safe: for that belief you alone are therefore responsible, and I spent the night of the 25th to the 26th under my own roof only because of what I had from your letters number 4 and 5, received the 25th. In those letters you notified me of the sale of my charge;[7] I was stunned; 'twas impossible for me to imagine that such a dreadful piece of news could be announced to me on the eve of the day when I was about to be struck an even more dreadful blow, and I went to bed very afflicted[8] on the one hand, but very reassured on the other. Nevertheless, do not think that by this little reproach I am seeking to impute anything to you. That would be too much to bear: no, I should never accuse you; I would rather die a thousand deaths. But your mother, who could very well have fallen under suspicion here, did not once appear thus in my eyes; I expressly beseech you to tell her so, and to both of you I hereby swear 'tis my most intimate persuasion this foul deed[9] was done without either of you having any knowledge of it.

Before going into the particulars of this sinister adventure, I shall add yet a second reproach. You have been unsparing concerning some of the good and decent people who were my friends down there, and yours too, and when one needs the help of everybody, one must be

---

in 1774 as governess at La Coste. Her duties during that orgiastic winter were doubtless far broader.

7. Sade is referring to his post, passed on to him by his father, as lieutenant for the provinces of Bresse, Bugey, Gex, and Valromey.

8. Sade exaggerates. In a subsequent letter to his cousin he says, regarding the sale of that title: "It's simply a transfer of title. It was sold for what it was worth."

9. That is, his latest arrest; despite his words, he holds the présidente responsible.

tactful with everybody. The canon[10] complains greatly about you; you have written him ridiculous letters about a small affair he thought to entrust to your good offices in Paris. These people understand nothing of court flattery, and 'tis not with friends, and, I dare say, with sincere friends, one should act in the same way. You acted in similar fashion with Milli Rousset who, if 'twere possible, is even more attached to us and who, upon this latest occasion, sacrificed herself entirely for me: one day I shall convince you of it. You wrote her grand and foolish letters headed by *Mademoiselle*, all the while hers to you were filled with the greatest warmth for you. One day I saw her weeping at being thus treated by you, and that at a time when, out of the kindness of her heart, she had remained in the château and was doing me every service friendship could suggest, even, since I had no domestics, helping with the household chores as Gothon would have done. She stayed by me every instant the whole time I was at La Coste, and most assuredly was of great help to me. Is it because she and the canon helped me to see the light about Gaufridy's infamies that you have taken a dislike to them? and is there a chance you suspect them of acting with their self-interest in mind? Some of your letters have shown that, but you are greatly mistaken. Their staunch friendship for me, and the general scandal created at La Coste by Gaufridy's behavior, made them all the more zealous; and the proof that neither one nor the other seeks any advantage is that they each separately advised me to exercise patience, to refrain from having any showdown with that monster and, above all, when I did have it out with him, never to replace him, since I had no need of any businessman once my lands were leased. They were therefore completely disinterested and, as you see, had nothing in view either for themselves or for theirs. But at this point you will perhaps remind me that Gaufridy nevertheless behaved well at Aix . . .[11] Do not be fooled by that: there were too many eyes upon him, he had no chance to misbehave; yet even so he had some shady dealings with the five girls, which proves that he whispered all the evil he could, and that, if he did no worse, 'tis because he was not able to. Exactly what these shady dealings consisted of would be too long to go into here.

---

10. Canon Vidal of the neighboring village of Oppède. He was Sade's close friend and confidant.
11. "Behaved well" is not quite accurate. Sade is referring to Gaufridy's journey to Marseilles, during the Aix trial in July, to wine and dine the five prostitutes, as well as the apothecaries and surgeons whose testimony relative to the "poisoning" was paramount. In other words, to pay them off.

The gist of it is that he dealt very harshly with the most decent of them, whose depositions were the most favorable, and showered both kindnesses and money upon one who came to the confrontation[12] to stage a tragic scene, which greatly embarrassed the commissioner, and was of a mind to undo everything. Moreover, had that man[13] been my friend and truly honest, as I was led to believe, wouldn't he have agreed to do what was asked of him? Instead of that, he did the very opposite. He even went and revealed to M. de la Tour[14] one of the elements of the plan I was getting ready to put into effect, talked Ripert,[15] who agreed to take charge of everything (the said Ripert admitted to this publicly), out of doing so with great eloquence and fanfare. Finally, between him and his friend Reinaud[16]—who is no better than he and to whom I most urgently ask that you send nothing further—their combined efforts all told boiled down to giving me twelve louis, and, what is more, they proposed, beggars that they are, deducting them from a sum intended for you. If they had given me more— and they easily could have, especially because M. de la Tour had offered Gaufridy as much money as he liked—if, I repeat, they had given me more, I would have gone to Florence, as was my intention, and today I would not be here. Once I was home, I could have remedied matters, that I admit; anyone else but me would have done so. It was the time when my leases were up for renewal: by going to see my tenants one by one, I would have collected a considerable amount of money simply by renewing their leases at a third less than the going rate. I repeat: anyone else but me would have done that; but I, who am always the victim whenever I try to do some good, I, far from putting a crimp in my affairs, thought only of straightening them out. They could not possibly have been in greater need of being put aright, the moment could not have been more critical for me. . . . That is how I have been rewarded.

Let me come now to the particulars I promised you. On August 19th I was taking a quiet stroll in the park 'round about dusk with the curate and Milli Rousset when we heard someone in the little wood,

---

12. That is, to the trial, where the accused and the accusers came face to face.
13. He is referring to Gaufridy.
14. Count de la Tour, governor of the duchy of Savoy. Sade was under his benign jurisdiction during his incarceration at the Fortress of Miolans.
15. The Sades' steward for their Mazan property.
16. Maître Reinaud was Sade's attorney in the Midi and represented him in the Aix appeal.

which upset me greatly. I called out several times, asking who it was; to which I got no response. I stepped forward and came upon the guard Sambuc, the elder, a little tipsy from too much wine, who said to me, looking extremely worried and frightened, that I should make my getaway as fast as I could, for the tavern was beginning to fill up with people who looked most suspicious. Milli Rousset went down to check things out and an hour later returned, completely taken in by the speeches of two spies whose task it was to prepare the way, and assured me she would stake her life that these people were indeed who they said they were, that is to say silk merchants, adding that there was absolutely nothing to fear. You would not have made such a mistake, for one of them was part of the gang that arrested me in Paris at your house. So I was not all that wrong in wishing you were with me. When you were with me, nothing bad ever happened to me at La Coste. Little reassured by what I had learned, I left that same night and sought refuge with the canon. Milli Rousset forwarded my mail and twice a day sent me dispatches to keep me abreast of all the details. As these were becoming ominous, I left Oppède and came to a barn about a league away. The reports continued to be disquieting. You know who, from Apt,[17] spoke in the clearest terms, and, in spite of everything, as though impelled by a force superior to my own, for there is no escaping one's fate, on Sunday the 23rd I fell into a kind of agitation so violent that nobody with perceptiveness could have failed to see that this cruel state signaled the end of my unhappy period of freedom. The person the canon had appointed to take care of me was so frightened by this state that she hurried off to notify the canon. He soon arrived. "But what is the matter with you?" "Nothing; I want to get out of here." "Are you feeling ill?" "No, but I want to get out." "And where do you want to go?" "Home." "You are mad, and I shall certainly not go with you there." "I'm not asking you to, I can get home quite nicely by myself." "But stop and think for a moment, I beg of you." "I've already thought about it, I want to go home." "And you're totally ignoring the danger, everything that has been written to you! . . ." "Stuff and nonsense, that's all it is; there isn't any danger. So let's be off." "Let's wait at least another four days?" (Alas, the poor devil guessed exactly the number of days we should have waited!) "I don't want to wait, I tell you, I want to leave." Finally, we set off together, and arrive at La Coste. For fear of keeping me from getting a little rest, they

---

17. Gaufridy, whose home and office were in that town.

don't dare take me too openly to task for my rashness. On the morrow, they urge me to return to my hiding place. I hold stubbornly to the notion of staying. Your letters of the 25th arrive. I feel increasingly safe, and, on the 26th, at four o'clock in the morning, Gothon, in a state of complete undress and all aflutter, rushes into my bedchamber (the one where I sleep in summer) shrieking at the top of her lungs: "Run for your life! . . ." What an awakening! Clad only in my nightshirt, I make off in the only direction I can, racing mechanically up the stairs to a place which, despite my explicit instructions, had in no wise been prepared;[18] finding nothing there to help me, I dash into the Marchais bedroom, lately referred to as the Brun bedroom. I lock myself in; a minute later I hear such a frightful uproar on the stairway that for a moment I thought they were thieves coming to cut my throat. There were shouts: "Murder! Fire! Thief!" and then, in a trice, the door is battered down and I am seized by ten men at once, several of whom have their swords pointed at my body, while others are holding pistols clapped to my face. At which point, a flood of atrocious stupidities comes pouring out of the mouth of Monsieur Inspector Marais; I am tied up; and from that moment until Valence I had unceasingly to put up with that man's invectives and insults, the details of which I shall spare you. They were too humiliating relative to someone you love, and I prefer not to describe them to you. At Cavaillon, the whole town came out; at Avignon more than three hundred people,[19] and what most distressed me there was that, at the very same moment, my poor aunt, the Abbess of Saint-Laurent, lay dying. She had just had my cousin write me a charming letter full of congratulations. What a turn of events! It may prove to be the death of her. . . . I beg you to write to her and also to my aunt in Cavaillon, to express all my fondest regards, and to give me news of them. —There, my dear friend, is how I was treated.

But I would have thought at the very least, according to what your mother wrote, that, once I was back in prison, I would have all the amenities that were consistent with my safekeeping. Instead of that, I have not a fourth of the bare amenities I had before. They have put me

---

18. A storeroom on the third floor. Sade had intended that it be fitted out as a secret hiding place, where no one could find him. Obviously, the work was never done, doubtless for lack of funds.
19. Sade was by now so notorious, from the scandal sheets and local word of mouth, that he was a major celebrity. It was as if Satan were passing through.

in a new cell[20] where I can barely breathe, where all ventilation is blocked off, a cell in which 'twill be impossible for me to make a fire this winter. I am harassed and vexed on every score; I am much less well fed, and at completely different hours, which wreaks havoc with my stomach. In a word, I am treated like someone they don't know what to do with and would like to give up on completely. I have no more commission, I have no more trial: does it matter whether I live or die! Such was doubtless their reasoning as they worked out my unhappy fate, and all I need do now is die of grief. You clearly insinuated that if I asked to be transferred to the abbey, my wish would be granted. I most earnestly make that request; there we would at least be within striking distance of each other, if only they would allow visits, and I would at least be able to have the food and furnishings I liked. If cost is a consideration, I do not ask that one more penny be spent than what is being paid to keep me here, and with this sum I warrant that in any other prison, be it in a kingdom, I would be infinitely better off than I am here. Please be so kind as to ask your mother this one favor. If she is of a mind to seek it for me she will surely obtain it. I am going to ask it of M. Le Noir; and to make sure 'tis not mistaken as some momentary whim on my part, I shall most assuredly go on asking for it in every letter I am allowed to write.

In a letter you wrote me at La Coste, you told me that it was just as well I had escaped, since were I to return to prison 'twould be for at least a year, with exile afterward, and for three years at the most. Which of the two is it, then, one year or three, since the length of my sentence has been determined? And 'tis quite clear that it has been fixed. Since my sentence is a result of my trial, they can very well tell me what the sentence is. I most urgently ask to be told what it is. There is no longer any reason whatsoever to keep me from knowing it. This terrible uncertainty keeps me in a state of affliction that no words can describe. I beseech you and your mother to have the kindness to remove me from that affliction: all I ask is that one consolation: will they deign grant it to me?

You had no idea, my dear friend, how deeply upset I was over the loss of my charge.[21] What a frightful combination, to suffer such a loss and then find myself in prison to boot! Was it at least sold for a suitable

---

20. The infamous cell number 6, which Sade claimed unlivable. Sade began referring to himself as "Monsieur le Six," Mr. Six.
21. As noted, Sade could not have cared less about his loss of the royal charge or commission; again, he is simply playing on Renée-Pélagie's heartstrings.

price or was it simply given away for the assumption of the commission? You should at least have told me that much. I must confess that this arrangement, especially when I learned it was initially to be made with the elder M. d'Evry,[22] struck me as a trifle suspect on your mother's part. To transfer into her family the favors which the king formerly granted to mine did not strike me as very loyal. I suspected some other arrangement more advantageous to my children was being made, when I learned that it was going to someone bearing my name. That will not prevent me from feeling the most profound hatred for that pip-squeak of a gentleman; and despite the enthusiasm for this house you display in one of your latest letters, you will permit me to be completely convinced of the fact that I reported on them because I have it from the horse's mouth, [and] to consider him personally as a man both hard-hearted and lacking in sensibility for daring to enrich himself at the expense of his cousin, and most cordially to loathe him, him and his kin, for the rest of my life.

Moreover, from some phrases you let slip into your letters, from one letter written by your mother and sent on to me for some unknown reason, I was able to piece together—for with you one always has to piece together: candor and simplicity are virtues you simply no longer have—in any case, I was able to figure out that your mother was meddling with my property. She probably thought that since she had succeeded in stripping me of my commission without my consent, she could also sell off my estate as she liked and act as if all this were no more than the cabbages in her own garden. I believe she is incapable of ever making a mistake, and I would even go so far as to say I know her well enough to be certain that I could only gain from any arrangement she might make: nonetheless, I beg her to get it firmly into her head that under no circumstances do I wish to part either with La Coste, or with Saumane, or with Mazan; that from the moment I go on record as being formally opposed thereto, which I am and always shall be, I doubt whether anyone would purchase a property, given the fact that as soon as I am free my first act would be to lodge a complaint against him. Therefore, I beseech her not to meddle with any of those three objects, not wanting, no matter what they may allege my wishes to be, to part with any of the three. Let her sell Arles if she likes, and with the money and with what the commission yields, let her meddle to her heart's content. But as for the rest, no. Let her be sure that I shall always stand in opposition. In my next letter I shall include some

---

22. Madame de Sade's uncle.

details about what should be done instead, at least for the time being, regarding the renewal of the leases.

7. To Madame de Sade

October 4, 1778

So, 'twill be erasures, crossing out words, and every possible sort of scrawl that are going to replace the torture wheels! If, as you say, you are most eager to calm me down, to please me, and other high-blown phrases that flow from the pen without coming from the heart, if, I say, you are so bent on pleasing me, please be so kind as to spare me as well these erasures which I am willing to wager are your work and not someone else's, because some of them that I have deciphered are too indifferent to have been produced by anyone other than you and your charming adviser. They are further signals,[1] are they not? Well, I implore you, spare me such signals, for I solemnly declare I shall return every one of your letters wherein even the slightest hint of a signal appears. You wish to convince me that 'tis not you doing them? Well then, I am going to offer you a means to avoid inflicting that torture upon me. Send your rough drafts to *the scribbler;*[2] as one sends shoes to a bootblack; let the scribbler scribble away in peace, then return the scribbles to you. After which, you will make a clean copy, and I shall have no more erasures. If you had a little more spirit, I would tell you to go find the person who takes it upon himself to edit your letters and ask him by what right he arrogates unto himself this permission, when you speak neither about the king nor about the government, which are the only subjects that are forbidden. But you are not one to do that. Far be it from you to show such disrespect for Sir Scribbler! But while we are on the subject of this little gentleman, do go some fine morning and pay a visit to his master, I beg of you, and ask

---

1. As noted, Sade became convinced his wife's letters were filled with secret signals, meant to evade the censor's pen and to reveal something important to him that she could not say openly, such as when he would be released, the most burning question for Sade as for any prisoner. Renée-Pélagie denied she ever resorted to such signals; Sade simply refused to believe her.
2. That is, to Monsieur Boucher, Sade's personal censor at Vincennes.

whether 'twas following his orders that he informed Marais of everything I wrote, both to you and to your mother, during the last three
weeks before my departure for Aix, adding, in a bantering tone that fits
him to a T: *"You see how he goes on and on. One can tell he's a prisoner."*
Marais said—and he said it in the presence of the same four witnesses
I have cited in connection with his insolent behavior in my house—
that the person who receives my letters at police headquarters had
shown him two or three in which I most urgently requested both of my
mother-in-law and of M. Le Noir, not to be escorted by him.[3] And that
this secretary, with whom he was close, told him everything and
showed him everything. That is what Marais said in no uncertain
terms, adding several days later, when he talked to me personally, that
it was for no other reason he had been in a foul mood and his behavior
had been what it had been. Then he told me that this scribbler, who
out of decency I prefer not to call by any other name, hell-bent to see
me behind bars again, since he probably earns some fee from his scrib-
bling (it keeps leading back to my bootblack comparison; *M. Shoe
Brush* is never pleased to see his business decline); that this scribbler,
I say, had hied himself off to see Madame de Montreuil, and from her
slyly (for he is a sly one, the scribbler!) wormed out of her some clari-
fication regarding the name of a certain *Vidal*, whom they feared might
cause trouble as they went through Valence; that he had proceeded
with much art (for he is artful, this scribbler is!) in order to discover
what he wanted, considering that the said Lady de Montreuil had no
desire to see me recaptured; and that finally he had learned this and
passed it on posthaste to the aforementioned Marais. So much for the
facts! The truth of which should convince you that I am not making
them up, and also make you see the extent to which subordinates
whom their superiors believe are deserving of their greatest confidence, abuse it to perform the darkest deeds the moment they glimpse
the slightest gain therefrom. Would you be so kind, without wasting
your time over the second item—which I brought up merely to show
you I am aware of it—as to betake yourself to see M. Le Noir and talk
to him about the first matter only, essentially to lodge a protest against
the behavior of the man who, entrusted by him with my letters, pur-
veys their full contents to third and fourth parties, and then gloats over
them. If this letter does not come into your hands, and if I receive no
positive reply from you upon this article, then 'tis clear that *Martin
Scribbler* will have scribbled and consequently feels guilty, since he is

---

3. From Paris to the Aix appeals trial.

standing in the way of my complaints against him getting through. Then I shall know what I have to do. Never in my life have I been at a loss about how to punish insolents of that class, as long as I have found walking sticks to buy.

In the most recent operations of the *animal* I have just been referring to, I have managed to decipher only one word: *certificates*. I have no idea what that means. But if it refers to Marais, as it appears from the preceding lines, 'tis not astonishing that his dear friend the Scribbler would have scribbled that. *All those beggars are alike*, therefore always back one another up. Speaking of which, I am reminded of an altogether charming little remark you made. 'Twas with reference to the four hundred thousand francs: *"I am ready to pay them the moment you are let out, otherwise not."* But when I am let out, shall it still be your responsibility to sign and settle accounts? I thought it would be mine. You can see all the implications that your execrable phrases are forever leaving in their wake. And the word *otherwise*, where did you come up with that? *Otherwise:* that is to say, you foresee and cleverly imply there might be a situation where I shall not be let out. You see how deftly comforting you are in your letters! And then you come and tell me *that you do not understand why I can be upset by them, that all you're trying to do is soothe me, to calm me down*, etc.! Come, come now, Madame! your behavior toward me is horrifying. *If you had any possible way of telling me*, you add on another page, *how long my term is to be, you would do so; but your silence will shorten it, and your zeal is no less keen*, etc. Yes, once again, you must have lost all sense of honor and humanity for you to dare write thus to your husband. Your behavior with me is execrable. And mark you well, as long as a drop of blood still flows in my veins I shall not forgive you. I shall dissemble, because I have been taught to do so, but for the rest of my life I shall consider you as a heartless and unfeeling woman, *who is naught but a weathervane and is brought low by the slightest bump in the road;* in a word, as a lump of wax that anyone can give whatever shape he likes. *Your zeal, your efforts?* Well now, shall we strike a bargain? I shall relieve you not only of your *zeal and your efforts*, but also of whatever they might produce. And I want you to tell me the worst I should expect. I am resigned to enduring every last day of it, if only I have the satisfaction of knowing what it is. Come, come! Madame, you are behaving shamefully, that is all I can say to you. Yet this great secret is not all that inviolable, since at La Coste you wrote me that 'twas to be *one year or three*. Why can't you repeat to me here what you told me there? All I ask of you is: which of the two is it? It seems to me you must surely be able to tell me that! And, once again, what could be the reasons preventing me from being told? At present, there are no longer any at all. It is impossible, absolutely impossible, that there be any except for your dreadful and black spitefulness, or rather your weakness and your humbleness vis-à-vis the scoundrels who are leading you down the garden path. You tell me that the name *Albaret* is an enigma for you. What then are two letters signed *Bontoux*, and disclaimed by the said Monsieur Bontoux[4] that you sent me last year? They are indeed in Albaret's handwriting, that you'll not deny? Moreover, in the presence of the commandant of this Château, Monsieur de Bontoux positively denied having written them. Who did write them then? Until I have your explanation on that point will you get it out of my head that this strange dark fellow Albaret is not your adviser. Besides, Chauvin saw him at your house: he told me so.[5] Thus it is useless to deny anything so obvious. You used to write to me in Provence: *"Ah! dear God, oh, my good friend, you are upset by my letters. Verily, I know not why. You must have known that if I did not speak, 'twas because I could not."* And when you were able to speak, when you wrote *thirty letters in milk*,[6] why did you say nothing? And why were those mysterious letters even more stupid than the others? Eh? How do you explain that? You can't: the only explanation is your unkindness or your weakness. Ah! it will take some time before my bitterness is gone. Mademoiselle Rousset has my permission to tell you how angry I was when I spoke of you to her, and how, despite her friendship for you, she was so surprised when I gave her the full rundown of your horrors that she could find no word to justify you. I am deeply sorry that I prevailed upon her to come to Paris. She is going to adopt your tone, your language; 'tis a good friend I shall lose. Would that I have never told her to come! *"The most difficult part is over,"* but what in the world do you mean by that? And what do you mean it to imply? You can see for yourself that, far from offering me the least comfort in your abominable letters, you seek only to drive me out of my mind. And do you expect to

---

4. A lawyer engaged by Madame de Montreuil to help Sade in his appeals case in Aix. Bontoux's strong recommendation—perhaps instigated by Madame de Montreuil—was that Sade enter a plea of insanity, which he steadfastly refused to do.
5. Pierre Chauvin, Sade's steward at La Coste.
6. In an attempt to circumvent the censor's gaze, Madame de Sade resorted to writing, often between the lines, in invisible ink, to impart important information or advice. This "secret writing" was quite apart from the so-called signals Sade thought he detected in her letters.

reap some benefit from all that? No, Madame, no, take my word for it! You are making my character even more bitter and me a thousand times worse than I ever was. Ah! my God, why is it you are incapable to judge what you are doing and see what you are turning me into! But that sentence *"the most difficult part is over,"* you wrote that to me at La Coste, I remember it well. Therefore, you already knew at the time that I still had something further to do?[7] And if you did know, why did you not tell me? Why, far from urging most insistently that I not stay at La Coste, did you lull me into a false sense of security by saying, *"I advise you to finish writing your book"?* But that means you didn't know . . . And if you didn't know, why then did you say *"the most difficult part is over"?* I defy you to work your way out of that vicious circle. But to this you will not reply, isn't that so? That's the quickest solution, and *Beau Scribbler* will come to your rescue. *"You'll see. Someday you will realize that I love you,"* you tell me in your most recent letter. Yes, the way you loved me at Aix, isn't that true? And that lovely letter it took me two hours to understand, the one that began: *"Well there, my dear friend, now do you doubt that I love you?"* My God, I said to myself, what has become of me? I felt I was free. I pinched myself to see if I was dreaming . . . No, absolutely not. That wonderful love consisted of advising me to take certain measures that put my life at risk a thousand times over, and, what is more, you were unwilling to back me up! For to back me up, as soon as you knew there was still something that needed to be done—since you said that *"the most difficult part is over"*—to back me up, I say, you ought at the same time to have urged me most urgently to hie myself abroad, you ought to have sent me letters of credit and letters of recommendation, all that care of La Jeunesse, and my carriage. That is how one supports that kind of course of action, when one is of a mind to do so, and not by a banal letter, without a penny enclosed, and by a scoundrel of a business agent[8] who, although in only five months' time will owe you two thousand crowns, boldly offers you twelve louis. That, I say, is how you should have shown your love, Madame. And if the proofs of friendship that you tell me will be forthcoming are similar to the ones you have already shown me, do me the favor of opting for indifference. In a word, it appears from what you wrote to me yesterday that if you tell me what my term will be, it shall not help me one whit, and that if you remain silent, I shall be the

---

7. Sade doubtless means, "I still had more prison time to serve."
8. Gaufridy.

better for it. Well, I repeat once again that on this subject I do prefer to know. In a word, I beseech you to tell me. *Or I shall curse you as the lowest of creatures, and consider you, having refused me once again, a monster upon whom I shall never lay eyes again as long as I live.* These two trunks of Mademoiselle Rousset's, what do they mean? I bet one of them is for you, and that you are having your belongings sent up from La Coste. Tell me. And if 'tis so, and since you seem so bound and determined to explain things these days, explain to me why you have had my portrait sent up? Why did you send for the livery habits? And why have you sold my carriage? . . . Eh! Tell me, give me the whole story without any of your shilly-shallying. Tell me that I still have a long time to suffer, and that all this was a way, done in your own inimitable manner, of making me understand it. Oh! good God, why did I have the misfortune of going to Provence to find out all that I found out there, and see there all I saw? If Mademoiselle Rousset was destined to come back to Provence with me, and if I did not have a long time to spend here, she would not have brought such a considerable amount of luggage! But she sees that 'tis to be long and makes her arrangements accordingly. *"Do not worry. Do not be upset."* What! you told me all that when I had sixteen months of suffering ahead of me. Those are your eternal phrases! Of course they didn't calm me, far from it. From now on, when I ask you something, kindly refrain from answering: *"We will bring it up with the minister."* Because no minister is needed for me to have a better cell, for me to be allowed some fresh air, for me to have some writing paper. There are regulations for all that. Thus 'tis merely a matter of telling me quite plainly: "You'll have it in this or that amount of a time." As for my cell, *'tis a very great act of dishonesty* was done me when mine was changed.[9] 'Tis one more act to add to the others, and one I shall remember. Not only shall I be unable to have a fire throughout the winter, but, to boot, I am devoured by rats and mice, which keep me from getting a single minute of rest all night long. I have just spent six sleepless nights in a row, and when I ask if they would kindly have a cat put into the next room to destroy them, they answer that *animals are forbidden.* To which I respond: "Why, fools that you are, if animals are forbidden, rats and mice should be forbidden, too." To which they reply: *"That's different."* You see what the regulations in this execrable hovel are like, all of which tend to make the

---

9. That is, when he was brought back to Vincennes in August and reincarcerated in cell number 6.

prisoner's life ever more miserable, not one of them aimed at alleviating it. Since more suffering lay ahead, at least they should have allowed it to happen in Paris or Aix. That was all I asked. But no, Vincennes is all the rage! That is all they have to say. May those who keep me here, those who had me put here, and those who do not want to tell me for how much time I am to be here, all die a thousand times over. That is my last wish.

8. To Madame de Sade

October 21, 1778

*W*ell then, my dear friend, 'tis decided once and for all that, down to the very last moment, all of your letters will be for me so many knife thrusts. Ah! but good God, will you then never weary of this abominable torture, and do you absolutely want to force me, for my peace of mind, to ask to be deprived of what, one might suppose, ought only comfort and console me? 'Tis a most incredible persistence, that! Am I not already miserable enough at having been re-arrested, at having to recommence my suffering all over again, and even worse than before, to see the best years of my life wasting away in perpetual irons, without you allowing, nay, striving, to open the wound again and again, by the damnable poison of your venomous letters? When she is with you, ask Mademoiselle Rousset whether I did not tell her that my greatest afflictions have come from no one but you . . . you from whom I ought to expect naught but comfort. 'Tis from you I received and receive the most telling hurts. But who in the world is the person so barbarous, so completely devoid of good sense, as to suggest such behavior to you? And what does he—or they—want unless 'tis to plunge me into despair? First off, 'tis not your mother who is behind it, of that I am now sure. She would be incapable of calculated horror to this nth degree. No soul that ever knew tenderness could have conceived it or even conceive of it. What does this mean: *"Your children have gone away for two years; I promised them that upon their return they would join us again, you and me, wherever we might be; they left satisfied they would see you in two years"?* I should greatly like you to be in my place, for only a month (without knowing 'twas to be for so short a time), and

have someone write you a sentence like that! You can flatter yourself
that in the whole precious collection of lovely epistles I have been getting from you for nearly two years, you have not sent me any whose
sharp angles have stuck any deeper into my flesh nor perhaps wrought
such havoc in my mind as this, which for the last forty-eight hours it
has been my misfortune to have before my eyes. Is there any amphi-
bology, any logogriph, to match it, and did you heat it sufficiently in
the forges of the infernal demon who inspired you to write it? He
should be proud of his work. I had never yet felt such a deep distress,
and that was the final touch needed to finish me off after all I have just
suffered . . . And so it will never end and will therefore always be the
same thing! In short, what do you mean by that sentence? In God's
name, if there is still a bit of pity left in your heart, if 'tis possible that
you listen to it and for one moment free yourself from the demoniacal
rage of the scoundrel who is guiding you[1]—and who, say what you will,
I know on very good authority to be never out of your sight—and be
counseled (not by your mother, I know that) but by others, and by others than those who, I was warned of it, have hated me most cordially;
if, I say, 'tis possible you can remove yourself for a moment from their
tyrannical vindictiveness, do me the favor of explaining that sentence
to me, in clear and simple terms, whether you intended thereby to advise me *that I shall get out of here only in two years?* Is that it? Then say so,
say it at once. Oh! my God, yes, say it, and no more of this rubbing salt
into my wounds and driving me crazy, making me frantic each time I
lay eyes on one of your writings. At this point there can no longer be
any reason for not letting me know my term. 'Tis clear it has been set,
that 'tis a consequence of the verdict, and that like that verdict it has
been set. I was informed of the one, why should I not be informed of
the other? There is not any need to fiddle over the affair; it has been
judged; there is no longer any consideration that might detain, no
longer any secret efforts being made, no hidden scheme; in short,
there is no longer anything except blatant wickedness that can stand in
the way of granting what I so earnestly ask. Am I perhaps sentenced to
such and such a term and you hope to whittle it down to some degree?
Well, do not tell me what that "some degree" amounts to; I don't wish

---

1. Sade is grasping at straws. He cannot imagine his wife is capable of making
such epistolary lapses as telling him his children are being sent away for two
years—from which he deduces he will be at Vincennes at least that long—on
her own.

to know. If it comes to pass, so much the better! Tell me the worst. That is all I ask of you. In a word, I beg you in the name of your children, in the name of all you hold most sacred, to deliver me from the horrible state I am in, and to inform me of my fate, no matter what it may be. I shall hear it and I shall hear it without complaining, and when I know what it is, however long it may be, my state of mind cannot but be less dreadful than the horrible uncertainty in which I now find myself. Must you absolutely speak in riddles? And is it set in stone that that is the only way you can express yourself? Very well: in your reply to this letter repeat to me: *that my children are gone for two years to Vallery; that you don't know whether you've mentioned it to me, but in case you've forgotten to do so, you are hereby informing me.* Repeat that to me and I shall take it to mean that I have two more years here. Alas! dear God, 'tis only too likely that that is the enormous period I still must endure. If (as I dared hope) I had been exiled to my estates, since my children are at Vallery, who (assuming your mother's permission) would have prevented me, a few months from now, from paying them a twenty-four hours' visit, or at least from having them brought to me by the mail coach? The road is so nearby. And one way or another, I would have seen them then. 'Tis therefore clear, and clearer than daylight, that since they are for all intents and purposes on the road to Provence, and since you tell me I shall not see them for two years, therefore, I say, 'tis clear beyond all shadow of doubt that I shall not be traveling along that road for the next two years. Now, since 'tis impossible that, upon getting out of here, I shall go anywhere else than home, since to prevent me from going home would be ruinous, 'tis therefore obvious that, as I shall not be permitted to take the road to Provence for the next two years, that means I shall not be released from here for another two years. This relentless succession of consequences leads us unavoidably to the point, and after having fairly clearly given me to understand that, you therefore risk nothing by telling me that a little more positively, and at least allowing me to get straight in my poor mind something that is not one whit improved by being handled the way it is being handled, not by a long shot, you may be sure. Speak out then, speak out, for once in your life speak out clearly! I beg of you to do so, or you will end up reducing me to the final depths of despair.

Shall I tell you about the sad little castle in the air I have been building? Alas! I shall tell you about it, however much you may mock me for doing so; but what do you expect me to do here except lay my plans and give birth to fantasies?

Someone, and most assuredly a well-informed someone, whom I shall not name because he does not want to be compromised, in a word then, a man of substance and a very gallant man to boot, told me *that the court had dealt with my affair in accordance with the views of the minister.* 'Tis therefore clear that they also concurred on the sentence. Now, when the court pronounced three years' absence from Marseilles, in all probability that was the term the minister had in mind for my punishment, too. And so I said to myself: there will be three years in irons, but those three years will be *at the most six months in prison and the rest in exile on my estate.* That did not appear doubtful to me. Judge for yourself therefore the enormous impact your letter had upon me when it arrived. All the while I was free I could not refrain from holding to that opinion, and that verdict of three years was even one of the things which served most to reassure me, for indeed, from the moment there had been agreement between the ministry and the court, how could it make any sense that the court would forbid me from setting foot in Marseilles for three years unless it was certain that during those three years I might have the possibility of going there? It is in the context of this eventuality, I said to myself, that the court pronounced the sentence it laid down. Consequently, I shall therefore be free, for, if the intent was to keep me captive this whole time, what would be the purpose of this further restriction? It would be absurd, preposterous, beyond belief. Once it knows the king, by holding me prisoner, will effectively prevent me from going to Marseilles, why does the court therefore forbid me from going there? This excess of penalties is downright foolishness. Why, by so doing, go and mar a verdict? For that alone makes it look slightly suspicious. And it serves no useful purpose. When one has locked up a person inside a room, the custom is not to shout to him through the door: *"Sir, I forbid you to walk out."* 'Twould be a stupid persiflage, which one cannot imagine coming from our good gentlemen of Aix.[2] And yet, if the king's order is to thus bind me for three years, that is precisely what the judges have done. Therefore, when I was free nothing (and I said it and wrote it to everyone down there) encouraged me more in the belief I was to remain free than this verdict. And once I was rearrested, applying the same analyses, this same verdict persuaded me even more strongly that the king's chains could not last for three years, since the court had imposed its own verdict for that same period, and because it once again does not stand to reason that the latter would impose its restrictions when it saw

---

2. The judges of the appellate court.

that the former had already done so. That, I repeat, is a duplication of penalties, which is absolutely inadmissible. Hence it is clear: either I must be free and without restriction before three years are out, or else the high court of Aix has committed a blunder. And starting from that premise, I believe that it was quite reasonable to estimate six months in prison and a few more months in exile or, at the worst, exile for all the rest of the three years, ridiculous as that would have been. Assuming which, judge if you will the overwhelming effect of your letter suddenly hinting at two years behind bars without counting the exile. That is why I'm in such a frightful state and why I ask upon bended knee that you speak clearly to me.

And here's a little letter for those poor little creatures I love more than you can believe. Were I to be set free tomorrow, I would still find it a terrible torture knowing I must be another two years without seeing them. I was scarce prepared for this. I was right when all last year I dreamed that when I next saw them they would be all grown up. Ah, good God! Surely they'll not recognize me. 'Tis hardly worthwhile having children if you have no opportunity ever to enjoy them; for 'tis now the moment when they give true pleasure; later on, nothing but trouble. I ask you most earnestly to offer your mother and father my heartfelt thanks for the latest kindnesses they are bestowing upon those poor children. I cannot tell you how much this both pains and pleases me, for I find we are like those poor creatures who, in the presence of those who take care of their children, weep tears of gratitude and at the same time tears of despair at being deprived of their own through lack of fortune, and prevented from giving them the care they would like. I do not know whether my comparison will strike you in the way it affects me, nor do I know what name I could give the tears I shed as I write this.

What do you mean when you say that our eldest has promise of being employed after these two years of study? But, my dear friend, he will then be only thirteen, and at thirteen one's proper place is in an academy. Even assuming someone was recommending him, could he take up some position before he completed his schooling?[3]

In due course, you will explain that to me. Send your mother my thousand good wishes, if you will. Please assure her and reassure her of my fondness and my respect. I dare not write to her, since she does not read my letters, but I would consider it a great favor, and a great com-

---

3. Sade is doubtless recalling his own father's decision to remove him from school at the age of fourteen.

fort to me in my misery, if you could soften her heart, and get her permission for me to write her.[4] Let her judge me as I am since my return here . . . but why with such delay? because, alas! I was not enlightened until two days before my unfortunate catastrophe. But let her judge me since this return, and she will see whether or not I am true to my word.

I am distressed and surprised to hear that Milli Rousset is not yet with you. Give her my fondest regards when she comes, and love her well, hers is a most rare and precious heart. It worries me that she is so slow in arriving. That sets my mind to conjuring up further dark conjectures, not about her, God preserve me, but about my unfortunate and sad fate. Oh, how I need some fresh air! I am dying of migraines and vapors. I strongly approve of la Langevin[5] accompanying your children, and also of her taking care of the little one.[6] I don't know whether I shall become fond of her, I mean the little one, but she does not touch me like the two others. I have answered everything that concerns Gaufridy and business. I forgot to say that Ripert must be obliged to renew his lease, and that lots of vines must be planted at Piedmarin.

I enclose a kiss.

9. To Madame de Sade

[February 8, 1779]

*T*here you go again suffering a charming attack of deaf ear to the errands I asked you to do. 'Tis most kind, most clever, most gallant. The only thing is, it is becoming overly monotonous. This delightful

---

4. Madame de Montreuil had indicated that she would not reply to any further letters from her son-in-law, and indeed forbade him from writing her.
5. The Sade children's governess. Sade had three children, two boys and a girl. The oldest, Louis-Marie, was born on August 27, 1767. His second son, Donatien-Claude-Armand, was born on June 27, 1769. His daughter, Madeleine-Laure, was born on April 17, 1771.
6. That is, Madeleine-Laure, who was only five when Sade entered Vincennes.

signal recurs all too often. Thus it ceases to be natural as you would like it to be. Everything that is affected ceases to be natural, and remember the importance of injecting naturalness into the signal. For if I were so unfortunate as to venture a guess, if by mishap the signal made no sense, and if it no longer had this great look of simplicity so essential to everything we call signals, where would we then be? All would be lost, confusion would reign, lightning would strike, Madame la présidente would shit no more. 'Tis perhaps that I own the thing I most delight in seeing: that awkwardness with which you all—*all, for you are all signal-making animals—do your best to look natural: things are never done on purpose; 'tis always chance that produces them; and one can never fathom how I can perceive artificiality therein. There's the prisoners' mind for you: they see everything that way.* And other similar remarks with which they try to conceal the signal as soon as it is made. But once again, my worthy signal-makers, don't you really know that lies and nature are like oil and water, and that the more one strives to give the latter an appearance of the former, the more clumsy and ridiculous one becomes? But surely you do not know that, and there are doubtless many other things you do not know either.

For a signal-maker must by his very nature be exceedingly illiterate, exceedingly ignorant, dull as can be, very dim-witted, very clumsy, very pedantic, very idiotic, and a complete bore.

Fortunately, I still have the original copy of the errands you have been so kind as to keep putting off for almost six weeks. I shall therefore send it to you, but if I do I shall have no copy for myself. If you fail to have it taken care of this time I shall be unable to remember what they were.

So tell that rascal who scribbles, that ne'er-do-well blockhead, that he damn well better remember that when he was cleaning boots in front of the police station he would get only two half-farthings for a job poorly done. On the same subject, remind him that the présidente, who, they say, has him come every week to have his morning chocolate at the foot of her bed, is not going to pay him, or accord him her *ample favors,* when he performs so poorly. For his duty is to rub out the bad and to pass along the good to you: it follows therefore that no list of errands should ever be kept from getting through to you: for in a list of errands I do not say that Rougemont[1] is a m——f——, that the prési-

---

1. The warden of Vincennes. Sade's elisions are so obvious it is clear he is simply poking fun at his tormentors . . . or at his censors.

dente is a w——, that S[artine][2] is the son of an *alguazil*[3] of the Inquisition in Madrid, that Boucher is a toady, that Albaret[4] is a catam——. No, I say none of that in my lists of errands! I only say it in my letters. Therefore, only my letters are to be scribbled, and the lists should be left intact.

Kindly see to it that the attached bill is paid immediately, so that I am not made to ask for charity in order to obtain the things I need; which is always what happens until you pay the bill.

Kindly also send me the plays I already asked for, especially Petrarch's *L'Inconséquent* and *L'Opera*. I have the honor of giving you my most authentic word that all the plays I have asked you for are very much in print. I should hope that you have nothing so certainly stamped on your rear end as those texts are printed on paper.

10. To Madame de Sade

[February 17, 1779]

I answer you with my customary reliability, my dear friend, for nothing is easier for you than to count my letters and see whether any are missing: you have but to count your own.

I am most assuredly not incapable of writing you, and the day I am, for fear of worrying you, knowing how you feel about me, I shall manage so well that you won't even notice it. But please do tell me what you mean when you keep on saying, *"If you are unable to write to me, have a letter written?"* Doubtless, you think I have all sorts of secretaries at my beck and call: alas, I am a far cry from having such a luxury when my most elementary needs are scarce fulfilled! A man, always in

---

2. The former lieutenant-general of the Paris police, who took his orders directly from the king's ministers. For the past five years he had been minister of the navy.

3. Spanish for "policeman": Sade refers to those who acted as torturers during the Spanish Inquisition.

4. Albaret is a family retainer of the Montreuils, whom Sade disdains as a lackey of la présidente.

a great hurry, appears four times a day in my room, the first time being at dawn, to ask me *whether I had a good night's sleep* (you see how highly considerate they are); the other times, to bring me food, etc. Seven full minutes in all is the exact length of time he spends with me during these four visits; and then 'tis over: *Die, if you like, of boredom and a broken heart; for that matter, we couldn't care one whit.* What in the world were you thinking, secretaries at one's beck and call, when one is reduced to the state I am in! But, you may perhaps object, you didn't tell me such things in the past . . . Eh! maybe not, but in truth they used to take better care of me then than they presently do; in the past I was allowed more frequent walks; I was never left to eat alone; I was in a good room where I had a fine fire blazing . . . And at present, nobody keeps me company when I eat; many fewer walks; and lodged in the dampest cell in the dungeon (for 'tis from the humidity all my headaches stem). And, as a further pleasure, the impossibility of obtaining any heat: for as it is I have not yet lit a fire all winter, and I can safely say at this point that I'll light none. So that is how I am, my dear friend. But at present they have no further need of me: my case is closed. If I die, so much the better; good riddance . . . And I am quite convinced that, when all is said and done, they would just as soon be rid of me. And you don't understand that in such a situation one urgently asks to be set free or be told, at the very least, for how much longer one is to be here? One would have to be one's own worst enemy not to focus upon that sole idea, to be as much one's own enemy as mine are, both those who keep me here and those who refuse to grant me the unique consolation I ask for . . . You simply do not know, you are going to tell me! If you do not, how is it you try and indicate it to me? Don't tell such a lie, in God's name! Don't repeat it to me, it makes my blood boil. I shall prove to you beyond a shadow of a doubt that you knew as of February 14, 1777,[1] that I was going to be summoned before my judges on June 14, 1778.[2] Now, if you were so sure when the first part of my detention was due to end, how do you expect to convince me that you do not know the length of the second? But what am I saying? . . . Alas! you do not refuse to tell me what it is, and in fact you do tell me quite as emphatically and as expressively as you revealed the sixteen months to me with your number 22. Could anything on earth be clearer than the date

---

1. That is, the day after his arrest in Paris.
2. The date Sade left Vincennes, under the escort of Inspector Marais, for his appellate trial in Aix.

of *Saturday, February 22, No. 3 finally?*[3] After that, to doubt that the date of my release is anything but February 22, 1780, would surely be to labor under a very fatal illusion. But fearing that I not be sufficiently convinced, you had the goodness, very shortly thereafter, to send me three blank documents to sign, assuring me they were to run for *three years*. And today, renewing this charming signal once again, today, on the day when precisely two years have passed and one remains, you again clamor for my signature to another *power of attorney!* and you would have me doubt after such an obvious signal? No, no, no, not for one minute do I doubt that I have still another wretched year to endure here. 'Tis pointless for you to go on about it any further; I understand, pray don't remind me again of that dreadful memory. What I find outrageous, and what I shall never forgive those who do it, is to try and destroy this idea instead of bolstering it. When, from the very start, you made me understand so clearly those three years, why, whenever I alluded to them, did they reply to me: *What an idea! Three years, 'tis impossible! A few months at the very most . . .*

That is what is so foul, that is what is so odious, and that is what has been the cause of all the grief and all the misery of my situation. Would it not have been infinitely more humane to leave me to my illusion, since it was not such a pipe dream, instead of destroying it every day, thereby leading me to form a hope that was bred in me, fomented in me, simply for the sake of reveling in the unhappiness I perforce experienced at seeing it destroyed? I repeat, these methods are odious; they are also devoid of both humanity and common sense, and do but wear the emblem of an idiotic ferocity like that of tigers and lions. And when, more confirmed than ever in this very real idea that I still have one more year to endure, I say so in my letters—always harking back to the same old song, you people have the audacity, the infamy, to write to me, upon the subject of twelve jars of jam I requested back in the month of December: *Twelve jars of jam! Good heavens! what in the world are you going to do with all that? Are you going to give a dancing party? In any case, 'tis no great problem if some is left over.* In two words, such has been and still is the work of my torturers, for what other name can I give to those from whom I have received the most violent dagger-thrusts? Once you told me *three years*, once I had adjusted to the idea accordingly, what made you destroy my illusion? Why give

---

3. Again, Sade is reading in Renée-Pélagie's innocent numbers "signals" she never intended.

me a glimpse of my impending release when it was not true? And why, finally, take it into your head to dangle hope in front of me only to snatch it away the next instant? 'Tis this infamous game I decry; and those who, in playing it, serve as an instrument for the revenge of others, are playing a most mean and most despicable role, I might add a most barbaric role, for what have I done to these people? To one, nothing: I had never set eyes on him before in my life; to the other, naught but acts of courtesy and fair dealing . . . Well, I've heard enough for the nonce; they can sharpen their arrows for next year, if perchance my illusion is too optimistic; for as concerns this year, I declare to them that were they to talk and write to the devil, accustomed as I am to their abominable lying, I shall not believe I am to get out one minute before the 22nd of February, 1780.

Let's drop the subject.

There is however one sentence in your letter that could make me foresee a fate even more ghastly. Here it is: *Nothing proves that the release dates I indicated to you on the basis of my conjectures are false.* But the only date you have indicated is February 22, 1780. I vow and declare that I have neither seen nor been able to figure out any other indication from your letters. Yet in the sentence that comes immediately after you say: *To that you are going to reply: but why, when I was at La Coste, did you convey such and such a piece of information to me? The answer is that I was misled.* But what you conveyed to me at La Coste was that you had been told that I was to have three years once I had been judged, or one year plus exile. Now you say you are sorry you ever told me that. 'Tis therefore actually worse, since one is not sorry for having been overly pessimistic at first: you then have an agreeable surprise for him; you owe him no apology for having misled him in that way . . . And yet you apologize to me. The truth therefore is worse; and if 'tis worse, then I am still far off the mark in believing I'll be released on February 22, 1780! I would be infinitely grateful if you could explain that sentence to me, as it continues to worry and afflict me cruelly.

Tell me, I beseech you, do you sometimes ask the infamous scoundrels, the abominable beggars who take such pleasure keeping me dancing on live coals by refusing to let me know the date of my release, do you sometimes ask them what they hope to gain by so doing? I have already said and written a thousand times that instead of gaining thereby one only stands to lose; that instead of doing me good, they are doing me the greatest ill; that my character is not of a kind to be controlled like that; that in so doing they deprive me of both the capacity and the will to think things over and consequently to derive any benefit from the situation. I add and certify today, at the end of two years in this horrible situation, that I feel a thousand times worse than when I arrived here, that my mood has soured, I am more bitter, my blood is a thousand times more boiling, my brain a thousand times worse; and that, in a word, the day I get out of here I shall have to go live in the wilderness, so impossible will it be for me to live among human beings! —And what, in God's name, would it cost me to say that this is doing me good, if indeed such were the case? Alas, messieurs apothecaries,[4] now that your drugs are paid for and two-thirds taken, why should I not acknowledge their effectiveness if they have had any? But, believe me, their sole effect has been to drive me mad, and you are poisoners and not physicians, or rather scoundrels who should be broken on the wheel, to make you pay for keeping an innocent man in jail simply to satisfy your vengeance, your cupidity, and your nasty little personal interests. And am I supposed to put up with all this in silence? May I be struck dead a thousand times over if ever I do! —*Others have been their dupes*, you say to me, and have *said not a word about it* . . . They are animals, they are idiots; if they had spoken out, if they had revealed all the horrors, all the infamies of which they were the victims, the monarch would have been enlightened; he is just, and he would not have tolerated it; and 'tis precisely from their silence that these beggars' impunity derives. But I shall tell the truth, I shall open peoples' eyes, even if I have to cast myself at the king's feet to ask due reparation for everything I have been made to suffer unjustly.

Oh, you need not advise me against trying to make the numbers make sense and comparing your letters! I give you my word of honor that I no longer do that. I did it, unfortunately for me, for I thought I would go mad therefrom; but I would sooner be drawn and quartered than do it again. You turn a deaf ear to the number 22 . . . The question I asked you was simple enough, but you were unable to give me a satisfactory answer; let us speak of it no more. So remember, though, that I shall never forget your relentlessness . . . Ah! if you had a good memory you would recall whether all this worry about my character had ever succeeded in the past. The difference between what I was at La

---

4. Not to be confused with the apothecaries of the Marseilles affair. Here Sade is speaking metaphorically; the "apothecaries" are those, such as the Montreuils, the government, and even those members of his own family, including his uncle the abbé and two aunts, who prescribe prison to cure his ills.

Coste following the wonderfully witty and noisy scenes that went on there,[5] and what I had been before when I was left alone ... That should give you some idea whether all this is good for me. I don't want to mention anything except what you yourself used to say to me on the subject. If Mademoiselle Rousset is unable to say what she does not know, then let her say nothing: there's all I have to say; she will understand. If she's going to sulk, so much the worse for her; she is showing me as plainly as can be what age-old friends are, etc.

May one be told who married Mademoiselle d'Évry?[6] Mademoiselle de Launay,[7] you say, is not married, and *I shall not go to her wedding.* She is therefore about to be married, since you are getting ready not to go to her wedding? Consequently Marais did not lie to me as much as you claim. But to cite but one instance, he did lie to me when he told me I was to be here for only six months. And in doing that I find him an abominable rogue, for he knew full well 'twas not true and because 'tis outrageous to lead someone down the garden path in such a way; 'tis to prepare a man for the moment of deepest despair that comes when he sees his hope go up in smoke. —I have nothing to say about the power of attorney. 'Tis a signal. It has fulfilled its purpose; enough said. Haven't you received the money from Provence? Have it sent if you need it; but I shall sign nothing.

My one consolation here is Petrarch. I read him with a pleasure, an excitement without compare. But I read him like Madame de Sévigné read her daughter's letters: *I read slowly, for fear of having read him to the end.* How well written the work is! ... I am infatuated with Laura;[8] with her I am like a child; I read about her all day long, at night I dream of her. Listen to a dream I had about her last night while all the world was out dining and dancing.

---

5. The various attempts made at La Coste to harass and arrest him.
6. Renée-Pélagie's cousin.
7. Anne-Prospère, Renée-Pélagie's sister. And, of course, Sade's former mistress. Sade deduces that his wife's passing remark that she will not attend Anne-Prospère's wedding tells him she is in fact about to be married. What he doesn't know is that one of the conditions the groom-to-be lays down is that there will be no marriage unless he has assurances that Sade will be imprisoned for life.
8. Laura de Noves, Petrarch's great love. The Sade family claimed her as a direct ancestor, since she married Hugues de Sade in 1325. Recently some scholars have questioned whether Laura de Noves and Petrarch's Laura were really one and the same.

It was about midnight. I had just fallen asleep, her memoir next to me. All of a sudden she appeared to me . . . I saw her! The horrors of the grave had in no wise impaired the brilliance of her beauty, and all the fire of which Petrarch sang was still in her eyes. She was completely swathed in black mourning crepe, over which spilled her lovely blond hair. It seemed as if love, in order to make her more beautiful, wanted to soften the lugubrious garb in which she offered herself to my eyes. "Why dost thou groan on earth?" she asked me. "Come join me. No more sufferings, no more wars, no more sorrow, no more trouble in the vast space wherein I dwell. Have the courage to follow me there." Hearing which, I threw myself at her feet, I said to her: "Oh, my Mother! . . ." And sobs stifled my voice. She held out a hand to me, I covered it with my tears; she wept, too. "I was wont to look toward the future," she said, "when I lived in this world you loathe. I made out the generations that would emanate from me, until I came to you, *and I did not see you so unhappy.*" And then, completely absorbed by despair and tenderness, I threw my arms around her neck, either to hold her there or to follow her, and to water her with my tears; but the ghost vanished. Only my grief remained.

> *O voie che travagliate, ecco il cammino*
> *Venite a me se'l passo altri no serra.*
>
> Petr., Son. LIX

Good night, dear friend, I love you and I kiss you with all my heart. Do show me a bit more compassion, I beg of you, for I assure you that I am more miserable than you think. Judge all I am suffering, and the state of my soul is as black as my imagination. I embrace even the people who will have nothing to do with me, because all that I hate in them is their faults.

This 17th day of February, at the close of two years of dreadful bondage.

11.   To Monsieur de Rougemont

[March 14, 1779]

*I*t is to you, Sir, that I take the liberty of addressing the note included with the enclosed letter, requesting that you have it
promptly communicated to my wife via Monsieur Le Noir.[1] Were it to
turn out that the orders I have given therein relative to my business affairs were not carried out for having been withheld, I should be forced
to hold you responsible; and you, Sir, would not want to be held responsible for all the disorder that would ensue from your failure to
make sure they are both transmitted and carried out. I dare hope that
you will not be displeased by the liberty I have taken in taking you as
witness. You must understand, Sir, that I have no one else but you
here. If, however, you esteem this unseemly, you may, Sir, return the
note to me, and in that case be so good as to send me a notary public
so that I may more legally set forth my intentions. What I have done is
to try to avoid that complication, hoping that you would be willing to
testify in this matter if ever I am obliged to call upon you, which would
be as good as, nay better than, any public act.

I have the honor to be, with all possible sentiments, Sir, your most
humble and most obedient servant.

Would you be so kind as to send me my ordinary little provision of
writing paper.

Declaration attached to the preceding note.[2]

I the undersigned hereby declare that I shall neither discuss nor
conclude any matter of business as long as I remain under detention;
and to that I add my most authentic word of honor to systematically
nullify and undo all agreements, leases, contracts, settlements, etc. entered into, done, or made out during the said detention, whether the

1. Jean-Charles Pierre Le Noir, to whom de Rougemont reported, was directly responsible for Sade the prisoner. Both Sade and Renée-Pélagie used
him as intermediary when they wanted to ask a favor or for an improved condition, such as better food or more frequent walks.
2. The heading is Sade's.

said business matters have been concluded by my wife or by the lawyer Gaufridy, neither of whom has been authorized by me to conclude anything. I further certify by this note that if any of my business managers or leasers or farmers, etc., have disposed of any monies whatsoever belonging to me since the fourteenth of July seventeen hundred seventy-eight, the date at which I was restored to possession of what is rightfully mine, I shall make them pay twofold. I wish and intend that the present note, a copy of which I am keeping, has as much force as if it were done before a notary, and attesting to which I take as witness Monsieur de Rougemont, Governor of the said Keep, he being the sole person here I see, having every intention to cite him as such should the desires set forth by me in the said note remain unfulfilled. Done at Vincennes this fourteenth of March seventeen hundred seventy-nine.

DE SADE

12. *To Mademoiselle de Rousset*

[March 21, 1779]

*W*ell now, my dear Saint, New Year's Day has come and gone and you have not come to see me. I waited for you in vain the whole day; I'd dressed to the hilt, I'd put on powder and pomade, shaved myself close, I had no fur-lined boots but a fine pair of green silk stockings, red breeches, a yellow waistcoat and a black jacket, with a handsome hat trimmed in silver. In short, I was a very elegant lord. The jars of jam stood in battle formation. I had also made preparations for a little concert: three drums, four kettledrums, eighteen trumpets, and forty-two hunting-horns; all of which was set to play a pretty little romance I'd composed for you. Your ears, your eyes, your heart would have been truly delighted by the little party I prepared for you. But to no avail; I had got all dressed up for naught! 'Twill be for next year; but don't do that to me again, making my mouth water and then leaving me standing there, for all these preparations cost me a pretty penny.

Dearest and most amiable Saint, I shall not fill in your blank columns, and that for a very simple reason, which is that I would then have to send your letter back to you, and 'tis too pretty for that. You are like the man who wanted to make seaports of the whole of France, because seaports are profitable. Because I am fond of columns, you want to turn everything into columns! But don't do it, or else I shall end up without a single one of your letters, and they give me too much pleasure for me to want to part with them. In your letters, a separate sheet divided into columns, fine, upon which you can jot down the buffooneries or items of business: which these days are synonymous for me, for as you well know when they come to me here with talk of business 'tis pure buffoonery, 'tis Sancho Panza on his island being told that everybody awaits his commands. 'Tis a little mockery in which, let it be said without the least ill will, you indulge as you do in everything else. You have discovered the tone it takes *to lie to me* as you have learned that to make fun of me is the established norm; they have persuaded you that 'tis the thing for you to do as well, that there's nothing better, and especially nothing more apt to bring about a radical improvement in me than that. And so you do it, too . . . Yes, Saint Rousset, you have done it! and when we meet face to face, I shall make you admit that you have written to me *a number of most unwarranted things regarding my situation*. To which you will say, does that mean you want everything sugarcoated? Certainly not, Saint Rousset, that is not at all what I want. I want people to tell me the truth: that is the only favor I ask . . . But, you will say, people cannot . . . Very well then, if they cannot tell me the truth they must at least stop leading me down the garden path, making me believe I am in for a long stint, for to imply it without stating just how long, which would perhaps set my mind to imagining much more than it should, would plunge me into a state of utter despair. Thus, in such a case, 'tis better not to say anything, or else to talk straight, which is much simpler. In another letter, the one in columns to which I am replying today, you immediately switch to another tone and say: *Twelve jars of jam, that is a lot; in any case, no harm if there's some left over.* There's one of those contradictions that are unbearable, and I thought you were too close a friend to adopt such ridiculous language, about which you have heard me complain so bitterly. Tucked in amongst all that is another folly, one which Lady Sade, most sensibly, is beginning to forgo, but to which you still cling, and which I hope you too will soon abandon: 'tis to try and make me believe *that everybody's hard at work, writing letters, soliciting, still awaiting replies, that uncles, aunts, the devil himself* . . . Oh no, saintly and most holy Rousset, not another word about that! Be so kind as to sing some other tune if you want me to listen to you. Such stuff is fine for ordinary prisoners; 'tis what they call *keeping them entertained*. But I am not someone to be entertained. My time has been fixed; the day, the hour, and the moment are irrevocably set, and no uncle, no aunt, no Saint Rousset herself is capable either of increasing it or diminishing it by one minute. I ask to know *what it is;* 'tis my sole desire. They refuse to tell me, they keep me on tenterhooks. Bravo! But at least let them not believe they are *entertaining me,* nor that they are giving me food for thought, or by that tactic contributing to my welfare; because, on the contrary, all they are doing is irritating my mind, souring my character and unhinging my spirits, to the point where the unfortunate effects of all this will remain with me for the rest of my life. That is all they are doing, you may be sure of it. And, instead of that, had I known the length of my term I would have bent my efforts toward good things, because I would have had no need for vivid diversions; I would have had better and more solid reflections, and in the long run I would have been grateful to those who had given me the opportunity thus to focus my thinking. Instead, by completely disturbing it the way they are doing, by refusing to tell me the sole thing I want to know and the only one that can give me peace of mind, all I can do is curse and loathe them as long as I live, because I sense how much I am deteriorating and being undone here by frightful anxieties. Moreover, my dear Saint, if you only knew how your heart avenges me for the little wrongs your mind dreams up! how you, who write like an angel, become clumsy and stilted when your mind leads you to play *upon words, upon figures, upon signs* and all the other foolishness wherewith the Carmelites so liberally filled you! If, I say, you only knew how clumsy you were you would laugh at yourself and I would love you four times as much. Eh! Give it up! Go back to Voltaire's maxim in *Zaïre,* which he would have written expressly for you if only he had known you:

> *L'art le plus innocent tient de la perfidie:*
> *Qu'il ne souille jamais le saint noeud qui nous lie;*
> *Tu n'en as pas besoin.*

> *[The most innocent art derives from perfidy:*
> *May it never sully the sacred tie that binds us;*
> *You have no need for such.]*

There, I've unburdened my heart and I'll change the subject. You urge me to be reasonable, Saint Rousset! But is that a language you understand? 'Tis not made for women. That charming sex, which sends reason packing, must know neither how to hear it nor speak it.

And furthermore, how can you expect reason to prevail in someone who is treated as though he had none himself? Shall I mention that the sharp points of the candle-snuffers Lady Sade sent to me were very scrupulously filed off, for fear I would use them to kill myself? You can see that I am still a long way from the end of my misfortunes and that they foresee that I still have plenty of occasions for despair ahead of me, since they take such measures to withhold from me anything that might render its effects fatal! That's not any way to treat a man for whom twelve jars of jam are too many; 'tis the method they used with Damiens[1] and other famous scoundrels whom they prefer to keep alive, either to pry further information out of them or to keep them in a state of despair to which they are bound to succumb, thus not depriving the public of the example they want to give of their slow agony. And you want me to set my mind at ease! Have me ponder things, while they are resorting to such methods! Do you know my manner of thinking? 'Tis that the first man who ever took it into his head to dictate to his fellow human beings ought to have been broken alive. And when I see people just as narrow-minded as I take it upon themselves to steer me in the right direction, meddle with the matter of determining what ought to be good for me and what not, I have the feeling of being in the middle of the republic of asses, where each seeks to offer his advice and where all end up grazing in the same meadow! O man, how thou art tiny and vain! Scarcely have you had time to bask in the sun, scarcely have you touched upon the mysteries of the universe than you have nothing better to do than bend your cruel efforts in harrying your fellow man! And whence do you believe you have such a right? From your pride? But 'tis based on what, this pride? Have you any more eyes, any more hands, any more organs than I? Miserable earthworm, who has only a few hours to crawl, as do I, enjoy your lot and leave me alone. Humble your pride, born of naught but your foolishness; and if chance has placed you, really or *accidentally*, higher than me, in other words if you graze in a slightly better corner, profit therefrom to improve my lot. Saint Rousset, if amongst all the breeds of an-

---

1. Robert François Damiens (1715[?]–1757). A French fanatic who stabbed Louis XV on January 5, 1757, as the king was entering his carriage at Versailles. Convicted of attempted regicide, Damiens was sentenced to an atrocious death on the Place de Grève. He was publicly tortured, then torn to pieces by horses. Sade considers his endless torture worse than that of Damiens.

imals we know here on earth there were one that had built prisons for itself, and had then mutually condemned one another to this lovely little torture, would we not destroy it as a species too cruel to be allowed to subsist in this world? . . . I do not believe there has ever been any aberration like these prisons. First of all, it is an acknowledged abuse of both law and human nature that the *lettre de cachet* is in contradiction to the constitution of the State. Originally, prison was a place of safe-keeping, where the criminal was held prior to his execution. Later on, by some tyrannical principle, someone dreamed up the horrible idea of making the poor wretch suffer even more by letting him rot in prison instead of putting him to death. One day the Emperor Tiberius was asked to bring to trial a poor soul who had been suffering in prison for a long time. *"I would greatly regret it,"* the tyrant replied. *"How so?" "Why, he would be condemned to death and I should no longer have the plea-sure of knowing that he is suffering."* This Tiberius, as you know, was a monster. How is it then that we, who are *so gentle and meek, so civilized, so charming,* we who live in a *golden age,* are just as ferocious as that Tiberius? If I have deserved to die, then so be it, I am quite ready for it; if not, let them stop driving me mad here between four walls, and all that to no other purpose than to satisfy the vengeance of two or three ne'er-do-wells who would deserve a hundred strokes of the rod . . . and something else too I don't dare mention, and something else too I don't dare say plainly (isn't that how your little song goes?).

Prison . . . prison . . . nothing but prison! . . . That's all they know in France. You have a mild, a decent man; he made one unfortunate mistake, which his enemies have blown up all out of proportion in or-der to bring him down: *prison.* But, imbeciles that you are, when will you ever learn that there are as many differences in the characters of the human race as there are faces? that there are as many moral differ-ences as there are physical? that what suits one person does not suit an-other? better still, that what may cure one may be the undoing of another, and that with your prison at every turn you resemble Crispin playing doctor, who prescribes the same pills for all illnesses? "But to do what you are saying," you will object, "one would have to know something about human beings. Do you think that we are like the physicians and that we have nothing better to do than study your par-ticular needs? Eh! verily, what do we care whether that suits you or not? That which is unsuitable for one is just fine for others. Have you ever thought how wretched maggots would be if there were no more corpses? Study you! . . . Good Lord, believe that and you'll believe anything! And our pleasures? and our theaters, our shows? the young ladies we keep? *our wives* under lock and key? and, in our dealing with you, those little secrets we keep up our sleeves? . . . And what would become of all that if we had to go and focus on the study of man and rid ourselves of prisons? Come, come, dear sir, things are just fine as they are! And besides, the best reason of all for leaving them the way they are is that they have been that way for a very long time." —Eh! you have said it, gentlemen! you have said it and here is the reason why; those who are bound by no other laws than the Justinian Code must still think like Tiberius!

Well now, Saint Rousset, you see what comes of making me resort to reason: it tastes a bit of verjuice, my reason, doesn't it? . . . But what do you expect? 'Tis *fructus belli*[2] . . . But let us *have a brief look* at this letter with the columns, let me try to answer it if I can.

Tell me what this means: *"Your mind, let's not talk about it, you don't always put it to good use"?* I demand that you tell me what that means, otherwise I see trouble ahead.

You tell me that I listened to you for more than two whole hours when you talked reason to me. True, and 'twas even with greatest pleasure I listened to you. But then I was free, I was a man, and at present I am *an animal in the Vincennes Zoo*. At this stage I am merely unable to talk reason; soon, I trust, I shall be at the point where I will have lost the faculty completely.

This cot where I sleep will have a good many things to tell me someday! I am not quite sure what it will have to say, but I do know that when next I lay myself down upon it, I shall most certainly be filled with very wicked thoughts. If one fine evening you were to go there and, tucking yourself in, you were to find me there—eh? what say you, Saint Rousset? . . . You'd be greatly surprised! . . . Would you take to your heels? . . . You would, wouldn't you? Well, then, just see the difference between the two of us: I declare that if I were to come upon you in my bed, I'd slip myself into it as if it were perfectly normal. You women aren't much as philosophers; you always are frightened *by nature*.

You wish to become part of our *menagerie?* No, Saint Rousset, no, you are too old for that: to be in that group one must be between ten and fifteen. I, such as you see me, am only eleven; and so I feel quite at home. —By the way, tell me the honest truth now . . . you are as fa-

---

2. The fruits of war. Sade is implying he is a prisoner of war, a status that affects his manner of reasoning.

miliar with my room (for in referring to it as an "apartment" you do it too much justice) as if you had actually seen it: do you admit that you visit it daily and that 'tis you the magical mouse with whom I regularly do battle every night and who manages to elude my every snare? . . . 'Tis you, is it not? Tell me 'tis you, so that I cease trying so hard to get rid of you! and then 'twill be my bed I open to you, instead of the mousetrap . . .

"*A merchant's shop* . . ." That's just what it is! Yet, all told, I've only twenty-one crates or boxes, some big and some small; don't begrudge me them. But also don't send me any more, for I would not know where to store them . . .

You can picture me then, Saint Rousset, wearing my boots? *Oh!* I cut a fine figure in them! But I'm missing a sailor's jacket, you know the kind, one of those peajackets Marseilles sailors wear . . . A peajacket! Ah, Saint Rousset, send me a little peajacket and I'll have myself painted in it, since you want my portrait! Now, now, don't be cross with me because I told my wife that if I gave you the La Coste portrait it was because it didn't look like her. I say this in confidence to you: if I had a thousand paintings of her, I'd not give away a single one if they resembled her. So don't be the least bit annoyed with me; I'd refuse them to my own father, if I were so fortunate as to still have him with me. As for my own, that's different: I am as flattered by the request as I am anxious to procure you a good one. If you wish to make a copy of the large portrait in Paris, please do, or if you are willing to wait, then we'll have it done from life. Madame de Sade promised me she would have her portrait done in Paris: pray urge her keep her word as soon as possible, make her promise to go to the artist's, and you go there with her: 'tis the finest present she could ever give me. For God's sake, convince her to have it done toward Lent, so that she doesn't feel obliged to go outdoors until the weather is a bit warmer. You'll hold yourself responsible for that too, as you will regarding her health?

So, in two words, my daughter is ugly?[3] You tell me that in the gentlest way, but she's ugly, that's what you're really saying. Well, 'tis her bad luck! Let her have some wit and virtue, 'twill be better for her than if she had a pretty face! —How I'd like to have been part of the

---

3. In fact she apparently was quite ugly. Born on April 17, 1771, Madeleine-Laure was graced neither physically nor mentally. She retired early on to a nunnery, first to Saint-Aure, where her mother lodged. She never married, and spent her life in meditation and prayer.

game of hide-and-seek![4] 'Tis a game I adore. —From what account shall we take the money, you ask, to pay young Seignon?[5] Ah, let me ponder that for a moment . . . Shall I take from this account? . . . or from that? . . . hmm. This one or that? Ah, Good Lord! you are all thoroughly confused! I have it: don't pay him at all: then you'll not have to worry about finding the sum! —The chocolate is good. —Oh! I'm aware that they don't make wives like mine anymore, that is also why I beg of you to take good care of her for me. —My nonsense tales, you say, are only fit to amuse children? And what am I here, Saint Rousset, what am I if not a child? Your tales amuse me, interest me, and afford me the greatest pleasure: don't ever deprive me of them . . . As for mine, if they bore you I'll suppress them. But to talk naught but reason, that would be pretty dry . . . Adieu, I love you and embrace you as the second best and dearest friend I have in all the world.

13. To Madame de Sade

[March 22, 1779]

I wrote a long letter yesterday evening to Mademoiselle Rousset, the purpose of which, my dear friend, was to bid her farewell . . . for from what she says I gather she is leaving. That was the mysterious matter she did not want (or so you claim) to let you read in her letter. I leave it to you to judge whether 'tis an act of folly, and defer to your discretion and friendship both to her and to me to stop this ridiculous scheme. Moreover, it gives me a clear indication that my detention is slated to be much longer, for if 'twere merely a question of a few months, she would keep her promise to wait for me. It strikes me that when it comes to signals, 'tis impossible to give one any more forthright than this one, and I assure you that if 'tis not a joke, as I trust and believe, and that she is indeed leaving, then I shall in any case be in a state of great despair, upset not only at losing her but also at knowing

---

4. One presumes the Saint had been playing *cachette*, hide-and-seek, with Sade's children.
5. Unidentifiable. Presumably a teacher, or perhaps a tradesman. "Hmm . . . from what account?" muses the penurious marquis.

that there is no end in sight to my woes. Pray keep me informed about that, for I shall hold in abeyance both my attitude and my grief until I know the outcome. I expect to hear about it in your next letter, and meanwhile, reply line by line to the letter you have just written me, as is my wont.

I am pleased you are said to have gained a bit of weight and that the diet I recommended is working for you; it is unique, you may be sure, and I intend to adopt it for myself as soon as I am out.

Monsieur Le Noir did not increase the number of my walks. And it was pointless to strike out the line *"he appeared to me surprised that you were closely confined,"* because Monsieur Le Noir knows full well how confined I am, and because the commander here would not confine me in one way or another without orders from above; he does nothing on his own. Therefore, if Monsieur Le Noir appeared to you surprised, etc., he was putting on an act for you.[1] Certainly, I am much more restricted than I was before; I have already gone into the details for you two or three times. The hope you held forth in June made me suspend judgment, but if it proves empty, as seems all too likely, and if Monsieur Le Noir promises you to look into my situation and see what he can do to improve it, you should simply tell me to write down, in the form of a memorandum, the various things I need for my comfort, and I shall do it; ask that they be implemented. Meanwhile, do keep on asking for that third walk, which I desire more than ever, since now's the season to take advantage of it; but try to have it granted me in the afternoon, for 'tis only then that walks really do me any good. Certainly, if your hope of last June were to happen in everything except the extra walk I ask for, we could spare ourselves the trouble of asking for the rest. But if 'tis false, as seems very likely, then I most sincerely desire not to spend the summer as badly as I have the winter. Therefore I await your reply on the subject. You may dispense with any discussion of business matters, however brief, for most assuredly I shall not write one word in response. On that point, you must have received the notice wherein I give my word of honor, and I can tell you I shall not depart from it one iota.

Those verses are by Paulet, of that I am quite sure, and I persist in saying that the letter and the verses were sent from Paris, the lot through Saint Rousset or her intermediaries. You tell me that this

---

1. Knowing his fate is in the hands of M. Le Noir, Sade generally avoids attacking him, but here he loses control.

Monsieur Ives (another made-up name, like Bontoux's)[2] is a village wit who talks endlessly and who makes the two of you die laughing in the letters Gothon[3] has written. That's precisely where I catch you out, for there is nothing less comical and nothing less endless than Paulet's letter. The letter and the verses are very well written, in an easy and agreeable style, and are, in a word, the work of one of the Saint's lovers. For she writes even better than that, and she did not want it to be her style; I would recognize it, of course. 'Tis therefore one more clear signal that I shall not waste my time either scrutinizing or interpreting. The only signals to which I pay any attention are the good old-fashioned ones, solid and substantial like the almanac she gave me at New Year's, for example . . . Charming little New Year's gift, *more charming with each passing year.* And then the little looking glass shattered into a thousand pieces, which, without question, most clearly means that this is not going to be a lucky year for me, there being nothing more unlucky than broken mirrors. Those are what I call understandable signals. Oh! when they are like that I do understand them . . . But as for the others, in all candor I simply don't put myself to any trouble over them. I do not know how *to read her,* Mademoiselle Rousset says to me in her letter . . . Ask her on my behalf what one should do to know how to read her: do you turn the page sideways, or upside down? Let her at least tell me how if she would have me *learn to read her!* Is she implying to me that I do not know how to figure out the special *punctuation, the dots, the commas, the dashes,* etc., which, following your example, she has got into the habit of cramming into her letters? If that is what she means, she is right to maintain that I do not know how to read her; and, if such is the case, she may rest assured that were she to write me letters in that kind for a hundred years I would be no further advanced, for I would have made no effort to decipher them. She is wrong, she adds, to have told me twice the truth when I asked for it only once . . . Please do me the favor of asking her

---

2. The parenthesis is Sade's. Ives was Madame de Montreuil's envoy to Sade. He was hired to assist in Sade's appeal at Aix, presumably as a lawyer, but Sade staunchly maintains, in this same letter, that no such name was included in the register of Paris lawyers.
3. Gothon Duffé, a Swiss chambermaid the Sades engaged to service La Coste. From Sade's description in letter number 56, she was chosen more for the extraordinary proportions of her buttocks than for her chambermaidenly talents. Her lover at the château was Carteron, a.k.a. La Jeunesse (Youth), who was Sade's trusted valet. (See letter number 19.)

for me in which of the two sentences I copied out for her yesterday is this glaring truth recorded, for as one of them says white and the other black, 'twere well I be told which one contains the truth, so that, once I know which it is, I importune you no more upon this point . . . *The truth!* I'm most pleased that she dare assert that she told me *the truth*. Does she know it, the truth I ask for? It is short, it is brief; it is useless to drown it inside a jumble of nonsense about the hereafter. Simply write it down for me in a single line: *You will be released upon the ——— day of the month of ——— in the year ——— at ——— o'clock in the morning or afternoon.* As you see, what I ask for is short and to the point; no need to make so much ado about it. It required neither thirty blank letters, *nor* . . . etc. All it required was a single little note, which you could just as easily have delivered to me as you did your infernal blank letters. But you cannot, you tell me? . . . A lie, an atrocious lie . . . Say rather that you do not want to, and at the same time know in your heart of hearts that I shall never forget how you behaved on this score.

So you have written to Gothon telling her *to write to me every month* . . . Something to look forward to, indeed . . . *every month* . . . So I have a hundred more of them to spend here! . . . *Every month*, how nice it sounds. You wrote to her because I told you to—all well and good, but from that phrase *every month* Gothon will understand—'tis as plain as the nose on her face—that I still have a very long time to spend here, and no longer will she have the illusion under which I told you 'twas necessary we keep her, so that, thinking we were due to arrive from one day to the next, she would maintain the château at all times in a proper state and above all not raise any silkworms. Now find a way to make sure both those things come to pass.

A further bit of kindness. You are not going to send the stomachers back to me because *you hope* I'll have enough of them to last for the rest of my detention. Now, I very clearly informed you that I was supplied up until the end of May 1780. Thus you *hope* that at that point I shall need them no more. What a charming idea. Now, I do not wear them in summertime. Consequently, 'tis only twenty-one months from now that I might have a need for those in your possession. And YOU HOPE that by that time I'll not need them anymore. Verily, I thank you, Madame! When I look back upon the period of my sufferings, I shall be able to think of how well you fulfilled your duties toward me and to say that you were a source of great comfort to me. I know full well that your answer to that will be that I lack common sense, that I get upset for no reason and that I always see everything in the worst light. For two years now, Madame, you have been writing me those fine phrases, and yet you must admit that when they began to reach me, 'twas for good reason I got upset and I was not wrong in seeing things in the worst light. Inasmuch as I have been suffering ever since, who will assure me at present that more of the same is not in store for me? Am I in any way better off than I was at that time? Not by one iota; and 'tis a truly unusual and perhaps unparalleled thing, that with two years of suffering behind me, I have cause, both by the letters I receive and the treatment I endure, to consider myself worse off than I was in my first months here . . . And you believe I shall forgive those who have concocted this kind of torture to inflict upon me? I shall eat my own soul sooner than forsake vengeance . . . I shall prove to these unworthy monsters, to these execrable beasts vomited up out of hell to visit unhappiness upon others, that I am not their toy, and that if I had the misfortune to be it for a while, they may just as well become mine someday, no matter who they are.

Keep your bottle of Muscat wine. I asked whether Chauvin[4] had sent a lot of it, but since there is so little, I don't want any; and above all do not buy me any, because I'll drink nothing from any shopkeeper . . . it would be doctored stuff; I'll not touch a drop . . . Besides, my fancy for it is gone . . . This situation I am in is both horrible and extraordinary; and I feel something very strange that I had never experienced in the outside world. I would like to have some experienced soul-healer explain it to me. Twenty times a day you have an overwhelming desire for all kinds of things, and then the next moment, without having procured them, you have an awful sense of revulsion for them. That was the way it was about every one of the things I asked you for, and as soon as they reached me I found them disgusting: explain that to me.

What is all this nonsense you keep feeding me over and over that *you do not understand how the doctor can be so philosophical as to laugh at a sentence which you did not write to him?* I said that *IF you had sent that sentence to the doctor, he would have been philosophical enough not to be angered by it.* That is clear, is it not? Personally, I see nothing strange about it; and there's no point your telling me that I talk without knowing what I'm saying.

Nor did I say that the doctor's daughter was a beauty, but I did say that she was not dark-haired, that she was fair. Does that mean I said she is a beauty? As far as the duchess is concerned, still nothing at the bottom of your portrait: she looks as much like La Martignan as I do

4. Both Sade and his wife asked Chauvin to ship them local wines.

Sixtus the Fifth. La Martignan is a tramp, in large part the cause of my affair,[5] and who acted out of revenge because I would have nothing to do with her in the days when I first went to Provence. She is affected, short in stature, and has a common look about her, whereas the duchess, along with a very amiable character, has very noble features and the look of *Minerva*. I persist in telling you that there is no lawyer in Paris named *Bontoux*. When I tried to convince Siméon that there was, he brought me a register, printed in Paris, listing the names and addresses of all the lawyers in Paris, amongst whom I espied no one by that name. So don't talk to me any more about that brute. As for the unpleasant-looking countenance worn by the somber creature who was introduced to me by that name, let him go by whatever name he pleases, *Chivarucmarbarbarmarocsacrominecpanti*, if he likes, it's all the same to me; but may the Good Lord take whatever steps He must to make sure he is never alone in the same room as me. I impatiently await the four volumes of *Les Hommes Illustres;* when you send me those first four, let me know how many more there are. And the little candles, for God's sake, the little candles! Why do you persist in refusing to send them? I shall return Petrarch during the holidays, perhaps before. Does your father still go to the law courts? Bully for him! When one has a hundred thousand livres in annuities, one must be a fool to get up at five in the morning to go stick one's nose in other people's business! Is he by now presiding judge in his chamber? And your brother the knight, in what wretched regiment is he serving today? I find him mentioned nowhere in the almanac. Why do you never go to dine at your parents', young lady? ... For shame, you should be ashamed! *Honor your father and mother, says Moses, and eat often at home.* How is Madame de Plissay?[6] And give my regards to Madame de Chamousset.[7] I have always liked and respected her, and I would be willing to wager she does not dislike me either. It gives me pleasure to be told that I shall see Laure[8] when I am released ... That, for example, is one desire that has yet to turn into revulsion ... There are two or three others of the same sort, about which, Madame la Marquise, I shall inform you at the proper time and place. You did most positively

---

5. Meaning: my arrest.
6. Madame de Montreuil's mother.
7. The wife of Claude Piarron de Chamousset, an eighteenth-century French philanthropist.
8. Madeleine-Laure, his daughter, whose eighth birthday is less than a month away.

tell me, my sweet, that *"your children left satisfied they were to see you in two years"*—that, word for word, is what you wrote. Which means, I believe, that I shall not see them for two years. You now change your tune, so much the better, for I confess it would have sorely grieved me to leave the country without seeing them. Thinking about them drives me crazy. If only you could see me talking to them all by myself . . . You'd think I'd lost my wits. Not a night goes by without my dreaming of them. I'll write to them soon. I greatly appreciate all the charming things you tell me now and then about that duchess. I'd like to have sufficient wit to respond to them. Let it suffice that you know my heart is touched by them.

This portrait the Saint has done is quite unparalleled. 'Tis unheard of to have done it without a sketch . . . She does whatever she likes with those five fingers of hers. There was only one thing I wanted to get her to do at La Coste with those same fingers, and she never would . . . Well now, ladies, there it is, isn't it? You think you are about to hear a little remark, and 'tis the simplest thing in the world. 'Tis so simple and so proper I would say it to the Holy Virgin herself, were she to ask. When you ask me for an explanation, I'll be happy to provide it . . . Meanwhile, tell her I was even more flattered by her efforts than she supposes, and shall keep this portrait all my life. Tell her, too, that one must not leave when one loves someone to the point of enjoying painting their portrait. In addition to which, tell her that good though it is, I like to think it would have been an even better likeness if she had not worked from the painting, since I am sure there exists in her a little spot where I am more strikingly present than upon Van Loo's canvas . . . But if she does leave, I shall never see her again. So let her stay and we shall always be together, and live happily ever after. As for you, my little duckling, I kiss you upon the . . . then upon the . . . afterward upon the . . .

This 22nd of March, having eleven more months more to endure.

14. *To Madame de Sade*

[March or April, 1779]

*I*s it possible that they don't want to see and [words missing] revolt, and serves only to destroy to the very root all the good resolutions that the conclusion of my affair caused to well up in me . . . No, never shall I pardon their infamy in having me rearrested . . . 'Tis a horror of unparalleled dimensions. To sacrifice a man, his reputation, his honor, his children, to the rage, to the vengeance, and to the greed of those who wanted me to be clapped back in prison—since, knowing what lay in store for me, they hid it from me so that I would I fall all the more easily into the trap—that is an execration whose example cannot be found even amongst the most ferocious of nations. And when I have the misfortune to fall again into this terrible trap, to make sure I was even more unhappy than I was before, to keep me even more confined in my new prison, to increase my persecutions there, to lie to me even more recklessly than before . . . These methods make one shudder, and I dare not look upon them with composure . . . Tell those who think that this is the way to punish their fellow human beings, tell them without mincing words that they are greatly mistaken: all they are doing is making their victims more bitter, nothing more. Persecutors—be you male or female—tyrants, valets of tyrants, odious satellites of their shameful caprices, in short all of you whose only good is revenge or the hope of attaining honors by basely serving the rage of those whose influence is your sole support or whose money nourishes you, do you know what I compare you to? To that band of ne'er-do-wells who go, sticks in hand, to jeer at the lion held captive in an iron cage. 'Tis with a mixture of great fear and glee they tease it, poking their sticks through the bars. If the animal had broken loose, you would have seen them running helter skelter, trampling one another as they all fled, and dying of terror before the lion had caught up with them. There, my friends, in such wise do you behave: judge what I think of you from the comparison, and your infamies from its accuracy.

I am infinitely gratified by the news of my son's progress.[1] You must sense to what degree that makes him even dearer to me . . . Whatever the prior may think, this translation strikes me as most commendable in a schoolboy in his first six months of study. That does not lessen my affection for the *chevalier.*[2] You know that till now I was fonder of him than of his older sibling. But I am so delighted by the good things I hear about the elder, rendering him even so dear to me, I shall as you say write to the *chevalier* to encourage him. Please be so kind as to thank your mother for her attentiveness in wanting me to share with her the joy this child's progress affords us. To inform me of the news by such an agreeable channel is, in a way, to make it twice as

---

1. Louis-Marie, his older son, who was doing very well in school.
2. Donatien-Claude-Armand.

welcome. What a pity that this child cannot be given a broader education . . . And how truly sad I shall be if I don't have the chance to see
him when I am released from here. I have no further work for La
Jeunesse.[3] What can you expect me to do without books? One must be
surrounded by them in order to work, otherwise one can concoct nothing but fairy tales, and I have no talent for that. Therefore answer me
about that book I asked your father for, and the little candles which I
asked for centuries ago; I have been out of them for over a week.

I embrace you.

15. To Mademoiselle de Rousset

[April or May, 1779]

*T*here has been a veritable torrent of meaningless words on both
our parts for a very simple discussion; it has gradually led us to
bitterness, and I do not want our friendship ever to become embittered. Whether or not you reply to this final accusation, I care not; it
shall be, if you so desire, the concluding piece of evidence in the case,
and once we have got past this I would prefer not to mention it again.
First of all, I am going to lay out the wrongs you have done me, and excuse them by invoking the one motive that I consider an attenuating
circumstance; after which I shall set forth the wrongs you accuse me of,
and justify myself with great ease.

Your wrongs consist of: 1) Having told me that I have no friends.
Three months ago I replied to you in great detail upon that point and
proved to you that misfortune rarely leaves a man any; I shall not harp
again on what I have already said, for nothing bores me as much as repetitions. 2) Having tried to persuade me that my mother-in-law was
the cause of my second detention. Whether she was or not, 'tis wrong
for you to try to work up my feelings against her. If I believed her innocent, 'tis because my wife, writing to me at La Coste, asserted in no
uncertain terms that she was; consequently, your remark tended on

---

3. Sade's valet served, among other things, to transcribe Sade's writings into
fair copy.

the one hand to make me look upon my mother-in-law as *suspect* and, on the other, my wife as *a liar.* Is it befitting for you to play this role? 3) Having tried to deceive me by giving me false hope for this spring. At La Coste I told you that the worst torture in the world was that of a wretch to whom hope is given then taken away. I maintain that there is no torture in the universe to equal it, and were one to delve into the cause of all suicides, twenty-nine out of thirty would stem from that alone . . . 'Twas proven long ago, and if I were called upon to do so I could cite a thousand examples. Although you knew very well from me that I considered it a horror, an abomination, you did it. At this point I ask but one thing: if they are of a mind to beat me . . . *is it for you to furnish the rod or the staff?* I have been insistent on this subject, perhaps even violent, insolent, dishonest, harsh, whatever you like, but there was nothing I wouldn't have done, no matter what the risk or peril, in order to find out whether they were lying to me and in order not to push the error to its extreme; I know what it once cost me in order to do that . . . what I suffered from it . . . what I felt . . . and I do not want to go through that ever again. I have already suffered near fatal traumas from my past misfortunes, and I'm now at the point where it would perhaps take but one more, whether the news be good or bad, to kill me off. Here is one recent example to prove my point. Yesterday night, they came into my room at an ungodly hour, 'twas for a perfectly simple matter but one I was not expecting. For three-quarters of an hour thereafter I was ill over it. And so 'tis not a figment of my imagination, a mere caprice, a misplaced curiosity that makes me want to find out how long my term is to be, 'tis life, 'tis nothing but life I am asking for. But, to that you will reply to me, twenty-four hours' notice is quite enough. I agree; strictly speaking, that is all I ask, and if it appeared I was anxious to know further in advance—and I've told you so a thousand times—'tis in order to profit from this period of retreat and spend it improving my mind or my attitude, something absolutely impossible for me to do when this constant feeling of uncertainty leaves me troubled and in a state of perpetual agitation. At long last you gave the lie to this springtime fantasy, for which I am grateful. You would have played me a fatal trick had you left me believing it until the last moment. What I do dislike is the ridiculous way—allow me the expression—you chose to destroy it. *"Had you been less cantankerous, had you not written,"* etc. So I am to be punished like a little boy whose hands are beaten when he has not recited his lesson properly? There is yet another very stupid course: I have told you so often enough, 'tis not by using such methods they'll make me any better. Severity embitters me, period. Do they really think I shall be made to love a government, which in this case is acting unjustly toward me, by keeping me arbitrarily in prison, and respect a tribunal that has no jurisdiction over me? Do they truly believe, I say, that prolonging my detention will result in my improvement? They are mistaken. If they kept me here for life I'd still say the same thing and always talk in the same way. I am both firm and courageous. Blasé when it comes to misfortunes, I have little or no fear of whatever new stroke of fate might befall me, and the threat of the scaffold does not turn me into either a rogue or a traitor, nor does it humble me. And despite this unshakable resolution, this solid character of which I pride myself, a mere nothing, a mark of *real* friendship, a proof of confidence would turn me into whatever they wanted me to be; with kindness I could be made to move mountains; severity could make me dash my brains out against a wall. Such is my personality, which has never changed since I was a child—Amblet, who brought me up, can attest to that—and will surely never change. I am too old to make myself over. So let them abandon their project of *maturing my mind:* twenty years from now 'twill be no more mature than it is today, on that you have my word . . . more unruly perhaps, but certainly not more settled. Only let me out of here, offer me a show of friendship and trust, and you will see an altogether different man emerge. Let them not tell me: *we tried it and it did not succeed.* I shall prove that though they pretended to be trying it, all they were really doing was setting traps for me, to have the pleasure of crushing me once I fell into them . . . At any rate, the die is cast, I am not to be set free this spring . . . Come now, do admit that it was wicked on your part to have tried to persuade me I would be, and ridiculous of you to come and tell me now, *"Oh, you would have been freed if you had been better behaved . . ."* Oh! good God, my dear friend, you must think me both stupid and credulous, simply because I have the misfortune to be behind bars!

Your fourth and final wrong is to have told me that horrible contradiction about *my children at the feet of the king,*[1] sufficiently discussed in my last letter so as to require no further comment here. There are all your wrongs: mere trifles in the outside world, they become exceedingly serious vis-à-vis a poor wretch who sees nothing, hears nothing, and for whom letters are the only horoscopes wherein he can try and

---

1. There was a plan afoot that, if all else failed in the efforts to have Sade released, all three children would be dispatched to Versailles to beseech the king to do so. Sade was appalled at the idea.

read his fate. The excuse I give for them is this: you have been seduced *by my torturers*, and you have been so stupid as to believe, as they do, that all those little pesterings to which they subject me were to bring about in me the most wonderful effects. *Weakness* and *credulity*, they are the origin of your wrongs. I forgive them. Let us renew our love for each other, let us resume our correspondence, and let bygones be bygones. But do not use such weapons in the future: you can see how useless they are. If you love me, do not risk the bitterness and inevitable chilliness that must emanate therefrom. I shall be set free when God so chooses. If you care to tell me when that is to happen, it will please me no end; otherwise, tell me nothing; I would prefer knowing nothing than to be deceived; and there's the origin of my phrase, *let there be silence*, which shocked you so. *Let them speak the truth or let there be silence*, that is what I said, and say again, and so saying I see neither the slightest harshness nor the slightest dishonesty. Moreover, if all you implied in your last letter is true—which I must believe, since you maintain it is—invoking the truth, your candor, etc., then I am most unhappy. I must now anticipate a very lengthy detention, and I can clearly see that I have been made a sacrificial lamb. In that case, I am wrong to have blamed you for having told me what you did; I can only praise your candor; there are certain truths that must be expressed bluntly and without mincing words; that is one of them . . . That you did the right thing . . . But if 'tis true that my fate is as ghastly as you tried to intimate to me, why did you announce to me that my freedom was around the corner? And if indeed it was, why did you offer me the picture of so many swords still suspended above my head? I keep coming back to the same point; be frank as long as you like, but be consistent, for inconsistency is the surest emblem of deceit.

As for your reproach, *"he says everything,"* you will explain it to me whenever it suits you, for I do not understand it, nor do I understand any better the ways you say you have used to get through to me. The only others I know are the deleted lines: 'tis from there I have taken everything I have said. This I am ready to prove. If it pertains to something else, then I do not understand what you mean, and indeed do not believe there is even any possibility of something else. If there were, or were it to come to pass, I swear to you that I would be the first to divulge it, knowing full well there is never any change in the rules except to impose one more torture. I have learned it all too well from harsh experience to seize the bait anymore, and I do not advise anyone to put me to any such test, for I would very quickly ferret out what was afoot. Here I gloss over a very cruel invective on your part: *"Your friendship has tarnished my good name."* Mademoiselle, I have the highest opinion of your good name. But I am not yet fallen so low as to fear that my friendship might tarnish it . . . You may perhaps have had some other friends, before me, who . . . How is your health today, Mademoiselle Rousset? You see where all these empty amenities must lead us both: to bitterness, and thence in the long run to hatred. I am therefore right in declaring to you that no matter what you may say or reply to that, I shall hold my tongue. In general, that is what I plan to do in the future; therefore receive from me *the most solemn oath,* and overlook this letter and the one I am going to write in response to Madame de Sade. I hereby declare to you that I intend to limit myself to asking for things I absolutely need and to talking about the weather. Go back to the first of April; examine my letters written during that period, and if they do not bear out what I say, you can call me all the names in the book. If I am to be caned like a schoolboy, at least it will not be for my letters, and I shall eliminate that pretense from my torturers. You want to deprive me of the single consolation I still have in the midst of my misfortunes, that of believing there is a fixed date to my term . . . 1) 'Tis a foul thing to do. Why break a child's toy? 2) 'Tis false to tell me the contrary, because there is nothing more clear and obvious in the world; of that I have the most compelling proofs, and were you not yourself convinced of that I'd convince you in short order with unanswerable arguments . . . But when is the fixed date? Ah! that is what I know not, and what I do not flatter myself that I do. Thus you may without fear say on that subject that my calculations are wrong, for I have given up making any. What you tell me that I should say about my mother-in-law is precisely what I have said, and all you have done is ape me. You overly complicate, change, demolish, augment my sentences as you see fit, and all that simply to annoy me and worry me to death, isn't that so? Well, I say to you once again that you will not succeed. And in the future, my profound silence will demonstrate how greatly I scorn all these half-starved little subterfuges that I regard as the effect of the hysteric vapors to which the people of that house are sorely prone. *They make fun of your threats,* you add, *nor do they fear them* . . . That I believe. However, the proof that they do indeed fear me is shown by the tight leash on which they keep me; one does not keep chains on people you despise. *I want to call Peter to account for cheating Paul* . . . That's a rich one! What! do you fancy that because I am in prison my business advisers have had the right to rob me blind without my calling them to account? Think again; I shall call them most severely to account, and if they have stolen from me I shall get rid of them, that I swear to you. I conclude not with *Mademoiselle* but with *my dear friend*, and to that I add a further most urgent request not to leave without me, no matter how long they may keep me here; I beseech you in the name of that friendship of which you assure me some spark still remains in you; I beg of you to restore it to me in full, and as proof thereof to wait for me, and not to increase my misfortunes and my despair by this threat and by the bitterness of your letters.

16. *To Madame de Sade*

May 16, 1779

I have no idea what all this endless repetition is about, nor why, when I ask you for objects that would make my life a trifle easier, all I get in response are crossed-out lines. You must be very weary of all those platitudes, for they are very boring. The fact is, I still am without everything I asked you for, and there is nothing to suggest that 'tis about to be granted to me. If my former room[1] is unavailable as you indicate in your crossed-out lines, let them give me another. That one or another one, I care not. 'Tis not to the room I was attached, for most assuredly it was dreadful, but to the view and to the fresh air one could breathe there. Any room on the same floor will have the same advantages, and I am very sure that many of them on those floors are empty. I have already told you twenty times over that this past winter in the room where I presently am I suffered all one can suffer; that it is extremely humid and unhealthy, that from this room you can barely see the sky, and that its air passages have been stopped up for fear that the prisoner might fly out of them. *For in here 'tis the one thing they fear most.* And so I ask, and ask most urgently, to be shifted to another. I ask for a room on the upper floors, I don't care which, provided one can have a fire there in winter, which is impossible in this one, and that it have air and light; that is all I ask of it. As for the walk, which you say cannot be granted to me more than four times a week, one should start by

1. That is, cell number 11, where he was incarcerated on February 15, 1777, two days after his arrest at the Hotel de Danemark. The cell was higher than the dungeon walls and therefore was literally "a room with a view."

giving me my walk four times a week, for at present 'tis only three; but even assuming there were four, I would still complain, considering that, for my health's sake, I have the most urgent need of fresh air at least an hour each day, and that is what I am asking for. For the past fifteen nights in a row—I took the trouble to count them—I have not had a wink of sleep, or at most what they call a cat nap each night, and I hope and trust I shall soon be ill from it. If 'twere the death of me, nothing would suit me better. Farewell. I tried to drink some barley water, my stomach couldn't take it, I had to cease and desist.

And so I very urgently request that I be allowed at least an hour of fresh air every day. Why are some granted this favor, and not me along with the rest? Oh! verily, I am well aware that those are the commandant's[2] *little pet doggies* and that for having spoken out too truthfully I'm not one of the happy few. Let him take his little revenge, but he still does not have leave to allow a man to die! When one asks for more frequent walks, they raise the objection—or so you tell me—that 'tis out of the question because there are so many prisoners. 'Tis an outrage that the vigilant eye of the minister does not take steps to remedy the shameful and odious abuse that goes on here in this regard. Why, given the miserable little courtyard of this dreary dungeon, which is about as big as your hand, does the worthy commander begin by walling off three-quarters of it, and then forbid anyone to set foot in it? That's the kind of horror they perpetrate here and nowhere else. In all the prisons one can name the wardens have gardens—nothing more simple, they take therefrom whatever is produced—but they are open to the prisoners, who are allowed in them as much as they like. And 'tis this abominable constriction of space here that makes the prisoners' walks so few and far between. With the little land there is, divided as it is, four prisoners guarded by sentinels as everywhere else—and not by the employees who serve the food, which is another abuse that explains why walks cannot be granted more often—could have walks four at a time, and if I were in charge here, even with thrice as many prisoners I'd have all of them out walking twice as much as they do now.

Does the commandant fear that his apples and pears may get eaten? I do not say that hunger cannot sometimes tempt one to such an act, but one would have to be what is known as a very *ill-bred fellow* to go and steal the fruit from a garden where one has been allowed to walk. Such a fear most assuredly does not attest to the high opinion of the people he is accustomed to have here. It seems to me that if I were

2. The warden, Monsieur de Rougemont.

in his shoes I'd have a very strong aversion to eating any fruit from a garden whose preservation I knew was being *bought by the health of some miserable inmates*. Those pears may aptly be called *choke-pears*. Such then, my dear friend, are some of the little infamies which, together with a good many others, put me in such ill humor this past winter, at this very moment, and will continue to do so—*a little more fruitfully, I hope*—anent this odious place, and which makes me say and say again that amongst all the methods your mother has used against me, the one I am least apt to forget is that of having allowed herself to be blinded *by the entire clique* that has an interest in stocking this house, and of having had me incarcerated here. It seems to me that I have written enough about it from Aix so that at least they ought to have put me somewhere else, since I was destined to suffer even more. But in a word, I beseech you to obtain for me the objects I have so often asked you for in my more recent letters, or at least to have me transferred to another prison, since I absolutely cannot cope with the abominable existence in this one, suffering as I am here like one of the damned.

The breeches fit me very nicely; the little cookies are as always excellent, and 'twill be quite some time before I tire of them: please keep sending them and feel free to increase the quantity; the pens are detestable: I ask you for big quills from "Griffon's,"[3] which cost a penny; Griffon's does an excellent job of sharpening the points. The sponge cake is not at all what I asked for: 1) I wanted it iced everywhere, both on top and underneath, with the same icing used on the little cookies; 2) I wanted it to be chocolate inside, of which it contains not the slightest hint; they have colored it with some sort of dark herb, but there is not what one could call the slightest suspicion of chocolate. The next time you send me a package, please have it made for me, and try to have some trustworthy person there to see for themselves that some chocolate is put inside. The cookies must smell of chocolate, as if one were biting into a chocolate bar.[4] And so in the very next package: a cake like the one I have just described, 6 ordinary ones, 6 iced, and two little pots of Brittany butter, but well and carefully selected. I believe they have a shop for that in Paris, like the one selling Provençal goods where you go for oil.

---

3. A stationer, the quality of whose merchandise Sade admired.
4. Sade loved sweets of any kind, but chocolate in any shape or form he held in the highest esteem. His ravenous appetite for sweets and his enforced sedentary ways resulted in his increasing problem of obesity, which was to plague him the rest of his life.

When you have proved to me that you are taking care of me by obtaining the articles I ask for, I shall do the same for you by returning posthaste the notice you wish. Meanwhile, I cover your hands with kisses.

Please do send me as soon as possible a pair of steel buckles, only shoe buckles, no other. I only want you to pay three francs at the most, since when I am free I shall buy some stylish ones. Mine have just broken; and buckles at the price I request will do just fine here. Pick a pair that La Jeunesse will like, because when I get out they shall be for him.

17. To Madame de Sade

[May, 1779]

*Y*e gods! What on earth did the présidente eat during Lent in order to produce such an outburst between Easter and Pentecost? What a flood! It ends up being charming. Just look at her! Patience! *He who laughs last laughs best.* It will be my turn to laugh one of these days, and I'll do more than laugh, of that you may be sure. During my idle moments here, I have fun drawing up plans. I have some unique ones. And, like her, I shall not really be making up anything new. I shall confine myself to imitating. Some paper, some ink, and a few bribed rascals, that's all it will take. I won't need any police or ministries, not I. A few stout memories, a bit of money, and the printers in the Hague.[1] Oh! what delight! The pleasure to which I look forward alleviates all my pains. Gone in a flash all my pain and sorrow the moment I think of my revenge.

> *Une brochure unique, un ouvrage admirable,*
> *Bien scandaleux, bien vrai: le style n'y fait rien,*
> *Et pourvu qu'il instruise, il sera toujours bien!*
>
> (Le Méchant)

---

1. Where uncensored works could be printed and then shipped clandestinely into France.

[A unique pamphlet, an admirable work,
Most scandalous, true as can be: the style matters little,
And provided it teaches, 'twill always be good!]

(The Spiteful One)

I change nothing except to underline. And, whoever would have told me that, when she and I[2] were playing that together, these very sentences would someday pay her back for the way she behaved.

Well, well, so there you are, lodged with her, and lodged there ever since my return.[3] I offer you my congratulations. Simply bear one thing in mind, and that is that as far as I am concerned you have either the semblance or the substance of a great many wrongs, and though my friendship for you will doubtless efface them the instant I see you, *that one I shall never forget.*

I promised you the *Maintenon*[4] volumes as soon as the books for rereading appeared. You can see that I am a man of my word. Here are 320 pages. 'Tis quite good in my humble opinion. You didn't expect such a great quantity. Oh! I like to spring surprises on my friends, especially pleasant ones. Read this *Maintenon* if you are not familiar with her. 'Tis a delight and charmingly written. Madame de la Vallière made me weep like a child. How I should like to have been at the Carmelites' to see her splendid portrait! Remind me to go and see it as soon as I can. Verily, do read this book. I seem to recall that you have (as did I) some mistaken notions about the early stages of the king's love for Madame Scarron. Think again. I won't keep you waiting for the volumes. Each week you'll get two, I promise you. 'Twould go faster were I not rereading other things from which I am taking a great many passages.

'Tis a fine collection of books I've just received. Two or three at the most from my list, the rest doubtless chosen by Monsieur de La Jeunesse. That makes no sense. More books that will stay here forever,

---

2. In the early days of her daughter's marriage, Madame de Montreuil sometimes took parts in the plays her son-in-law staged.
3. To Vincennes following the Aix appeals trial.
4. Françoise d'Aubigné, the Marquise de Maintenon. She was put in charge of the children of Louis XIV and Madame de Montespan, and after the death of the latter, she secretly married the king, probably in 1697. After the king's death in 1715, she withdrew to her estate of Saint-Cyr, which was devoted to the education of young women.

since I'll never bring myself either to send back any that are unread or to read those that are just plain stupid. For God's sake, have Amblet make up my lists and send only those he chooses.

I believe in Mademoiselle Rousset's departure the way I do in Balaam's ass[5] and won't believe it until I've received a letter from her postmarked Provence. She promised me she would wait for me. She is a woman of her word and is incapable of failing me. Her with you, I'm totally confused, *which harms me more than it helps me.*

If only you had seen me Saturday and Sunday. I was a sight to behold. I was expecting Monsieur Le Noir. Ah! by God, I had decked myself out for the occasion. No, you could not have resisted. If only you had laid eyes on me, I would have chased all the Albarets, all the *Lefebvres,*[6] from your mind. I must say, I was as handsome as a Greek god. And then he didn't come. Fie! To treat the poor old likes of me that way! All right, I'll get back at him, for whether he comes or not, I won't put on my Sunday best. And, while I'm on the subject, 'tis time you came to pay me a visit, cease all this idle prattle and come to see me. All joking aside, I earnestly declare that I very much want to see you. How we are going to study each other, eye each other contemptuously, after all this time. But, damn it all, the problem is we won't be able to *measure* each other. And why not? The bailiff? Why, what do we care about the bailiff?[7] He will hold the candle; he's quite adept at that sort of thing. As for me, I am doing some *measuring* ahead of time, I must warn you, like the Huron with the fair Saint-Yves. You know that it turns one into a strapping devil of a fellow to go for such a long while without *measuring.* 'Twould be a whole other matter if, like the bailiff, one could have recourse to *a little darling in the shape of a turnkey* to whom one tells all, in whom one confides everything, even the complaints one has heard about the fraudulent practices of the various Cer-

---

5. See Book of Numbers, verses 22–24.
6. Lefèvre, whose name Sade pointedly and disdainfully misspells. A Provençal peasant who was once a valet of Sade's uncle the abbé, who had taught him to read and write, Lefèvre had been brought to Paris by Madame de Sade as a servant. Seizing on an allusion to the man in one of his wife's letters, Sade jumps to the conclusion that Lefèvre is her lover. "Where in the world does he come up with such ideas?" she writes to Mlle de Rousset.
7. During Madame de Sade's visits to Vincennes, the warden ordered a guard—usually the Scribbler—to be constantly present. By "measure," Sade's meaning is obvious.

berean creatures[8] who guard the gates of Hell here, so that he can go ahead and offer insolent rebukes to them who may one day perhaps be in a position to take your sword and slash the face one adores, and that without any respect for the temple, for the idol, or for the worshiper.

I am not impugning the motives that led you to select these very soft towels. They are *charming*. But I'm afraid that the linen might be of inferior quality. I've received the rest: 'tis excellent, and I thank you. It seems to me I am missing six more handkerchiefs, to round out the dozen of each item, to wit:

Wardrobe towels	12
Shirts	12
Shaving-cloths	12
Handkerchiefs	6

I think my calculations are correct. In which case, I beg of you to send me another six handkerchiefs just like the others, which are very fine; and that will see me in linen at least for half the remaining period of my detention.

This white jacket you sent me is as wrong as wrong can be, because 'tis without sleeves. You know full well that the similar jackets you sent me earlier had sleeves. Finally, the [. . .] is very pretty, but everything was to have been the same, both sleeves and back.

So tell me when this farce will end. It has already gone on for two months. That's a long time, you know, and even so I get the distinct impression that not everything is settled: there will be another unpleasant surprise during the early days of next month; and then I hope you'll leave me alone, all the more so because I want to pack in an enormous amount of reading this summer. Do let me see that project through. And 'tis far better, if I do say so, than all of yours. At least I have something to show for it, whereas nothing you have undertaken has ever produced, and never will, anything but blather, platitudes, and perhaps a few crowns in the pocket of the bailiff or his colleagues.

That idea that popped into your mind concerning Mérigot[9] is neither new nor yours. You must kindly excuse me, but things of value are

---

8. In Greek and Roman mythology, Cerberus is the three-headed dog that guards the gates of Hades.
9. A Paris bookseller.

subject to claim. I had suggested that to you ages ago. In the future, that's the way it should always be.

Tell me, my fair queen, if instead of spending so much time and effort trying to obtain permission to come to see me, you had worked as hard to solicit permission for me to come and see you, wouldn't that have been time better spent? Hasn't all this gone on long enough? And what the devil can they, in honor and in good conscience, be hoping to gain by keeping me so many years inside a room? For quite some time I have both seen and experienced the most frightful drawbacks, but so far I have neither seen nor felt the slightest benefit. Ah, good God! After all the time that people have known the other side of the story relative to those sentenced to prison, since it has been acknowledged that prison has never served any purpose except to make a man worse, and that its sole purpose is to provide nothing other than gratifications, which ministers enjoy distributing at the expense of families, to their pimps or their whores, after all this time, good God, should they not have revised their opinions about prisons? And is it possible there are still some relatives low enough, cowardly enough, stupid enough to sacrifice their kinsmen to such infamies? I look forward to some fine day in the future when somebody comes to take my children away, so that Mme or M. So-and-So might pocket some money therefrom, and only hope that at that moment I were to have a loaded pistol in my pocket, either to blow their brains out or else to dispatch their victims, if such were to be their fate, and no matter how things came out I would have done the State a great service by destroying the former, to humanity by preventing the latter from suffering and turning bad, since nothing is more certain than that prison is bound to turn someone bad.

I am most appreciative of what you say about my manuscripts. I shall surely never ask for them back, since they seem to offer you a modicum of pleasure. But to convince me of that more thoroughly, you must at least explain to me the following sentence, which, as you can see, is meaningless:

"The baroness was a good friend, but her motives are somewhat dubious, sufficiently so as to obscure the ends she clearly implies at the beginning of the 2nd act."

You do of course see that this sentence is unintelligible. Explain it to me and tell me in plain and forceful language whether her behavior surprises or not, whether or not one foresees what she is going to do. That is what it is absolutely essential for me to know. Have no fear about telling me what you think, for 'tis the simplest and easiest thing in the world to correct. 'Tis a simple matter of either suppressing or reworking the monologue that opens Act 2. I have cast about for a similar character. The only one I found is Julie in Destouches' *Le Dissipateur* [*The Spendthrift*], who reveals herself in the same way, and for the excellent reasons that Destouches sets forth in his preface, and which have served as rules to me, the circumstance being more or less the same. Do let me have your thoughts thereon, and then I'll truly believe that my writings afford you some pleasure. If that were so, you would at least have mentioned the speeches or the couplets that most pleased you. But I've run on too long upon this subject, and besides, I've come to the end of the page, so I close with a kiss. *And come visit me.*

18. *To Mademoiselle de Rousset*

[May, 1779]

This Sunday evening, having just received yours.

You are leaving, Mademoiselle . . . the stroke is new, I did not expect it or rather I seem to have been a complete fool not to have counted upon it: can one be so indiscreet as to ask what brings you to such a formal violation of the promise set forth in the following lines:
"You wish me to promise that I shall not leave Paris without you and that you will never be at La Coste without me . . . Very well, I grant you the first," etc.: Letter II, dated January 23.
In any case, Mademoiselle, as I do not fancy there is anything I can do to keep you from going (however great my desire for you to stay) I now feel obliged to deal with the two subjects I have promised myself to address, under a circumstance I foresaw only too clearly, the first being to declare to you that if you do leave before I am set free, *I shall not see you again as long as I live.* The second is to prove your failings to you, so that you do not take away with you the notion of an untrustworthy and irresponsible man, a slanderer, a man who is unjust, whose misfortunes have embittered him to such a degree that he has become unsociable; and 'tis with paper laid out in front of me that I shall initiate the discussion, when I am through I shall let you be the sole judge . . . But you will look high and low for excuses, won't you? Instead of justifications you will come up with jests . . . and you will tell me that 'tis not you, but your double . . . I quite agree; but at least you will have to admit that the false one, the double, has been playing a most despicable role, and that the Jupiter who pulls the double's

strings is a great rogue . . . But our armor remains undented from such
qualifications . . . and we enjoy earning them . . . And are we then convinced that this is the way to later put a good face on things? . . . Well
now, Mademoiselle, before you leave I beseech you to do me the one
last favor of assuring me that it is *not* . . . Otherwise, I swear by everything I hold dearest in this world that when I get out of here it will be
with naught but rage in my heart, and with the utmost desire to vent
it. But enough of this, let us to our subject, 'tis high time we did. The
simplest of all secrets, which I believe is well known to every twelve-
year-old schoolboy, is that when one crosses out a line, the deleted line
becomes the meaningful one in any passage, that letters that are mixed
up make sense when one reads what has been crossed out, and that not
so much as a comma is lost when the thing is done carefully; they who
cross out lines in my letters are too well educated not to know what
they are doing, they want to provide me this one further little pastime . . . I thank them, nothing being worse than idleness. The lines
from you that I am about to transcribe and confront, which are here before my very eyes, come from two different letters, both dating from
roughly the same period; and without making the slightest alteration
to either, I have rendered to each its real meaning. I shall keep them
very carefully, and you will be surprised when you see them. Such
then is my text, Mademoiselle, and starting from there I shall convince
you not only of your atrocious lies, but of your cruelties toward me, and
above all your frightful inconsistency which I am not wrong to call *the
product of your heart* and not of your mind, because the plot is too carefully woven not to recognize therein a veritable desire to hurt and to
harm: a plan as infamous as it is odious, the fruit of an evil heart if it
comes from you, most basely and vilely complaisant even if you have
only been an accessory to the crime. 'Tis that I prefer to believe.

1st Letter . . . September '78
Crossed-out lines reassembled so as to reconstitute their meaning.[1]

   "I have seen the high priestess.[2] I shall see her again, I am not displeased, to rush ahead with things at too fast a pace would be to make
certain they failed, minds are still too biased. Moving slowly but

---

1. The headings are Sade's.
2. Madame de Montreuil.

surely, and with solid arguments, we shall win out and your detention will not last *at the very worst* beyond springtime. Mme de Sade is less well informed than I, they keep everything from her."

Spring ends the 22nd of June, and consequently, till then we have nothing to say save about the phrase *at the very worst*. But let's not quibble over such details. Will you be so kind as to tell me, Mademoiselle, whether I am not to deduce from this phrase that I shall most assuredly be free in June?

2nd letter . . . January '79.
Crossed-out lines restored to their proper meaning.

"I cannot tell you when you will be let out . . . at worst, we have one resource, 'tis that your wife and your children cast themselves at the feet of the king, the one will beg to have her husband back, the others their father, etc."

Proven contradiction.

First: If my detention is not to extend beyond the spring *(at the outside)* which, you say, you know for sure, then why, considering that you are better informed than Madame de Sade, do you say *that you cannot tell me when I shall be let out?* and if you cannot tell me when I shall be let out, why do you tell me *that my detention will not last (at the outside) beyond springtime?* Second: If *at the outside* I am not due to be here later than the end of spring, why do you tell me that *in order for me to be released my wife and my children are going to cast themselves at the feet of the king?* And if in order for me to be released my wife and children must go and cast themselves at the feet of the king, why do you tell me *your detention will not last (at the outside) beyond springtime, I know more about the matter than Madame de Sade, from whom they keep everything?* Worm your way out of that, Mademoiselle, devote all of your multi-talented resources to finding your way out of this labyrinth. Can one put one's mind to better use than to justify one's heart?

Sheer hatefulness proven beyond all doubt.

I have sometimes said to myself that 'tis entirely possible an even greater misfortune might yet befall me than all those I have thus far endured . . . What might that be? 'Twould be to receive a letter urging me to try to escape if I can, or that someone sneak into me some poison or a file. The situation would then be clear . . . 'Twould be proven once and for all that, being sentenced to a lifetime of imprisonment here, these were the only means left to deliver myself from my grief, and I should use them. If there is anything in the world synonymous with the *file*, the *poison*, or *advice*, 'tis assuredly the ingenious and charming *resource* that you seem pleased to have discovered, Mademoiselle, *that of having my wife and children cast themselves at the feet of the king.* If I had read this phrase before going to Aix, had I not seen and heard what *I saw and heard* in that part of the world, I do swear to you on my word of honor and in good conscience that the effect of your phrase would have been to take without further ado a pane of glass from my window, and swallow it with a glass of water . . . and of that I again swear to you on my most authentic word of honor. But convinced as I was, and still am, that 'tis physically impossible for my detention to be eternal, for a thousand reasons it would take too long to detail here, of which the best of them is that when it comes to life imprisonment the procedure and the conclusions were completely pointless, and that if life imprisonment was what was to ensue, this same sentence, assuming they would have taken the trouble to pronounce it, would have been infinitely less harsh. Convinced, I say, of the soundness of this argument, certified to me down there by Messrs. Siméon, Reinaud,[3] Gaufridy, by the advocate-general and by Monsieur du Bourguet, my recorder, I confined myself to saying to myself, upon seeing Mademoiselle Rousset offer as a final parting a means that is never employed except in the most extreme cases and in those where lifetime sentences have been most pronounced without hope of parole, *here's a friend who is abandoning me, who is becoming the echo and marionette of my tyrants, and who, once a frank and honest person, is turning into someone most wicked and most traitorous.* Yes, Mademoiselle, that is what

---

3. Maîtres Siméon and Reinaud were Sade's lawyers in the Midi. Both had been involved in his Aix appeal and both had advised Sade against going to Paris in February 1777.

I said to myself, sprinkling this speech, by your leave, with a few tears, not out of fear, none being present in that case, but out of sorrow to see a friend willingly take it upon herself thus to thrust a knife into me at such a vulnerable moment, that the futile seductions of my torturers could compensate her for the loss of an unfortunate friend who was wont to love her as a sister.

My wife and my children cast themselves at the feet of the king! But are you aware, Mademoiselle, that I so love these children that I would rather choose a lifetime in prison than expose them to the certain dishonor wherewith such a maneuver would visit upon them forever? Do you think Madame de Montreuil a total fool, a woman capable of exposing her grandchildren to rack and ruin, do you think that, my case once heard, my trial over, she would not have sooner enlisted fifty armed men, if that was what it had taken to free me at the time, than (to attain that same end) compromise both her daughter and her grandchildren? A woman by the name of Madame de Sade cast herself at the king's feet, together with her children . . . Ah! are you aware, Mademoiselle, such an act would go down in history, nor are there many like it to be found in any reign? . . . That of Louis XV offers but one instance of it: a certain Monsieur de Lali[4] . . . But I am being very kind wasting my time refuting such a fantasy . . . which owes its existence only to the vile deference you have had for those who are persecuting me, and who doubtless told you, *Write that to him; it will be charming, you'll see the effect it has on his mind.* They are wrong, Mademoiselle, 'tis not in my mind it has hurt me . . . *'Tis a little lower down* . . . (as you used to say in a happier time) yes . . . 'tis there the knife went in, and went in deep, 'tis not a pinprick it made, 'tis a gash, and the venom the blade was infected with will make the wound incurable.

I have said all I have to say, Mademoiselle . . . I have now but to wish you a good and pleasant journey . . . If I wished to go on harping on the same old thing, I would say that since you are leaving without me despite your promise, 'tis the clearest indication that my sorrows are not at an end. The end of your letter—*a time will come . . . make sure*

---

4. Sade is probably referring to Thomas Lally, who was governor-général of the French colonies of India in the eighteenth century. Defeated by the English armies in India, he rendered his sword at Pondicherry, and upon his return to France was condemned to death and executed. The case to which Sade refers relates to Lally's son Gérard, the Marquis de Lally-Tollendal, who with the help of Voltaire besought Louis XV to rehabilitate his father's good name.

I hear how you are faring, etc.—exhales an odor of great length, which leads me to think that I still have a long while to suffer in this execrable prison, and that you deceived me most cruelly when you implied that the end would coincide with the end of spring. But I do not want to put a further tinge of gall and blackness upon thoughts which are already dismal enough . . . You yourself must be well aware of all the pain this departure causes me . . . *I feel it to the depths of my heart!* . . . And (in spite of your behavior) 'twas a kind of consolation for me to breathe the same air as you . . . But 'tis unfair of me to take advantage of your indulgence for so long . . . besides, what good can you do for me by staying here? You see how it is dragging on, as you see there is still a long road to hoe before 'tis over! Go, Mademoiselle . . . go . . . return to your own affairs . . . After having devoted yourself to your friends, 'tis only right and proper to think of yourself . . . Do think of me from time to time . . . even in the midst of your pleasures; go to La Coste in the month of August, I sentence you to do so, sit down upon the bench—do you know which one I am talking about? . . . Yes . . . and when you are there, say, "A year ago he was here, next to me . . . yes, I was here . . . and he was there . . . He opened up his heart to me, with that candor and that naïveté clearly proved how much I meant to him . . . I asked him to promise me . . . . he took my hand and said to me, 'My dear friend, I swear to you' . . . 'Ah,' said I, 'twill be for your own happiness . . . ' And his reply to me was: 'Ah! was there any other advice you could give me?'" . . . And then you will go into the little green sitting room . . . and you will say: "My table was over there . . . there was where I wrote all his letters, for his life was an open book to me . . . Sometimes he sat in the armchair . . ."—you know which armchair I mean? —"and from there he would say, 'Write . . . *We shall do* . . . ' 'But, Monsieur, *we?*' 'Yes, dear friend, *we:* our phrases must be formed like our hearts . . . So please put *we* . . .'" And then you'll go and set the clock . . . Then you'll take two or three turns about the big drawing room, and you will say: "Even if I had lost him forever, still . . . how precious all these places for me! . . ." Yes, do all that, and I, ever sad and unhappy, ever caught between hope (perhaps the most frivolous hope) . . . and the desire to have done with my woes . . . I shall wander with you during all those little walks and those little memories . . . perhaps I may squeeze your hand again . . . Do you know how powerful an illusion may be upon a sensitive spirit? . . . You will think you are seeing me, and all it will be is your own shadow . . . you'll think you are hearing my voice . . . and 'twill only be the voice of your heart . . . Who knows whether some misgivings may begin to creep up on you: you will remember these letters . . . yes, these cruel letters which you leave with me . . . and which will be all I have of you . . . like those wretches that poverty compels to eat the most contradictory fare, I shall read them . . . because you have written them . . . I shall cherish them, because I know you wrote them without thinking . . . Adieu, Mademoiselle . . . yes . . . adieu . . . At least I say it without tears in my eyes as I utter those words . . . Give me news of yourself via Madame de Sade, and she will pass mine on to you . . . But please be so kind as to write me another brief letter before you leave . . . to tell me the day . . . yes, the day . . . For I absolutely want to know what day you are leaving. Once again, adieu. You can see that I refuse to resort to a formal closing.

Open . . . open your heart and you will see the feeling that replaces it.

DE SADE

19.   To Carteron, a.k.a. La Jeunesse, a.k.a. Martin Quiros

[October 4, 1779]

*M*artin Quiros . . . you behave most insolently, my son, if I were there, I'd play a dirty trick on you . . . I'd snatch off that frigging wig of yours, which you replenish every year with ass-hairs gathered from bidets on the road between Courthezon and Paris, then what would you do, you old monkey, to fix that? Eh, speak up, what would you do? Would you go around like some person from Picardy foraging for nuts fallen off a tree, and peck and pluck about to right and left amidst all those black old *things* aligned in the evening outside the shops up and down the rue Saint-Honoré, and then the next day, with a bit of strong glue, you would set it back again upon your scaly brow so that it would be no more visible than a crab-louse on a slut's beard, would you not, my lad . . . Come . . . let's have a little quiet, if you'd be so kind, for I am tired of being insulted for so long by riffraff. True, I do as dogs do, and when I see that pack of mongrel bitches barking at my heels, I lift a leg and piss on their noses.

F——me, I say, you are as learned as an in-folio, where have you picked up so many pretty things? . . . These elephants killing Caesar, this Brutus stealing cattle, this Hercules, this Battle of Prunellae, and this Varius! . . . Oh! that is fine stuff indeed! You stole all that one evening, on your way home with your mistress after having taken her to supper with her old mum, you slipped it in from behind under her petticoats, piece by piece as you got hold of it, and then you acted as if you were eating cherries, so that the poor marquise arrived home that night with elephants, Herculeses, and steers inside her dress, which made her hold herself stiff and bolt upright quite as if she were not a magistrate's daughter. Sometimes you prattle to me about some woman with child, but, ah, I didn't teach you my tricks for pregnant ladies, no, but for yourself . . . Are you with child, my lad? Is it Mme Patulos who is? Or is it Milli SPRINGTIME?[1] Tell me . . . tell me, who is it, then, who's heavy in your house? Forsooth, let them be, if they like it, and bear in mind my little song, *Go f——k away the live long day* . . . Well, that's the song I sing here, six times a day. And I whistle it four.

What, you good-for-nothing monkey, with your face of a scrub brush smeared with brambleberry juice, you pole in Noah's vineyard, you rib in the belly of Jonah's whale, you used matchstick, from a bordello's tinderbox . . . you evil-smelling ha'penny candle, you rotten cinch from my wife's donkey . . . what, you've found me no islands? You dare tell me that, you and your four comrades of the frigate sailing the shores around the Port of Marseilles, you've not made the least effort to discover me any islands and you've not found me seven of them in the space of a morning? Ah: you old pumpkin pickled in bug juice, you third horn on the devil's head, you cod face with two oysters for ears, you old worn-out shoe of a bawd, you dirty linen full of Milli Springtime's *red unmentionables*, ah: if I had my hands on you now, how I'd rub your dirty face in them, that baked apple of yours that looks for all the world like a burning chestnut, to teach you not to tell such lies.

How kind you are to remind me that you're never seasick. What can I tell you on that score, my boy? I've long known you carry your wine and your water better than I. But while you make such a brave show up there on deck, all it would take is a pasteboard sea serpent to send you flying into the water or into hell if it opened up beneath your feet . . . Each of us has his little weaknesses, Quiros my son . . . happy is he who has the fewest. But what's all this talk about Venice? I've never been to Venice; 'tis the only city of Italy I'm not familiar with, but someday I'll go there, or so I hope. As for skipper Raviol, that's a whole other matter. I do know him. I had the honor of having him

---

1. Mademoiselle de Rousset.

serve under me for a period of three weeks, I remember how we attacked the bridge at Arles together, during which battle we suffered serious losses, and I was obliged to retire with dishonor and without having managed to board. During that same time, you who like me don't know how to swim and who therefore has no stomach for naval combat, you were slinking along the shore, your saddle on your back like a tortoise, your hands thrust deep into your boots as if they were gloves, trying to get together with some Réstif gentleman, ah: I haven't forgotten all your wonderful feats and achievements.

I was most gratified to learn my squadron was in the roads. I'll be joining it soon, with my sloop *Blaster*. All I am waiting for now are sixty or eighty cannons, and there are forty mules' pizzles I want to fly from my top, to make us look more formidable. And then I'll unfurl my sails and set forth on a cruise this spring.

So your view, Martin my boy, is that you don't like the way I write? Hear me out upon this matter, and follow my line of reasoning.

I write only for my wife, who can read my writing very well, however poor it may be. Those who without the slightest authority or right to do so want to stick their noses into this writing, which displeases you, if 'tis not to their liking they can go f——k themselves. If at this point you would like a bit of erudition upon the matter, well then, here it is, my boy: both the male and the female who take on these airs, far from taking offense at being sent where I recommend they go, if they dare be honest with themselves will answer me as the regent replied to a woman who complained to him that Cardinal Dubois had sent her where I am sending them. *Madame, the Cardinal is insolent. But his advice is sometimes good.* Farewell, Quiros. My compliments to Gautruche[2] when you see him; tell him I am altogether delighted by his resurrection;[3] and I particularly commend myself to Milli SPRINGTIME.

This evening of the 4th upon receiving your 3rd letter, or, as Milli Springtime says, in the nick of time.

---

2. Sade's pet name for Gothon.
3. Sade is turning Gothon into a male, doubtless to confuse the censor.

20. To Madame de Montreuil[1]

[October 29, 1779]

I have tried, Madame, insofar as possible and despite all I have had to suffer, to avoid importuning you, hoping that when I did so rarely take that liberty you would necessarily be more sensitive to the important reasons that might oblige me to break the silence. Your venomous hatred for me notwithstanding, of which I am the recipient of too many obvious marks for there to be any doubt, I flatter myself that simply as a most miserable human being, and asking naught more of you than the milk of human kindness, which even the lowest of the low could rightly expect from your good soul, I should hope that you might well be touched by all my pain and suffering and moved to alleviate the woes, which by now they must be weary of imposing upon me for so long and so pointlessly.

The air in this place, Madame, and the way of life the commandant has chosen to subject me to, are so prejudicial to my health that my chest is already affected to the point where I am spitting up blood, and I truly fear a serious and perhaps fatal lung disease is likely to follow, from which I may not recover if I have the misfortune to spend the winter in this execrable place. If you ask me the cause of this physical disorder, which they doubtless will keep from you, and of the stage to which it has evolved, all of it traceable to little reasons of ego that you can easily imagine, I shall have the honor, Madame, of setting it forth for you in four words, hoping that your many kindnesses to me in the past will enable you to overlook the banality of these details, render you more sensitive to the increased sufferings as real as these, and will finally incline you to take measures to remedy them.

During my first detention here[2] I was in a healthy and airy room, I ate at three o'clock and could consequently link this meal to the milk

---

1. As noted, Madame de Montreuil had declared she would neither write her son-in-law nor receive his letters. In a letter that January (1779) she wrote to Renée-Pélagie: "The indelible memory of an entire past prevents me from having any direct contact with him." Still, as he nears the beginning of his third year of prison, increasingly desperate to see if not an end to his imprisonment at least an alleviation of its harsh conditions, he turns to the one person he thinks can, by word or deed, offer a change.
2. That is, from February 1777 until his return from Aix in mid-1778.

which I have been used to drinking every morning for more than ten years. During my meal, someone would be there to keep me company, which helped me eat a bit less bitterly, and to digest more easily. At the time I set out for Aix, Monsieur de Rougemont, a soldier honestly to be commended for his candor, which is to his honor, assured me that if ever I were so unfortunate as to return here—which was by no means certain then—I would be infinitely better treated upon my return and I would have all the comforts and amenities I might desire. And yet, as though this gentleman, who only needed to be candid in what he promised me, had reveled in playing the scoundrel, not only by not keeping to any of these promises but even going so far as to deprive me of the few amenities I had previously enjoyed, he took it upon himself to put me in another room, deprive me of the pleasure of a moment's distraction during my meal, and make me dine at eleven in the morning; and all that to make life easier for other prisoners and especially for the comfort and convenience of his faithful Cerberi to whose interests everything here is sacrificed.

What resulted from all this, Madame, is that from spending last winter in a very poor room where fresh plaster would have never dried, in a room completely devoid of air, a room exceedingly damp and in which 'tis quite impossible to light a fire, that to be deprived of the little distraction I enjoyed during my dinner,[3] and more than anything else, from having stubbornly insisted upon changing the hour of that meal, which made it impossible for me to continue my milk and obliged me to give up taking it for over a year, what has resulted, I say, is that my health is totally destroyed and in tatters, and I am spitting up blood. This illness, Madame, which care and a supervised diet would cure anywhere else, is not only not improving here but growing worse by the day, as much from reasons of morale—about which you know more than I, since you nourish the serpents which occasion them—as from a physical defect in this place, something in addition to everything else I have described and which, being present in all the rooms, is a drawback tending to produce this sickness in those who did not yet have it: just think what it must do to those who already do! The defect to which I refer, Madame, is that the floors in these rooms are not tiled, that one cannot take a step without raising a dreadful cloud of dust, plaster, and saltpeter, fatal for the chest and lungs. You can therefore see, Madame, that here, instead of the illness abating, it tends only to

---

3. Following his reincarceration, Sade was prohibited from having anyone remain with him while he ate.

become more irritated and worsen in every sense. If this dreadful defect has been here for centuries, 'tis still very real and very dangerous, and if they do not repair it, the reason is obvious: whether one is comfortable here or not, it matters not one whit, the point being that you are *here*. 'Tis like those innkeepers who never have their inns repaired for fear guests may stop coming while the masons are there. Therefore, for all these reasons, and calling upon the feelings of your heart, which my sufferings must reawaken even if that heart has been alienated by my faults, I take the liberty, Madame, to point out to you that my suffering has gone on for a very long while, and that 'tis high time, it seems to me, that I at last be allowed to breathe. But since I have every good reason to believe that your pact is set in stone and that nothing can either increase by one day more or decrease by one day less the arrangements you have made, I would therefore request of you, while awaiting a freedom which after eight years of suffering I have every good reason to hope for, that I at least be transferred to another prison. That favor, Madame, is refused to no one when reasons of health authorize it. Now, can there be any more forceful or more legitimate reasons than those the prison doctor will vouch for; since I made him aware of my symptoms, he has seen me and after what he saw prescribed a diet I am following; what better reasons can there be, I say, than the fact of my spitting up blood, as a result of my being unable to stand the way of life and the air of the place where one happens to be? This transfer will not be a burden to anyone, Madame, I shall pay for it out of my own pocket. If they fear for my safekeeping, instead of six men let them assign a dozen to guard me if they like, I shall pay for them. If they care not where I am to be sent, as I imagine must be the case, I ask that preference be given to Lyons, although I am aware that Monsieur de Bory[4] is no longer there. The air that such a decent man breathed there for so long must be impregnated with his virtues, some traces of which must still exist. Moreover, Madame, there is a further reason joined to the earlier one: 'tis the air in that town, enriched and thickened by the mists of the Rhône River and the mineral coal vapors, which are especially recommended for people suffering from infections of the lung. Nothing easier than this transfer, Madame; from here to the suburb, where the Lyons coach passes, is not far. I can be marched there surrounded by forty men, if that would please them

---

4. The former warden of Pierre-Encize prison, whom Sade respected as much as he respected anyone in the prison system.

to do so. I agree to such an arrangement and will defray the costs, firmly believing that I could never pay too much for anything that would get me out of here, even were it to land me in Hell itself. As for the journey from Paris to Lyons, all they have to do is pack the entire coach with people to guard me. If I did not run away when I came here with five,[5] 'tis unlikely that I would try to escape when going away with eight or ten. As I finish my letter, Madame, which my present suffering prevents me from going into in further detail, and which may already contain more than enough to try your patience, I most earnestly and most insistently renew my request to have me transferred, and I beseech you, if that is to happen, that it be done before the onset of cold weather, since later on I would not be able to endure either the cold air or the journey. Do not wish for the death of the sinner, Madame, he may yet see the light; it strikes me that his conversion will prick the pride or sensibility more than will his destruction. In a word, Madame, I beg you to consider that what I am asking is neither for a reduction of my sentence nor for the recovery of everything that was ridiculously taken from me, but for transfer into a wholesome place and one where, although locked up, I can at least catch sight now and then of human beings, get some fresh air when I want to, and live according to my own rhythm rather than that of others, things which are not denied to anyone after so many trials and tribulations and such a long confinement, that, if worst came to worst, I'd prefer the Montboisier Tower at Pierre-Encize[6] to all of the Vincennes dungeon. And, if you refuse me such a slight favor, my frame of mind is such that, were I to have the misfortune of spending another winter in this place, verily I believe 'twill be the last, in which case, Madame, 'tis very likely this will be the last time in my life I shall have the honor of conveying my most respectful regards, with which I have the honor of being, Madame, your obedient and most humble servant.

I take this opportunity to assure Monsieur de Montreuil of my sincere respects, and to thank him for the books he so kindly lent me this past summer.

This letter has been written the 29th of October, but shall be dispatched only when I know for certain that they intend to make me

---

5. After his recapture at La Coste on August 26, 1778, he was escorted back to Vincennes by five armed guards.
6. The prison near Lyons where Sade was confined from the end of April 1768 until November 16. Relatively speaking, it was an indulgent prison.

spend the winter here, which shall be determined when I see which of the latest objects I requested are indeed dispatched.

21. To Madame de Sade

[December 2, 1779]

*I*n truth, Madame, I believe you think I complain for no reason . . . to make myself interesting. Ah! great God! what would I stand to gain from resorting to such a stupid trick? What use could it possibly be for someone as convinced as he is of his own existence that his term has been fixed and determined, and that were he on his deathbed, nothing could either shorten it or make someone tell him what that date is? Am I not painfully aware of what an old idiot's stubbornness can lead to? . . . Have no fear that I shall ever try to overcome it . . . 'Twould be a stain on my pride . . . Since 'tis absolutely impossible for you to believe that the ills about which I complain are true, 'tis necessary, in order to justify the lack of interest you take in them and your continued stabs in the back, even in my present state, 'tis necessary, I say, that they who ought to describe those ills to you as they truly are, are instead offering you a watered-down portrait . . . And coming from them, this does not surprise me . . . In truth, they are not such fools as to report the situation accurately: to do so would have the effect of arousing people's concern, and cost them their prisoner . . . And with him, their salary! Must blood not forever flow into the gullet of the cannibal who feeds himself upon it? What would become of him were the flow to be stemmed? Yes, Madame, I am suffering, and what is worse, suffering more and more every day. On this score, would you like me to tell you a little story that illustrates the humane rules which govern this establishment? Last night, having felt much worse over the past several days, I thought I would write a little note to the surgeon, in which I asked him for a new medicine I hoped might make me feel better. I went to bed and fell asleep feeling slightly calmer in the hope that he would shortly give me what I asked for. When I awoke in the morning, I said, "So have you brought what I asked for?" "Not another word," was the reply, "I am returning your note to you." "My note?" "Yes, Sir, your note: you addressed it to the surgeon, and that is a crime . . . The note has to be addressed to the commandant." "And the medicine?" "Oh, the medicine! When you've addressed your request through the right channels . . ." So! what do you say to that? Is it nice? is it kind? is it attentive? But in all fairness, 'tis not the fault of those who carry out the orders, and I save my curses for the inexcusable stupidity of those who give them . . . Would you like another little example, piping hot? . . . Three or four days ago, because of the cold, I had not been able to go down to the garden. One day the weather waxed warmer . . . Down I went . . . While I'm there I'm informed the surgeon is on the premises. "Very well," I say, "have him come to the garden." "Sir," I am told, "he'll do nothing of the sort; the rules strictly forbid him from doing so. The choice, Sir, is up to you: either lose the surgeon's visit or lose the walk." "Alas!" was my answer, "the fact is, both of them would do me a great deal of good." "That may well be, Sir, but 'tis not one's good we are concerned with here, 'tis the rules . . ." So what do you say to that, Madame Marquise? A surgeon unable to see a sick man in the garden! . . . As though you absolutely had to be at death's door in order to have the right to consult a doctor! What an infamy! . . . And is the eye of the government completely blind to such abominations? And is there no one to reprimand a little subaltern capable of subjecting proper gentlemen to every tyranny on the books, to every whim that passes through his imbecilic imagination? And the whole world is not to hear about this someday? I would rather have both my hands cut off than not serve the nation by enlightening it about such abuses . . . And how could such abuses fail to exist, when the person on whom everything depends, Monsieur Le Noir, and whose duty it is to keep an eye upon such matters, blindly takes his cue from a subordinate[1] who has every reason in the world to deceive him? Oh! I shall unmask them, indeed I shall, these horrors, these odious schemes, these plots concocted by greed and rapacity! I am now familiar with them all, I have learned about them at my own expense: all France must know about them as well.

Why have you not sent me the books from the new list that I had sent to you? 'Tis passing strange that you have not received the old ones, for 'tis more than a fortnight that I sent them to you. They were a treatise on the Inquisition; I'm not surprised if it was waylaid by the Reverend Father Inquisitor; but whatever horror this treatise contains, whatever iniquitous law may be found therein, whatever the measures

---

1. That is, Monsieur de Rougemont.

every wise nation may have taken to proscribe this tribunal—I defy him to find therein anything he didn't already know, and after having read it he will still be able to say, like the pheasant in the fable: *Ah! I knew a great deal more about it than that!*

And here is another startling example. Just as I was writing you this letter, the letter to the surgeon was returned to me because the address, made out at first to him, then later to Monsieur de Rougemont, appeared scrawled. *Take care how you address your letter, or no remedy . . .* I do believe the dear man is going mad; one has to twit his little vanity, and that I am going to do in a letter I shall enclose with the other. You have told me that I was allowed to write to whomever I so pleased. 'Twould be most unusual if I were able to write to my friends and yet could not send a note about my state of health to the doctor. One does not at all enjoy having to deal with madmen who, all puffed up with pride from hearing themselves called *Commandant* by soldiers and jailers, think themselves entitled to add even heavier chains to their betters when chance or misfortune brings them to their inn. Be good enough to have them make up their minds, yes or no, whether or not I can communicate in writing my state of health to the doctor, at other than the prescribed hour or when I do not feel it necessary to have him pay me a visit but only want to check with him on some matter. What a place! What a man! If only he knew how I despise and detest him! If only he realized how stupidity disgusts those who have a little common sense! But I hope that I shall someday have the opportunity to tell him all that. Only that sweet hope keeps me going.

Do send me the books listed in the little note I recently had forwarded to you. 'Tis incredible that you don't want to send them. I'm distressed to learn that the author of *Le Voyageur français* is ill. He is a charming writer. Read that book if you want to have a delightful time. I know nothing so instructive and at the same time so entertaining. I promise you that 'tis the first book my son will read. Send me whatever you can find out about this author. I am especially interested in him because of the delightful evenings he provided me, both last winter and this . . . A Father Inquisitor, a familiar of the Holy Office, an Auvergnat scissors grinder, all that vile scum of the human race will live to the age of eighty, as it is well known 'tis the characteristic of all useless and noxious animals to outlive the others, and a certain Abbé de La Porte, a delightful and charming author who must charm the social world as he does those who read him, will be snatched away in mid-career and not know the pleasure of completing his work! . . . And

Providence is just! . . . Oh, upon my honor 'tis not! My chest, worse than ever . . . How could one get better with such scenes taking place day in and day out? And yet, 'twill one day be over, and I shall still have full use of both my arms.

I beg of you, if 'tis not too late, please include in the package a pot of beef-marrow ointment, or ordinary ointment, a pound of powder, not of plaster like the last time, and a pair of fine leather gloves similar to those you previously sent.

22. *To Carteron, a.k.a La Jeunesse, a.k.a. Martin Quiros*

[Early January 1780]

I hasten to take this opportunity, Monsieur Quiros, at the turn of the New Year, to wish you and all those near and dear to you the happiest of years. At long last my trials and tribulations are coming to an end, Monsieur Quiros, and thanks to the many kindnesses and the unstinting protection of Madame la présidente de Montreuil, I hope, Monsieur Quiros, to be able to offer you the same good wishes *in the flesh* the day after tomorrow five years hence. Long live influence, Monsieur Quiros! If my unlucky star had allied my fortunes to any other family, 'twould have meant I'd have been in here for life, for you know, Monsieur Quiros, that in France 'tis not with impunity one shows disrespect for whores. One may speak ill of the government, the king, religion: all that doesn't matter. But a whore, Monsieur Quiros, gadzooks! be careful never to offend a whore lest in a flash the Sartines, the Maupeous, the Montreuils, and other brothel-lovers arrive in *soldierly* fashion in defense of the whore and *intrepidly* jail your gentlemanly self for a dozen or fifteen years, all over a whore. So there is nothing finer than the *French police*, you see. If you have a sister, a niece, a daughter, Monsieur Quiros, advise her to become a whore; I defy her to find a finer profession. And indeed, how can a girl be better off than in a situation where, in addition to a luxurious and easy life, plus the constant intoxication of debauchery, she also has quite as much support, influence, and protection as the most high-minded bourgeoise? That's what they call encouraging high moral standards, my friend; that's what is meant by discouraging decent girls from ending up in the gutter. God be praised! 'Tis well thought out! Oh, Monsieur Quiros, what an enlightened age we live in! As for myself, I give you my word of honor, Monsieur Quiros, that if by heaven's hand I had not been born in a position to feed my daughter, I swear to you by all I hold most holy in the world that I'd turn her into a whore this instant.

I hope, Monsieur Quiros, that you will allow me to offer you as a New Year's gift a new little work, selected by your dear mistress's little lackeys and fully worthy of their taste. I was quite convinced that this little work would be of interest to you, and so I am relinquishing it in your favor. 'Tis anonymous; great authors, as you know, preferring to appear clandestinely. But as book lovers like ourselves like to guess who is hiding behind the mask of anonymity, I believe I have ferreted this one out, and if 'tis not by the drudge at the corner of your street, at least it's safe to say that 'tis by none other than Albaret. That worthy child must have as father one or the other of those two great men, *the marketplace or the courthouse*, there can be no other. My error stemmed from the fact that they look so much alike, for 'tis so easy to attribute to the one what comes from the other that the chances are great of making a mistake. 'Tis like the pictures of Carracci and Guido: those two renowned masters ascend so equally into the sublime that one may sometimes mistake their brushes. Gadzooks! Monsieur Quiros, what a pleasure to discuss the fine arts with you! The Palmiéris, the Albanos, the Solimenos, the Dominicanos, the Bramantes and the Guerchinis, the Michelangelos, the Berninis, the Titians, the Paolo Veroneses, the Lanfrancos, Espagnolets, Luca Giardinos, the Calabreses, etc., all those people are as well known to you as are whores to Sartine and pimps to Albaret. But here, when I try to talk about such things, no one can follow me. There's only the excellent *Lieutenant Charles*,[1] a very learned person, who will tell you at the drop of a hat that in the *twelfth century* the keep of his fortress was besieged *by cannon fire*. However, one does not unfortunately have a chance to chat with him as often as one would like . . . He is like *Molé*,[2] he only performs on the important days.

To enrich the enclosed book I have appended some notes in an effort to enlighten the text, which, I trust, will not displease you, Monsieur Quiros, and I like to think that you will keep this little gift all your life. I have included with it a little song, a trifle old and a trifle

1. Monsieur Le Noir.
2. François-René Molet, a.k.a. Molé (1734–1802), an actor at the Comedie Française whom Sade greatly admired and who, he hoped, would one day appear in one of his plays.

bawdy, but which, even so, ought to brighten your evening when you and your friends, Monsieur Quiros, come out to Vincennes to dine on a veal stew or one of rabbit-and-bacon at Vincennes, La Rapée, or La Redoute.

By the way, Monsieur Quiros, be so kind as to tell me if you are in tune with the fashion, do you have running shoes, harness buckles, or are you wearing a windmill on your head. I have a very great desire to see you in such an outfit, and am certain 'twould give you a most interesting appearance. Just the other day I felt like decking myself out in one of those windmills. 'Twas the one belonging to Lieutenant Charles, who happened to be *performing* that day ('twas quite a day); well, Monsieur Quiros, you'd never believe how much I looked like a cuckold as soon as my forehead was covered with a bit of felt. Oh, yes! Where did that cuckold look come from, Monsieur Quiros (for it did come from somewhere)? From the hat? From my forehead? From Lieutenant Charles? 'Tis a question I leave for you to answer.

I would be most obliged to you, Monsieur Quiros, if in return for all the many favors I have lavished on you, you would be so kind as to send me, in paper, a little model of your friend Monsieur Albaret's dunce-cap. I've a pregnant woman's whim to see a sample of that diadem. Kindly find the address of his hatmaker, for the first thing I intend to do when I get out is to go straight there and have myself properly hatted.

And how do your pleasures go, Monsieur Quiros?

> *Which of the two, Bacchus or Cupid,*
> *Crowns your day with victory?*
> *What! . . . by toasting each in turn*
> *You think that glory you will earn?*

I have every confidence you are fully capable of it, and the wines of Meursault, Chablis, Hermitage, Côte Rôtie, Lanerte, Romanée, Paphos, Tokay, Sherry, Montepulciano, Falerno, and Brie tickle your organs lubriciously, next to the chaste flanks of your Pamphilia, your Aurora, Adelaide, Rosette, Zelmira, Flora, Fatimah, Pouponne, Hyacinth, Angelica, Augustine, and Fatmé. Wonderful, Monsieur Quiros! Believe me, that's the way to spend your life; and when Mother Nature created vines on the one hand and c———nts on the other, you may be sure 'twas for the sake of our pleasure. As for myself, Monsieur Quiros, I too have my little pleasures, and though they may not be as lively as yours, they are no less precious. I trip about to and fro in my room; to keep up my spirits at dinnertime, I have (and they consider this a great favor) a man who, regularly and without the slightest exaggeration, takes ten pinches of snuff, sneezes half a dozen times, blows his nose a dozen times, and hawks up thick phlegm from deep down in his throat, at least fourteen times, all that in the space of half an hour. Makes for a very clean and entertaining meal, wouldn't you agree, especially when I am downwind? . . . 'Tis true, to keep me entertained, there's the tall, disabled soldier who comes once a fortnight bearing an official form to fill out, which I have to renew, and once a year I receive a visit from Lieutenant Charles, who struts like an insolent peacock. Come now, Monsieur Quiros, you have to admit, these pleasures are worth every bit as much as yours: yours but befoul you in every vice, whilst mine lead to every virtue. Go ask Madame la présidente de Montreuil whether there is any better means in the world than locks to bring a person to the straight and narrow. I know full well that there are animals—you for example, Monsieur Quiros (and please do forgive me)— who say and maintain that one may give prison a try and, if it doesn't succeed the first time, 'tis dangerous to try it again. But that's sheer stupidity, Monsieur Quiros. Here's the proper way of thinking: prison is the only remedy we in France know; hence prison can only be good; and since prison is good, it ought to be utilized in all cases. But it failed to work, not the first time, not the second time, nor the third time . . . So? In which case, they reply, 'tis a good reason to try it a fourth time. 'Tis not prison that's at fault, since we have just if not proven at least established that prison is good. Hence the problem lies with the subject, and consequently back to prison with him. Bleeding is good for fever; in France we know nothing better; so bleed away, bleeding reigns king. But for Monsieur Quiros, for example, who has delicate nerves or a rare type blood, bleeding is not the solution—one must try to find something else for him. Not at all! your doctor will rejoin, bleeding is excellent for fever, that much we know for sure. Monsieur Quiros has fever: therefore he must be bled. All of which is called *the power of reason* . . . On that score, people far more sensible than you, Monsieur Quiros, who (with my most profound apologies) are an oaf, people say: *Pagans! Atheists! impious souls!* can you not tell the difference between physical illnesses and those of the soul? Do you not understand that there is no connection between the soul and the body? As proof of that, taking you as an example, *whoremonger, drunkard,* your soul's gone to the devil while your body is rotting away in Saint Eustache's cellar! So there is a very great difference between the soul and the body: therefore, there is no way one can make a connection between the treatments for the one and treatments for the other. More-over, I, a doctor, earn my money from bleeding you, I am paid *so much* for each prick of the lancet; therefore you must be bled. And I, Sartine, earn money from clapping you in: I am paid *so much* per prisoner; therefore, you must be imprisoned. What do you have to say to that logic, Monsieur Quiros? If you want my advice, hold your tongue, and don't get involved in dredging up your trite objections: prison is the fairest institution whereof the monarchy is adorned . . . If I had not kept my son-in-law behind bars, Madame la présidente de Montreuil will tell you, how could I have married 5's, 3's, and 8's together, could I have squared 23's with 9's? and so arranged things that when my daughter visits her husband for the first time, when she pays him a last visit, and when finally she goes to bring him home, more than eighty numbers will all be the same? Eh, you big oaf, the présidente will go on to tell you, could I have done that if I had been worrying my head about my son-in-law's happiness, about cleaning up his ideas or trying to bring him back to the straight and narrow? And isn't my matching of numbers worth far more than these foolish suggestions you are recom-mending to me now? *Happiness, virtues, head cures,* you see that every-day. But the squaring numbers, figuring out their relationships, and resemblances, only my Albaret and I can carry out such things. Faced with such profound reasonings, Monsieur Quiros, your arms go slack, your large mouth grins from ear to ear, your right eyebrow makes a move toward your left, your nostrils swell, your brow breaks into a sweat, your knees knock together, and in your enthusiasm you ex-claim: *Ah! I had always said that that bitch was smarter than I and my cousin Albaret, too!* Come now, Monsieur Quiros, cough, blow, spit, fart, and hum me a few bars from *Margot's in the Stockade Now.*[3]

23. *To Monsieur de Montreuil*

January 6, 1780

I kindly request that Monsieur le président de Montreuil be so good as to remit to Madame la Marquise de Sade, his daughter, the sum

---

3. Rough translation of the title of an irreverent army song popular at the time: *Margot a fait biribi.*

of one hundred livres, of which I shall be accountable to him in the manner and at the time of his choosing; said sum to be employed by the aforementioned Marquise de Sade, my wife, for the deliverance from prison of one or two persons lying there for debts or fosterage; the sum remaining after the deliverance of the one, or of both, to be employed by her for whatever charitable purpose she so desires; all this in celebration of the greatest and most pleasing piece of news in the world, and of the finest act of justice, wisdom, and insight that the best of kings could implement in the course of his reign: the fall from grace, the dismissal, the shame, and the downfall and degradation of Sartine.

DE SADE

24. To Madame de Sade

[Sometime after April 21, 1780][1]

I know of nothing that better proves the dearth and the sterility of your imagination than the unbearable monotony of your insipid signals. What! valets still sick of cleaning boots, workers reduced to idleness? And that's all you can do, with a dozen of you toiling away, racking your brains, making up one thing after another, and only to come up with the same nonsense every day? What stupidity. I blush with shame for all of you!

The other day, because you needed a 24, some fellow, sent to impersonate Monsieur Le Noir, and in order to make sure I wrote to Monsieur Le Noir, *came* on the 4th: and there was the 24![2]

Recently, because you needed a 23, walks reduced by one and restricted to between 2 and 3: there's your 23. Beautiful! Sublime! What a stroke of genius! What verve!

---

1. We know that on April 21 Sade received a visit from Monsieur Le Noir, during which the police official informed Sade that in the near future his wife would be allowed to visit him.
2. An example of Sade's reading signals into many of his wife's letters. Only he knew how to "read" them. Most signals were figments of Sade's mind, therefore impossible to clarify, though in some instances here he does offer the source for his deductions.

Ah! my God, read, keep busy, and if you had read nothing but *Little Tom Thumb* and spent all your time learning to tie knots, your time would have been less wasted than it has with such stupidities. If 'tis true that one must account to the Lord for one's time on earth, what embarrassment awaits you in the next world!

But if you must make these signals of yours, at least do so with honest intent, and not so they are forever a source of vexation! 'Tis only the executioner who torments or mistreats a prisoner. Is that the profession you or your family intend to exercise? Is it baseness or sheer stupidity that keeps you from turning your signals into a source of comfort instead of always making them a source of constant vexation? If 'tis the former, then I have nothing to say, and I shall pay you back in the same coin, on that I give you my word. Of what use would your school be to me if I did not learn something from it? If 'tis the latter, then cast your eyes if you please upon this little example and you will see how easy it is to do the same things properly instead of doing them wickedly and stupidly.

When I want to form a 16—since, according to you *sixteen* and *ceases* are one and the same,[3] and since you arrogate unto yourself the right to corrupt both the language and the ideas to such an extent—when, I say, I wanted to form a 16, from amongst the thirty or forty uniformly ridiculous chains Monsieur de S. has when I would subtract one, there would be a *cess-ation*. He desires an open door: when a 16 occurred I would open one for him to have 3 men bring him his food, as is done with the insane: he finds it both insipid and stupid. When the 16 comes around, I'd have this foolishness cease.

When I wanted to form a nine, I would tell him some piece of news or feed him some pleasantry. And the same with every other number. I want a 24? On the 4th I would grant him the pleasure of chatting with someone on the 2nd. I want a 33? I give him three hours of walks, and he writes back to me: "On the 3rd I had a three-hour walk," and there's my 33.

I want to mark some outstanding event, say a quarter, a third, etc.: I have him take a walk in the company of the major or the doctor for two or three hours in some other garden; now that's an event. And why is it that, of the miserable less than half-acre they have here for taking walks, the commandant perforce takes three-quarters for himself? Is that fair? Have you seen Monsieur de Bory resorting to such infamies?

---

3. A pun lost in translation. In French, sixteen (*seize*) and cease (*cesse*) sound very much alike.

There, in a highly abbreviated form, is the way in which you should go about making your signals. This one little example can serve for five hundred numbers as it can for two; at least I shall not sink into a state of utter exhaustion as I am presently doing here, from never seeing anyone or having anyone to talk to. Yes, that is the way you ought to act if you had a shred of kindness left in you, and any other projects or desires in mind except those of imitating all the hangmen in Hell or driving me completely mad.

Not only must the signal be made in complete honesty, it must absolutely and very distinctly stand out from the ordinary parts of the letter, failing which 'tis but a horror, a heinous and spiteful act deserving of vengeance.

25.   To Madame de Sade

[April, 1780]

So 'tis decided once and for all that you do not want to send me those two comedies I have been asking you for so insistently and for such a long time. Or else, if you are sending them, they simply will have to await their turn and fall in line with the sublime signals that govern everything. I had begged you to send them in the simplest way, without bothering to enclose a letter, without anything, just sent in a plain envelope, nothing could have been easier. But apparently the *Sublime Council*[1] has decided otherwise. All right. Come now, since I find myself without anything to do, I therefore might as well write to you. That will keep me busy for an hour, and 'twill be one more hour taken care of. As a first piece of news, I hereby inform you that my health grows worse and worse. The day before yesterday the stove finally did me in and gave me such a terrible headache I was ill. I would have given ten louis to have been able to have fifteen minutes of fresh air; and, of course, I thought this would be a good time to make an exception to the rules, but 'twas not my day, and people who think that at the very least they risk being hanged if they depart in any wise from their duty or take the slightest initiative, such people, as you can well

---

1. Madame de Montreuil and her advisers.

imagine, would not lift a finger to help you even if you were on death's doorstep. But in that case, Sir Sublime Director,[2] insolent little despot who doubtless think that you're in charge of a menagerie and not of people who are your betters—may I be allowed to address this to you— but in such a case you therefore must stay home, so that when such an emergency as the one that has just happened to me does occur, you can issue the necessary orders. And not take off at six o'clock in the morning, without anyone having the faintest notion where one can get hold of you for the rest of the day. All so that you can have your nasty little body purged *somewhere on the other side of the mountain. We know you, you clever scoundrel, we know all about you!* What does one do in Paris at six o'clock in the morning? 'Tis not at that hour of the day decent folk opens their doors. On the contrary, 'tis the hour of the lowest of the low, and 'tis they you are out looking for, is that not true? Yes, those are the ones you want, and we know at what price you frequent such people with impunity, and how you procure the sums necessary to pay for the pleasures they provide you. Yes, we know all this and have known it for a long time. And so when one prefers not to stay at home, one at least ought to have an adjutant who can act in one's stead and make decisions when someone might be in dire need. But providing you are told in the morning, or once a week, that none of your wards has either *escaped* or *died*, that's all you require. For since that is the only thing that guarantees your income and consequently *your little pleasures at six o'clock in the morning*, that is all that interests you.

Oh! 'tis a fine mess we have here, dear friend! Good God, if only you could see it for yourself! But of such shenanigans and of my health who will ever give you an accurate report? Ah! perish all thought of ever finding out the truth! Can you hope to get it from this kind of au- tomaton who, twice a day, brings me food and drink as if to a dog in its kennel? Certainly not! The rascal to whom I'm worth more than forty pence a day would be the last person to let you know that I am at my wit's end here and that 'tis killing me by slow degrees. Do you think you'll find out from His Highness the *Chief Jailer?* Even less likely. Ah! Good Lord, since no one is going to make the slightest move to have them all released until word gets out that everyone is at the end of their rope, we are in a position to do some fine business! I sometimes imagine I can hear him say:

2. The warden, Monsieur de Rougemont. When Sade felt ill and called for the doctor, he was informed that his request would have to be approved by the warden, who had left Vincennes at six in the morning.

"You bore me to tears, Sir, with all this talk of yours about human kindness; I have a hard time feeling sorry for you. I, Sir, I need to drink, eat, sleep, and have myself . . . shaved. I am the youngest son in my family, *slightly depraved*, and to whom this post was given in the days when everything went to pimps, and because that's what I was like any other. I got to where I am by the sweat of my brow, and in times as perilous for us as these, considering that the State is no longer honored as it deserves to be, you want me to subject myself to that ridiculous human kindness and report to your family on matters that might be of interest to them and so deprive me of my few remaining pleasures! Ah! you may be sure I shall do no such thing."

In short, the upshot of all this is that your ever-witty présidente has been screwing around full-go twice over; one, the Langeacqueries[3] can at least be taken care of by payoffs, but this one is much worse, since keeping one here is the source of one's income. Oh, the decent woman, the good woman, the ingenious woman, that présidente of yours! What a sharp mind, what a genius, how adept she is at making things work! Sometimes when I reflect upon that woman's vast capacities—I mean her genius—I am simply stunned. How quick she is to foresee things once they have happened! What a talent she has for averting calamities when they have already occurred! . . . 'Tis an obsession with her, a veritable innate predilection! What that woman wants is not to prevent evil, 'tis that it come to pass and she then has the pleasure of taking her revenge afterward . . . Oh, she is the most generous of souls! She reminds me of that madman in Athens of whom Plutarch speaks, who stood in the street watching his house burn. "What, don't you want to save your house?" people shouted at him. "I'd like nothing less," he replied coldly. "I want the house to burn down so that I may have the pleasure of punishing those who set it on fire." He and your mother are like two peas in a pod. Hark back upon almost all the events in the history of that prude's behavior toward me, her falsehoods, her ruses, her infamous maneuvers, both past and *present*, and you will see whether 'tis not the same thing, word for word.

Oh, that reminds me, kindly tell me what this little *virtually* stands for in your remark, "virtually everything at home remains in the same state in which I left it." I am most curious to know what that means. Is it one more witty comment from your *lovely little mother?* Oh, I'm sure it is, but it won't work, my darling présidente, it simply will not work.

---

3. Sade refers to the shenanigans of Madame de Langeac, a friend of Madame de Montreuil.

You already saw it didn't work once before; it won't work the second time either. All your efforts on that front are in vain . . . 'Tis an affair of six months at the most . . . Don't you know how the spider spins its web? And this will be better, for your plan was shapeless, unpolished, a kind of rough canvas, what we painters call a *rough sketch*. 'Tis the froth which bubbles out of the pot before you get the clear soup. If you had been a trifle more patient you might have ended up with something *noble*, something *fine*, something *clean* . . . But you prefer that your work bear a close resemblance to yourself, don't you? That is why you are so eagerly keen for the kill. My self-respect suffers therefrom, but, my beloved présidente, I gladly sacrifice it to your tastes.

Another question that I should like you to resolve for me at long last, my dear friend—for, despite my insolent digressions, 'tis always to you this letter is addressed—and that is to tell me once and for all how 'tis possible to resort again and again to the same old things, the same maneuvers, the same old methods, when one has so clearly seen that they all failed miserably the first time? What good did Pierre-Encize do me? What good did Miolans do me? What good did my first detention in Vincennes do me?[4] All it did was make my temper and my mind worse, heat up my bile, my brain, my temperament, lead me back into the same errors, for the simple reason that 'tis part and parcel of my being never to admit or to say that punishment affects me other than to make me worse. Once that is clear, once that is acknowledged, once 'tis understood I would rather perish than prove the contrary, and that, accordingly, if a kinder and better means be employed in dealing with me, one can turn me into whatever one would like me to be, why then always resort to the same old thing? . . . Because S[artine] must pay his wh——, right? Of course!

26. *To Madame de Sade*

[May, 1780]

I find nothing in the world as enjoyable, nothing quite so entertaining, as those mechanical fools who are so idiotic, so dull-witted they are unable to come up with anything better when they refuse a

---

4. The three prisons where Sade was incarcerated for libertinage and outrage to morals in his younger days.

request than: *"That's never been done, I've never in all my life seen it done."* In the name of God, if chance ever puts you in contact with such louts, tell them as follows: "Stupid animal that thou art, if extraordinary things make such an impression upon thee, do nothing amazing thyself, for if thou dost not want to be amazed, thou must not amaze others."

That's never been done here, and I have never seen it happen, for example, 'tis as if at the age of eight and sixty years one donned an apple-green coat and had one's hair curled with six rows of curls.

That's never been done here, and I have never seen it happen, for example, is to prostitute one's own wife in order to take in prisoners, and to feed as one's own children one has never had the faculty of fathering.

That's never been done here, and I have never seen it happen, for example, is to take a filthy and disgusting turnkey and turn him into one's catamite, and to place such trust in the aforesaid turnkey as to make him both one's mistress and one's reader, both one's scribe and one's intimate confidant.

Rougemont, my old friend, when one carries strangeness to such an extreme one must not be surprised by other peoples' minor eccentricities, unless one is resigned to being taken for a f—— beast. But that is not what terrifies you, is it? Upon that score your mind was made up long ago; and this worthy resignation on your part is the only virtue I see in you.

Now that I have absolute certainty, through your very own admissions, that the handwriting is counterfeited, you will understand if I neither sign nor send anything further. When dealing with rogues and scoundrels, one must constantly be on one's guard. You may be sure I shall be on mine. In Provence, do whatever you like: *seize, loot, trim, clip away to your heart's desire.* No matter what you do, once I know for sure 'tis you who have done it, I shall approve it and applaud it, because 'tis only you I trust. But also that trust is total: it could not be greater.

Send me everything I ask for by the first of June without fail. I absolutely cannot shorten the list except for the six jars of jam. If need be, two will suffice until fruit is in season. On Thursday evening, or Friday morning at the very latest, the campaign volume on the military campaign and *Voyage de Ceylan* will be downstairs in the office.

If this supplement or postscript displeases, at least let this half-sheet go through: 'tis essential to my everyday business concerns.[1]

---

1. This remark is for the censor.

27. To Madame de Sade

[*Early June, 1780*]

*H*ere we are back to frightful winter again. I advise you to take out all your warm clothes again, if perchance you have changed out of them, for this most uncommon drop in temperature after the warm weather we'd been having can only most certainly result in people's falling ill if they fail to take proper precautions in keeping with this unseasonable weather. As for me, I know that my poor chest is suffering from it, the details of which I shall spare you, knowing as I do how *powerful* an interest you take in such matters. The result of the doctor's visit was an herb tea wherewith I'm to stuff myself and which, I am now in a position to affirm only too well, will have no other effect than to upset my stomach altogether. However, what I was able to piece together from his embarrassed remarks to me (and could it be anything but embarrassed, speaking as he was with a pack of spies on every side and also because when all is said and done he was far more concerned about the person who profits from my sufferings than about the patient he had come to relieve!), from all this, I say, one thing I was able to piece together was, that only the waters and plentiful exercise, two things which are of course absolutely impossible, as you know, would be of any help to me, given my necessity *to feed my little pigs.*

And so 'tis clear that prison not only has ruined my health but also prevents me from taking the necessary steps to improve it. Shall we now examine its moral effects? All right, you may be absolutely convinced, *you and yours,* that 'tis the poison most certain to wreak havoc on the soul, to make sure the qualities of character are actually destroyed, that except for *those who get their living therefrom or who thereby pay their mistresses,* there is not a person in the world who will fail to tell you that 'tis never by severing a person's every tie with society you will succeed in inculcating a respect for those ties, and that the remedy, in a word, may well serve to worsen, but surely never improve, anyone.

I remember a time when madame your mother was fully convinced of these principles: but in those days she was not as yet an affiliate and she had not yet learned (for experience always does teach us something) that 'tis far better to sell or sacrifice one's son-in-law and one's grandchildren than to deprive oneself of the single honor of being affiliated with the police *on the distaff side* and to be able to say, along with *the bumbailiffs, officers of the watch* and *ladies of the bordello:* "I'm here in the name of the crown court." I remember. In those happy days of which I speak that praiseworthy passion was still in its early stages, the effects of which have since proved to be so brilliant. 'Twas a profound admiration for sublime official decrees that emanated from law courts, and especially for that kind of pretentious charlatanism that claims omniscience, which fools and provincials never fail to find so amazing . . . But what progress we have made since then! 'Tis our own flesh and blood we now want to be our victims and, all puffed up with pride triumphant, we ourselves lead them to the altar, their brows adorned with the bandages of infamy, which our stupidity has placed there.

How wonderful! Let us then hear from these unfortunate victims, since hear them we must and since 'tis set in stone that no matter what government we live under, the best of all laws will always be that of the strongest! But at least let there be some variation; for you will perforce agree with me that 'tis difficult when the victims are always the same. I agree with you that *the little larder* must always be kept filled, for otherwise how would one maintain one's *carriage* and one's *dressing-gown?* . . . Even so, let there be some differentiation in the choice of victims! Ah! I hear your response, *"'Tis not on every street corner you come across mothers as idiotic as mine, and who, although already caught twice, are absurd enough to let themselves be caught a third time. You have to take whatever you can get. You need about fifteen, don't you, to fill your quota? And where the devil do you expect us to find, with the desired variation, sixty or eighty families per year in a state of such a stupor as to imitate my mother?"*

Yes, my dear friend, I understand you very well, and with a complete feeling of resignation in the face of such sublime arguments, I shall cry out as did the Prophet King: *Quot sunt dies judicium? Quando facies de persequentibus me:* judicium? (Psalm 118)

[Included with this letter was the following request for items, dated June 15, 1780:]

The succeeding volumes of d'Alembert, if you please. I'll send them back in short order. Some trash for my secondary reading, since I am absolutely unable to read anything serious at night, what with the periodic headache I get immediately after I have eaten, and seeing that I am kept from taking any exercise, which you know I am accustomed to. Some marshmallow syrup, passably iodized, and the same sort as before, for 'tis very good. Above all some jam, which I am in the habit of eating, and which you really ought to have sent me instead of the little candles for which I had no use, since I have more than I have need of, both the short and the tall, until the 1st of July. Do please contact the dentist, for I fear I shall need him within a fortnight, and as soon as it becomes pressing I shall write you a little message telling you to send him to me forthwith.

I recall that on the 15th of June last year you sent me an excellent eel pie which, despite the warm weather, was a great success. As I have been allowed only a small amount of both roasted and boiled meat, I have to believe one can mix in a bit of fish as well, but one has to be extremely careful about one thing that will hasten its going bad, and that is to make sure no spice whatsoever is added to it, for if there is the slightest bit I shall simply refuse to eat it. It won't keep, I know; in which case, the only wise thing to do is make it a very small pie, and I'll make the best of it. If you want me to try the first strawberries of the season and feel you are in a position to send me some, I shall be most pleased; but that is just a fantasy pure and simple on my part, to which you need pay no attention.

I embrace you with all my heart.

28. *To Madame de Sade*

June 25, 1780

"*W*hen you get out I shall lock you up in my bedroom," etc.

"When you get out you will go abroad," etc.

"When you get out you will be exiled," etc.

"When you get out you can do your own browsing in the book-shops," etc.

Oh, my God! won't I have my hands full, and how clever I shall be if I am able to fit them all in! Why did you not add, "When you get out you will embark on a ship"? *"And when you reach port, I shall be happy beyond compare"*—a sentence as full as the one that said: *"Seventeen seventy nine will be a very happy year for me."*

Admit it, yes, please do, 'tis that last *"when you get out"* is the one you are keeping from me. Several sentences in your letters like the one I just quoted, the same old tunes mumbled to La Jeunesse and also appearing in his own letters, a note countersigned *"rigolei d'aqui"* and postmarked Boulogne-sur-Mer, embellished as usual with numbers (a note they just happened to drop off in my room back in March of 1778), a casual question Marais put to me on the road, *if I was afraid of the sea*,[1] and, most of all, something analogous to that project, which you mentioned to me after one of your returns from Paris, in the early stages of my affair: these are the grounds for my suspicion, which alas is doubtless all too well founded, about how this dreadful business is ultimately going to come out: a sinister end, of which you have to give me unmistakable hints in all of your letters, in everything they have done in my regard, in the packages you send, etc.

Please pay close attention to what I am about to say, keeping in mind that I am writing this letter in a state of total calm, and, make absolutely sure it reaches you, making sure 'tis free of any kind of invectives, to prevent the censors from finding any reasonable motive to confiscate it; so, once again, pay close attention if you please to what I have to say.

I have always dreaded and prodigiously detested the sea. La Jeunesse, who has seen me brave the sea, knows that this antipathy stems from my basic nature and that I absolutely cannot bear sailing. You may be sure that with the sad state of my already wasted chest, that is all it would take to finish me off. Even if it were a question, not of a post, not of the command, but of crowning me the *king* of an island, I would turn it down. I feel bound to declare it in no uncertain terms; to which I add something else concerning which you may be sure I shall remain firm, and from which I shall most assuredly not waver, and that is, certain as I would be that such a project holds nothing for me but a very swift death, I shall most certainly never agree to it of my own free will. And that if I am forced into it, I would sooner be chopped into pieces on the shore than forced onto any sort of ship, preferring, between two possible deaths, the one that will deliver me from my sufferings at one fell swoop rather than one which, simply prolonging them, would be more than dreadful in my view. In testimony whereof I sign this present writing, so that those who might have concocted this dark design against me may be convinced of my position.

DE SADE

---

1. Sade is referring to the possibility that when he is released he might be sent abroad by ship into exile. Since he cannot swim and hates the sea, he is haunted by that possible fate.

I have not often asked you to dispel all the fears or nightmarish fantasies wherewith my unfortunate situation has filled me. Furthermore, there are five or six other worrisome aspects to this ridiculous scheme you leave me with, regarding which I ask you for no *reassurance*, if one may employ that expression. But as for this one, it has afflicted me so long and so cruelly that I believe the anxiety it has caused me, and the sleepless nights it has made me spend, are doubtless the reason behind my failing health; and I ask you with the greatest urgency to reassure me on this score. If you fail to reply to me, if you choose to remain silent on the matter, I shall be forced to believe that nothing is more true, and in that case I shall not hide from you the fact that . . . For God's sake, erase this doubt from my mind, I ask you most humbly. It does not surprise me that a knave* whose situation is so precarious that he stands to be shipped off to the islands for any misdemeanor, perhaps from having been afraid [of the high seas] more than once in his life, either that or being sent to the galleys, made such a suggestion to your mother. The desire he has always had, which you yourself have admitted, to go down and manage my estate for my own good, in order to steal to his heart's content, more than justifies this advice. But I hope your mother will not be weak enough to acquiesce to it. You are fully aware, and you must constantly make every effort to remind your mother, what a complex and thorny matter it is to manage my estates, and what a singularly easy opportunity they offer for thievery, something my father painfully discovered, since during the last years of his life—may God keep him close beside Him or send him back to me—he derived absolutely no benefit therefrom. During this latest absence,[2] you have also seen it for yourself, since the leases in the surrounding areas rose by a third while mine fell by a quarter. And yet in spite of all that, I swear, under whatever penalty it may please you, that I intend to leave them to my son worth twice what they were when I inherited them from my father, if for once in my life I am left alone and am allowed to go and live upon them when I get out of here. Those are things of which you must constantly remind your mother,

---

* I am of course referring to Albaret, having promised myself to refrain from letting any invective slip into this letter, aimed at those who believe they are sheltered therefrom. But I trust that one can well imagine that this individual can never avoid being treated in a manner he so thoroughly deserves. (*Sade's note*)

2. From La Coste.

who I believe will, when she takes all this into account, see a far greater need for allowing me to remain peacefully at home rather than shipping me off to some distant place. I dare say that Gaufridy, another scoundrel of the first order—of which I think you have had more than ample proof—keeps sending your mother all sorts of plans and proposals, to convince her that, no matter how far removed I may be from the scene, she can direct everything perfectly well from her own hearth and home, and that her every wish is his command. But to that there is only one reply one need make to him: *"Sir, so what about the La Coste lease?"*—you will soon see him blush and fall silent.

In a word, I ask you for no greater consolation than to assure me that when I am released from here I shall be allowed to go and work for the future of my children: regarding that next step in my life, leave me to fret as much or as little as you please, 'tis a form of existence I have grown used to by now, and which has convinced me there is nothing truer than that one can adapt to any situation. All I ask is that you allay my fears *upon the single matter of shipping me off to sea*, which I consider a deliberate act of killing me off in a tortuously slow manner. The shorter way would be to send me a stout dose of opium, and the matter would be done. I shall sign the request in my own blood if need be.

Until I hear from you positively upon this subject I shall be in a terrible state of anxiety. And if you persist in remaining silent for more than a reasonable period, I warn you that I shall order them in the future that under no circumstances are they to bring me any more of your letters. I have no need for a correspondence that causes me naught but anxiety without ever reassuring me on any given subject. A long time ago I first warned you of my desire to break off our correspondence, but I have been patient till now and very certainly foresee the day when 'twill be a thing of the past if you do not give me satisfaction. Once I have forbidden further letters, will they decide to pass them on to me all the same? *Woe to him who dare to do so*, 'twould cost him dear; despair stops at nothing. What will result therefrom? To be deprived of your kind favor? . . . No matter! I had no trouble doing without it early on here, I shall do very well without it again . . . Till then I beseech you to send me once each fortnight—at least until the time when, desiring to make anything you send conditional upon the exchange of letters, offended because I want no more of your letters, you are unwilling to send anything anymore—till then, I say, kindly send me some books, candles both large and small, jams, some cotton stockings, and as always both kinds of marshmallow. The doctor, to whom I have spoken highly of that marshmallow, would be obliged if you would send me the address for it. Your paté was a veritable firebrand of spices, the benefits of which I left to those who serve me here. Herewith my thanks and much love.

29. *To Madame de Sade*

[*July 27, 1780*]

*W*ell, well, there you go, withdrawing into one of your great silences . . . 'Tis well done; 'tis only right and proper to rest upon one's laurels at times. I have just done a bit of the same. But the difference between us two is that I have nothing to talk about and consequently there is little or no point in my writing; whilst you, if you so desired, or if you were able, would have a great deal to say. Please note that I say, *if you were able*, and by that remark you can see the full justice I render you and to what point I am convinced that you are no freer to avoid all the absurdities you are made to commit than I am to receive them. That should make you clearly understand once and for all that my feelings for you will never be affected by all this. My portion of hatred will remain undivided; if it were apportioned, I fear some might get lost, and I am too desirous of reserving every last bit of it for her who so thoroughly deserves it. Whatever may come of all the kindnesses and all the charming signals, I can tell you that they hasten the decline of my health. 'Tis impossible for me to exist without getting out for some fresh air, especially in a season like this. I absolutely am unable either to eat or sleep. At least if they are going to prevent me from getting any fresh air, they should leave me alone at night. But to give me the most horrible headaches all day long by depriving me of sleep, and to prevent me from getting any fresh air, which is the only thing that makes them go away, is to inflict upon me ills of every sort all at once, and these charming tactics shall rest engraved in my mind. At least send me the flask of eau de Cologne I asked you for so long ago: if only I had some these past few days, when I suffered so from nerves and headache, it would have been of great comfort to me. That one example, you have to admit, denying me even this slight aid, is a needless annoyance. Ah! what a lovely lesson that teaches me! and how I shall put it to good use! Keep in mind when I say that I would much rather dash my brains out against the wall here and now than not oblige your execrable mother to say one day, *"How right he was; I am sorry for what I did. These were not methods one should have used in dealing with a head such as his."*

The other day I came to the firm conclusion not only how much they want me to suffer, but also how upset they would be were an illness to come in the way of all the infamies they visit upon me. By actual count, I spent seventeen nights without closing what is referred to as one's eyelids for a single minute. I looked as if I was newly risen from the grave, so much so that I was frightened myself by the way I looked. The doctor breezes in and asks me how I'm feeling. "My face will tell you better than I," I answered. "Why, not at all, not at all," he said to me. "In truth, I find you looking fit as a fiddle." Good, I said to myself, that's all I need to be convinced that this man views me like the Inquisitor's doctor, who takes the victim's pulse during the torture to see whether the torture can go on any longer, and who always says: "You can go on." This man (so I believe) has orders to find out how I am; but do you for a minute believe that he doesn't see, from the way they talk to him, that they want nothing more than for him to find me well so they can go on with the torture? In consequence whereof, this man, who couldn't care less, will always reply that I am doing just fine so long as he doesn't find me suffering from a stroke. And moreover, you should get it into your head that as far as they are concerned, all these vile people have everything to gain from making the families believe that their charges are doing just fine, and so they deceive them; in a word, the horrible malpractices which, under cover of this lovely secrecy, are routine in these houses, are one thing that ought most to be brought to the attention of people in high places if there were really any equality in France, and if the interested parties were not so careful to stifle any outcry with well-placed gold and pretty women. All is well, all is in order, everything in the world is just fine when one is well-bedded and one's purse is full. Gold and c——ts, these are the twin gods of my native land, and I am supposed to stay here, I who have never had much of the latter, and who am not in the least interested in defiling myself to the point of prostituting the former in those I hold dear? . . . No, no, I shall not stay! . . . I swear I shall not, I would rather go and live in Japan; there, I am sure,

I would find more good faith and would surely not be witness to so many horrors ... And, what is more, those who commit such horrors are punished there.

What I would most like is that, for once, a comparison be made, and made fairly, between the life of the wretched victims they keep imprisoned here and the infamies of those who are their keepers; and then see who better deserves to be in charge of the keys to the cell doors! An unfortunate incident, a brazen act, some kind of betrayal on the part of valets or friends—put that on one side; and on the other, put a thousand injustices, a thousand vexations, a thousand atrocities, all of which are covered up and kept from the public by money or influence ...

Enclosed herein a great many books I'm returning to you. Two volumes of Abbé Prévost, the rest of Monsieur d'Alembert's works ... What a man! What a pen! 'Tis such people I should like to have as arbiters and judges, and not the wretched souls that presume to govern my fate! I would have no trouble at all clearing my name in tribunals made up of such people, because just as one has little to fear when one is in the hands of philosophy, so one must tremble when one sees that one is prey to bigotry and rapacity ... Also, the first two volumes of *Les Cérémonies;* I am sending them to you quite smartly, it seems to me. I never told you it was a book that could be read in a fortnight, and when you sent it to me I saw right away that that was a witty way of letting me know that my sufferings were still far from over. But I am now quite used to all your imbecilic jargon, I remain indifferent to it, it no longer affects me in the slightest. It remains to be seen whether or not trying to dry up a man's ability to feel is a sound means for bringing him back onto the path of virtue, goodness; and whatever else may be said about your *Cérémonies*, so little did they terrify me that, if it is what people want, I shall agree to stay here until the book has been read: proof that my reckonings go well beyond this term. [As for] the rest of the books that I still have, [I] do not, I warn you, intend to rush through them, because, like *Les Cérémonies*, they can only compose my primary reading. So progress will be slow. As for my secondary reading, all I have left is your *Troubadours:* that will take me about a fortnight, therefore till August 15th. For the aforementioned secondary reading, I would ask you, in accord with Abbé Amblet, to try to find me some novels that are both interesting and philosophical but neither too depressing nor too languorous, since I absolutely detest both of those two extremes. I repeat: novels; for in the evening 'tis impossible to read anything serious.

For the first of next month: a bar of marshmallow (no syrup) and above all, I beg of you, my bottle of eau de Cologne; do not forget it, I ask you on bended knee. If you care to send me some figs, I shall be most grateful: those you sent me last year, at about the same time if memory serves, arrived safely and did me a great deal of good. I leave it to you to shower your blessings upon me once again, and beseech you not to forget me when the Charterhouse peaches are round and ripe.

In addition, you would do me a great favor if you could get them to reinstate my walks, for I report to you a thousand times over that I am suffering horribly from my lack of fresh air, and that 'tis an infamy to deprive someone of a basic right granted to even the lowliest of animals. Can surplus alone suffice to make up the signal? And will it not be just as witty and affecting, when that extra episode is not included? Neck-deep in refuse and filth, eaten alive by bugs, fleas, mice, and spiders, served like a pig because of the incredible speed wherewith they light out of my room as soon as they have brought me my meals, I never have the time either to remember what I need or to ask for it, and our innkeeper's three scullions, always ready to open fire the moment my door is unbolted, does not all that constitute a charming signal? . . . a truly pathetic and touching signal? Do you need to add the torture of the pneumatic machine? I won't even mention the problem of my hair, which has been steadily falling out ever since one of the signal episodes called for no longer taking care of my hair: I shall not even bring up the subject, because I no longer have any vanity as far as my hair is concerned, thank God, and because the minute I am out of here I shall most certainly wear a wig . . . that is a firm decision . . . Ah! verily, my true love, have the years not taken their toll? . . . No more illusions, I've reached the age of forty, this charming age when I always promised I would renounce Satan and all his pomp . . . forty years come and gone, and 'tis time to begin, by slow degrees, taking on *a slight tint of the grave:* one is taken less by surprise when it comes if one is prepared for it in advance . . . Let it come, let it come whenever it likes; I await it, without desiring it but also without fearing it. 'Tis only those upon whom fortune has shone who are sorry to depart this life; but the man who, like me, counts his years only by his misfortunes, perforce looks forward to his demise as naught but the happy moment when his chains are at last lifted. May the dearly beloved friend, who is the only one who could yet temper the end of my career, not leave me with the pain and sorrow of surviving her, and may those poor creatures who owe us their existence enjoy a happier one than we! Those are the only prayers I still dare address to the Eternal, and the only ones whose fulfillment would cause a few more roses to bloom amidst the thorns of my life.

30. *To Madame de Sade*

[September 17, 1780]

I was on the point of writing you a lovely letter, my dear, thanking you for having seen to it that my walks were restored. But I was dead wrong; I have just been told that I am in error.

This morning the so-called adjutant arrives and informs me that *the king* has restored my walks. "Most obliged, Sir; I thank you and his Highness as well." "Ah, but that's not all, Sir, for you have no right . . . —" "What's this?" I broke in, "a little sermon? Please spare me; in matters of morality I know all there is to know." "But, Sir, 'tis only that—" "Sir," I added, "as long as the man of whom you are speaking (the jailer) is civil, he will find me polite to a fault; should he cease to be he will find someone quite disposed to teach him a few lessons, the cut of my jib being such that I brook no insolence from anyone, least of all from a rogue of a jailer . . ." At which point the siege was lifted; and as I refused, so they claim, to hear the old soldier's lesson in morality to the end . . . no more walks. And therefore, dear friend, I withdraw my thanks to you, and I save my gratitude until the favor is granted unconditionally and, above all, with no lesson in morality.

I saw the moment when, if I had gone on, they would not, I do believe, have minded asking me *to apologize* . . . But who in the world are these people, and who do they think they are dealing with, or rather who are they used to dealing with?

Moreover, I write all this so that it is very clear what I have said word for word, to make sure they do not go and falsify my words, which this great lout of a sick old soldier is fully capable of doing. In writing about them to you, I bring them back to life, and I solemnly declare and swear by all that is most holy in the world that were they to disembowel me alive I should never change my maxim one whit: *mild and polite to a fault as long as others are the same with me; barbed and very strict when others are lacking in proper respect toward me.*

I've received everything. I plan to send back a great number of books between the 20th and the 22nd, and at the same time I shall write to you about books and errands. Until then, I embrace you with all of my heart.

THE MORNING OF THE 17TH

P.S.—As best I could make out, judging from the initial period of the oratorical speech of the tall, thin individual they unleashed on me this morning, I gather the piece meant to treat of the moral and physical essence of that contemptible atom that goes by the name of *jailer.* I saw that the orator was going to be cold and tedious, that his speech would be chock full of catachresis, totally lacking in metaphors, and equally abounding in pleonasms, that his text was poorly constructed and his epigraph incorrect, that each member would be uniform, grace-less, and devoid of that salt and those nuances so necessary to the soul of discourse, as Cicero so highly recommended; moreover, that the matter, in itself rather dry, was totally foreign to my existence and to the kind of art I cultivate. In consequence whereof I sent the orator packing. However, if 'twere absolutely necessary that I know every-thing there is to know about a foul heart who earns his living by doing what would dishonor the life of any honest man, then, to spare me from the repercussions and strew a few flowers upon this unpleasant lesson, have the piece in the *Encyclopedia* copied out for me, I'll learn it by heart; that's the most I can do. And do let me have my walks! I beg it on bended knee, for I need them most sorely, and my head, I've already told you, will never ripen in the shade.

31. To Madame de Sade

December 14, 1780

*T*oday, Thursday the 14th of December, 1780, *the 1400th day, the 200th week,* and *the end of the 46th month* we have been separated, having received from you sixty-eight fortnightly packets of provisions and one hundred letters, and this one being the 114th of mine. These last three articles pertain only to my second detention. As for the first three, for me they are one and the same, since I count my real misfortunes from the day when our separation began, having always made, and always making, all my calculations from this period.

Either I do not know my p's and q's or that's what I call pinning down dates for you! And so 'tis to this hundredth letter from you, which I have just this minute received, that I am replying, my dear. There, at the very beginning, I see the proof that my manuscripts have reached you, which pleases me. You have chosen some very strange verses; I dare say they contain one solid truth, constitute a maxim new to the stage, so I believe, but which, like all the others that are offered there every day, will never have any positive effect on anyone. As for the line of prose, you certainly did not select the most striking one in that scene, which is one of the least bad in the play; still, I like the fact that you chose it, for it shows that you always agree with me when it comes to the happiness of our children. Rest assured that I shall always agree with yours, but also know that my view will rarely coincide with that of my tyrants;[1] I shall always be suspicious of everything they suggest doing on our children's behalf; they have given too many proofs of their undying hatred for the father for me ever to believe they can love the children, and you may take it for granted that either I must cease regarding them as my flesh and blood or those infamous people shall never be allowed to interfere with them. So there you have it; just look at the fine results all this has already produced: hereditary hatreds, endless dissensions, goods and properties ravaged beyond repair, irreparable disorder, ruined educations, a family deprived of all outward consideration, and children forever condemned to a life of unhappiness. And all that because one woman, furious to see the consequences of an event she lacked the intelligence to foresee, angrily declared before a gathering of three or four cronies (what is called a family gathering): *"Yes, no matter what the outcome, no matter what the fateful consequences may be for my daughter and for my grandchildren, however certainly 'twill be the undoing of them all, I shall be ten, twelve, fifteen years, etc., before I see the end of this affair."* Oh! Great God, did the Hurons, the Hottentots ever reason thus! And do these barbarians, these savages in their rustic huts, do they ever provide us with any examples of like atrocities? But let's return to the subject, for I'm not myself when I begin to dwell upon such infamies. It strikes me as so horribly unfortunate to

---

1. That is, Renée-Pélagie's parents and family.

have been born only to spend a third of my life as the plaything of a woman's fury—and an idiotic one to boot—that I must constantly remind myself of what I owe to the ties I have contracted so as not to curse them altogether. There I am, brought back to you, dear friend, you whom in spite of all I shall love as the best and dearest friend the world could have ever given me.

I adore looking at copies written in your own hand; you would not believe the pleasure it gives me. I shall always remember that, when I was in Italy, you began to copy out *Le Célibataire* for me, because there were places in it you thought I would like; that thoughtfulness on your part has come back to me a hundred times over. When they are my own verses, I like it even more. How I would love to have you make a copy, in your own hand, of my entire verse play, with little marginal notes praising or criticizing those passages that called for one or the other, and if it were you alone had done it without any outside help. I would wager whatever you like that such a manuscript, if shown to some discerning soul, would conform to his opinion throughout. But I just throw that out; don't go and try doing it, 'twould tax you and tire you. We shall discuss the idea when next we see each other, 'twould be a better time and place.

I am, my friend, going to renew an old request, which, since 'tis most reasonable, I trust you will do your best to convince those who might oppose it to change their minds. The years roll by and yet I never get a chance to read *Le Mercure*,[2] when I leave here 'twill take me a good year simply to read all those back issues, and yet I shall have many other things to take care of. This is what I propose in the matter, and I like to think 'tis not too much to ask. I was out in the world in [part of] 1777 and at the end of 1778. Consequently I was able to keep up with, and I did keep up with, the principal events of those two years: what harm is there in sending me the issues of those two years, so that I have less to read when I get out? That is all I ask. Mérigot rents them, you can borrow them from him; do send them to me, I beg of you. Still, if perchance one of these volumes happened to include, in the section on current events, which I never read, if, I say, some issue contains a report on some event that you did not want me to read about, tear the page out and pay Mérigot for the volume; thirty sous should take care of it nicely. You see that I don't care a whit about such things. All I'm interested in is the part dealing with the theater and literature. Whatever kind of work you choose, 'tis absolutely impossible

---

2. *Le Mercure de France*, the leading literary monthly magazine.

to do anything that makes any sense unless you keep up with the newspapers. There are probably better ones, but I followed *Le Mercure* for a good many years, and found it to my liking. As a favor, then, dear friend, a very great favor, do send me *Le Mercure* for the past two years '77 and '78, and tear out, cross out, to your heart's content, and be sure that I shall neither complain nor ever ask you why such and such a page was deleted. Also, I beg you to send me for the 1st of next month the three yearbooks: military, royal, and the one devoted to theater, which you have been so kind as to send me every year. These two articles shall be at the top of my list of errands, with which I shall end this letter or which I shall enclose on a separate sheet.

This, thank God, makes the third straight day that I have gone without lighting a fire in my charming stove, and God knows how much I've been coughing and in what a terrible state my poor chest is. One must be like Cacambo,[3] not a quarter Spanish but a quarter *English*,[4] or German, to even envisage locking up poor wretches in a room with a stove that belches and gives one a headache; and that when for a mere two louis, without damaging the thick walls in any way, one could install a fireplace in this room. I am prepared to pay for it; just say when; better yet, let them give me some bricks and mortar, I'll do it myself if that's what they want. Such an inconvenience is but a bagatelle in the outside world, because all you have to do is open your door or switch to another room: but just think how it is for the poor wretches who can neither change to another room nor open their door. You keep telling me over and over again (in guise of a signal) in your own sweet way that they are going to give me a different room and restore my walks, etc. But all that is to the tune of *Go, Johnny, go and see if they are coming*, etc., in consequence wherefore I count it amongst the articles in your letters I simply refuse to read. Still in all, I can't go on, I simply cannot go on; you have no idea of how this [stove] affects me. This damned odor of hot metal gives me migraines that drive me mad, and the smoke is ruining my eyes beyond repair. I would like to oblige that mongrel bailiff to spend three or four hours here, and make him dance me an *English saraband:* ye gods! what fun that would be! and how he would jump about!

I have received all your parcels; this time they are charming, my love, and I thank you from the bottom of my heart: candles, pheasant

---

3. The reference remains elusive. From the context, one might assume a connection with Sade's pet hate, the Inquisition.
4. De Rougemont was one-quarter English.

worthy to grace the table of *a commander of a castle or keep*, exquisite orange flower, and thoughtfully chosen preserves. All joking aside, 'tis all
excellent in every respect; I commend you to do as well in the future.

You did well to have your older son shaved, and 'twas a great mistake not to have the other shaved as well. I owe my head of hair solely
to the fact that I took that same precaution the minute I had chicken
pox. As for that elder's face, have no fear, 'twill end up just fine;[5] I can
see him from here, he will be thin, supple, nimble, well built, he will
have the devil's own wit. With those qualities, a man always finds more
than enough women to ensure his unhappiness. Further charms only
double the dose of misfortune; they are not to be desired. After I had
chicken pox I was a great deal more unsightly than he: just ask Amblet;
I would have given Satan a good scare; and even so, I think, I can say
without boasting that I turned out to be a handsome enough f——.

And so, therefore, send me the rest of the comedies. Not to do so
is a misplaced act of mischief: as long as I had a healthy chest and good
pair of lungs, those who today have the gall to refuse me those plays
know very well that I used both one and the other[6] to read aloud to
them, to entertain them because—and here again I'm not being boast-
ful—no one in their brilliant society was as talented at reading aloud as
I. I can say that now, because I am no longer able to read aloud, thank
God. So 'tis like that sixty-year-old woman who had hung above her
head the portrait made of her when she was fifteen, and who would say
to everyone who came to visit her, "*See how I used to look.*" Therefore
send me those comedies; don't force me to say there is no gratitude in
your family, and rest assured that all the works I am asking you for are
unquestionably in print. Moreover, if you want to hold on to them for
the purpose of using them to compose some sort of signal, don't bother,
'tis not the end of your errands, and once the present list is attended to
another one will soon appear: I'm a man of many resources.

I am most pleased you bought *Le Père de famille.*[7] I shall make an
emendation of the work in due course, and I'll send them [*sic*] on to
you one of these days. 'Twill not be much: a few words, a situation, no
real changes, sorry to say. On that subject, it seems to me, judging from

5. Actually, Louis-Marie's face was disfigured by the disease.
6. His chest and lungs. As noted, during the early days of his marriage, Sade
loved to recite or perform plays, and from all reports was head and shoulders
above his peers.
7. A popular play.

the plays you sent me, that no one stands on ceremony these days, and when they go so far as to lift entire verses from Racine, I do believe one can leave a particular situation in a play even though it may resemble a similar situation in some other play. All the same, I shall change the main element of the plot and send it on to you. Please be good enough to enclose the sheet with the manuscript and verify the changes that Monsieur Joseph Quiros[8] makes thereon.

Apropos of this *Père de famille*, you haven't read the epigraph: 'tis a masterpiece. Do read it; although addressed to a princess, 'tis a code of instructions to all mothers, and 'tis truly sublime. When you have a chance, have it read to your son. You'd think it was Diderot.

Thank you for the medical advice; I intend to act upon it. I've had no visit from the doctor. The problem does not keep me from walking, but it hurts a great deal when I'm in bed, and 'tis even worse sitting down;[9] and yet it's been going on for two months. You were quite right to warn me against *eau de boule*, for they were on the point of prescribing it to me here. There is no inflammation, 'tis like a bad bruise.

Let's see, what's next in your letter? . . . *"draft made out to my mother . . ."* Ah, yes! *Signals?*

    Chanson, chanson

       Il vous faut, dites-vous, poulette,
       Pour vous rendre plus grassouillette,
         Un mandat? —Fi!
       Ah! bon dieu, comme elle m'en flanque!
       Je sais bien que rien ne vous manque,
         Même un gros——.

    [Ditty, Ditty

       You must have,
       Or so you say, my little chickadee,
       Unless you do you'll fade away
       A draft? For shame!

---

8. Another name for his favorite valet, Carteron, to whom Sade attaches nicknames at will.
9. For some time Sade had been suffering from hemorrhoids.

You must be daft!
I know full well
You've all you need
Inclusive of a big
fat p——.]

Well, what say you, I am right, no? Yet I trust I'm not; may the devil take me if ever I were to hear any raillery on that front!

Do not say another word about *my fat serving-girl;*[10] you are forever confusing me. First, you described her as ugly: one can deal with that, and you say to yourself that chances are she'll console herself by worshiping more fervently at *the altars of virtue.* And now you tell me she's pretty, and consequently a wh——. No matter, I shall try to come to terms with that, too; but don't come and confuse me again on that matter; for 'tis a real pain to have to change one's idea with every new moon.

And I too, dear friend, I assure you that my only moments of happiness are those when I think of our being together again. But what a damnable long time they are making me wait for it. Oh! 'tis too long, far too long, and when one sees that things are growing visibly worse, and when 'tis proven that both physically and mentally naught but a very great ill and a very great danger can result, one should not drag all this out to such a degree. Damn it all! —I've already said this to you— we pay these people and let's be done with it! Money, money, as much as you like! Wounds to one's purse are not fatal; but not so with anything that contributes to destroying the mind, the temper, the character, and the basic elements whereof a man is constituted. These things are irreparable, and 'tis outrageous they be sacrificed to a woman's vengeance and to the fattening of a half-bred swine.[11]

Good night, I've rattled on long enough. I was encouraged by your letter, which is one of those I most cherish; but I must not overdo it and end up giving you vapors. So I stop here; I shall not write again except to acknowledge receipt of the things requested for the first of next month, whereof here is the list.

. . . .

[The remainder of the letter is missing]

---

10. He refers to Renée-Pélagie's unkind, but not inaccurate, description of their daughter.
11. Again, de Rougemont, whose bastardy Sade brings up whenever he can.

32. To Madame de Sade

"*T*his most surely is the last New Year's letter I shall write to you at Vincennes, my sweet . . ."

"Oh! I assure you that the year shall not end without my having the pleasure of holding you in my arms . . ."

"One must never give up, the year is not yet over, and I see nothing standing in the way of the hopes I gave you for '79."

"This shall surely be the year of grace, the end to our woes . . ."

"The Provost and all his crew have just assured me that the year '79 will be a very happy one for me, and he said it in such a way I quite believed him." (That one I believe, because your happiness consists of my being behind bars; 'tis a touchy matter!)

There, Madame, is a fair sampling of your abominable lies. And don't blame them on others who lied to you. Either you should not have said a thing or you should have spoken only when you were sure of your facts. In two words, you are an imbecile who lets herself be led around by her nose; and those who lead you, monsters who deserve to be hanged and kept hanging on the gallows till the crows devour them down to the last morsel.

I sometimes visualize your loathsome mother before the abscess of her stinking black bile burst and began leaking on me drop by drop. She must have been as swollen as the peasant in *Doctor Crispin* who downed three bushels of pills. I'm amazed it didn't kill her twenty times over, but alas for me heaven was not so inclined. I've made a little sketch of that, from which I want to have an engraving made when I get out of here.

In it one sees the présidente *naked*, lying on her back, looking for all the world like one of those sea monsters sometimes left high and dry on the shore . . . Monsieur le N———,[1] who is taking her pulse, says: "Madame, 'tis a puncture you need or the bile is going to suffocate you." Whereupon the dandy Albaret is summoned, who gives a puncture to his sweet mistress. Marais, who is holding the candle, and who from time to time tastes the matter to see whether 'tis worthy; and

---

1. Monsieur Le Noir.

there's little R———,[2] who is holding the plate and who—well-filled though it be—cries out in a falsetto voice, *"Courage! courage! That amount won't even pay for three months' lodgings in my little house . . ."*

That will make a delightful print.

Why have you not sent me the *Theater, Military, and Royal Almanacs*, as well as the *Mercures* I asked you for? If I do not have them without fault by return I protest and declare that I shall refuse to accept any more letters from you. 'Tis cruel never to want to do anything except what is hurtful to me, and never anything that might bring me a bit of comfort. There's your ——— of last year, the crowning examples of your falseness and lying: I send with it my best wishes to you, Madame, for the New Year.

May the lot of you, you and your execrable family and all their vile valets, all be put in a sack and thrown into the ocean depths. Then let the news be brought to me with all due haste, and I swear to heaven 'twill be the happiest moment of my life. There, Madame, I send both my best wishes and my greetings, including those to your wh——— Rousset, from head to toe.

33. To Monsieur Le Noir

February 20, 1781

Sir:
         So long as my punishment was limited to a period of time that might be found reasonably commensurate to some slight misconduct, I suffered in silence. But now that I see that 'tis extending far beyond what fair-minded and equitable people would doubtless have prescribed, and that for this reason I am fully convinced that to vengeance and calumny alone the government offers its protection, I have the right to entreat you, Sir, to come and see me, so that I can prove to you beyond all shadow of a doubt that I do not deserve a treatment as harsh as that to which I am being subjected.

You are not unaware, Sir, that the royal constitution, already completely opposed to everything called *lettres de cachet*, must be even more strongly opposed when one dares use them for the sole purpose

---

2. Monsieur de Rougemont.

of serving the secret hatred between families, or perhaps to further the special interests of their friends. Nor are you unaware that we are not living under an Inquisition in this country, and yet 'tis nothing but purely inquisitorial methods they have used against me these past four years, without ever once deigning to show me any order of the king. In a word, Sir, you know better than I that this is in violation of our laws, and I dare say even against the authority of the monarch, to punish one of his subjects without a proper hearing. If you had been unfairly slandered by unworthy enemies, would you, Sir, be pleased to be denied any opportunity of vindicating yourself? That vindication put a famous magistrate back on the bench. Find it in your heart, therefore, that my vindication also be given a hearing, and that it render unto the State, someone who, if not so beloved and so esteemed, is at least a subject who, like you, yet considers it his greatest glory to devote his attentions, his life, and his children to his country.

If I deserved to lose my life upon a gallows, I ask no pardon, and if I am guilty only of what everybody else indulges in,[1] and of which, in the position you occupy, you witness a hundred examples every day, I should not be treated so unjustly.

Were you unable to find it in your heart to reply to my letter by a visit, Monsieur, you would lead me to believe that rather than being a father and protector of the downtrodden, you are the agent of their relatives' tyranny. In which case, you should not be surprised if, once I am out of this place—even if I am compelled to cast myself at the feet of the king to obtain my vengeance—I take matters in my own hands and do whatever it takes, both to recover the honor of which you seem intent on robbing me, and to subject my oppressors to the same treatment I have received from them.

I have the honor to be your most humble and most obedient servant.

DE SADE

---

1. Namely, consorting with whores. Since the Aix court threw out the more serious charge of poisoning and sodomy, Sade plays on the fact that he is no more guilty than a goodly portion of the aristocracy.

34.   To Madame de Sade

MY GRAND LETTER

[February 20, 1781]

I truly do believe, my dear friend, that your intention would be to instill in me that same respect for your little divinities that you yourself possess to such a profound degree. And because you are going to grovel before that entire crew, you would demand that I do the same! that a ———, that a ———, an ———, a ———, and ——— be my gods just as they are yours![1] If unfortunately you have got that idea into your head, I beg you to remove it forthwith. Misfortune will never bring me so low;

> *Though enchained I may be, my heart is yet free.*
>
> *(Les Arsacides)*

and always will be. Even if these accursed chains, yes, even if they bring me to my grave, you will always see me the same. I have the sad misfortune of having received at birth a staunch soul, that has never bent nor ever will. I have no fear of offending or embittering anyone, no matter whom. You have given me too many proofs that my term is set for me to have any doubts on that score: consequently, no one is in a position to either lengthen it or shorten it. Moreover, were it not set, I would not be dependent on these people, but on the king, and he is the one person in the country I respect—he, and the princes of royal blood. Beneath them, I see naught but a blur so indistinct that in this circumstance it were better for me to refrain from looking too closely, for it would reveal a superiority so much in my favor that it would only serve to further confirm my already profound contempt.

You have to feel that 'tis unimaginable to want to treat me as they do and then expect me not to complain; for let's add two and two for a moment: when a detention has to be as prolonged as mine is, is it not a veritable abomination to try to make it even more horrible by every-

---

1. To escape the censor's possible charge of blasphemy, Sade gives us no clue to which deities he refers.

thing your mother has chosen to dream up in order to torment me here? What! 'tis not enough to be deprived of everything that makes life pleasant and worth living, 'tis not enough to be kept from even breathing clean fresh air, to see all one's desires forever being shattered against four walls, and to spend one's days so alike one to the other that they resemble those we can expect in the grave? This dreadful torture is not enough, according to that horrid creature: it must be made even worse by everything she can think of to redouble all the horror. But you will agree that only a monster is capable of carrying vengeance that far ... *But 'tis all in your imagination, you are going to say; people aren't doing any such thing; all these are figments of your imagination that people in your situation often have.* Figments of my imagination? Really! I shall go to the top of my notebook of observations, which contains no fewer than 56 proofs of the kind I am about to cite to you, from which I shall take only one, and you shall see whether 'tis not venomous rage of an odious shrew that lies behind all these maneuvers that I impute to her, and whether one can properly call them figments of one's imagination.

You should not for one moment doubt that a prisoner, although he may have good reason to believe his release is still distant, will leap like a starveling at anything even faintly suggesting his term might be less long: 'tis human nature, that, there's nothing wrong about it: thus 'tis not something someone should be punished for, but rather pitied. Therefore, 'tis an act of manifest cruelty to foment, foster, give rise to initiatives that tend to mislead him. One ought to be exceedingly careful to do the opposite, and basic humanity (were there any here) should at all times act as a constant reminder not to [toy with] the most sensitive of a poor wretch's feelings; for 'tis clear that the cause of all suicides is hope betrayed. Therefore, one must not foster that hope when it will not happen; and whoever does so is visibly a monster. Hope is the most sensitive part of the soul of him who suffers and is in pain; he who holds out this hope to him, then destroys it, is acting like those demons in Hell who, they say, are forever reopening the same wound, and who take pains to focus on an already open wound rather than on others. That is precisely what your mother has been doing to me for four years: a multitude of fresh hopes month after month. To judge from what these people say, from examining your parcels, your letters, etc., my release is always just around the corner; then, when we come to that corner, all of a sudden, a well-aimed dagger-thrust: and we are off for another long round of jokes and gibes. It seems as though this wicked woman enjoys nothing more than having me build houses of cards, to have the pleasure of knocking them down the moment they are done. Forgetting for a moment all the negative influence this has upon hope, not to mention the great possibility 'twill have of denaturing it, not to mention the certainty that one will write off hope for the rest of one's life, there is, you will agree, the far more serious danger of the final excess of despair; and at present I do not for one moment doubt that this is her sole and unique objective, and that, having failed to have me killed, and having left me in the dreadful situation I was in for the five years before I was in prison, she has decided to work on doing me in for perhaps another five years, under more propitious conditions. From the multitude of proofs I have just told you that I have of this barbaric little game she has been playing with me, which consists of lifting me up and then knocking me down, I shall cite you one of the more recent, in order to convince you of what I say.

About six months ago you sent me a curtain for my room; I kept asking the people here to put it up; they never wanted to. What must I conclude from this? *That there is no need to*, which gives rise to hope; they will leave it at that until they figure I have had the time to build my house of cards, and when that day comes, they hang the curtain—and my castle is dashed to pieces. Such are the little games Madame la présidente de Montreuil plays, games she has been enjoying for four years along with the lackeys she is paying to aid and abet her in these kindnesses, people who laugh at her behind her back (at least that is what Marais told me in no uncertain terms, he doubtless being jealous at not being a member of the inner circle) as soon as they receive their presents or money. There are 56 maneuvers of this kind, not counting those yet to come; not that I have entertained 56 different opinions about my release, God forbid! I would have spent my entire life counting and calculating, which I have carefully refrained from doing (you have the proof of my more serious occupations),[2] but I have kept a close eye on matters and I have duly noted that in all likelihood, instead of sand castle number four, the one I am presently on and which, far off though it be, will doubtless crumble like the other three; instead of four, I say, she has been involved in trying to get me to build a good 56. I can't help wondering whether this is how a sensible woman behaves, an intelligent woman and a woman who, if for no other reason than the ties that bind us, ought to lessen my sufferings instead of aug-

---

2. That is, his writings, which he carefully sent on to his wife for safekeeping and often for her opinion, which he frequently derided but inwardly cherished.

menting them? *But she is offended, you tell me.* First of all, I deny that; she has been done no injury except insofar as she wanted to be injured, and if she has a quarrel on that score, 'tis solely to her own genius she must look for whatever she may take as a personal affront. But let us suppose that she actually has been offended: does that mean she must seek revenge? A woman so pious, who *outwardly* seems to fulfill all the ceremonial part of her religion, should she turn her back on the foremost and most basic of all its dogmas? But let us allow her vengeance, I shall concede that; but, a prison sentence of this length, a sentence so harsh, is that not revenge enough for her? Does she need more? *Oh! you are missing the point, you will cut in; all this has been necessary; that's what it takes for us to win!* To win! Come, in all fairness now: even supposing I were to get out tomorrow, would you dare say I had won, without fearing that I accuse you of a most furious insolence? Win!—to put somebody in prison for four or five years *over a mere party involving some girls,* exactly like any one of the eighty others that take place every day in Paris! And then to come and tell him how lucky he is to get off with only five years in prison, and that if he has been driven crazy the way he has, 'twas in order *to win!* No, I banish the very idea, for I am too disgusted by it and I am quite sure you shall never be so brazen as to bring it up again.

Let us go back to something I spoke of a short while ago, *a mere party involving some girls* which, I can see from here, affrights those who despair at being unable to convince me that all the calumnies they accept against me are the gospel truth. My adventures can be reduced to three. I shall pass over the first: that one was wholly Madame la présidente de Montreuil's doing, and if anybody should have been punished for it, 'twas she;[3] but in France one does not punish those who have a hundred thousand livres a year income, and below them are *the little victims* whom they can hand over to the voracity of those monsters whose profession is to earn their living from the blood of the misfortunate. They are asked for *their little victims,* they hand them over, and the debt is discharged. That is why I am in prison. The second adventure was the Marseilles incident: I believe there is no point in discussing it, either. I think it has been sufficiently established that nothing but libertinage was involved there, and that whatever of a criminal

---

3. The so-called Arcueil affair, which, claims Sade, would never have amounted to anything if the présidente had not been so worried about it sullying the Montreuils' presumed good name.

nature they saw fit to insert into the affair, in order to slate the vengeful thirst of my Provençal enemies, and the rapacity of the chancellor who wanted my title for his son, was nothing but pure invention. And so, as for that one, I think it entirely taken care of by the Vincennes detention[4] and the banishment from Marseilles.

Let us then move on to the third. Before starting, I ask your forgiveness for the terms I am going to be obliged to use; I shall do my best to moderate them by using abbreviations. Moreover, between husband and wife one may, when the case requires it, express oneself somewhat more freely than with strangers or ordinary friends. I also ask you to excuse my confessions, but I prefer you think me a libertine rather than a criminal, laid bare, with no effort on my part to disguise it one iota.

Seeing myself reduced to spending a fair amount of time alone in a remote castle, almost always without you, and having the minor failing (it must be admitted) of being perhaps a tad too fond of women, I contacted a well-known p——[5] in Lyons, and told her: I want to take three or four servants home with me, I want them young and pretty; find me some like that. This p——, who was Nanon, for that Nanon was a well-known p—— in Lyons—I shall prove it when the time comes—promises to find me these girls and does so. I take them home; I make use of them. Six months later parents come and ask to have these girls back, assuring me that they are their children. I turn them over to the parents; and all of a sudden I am charged with a suit for kidnapping and rape! But that is the greatest of all injustices. Here are the rules in this regard, and this I have from Monsieur de Sartine himself; he had the kindness to explain them to me himself one day, as he will be happy to recall: 'tis expressly forbidden any p—— in France to traffic in virgin girls, and if the girl furnished is a virgin and lodges a complaint, 'tis not the man who is prosecuted, it is the p——, who is subjected to rigorous and immediate punishment. Even if the man has asked for a virgin, 'tis not he who is punished: he is only doing what all men do. Once again, the p——, who gave him the girl and who knew full well 'twas expressly forbidden, is punished. Therefore, that first deposition made against me in Lyons, for kidnapping and rape, con-

---

4. Sade means his first Vincennes detention, before he was taken to Aix for the appellate trial.
5. Procuress. Not only did Nanon provide Sade the young whores he requested, she came with the package and joined the hardy little group of revelers at La Coste during the winter of 1774–1775.

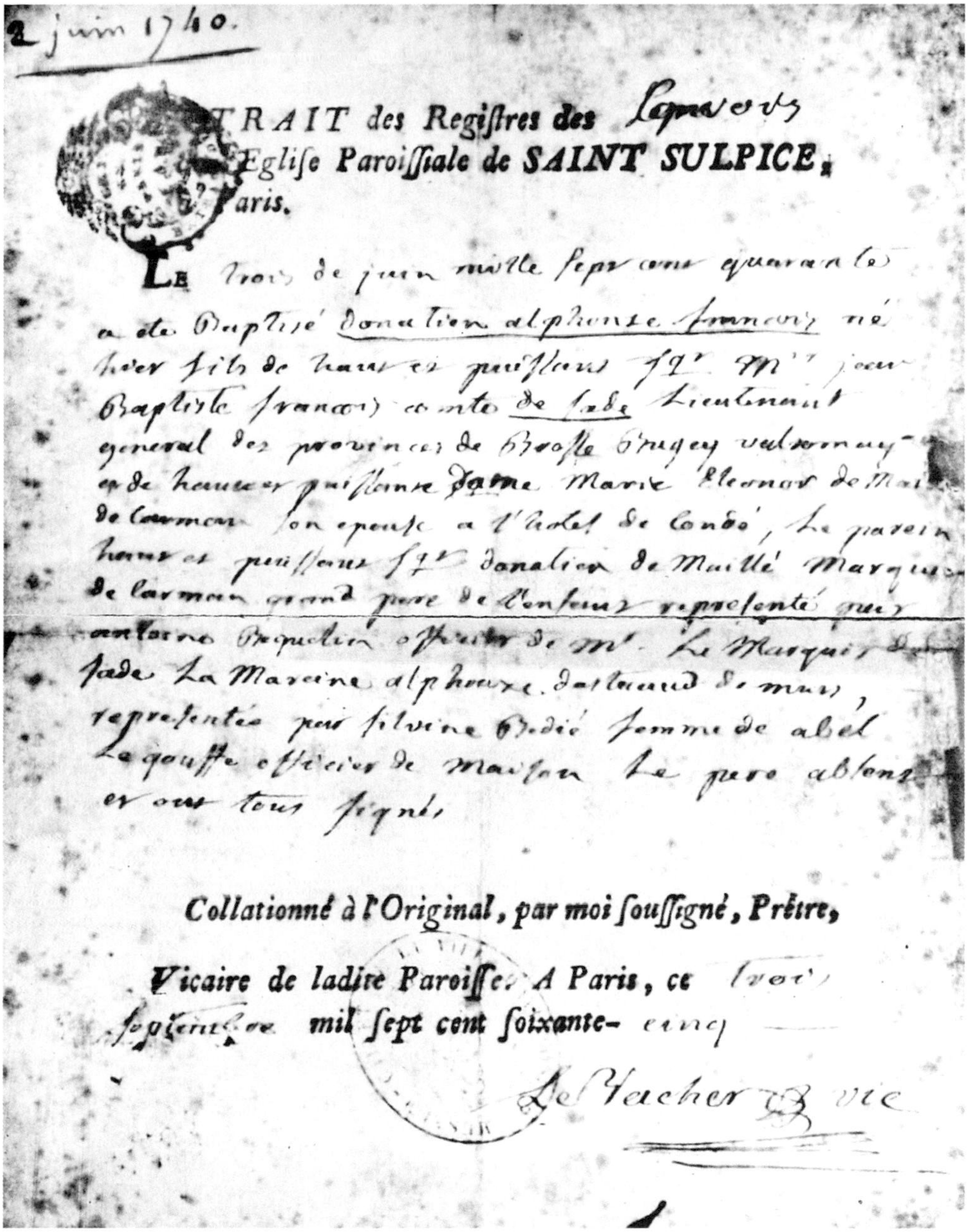

2 juin 1740.

EXTRAIT des Regiſtres des Baptemes de l'Egliſe Paroiſſiale de SAINT SULPICE, à Paris.

Le trois de juin mille sept cent quarante a été baptisé Donatien alphonse françois né hier fils de haut et puissant Sgr. Mre jean Baptiste françois comte de Sade lieutenant general des provinces de Bresse Bugey valromey et de haute et puissante dame Marie Eleonor de Maillé de Carman son epouse a l'hotel de Condé, le parein haut et puissant Sgr donatien de Maillé Marquis de Carman grand pere de l'enfant representé par antoine Prequelin officier de Mr. le Marquis de Sade La Mareine alphonse dalleman de mirs, representée par silvine Bedié femme de abel Lagouffe officier de maison le pere absent et ont tous signés

Collationné à l'Original, par moi ſouſſigné, Prêtre, Vicaire de ladite Paroiſſe. A Paris, ce trois septembre mil ſept cent ſoixante-cinq

Le Vacher vic

Sade's certificate of baptism, dated June 3, 1740. One day after his birth at the hôtel de Condé in Paris, he was baptized at Saint-Sulpice church. His parents had intended to name him Louis-Aldonse-Donatien, but then settled on Donatien-Aldonse-François. The parish priest misunderstood the old Provençal name Aldonse and instead substituted the more common "Alphonse" on the baptismal certificate. That clerical slip was later to plague Sade with the authorities, especially during and after the Revolution.

COURTESY MUSÉE CALVET, AVIGNON

Portrait of the libertine as a young man, by Van Loo. A full-scale painting of Sade by the same artist was lost and probably destroyed during the Revolution.

A nineteenth-century romanticized portrait of Renée-Pélagie de Montreuil de Sade, the Marquise de Sade. Despite her ultra-strict Catholic upbringing, she was madly in love with her seductive husband, and despite his many outrageous acts and endless infidelities, loved him selflessly and unswervingly for twenty-seven years.

Sade's father, the Count de Sade, was lord of the manors of La Coste (ABOVE) *and Saumane* (OVERLEAF TOP), *and co-lord of Mazan* (OVERLEAF BOTTOM)—*all in the Vaucluse region of Provence. Upon his father's death in 1767, the marquis inherited the three properties, although he considered La Coste his home. Sade spent several of his formative years, from age five to ten, at Saumane, the domaine of his uncle the Abbé de Sade. In some of his flights abroad as a fugitive, Sade assumed the title Marquis de Mazan, taken from his third domaine.*

PHOTOGRAPHS: LA COSTE BY ALAIN RESNAIS; SAUMANE AND MAZAN BY RICHARD SEAVER

Vincennes, the dungeon where Sade was imprisoned from 1777 to 1784, during which time most of the letters in this volume and many of his major literary works were written. In 1763, Sade spent a shorter (two-week) stint in this same prison as a result of a scandal known as the "Jeanne Testard affair." COLLECTION RICHARD SEAVER

Rauch del.   Skelton sc

dans le malheureuse situation ou je suis je ne puis par vou promettre rien de bien
satisfaisant en dédommagement de l'inquietude que je vou ... Car je vou calmer ...
ce que je vou promet en attendant que vou verrer d'ici l'exécution de choses qui seront
dans le cas de vou faire plus de plaisir ce que je vou promet dès ... cest des le moment le
un bien grand changement dans mon stile. D'ici vou pouvez compter aisement ce
conclurai en dans le verbe.

quand je vou ai demandé de connaitre pour moi les meilleurs caen a aller prendre au sorti d'ici
jusqu'a quoi je crain maide
je crois que vou pou repondre de cet article. autre preuve de ce que je crain maide
ce qui pourtant m'exécutera sûrement par au moins de mon vivant. on pourra m'embarquer mais
mort ou pas autrement je donne bien ma parole d'honneur.

lisez la petite lettre de la prochaine
De la bougie et le rate des comission
je prie qu'il y ... qu'on foute le flacon d'eau
de lavande.

ABOVE AND FACING PAGE: *The original of a letter from Sade to his wife dated June 25, 1780, in which he responds to a letter from her in which she dangles before him all the things he will do "when I get out." The only problem, Sade notes, is that she fails to mention just when that magic date might be. Sade expresses his fear that when that day finally does come he may be "shipped off to some distant place" in exile, for he has an obsessive fear of ships and sailing. See letter 28, p. 157.*

ABOVE AND FACING PAGE: *The original of a letter dated October 11, 1782, from Madame de Sade to Mlle de Rousset, who was back at La Coste trying to keep the long-neglected château from falling into a state of complete disrepair. The letter begins: "Since there is some hanky-panky going on relative to the [marquis's] study, about which I am quite convinced because of another matter altogether, which is no concern of yours, it is imperative we find another place, and inform me what it is, where we can store the most important things. I have therefore written to Gaufridy, instructing him to put all my letters in a locked drawer, without showing them to anyone." One can only guess what information, or indiscretion, those letters might have contained.*

cell on méprisable que leur individu
ce qui maffecte plus vivement cest dans cellique cest
la peur que vous devé avoir eu a la chute de
plafon cest lembaras et les peine que vous prenés
pour nous
a legare de mes papiers cachettés les dans un paquiet
etiqueté pour nestre remi et ouvers que par moi
ou un de S il y en a bien d'inutille mes il faut
que ce soit moi qui les brule parce que je connoi leur
 utilité et quil y en a d'essenciel qui ne faut pas
qui soit mengé par les ras. thas lormois de me et
la mienne mon linge &c toos cela a votre aise
cant vous vous ennuyez lenfermeri nesce pas au
colidor dem bau? et lautre audecu de la petite ecury
et audeu de lapartemene de monsieur?.
je nai que la place designer avec une croi au
dessou pour raison et onitot la reception de
celci repondé moi un mot sur le champ De Sade Montreuil

Jean-Charles Pierre Le Noir, lieutenant-general of the French police, held Sade's fate in his hands.
He succeeded Antoine de Sartine, a much harsher official whom Sade despised
and writes about in several letters in the most scathing terms.

REPRINTED FROM PAUL GINISTY, <u>LA MARQUISE DE SADE</u>

(PARIS: BIBLIOTHÈQUE CHARPENTIER, 1901)

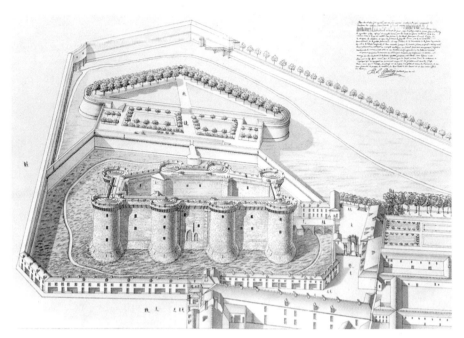

ABOVE: *A bird's-eye view of the Bastille. Note the extensive gardens where guards and family could walk. Prisoners' walks were confined to the narrow space within the high prison walls.*

EIGHTEENTH-CENTURY DRAWING BY PALLOY, COLLECTION RICHARD SEAVER

BELOW: *The Porte de Saint-Antoine, hard by the Bastille towers. On July 2, 1789, using a makeshift megaphone, Sade shouted from the window of his prison cell to the inhabitants and passersby below that the prisoners were being massacred and that the people should come and save them.*

EIGHTEENTH-CENTURY ENGRAVING, COLLECTION RICHARD SEAVER

Twelve days after Sade's rebellious act, the Bastille was stormed, and Warden de Launay and several of his aides were brutally murdered by the rampaging mob. By then, however, Sade had been removed to the insane asylum at Charenton.

EIGHTEENTH-CENTURY ENGRAVING BY DUPIN, COLLECTION RICHARD SEAVER

The Charenton Asylum. Sade was lodged on the second floor of the right wing of the hospital. Following his hasty removal from the Bastille just after midnight on July 3, 1789, Sade remained incarcerated in Charenton until April 2, 1790, which was Good Friday—a day, noted Sade, he intended to celebrate for the rest of his life.

PHOTOGRAPH: RICHARD SEAVER

A letter from Sade to his longtime Provençal lawyer, Gaspard Gaufridy, written shortly after his release from Charenton. Dated only "May 1790," it probably falls between letters 108 and 109 of the present volume. Sade, setting up his new household in Paris, is asking Gaufridy to go to La Coste and send him posthaste some silverware, sheets, and napkins, as well as, needed even more urgently, money. He also notes that he is ill, "shaking with fever."

il etait impossible mon cher avocat que dans le tourbillon
de la multitude de choses que j'avais a vous dire dans ma derniere
lettre, j'eusse debrouiller suffisament mes idées pour vous
expliquer clairement de combien precisement mon dd me
derange, c'est-à-dire quelle est jusqu'au 1er janvier la somme
exacte qu'il me faut en raison de ce vol.

je vous avois demandé 2 mil francs pour finir mon année
j'en avois assés; à ce compte j'aurois pu avoir pour de 600tt de vente.
au moyen de cette terrible breche, c'est au contraire 1000tt juste qu'il
me faut encor pour finir mon année

                    Compte
D'ici au premier de janvier j'ai à depenser ou a payer de dettes
pour   2640tt

        et j'ai pour payer cela

en poche environ   640
j'attends les cent juilles premieres   1000
                                                            ____
                                                            1640
                                                            1000
                                                            ____
Donc il me manque encor   2640
                                    (francs)

je vous conjure donc mon cher avocat
de m'envoyer au plutot ce surplus, et de me croire avec tous les
sentiment que je vous ai voué, votre tres humble et tres obeissant serviteur de Sade
                    ce 16 8bre 1790

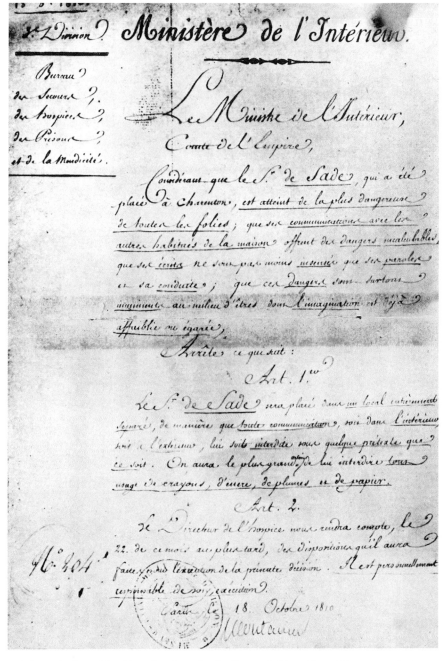

Copy of the order issued October 18, 1810, by the Count de Montalivet, Minister of the Interior, ordering that Sade be isolated from the other inmates at the Charenton asylum. By the time of this order, Sade had already been back at Charenton for seven years.

Among other things, Montalivet deprives Sade of all writing materials and concludes the "harsh order" by making the director of the asylum, Monsieur de Coulmier, "personally responsible for [its] execution." A week later Coulmier, who liked Sade, responded: "I credit myself with being head of a humanitarian establishment and would find it humiliating to see myself become a jailer or one given to persecuting a fellow human being." Count de Montalivet's order was never enforced.

COURTESY MUSÉE CALVET, AVIGNON

Sade's death certificate, signed December 3, 1814, "at twelve noon."
It lists Sade as a "man of letters."

tained not a shred of anything legitimate; I am in no wise guilty; 'twas the p—— to whom I applied who should have been punished and not me. But you can't get blood from a stone, they know, and the parents hoped to squeeze some money out of me. Point made. Earlier on, I had had an amorous adventure in Arcueil, in which a woman,[6] also a liar and a double-dealing swindler, had, to get money (which was stupidly paid her) spread word to all Paris that I conducted all sorts of experiments and that the garden behind my house was a cemetery wherein I buried the bodies I had used in my tests. This tall tale was just too good to be true; 'twas made to order for my enemies' rage, and they never failed to bring it up and embellish it whenever anything happened to me. As a consequence, at the time of the Marseilles affair, 'twas also some experiment I'd been trying, and here again the subject of my experiments would doubtless be the one girl who would never be seen again. But if all the girls did not turn up again at Lyons, they all did resurface sooner or later somewhere else. Let us examine the situation. Those girls from Lyons were five in number, that we know. One, terrified by the solitude in which she was being kept (not to perform experiments upon her but because decency compelled me to do so) escaped and took refuge at my uncle's. And so we *have accounted for her.* One remained in my house, as a domestic, and there she died a natural death, in full view and with the full knowledge of the entire province; she was cared for by the public health director. There's *another who's accounted for.* Two were handed back over to their mother and father. *Two more who are accounted for.* As for the *fifth* and last, she was blatantly threatening to run away like her friend and to spread all kinds of gossip abroad if she were kept locked up any longer, and as she had no parents to come and claim her, I turned her over to a peasant in La Coste—whom I shall name in due course and whom you know very well—who in turn had her placed as a domestic in Marseilles in the house of one of that peasant's relatives; and as I have to hand complete proof thereof, I confess I would be more than delighted to produce the evidence. And so she was taken care of, put into service and left there, regarding which a good and valid certificate was brought back to me, and which I have put in a safe place and will also produce when the need arises. I heard later on that that creature had left the house and taken to p——.[7] And so that is what has become of the five

---

6. Rose Keller.
7. Procuring.

girls from Lyons, the details of whose lives are clearly established in such wise that I can defy the cleverest, or rather the most double-dealing jurisconsult, to prove me anything to the contrary.

Let us take this one step further. Three other girls, of such age and condition that they were beyond their family's jurisdiction, lived, either before or after this period, for several weeks at La Coste château. Let us tell their full story, and may this be a general confession, for such is my express intention, and I wish, if I possibly can, to destroy once and for all even the slightest suspicion of all the horrors that some people have enjoyed trumping up about me and that have led Madame de Montreuil to treat me as she has, both because of her extreme tendency to believe anything she hears, and because of the weapons these falsehoods have furnished her desire for revenge.

The first of these three girls was named *Du Plan;* she was a dancer at the Marseilles Opera. She lived openly in the château, and without incognito, with the title of governess; and when she left La Coste, she did so openly. More than a year later, I ran into her again at the Bordeaux Opera, and she was still living in a small provincial town that was pointed out to me when I went to Aix. Therefore, no concerns about her. The second came from Montpellier; her name was *Rosette.* She stayed for about two months at the château, keeping very much to herself. At the end of this period, she said she wanted to leave, and so we both agreed that she would write to a man she knew in Montpellier, and that this man, who, I believe, was a carpenter by trade and her landlord in the said city of Montpellier, would personally come to fetch her, just outside the castle walls. The appointed hour, the place, the day, the rendezvous, everything was specifically agreed upon. On the appointed day the man duly arrived, and I myself handed the girl over to the aforementioned man, the girl named *Marie* (she being the Lyons girl who had remained in my service) carrying her package of personal belongings, which was also handed over to the man, who, having brought along a mule, placed the girl and her baggage on the mule, and received from me the sum of six gold louis that the girl asked me to give him—that being the sum she had earned in my employ—and off they went. That event took place in June of 1775. In October, 1776, I spent a fortnight in Montpellier, as you know, and thence brought back the third girl in question. Rosette—for that was her name—was most certainly living in Montpellier at the time, the proof being that I saw her there, *saw her there in any event or, to put it more honestly, in the full meaning of the term,* and that 'twas she who suggested to this third girl, whose name was *Adelaide,* to come and follow in her footsteps, assuring her in the presence of two or three other women, not all of whom may be disinclined to testify when the time comes for me to speak out; assuring her, I say, that except for the problem of loneliness, she had nothing but good things to say about me and her dealings with her. 'Twas thanks solely to Rosette's recommendation that I owed the other who, knowing nothing about me, would otherwise most surely not have come. And so Adelaide arrives and remains until Madame de Montreuil's third scene, at which point the postmaster of Courthézon[8] escorted her away without further ado. Thus is the fate of that third girl clearly established. Two or three other girls, either cooks or scullery maids, including those you and I brought down from Paris, did at different times, during my contumacy, live at La Coste château, but they were there so briefly and their arrivals and departures were so well documented, that I see no need even to mention them. Also among them was a niece of Nanon, the p—— about whom we have just spoken, and whom we sent to a convent. Madame de Montreuil had her removed from it; therefore she knows what has become of her. That is the full story. That is my general confession, such as I would make it before God, were I on my deathbed.

What is the upshot of all this? That Monsieur de Sade, whom they doubtless accuse of all sorts of horrors, since they are keeping him in prison for so long, who has good and valid cause to fear being imprisoned, both for the reason he shall shortly reveal and because he has already experienced, on two occasions, what the public's malicious calumny could do to harm him, is nonetheless no more guilty of *tests, experiments,* or *murders* in this most recent story than he was in any of the others, that Monsieur de Sade has done everything that everyone else in the world has, that he has consorted with women who were either already wanton or furnished for him by a p——, and therefore seduction is simply not applicable as regards him, and yet Monsieur de Sade is being punished and made to suffer as if he were guilty of the most heinous crimes.

Let us now have a look at the proof brought forth against him: 1st: *The confessions of the guilty p——.*[9] But are the personal reasons she had for self-justification not powerful enough to make me think 'twas in her best interest to put as much of the blame as she could upon the shoulders of the person she thought to be her accomplice? 2nd: *The nonexistence of the girls:* I stake my head on this, and am prepared to lose

---

8. A nearby town.
9. Nanon.

it if I am wrong. 3rd: *Human bones found in a garden*: they were brought as evidence by the girl named Du Plan, she is very much alive and well, she can be interrogated; as a joke, be it in good or bad taste (in either case I offer it to you), they used the bones to decorate a small room; they were actually used for that purpose, and then put out into the garden when the joke, or rather the platitude, was over. Let them count and compare what they found against the list that I have in Du Plan's hand of the number and kind of those she herself brought from Marseilles: they shall see whether one more was found. All these verifications and confrontations are nonetheless necessary in an affair of this sort: has anyone gone to the trouble of making even a single one? Of course not! Verily, 'twas not the truth they were after: 'twas to send me to prison—and here I am. But I shall perhaps get out some day, and when I do perhaps people will give me sufficient credit to understand that I shall know how to vindicate myself and how to pass judgment on those who are treating me thus; or at least, if because of their wealth and their protection I fail to succeed in this endeavor, at least, I say, I shall know how to cover them publicly with ignominy, shame, and embarrassment.[10]

Let us go on; I want to leave no stone unturned. What more is to be added to all this evidence? *The testimony of a child?* But that child was a servant:[11] in his capacity as a child and as a servant his evidence is inadmissible. Moreover, there is another obvious element of prejudice here: this child was the dependent of a mother who was by no means disinterested, a woman who thought that by having her child report a thousand horrors she would earn herself a nice little nest egg for life; she knew all about the hundred louis of Arcueil. *Ah*, someone may object, *what makes you so sure that this child testified against you? Therefore the child did see certain things, knew certain things, since you are afraid of his admissions?* Yes, I was expecting you to say that, for 'tis precisely the crux of the infamy. First of all, who must have been afraid of him, knowing

---

10. Which of course he did, using pen instead of sword.
11. A young man named André, probably no more than fifteen, whom Sade and his wife hired as "secretary" for the marquis during their trip to Lyons in early October 1774. André was one of seven servants the Sades hired that month to come with them to La Coste. At a time when their finances were desperate, the hiring of seven new servants was strange to say the least—not so much for the profligate marquis but certainly for the level-headed, thrifty marquise.

that he had just been retrieved in the same way and by persons such as those who had already raised such a ruckus in Lyons? A first reason for me to be highly skeptical, for me to be sure he was making the whole thing up, just as the others had done and with the same ends in view. But that is far from the whole story, and here is what I learned and what I was told during my trip up from Provence, by someone who seemed to be so well informed that he could not be suspected of making it up. I gave him my word of honor that I would never compromise him, and so I shall most surely keep his identity secret. But I also give my word of honor that this secret shall not remain one forever. If he is dead when I come out, I shall no longer be bound and I shall say who it is; if he is still alive, I am almost certain I can get him to release me from my obligation to keep the secret, and at that point you shall know who it is. I shall tell you what he said in his own words, to give them their full force: "You have everything to fear," he said to me, "even though your Aix affair may be over. The child you had as your secretary in 1775 went, as soon as he left the château, with his mother to give a deposition in the chambers of the general prosecutor in Aix, and there, I can assure you as positively as if I had heard it myself, both of them were fed what they were supposed to say. Monsieur de Castillon,[12] fearing that once your case was finished you might attack his cousin, Monsieur de Mende,[13] who had brought the iniquitous Marseilles suit against you, hardly reassured by what he had been hearing from Paris on that score, and unable to figure out or learn what your intentions might be and seeing full well that the said Monsieur de Mende would be undone if you were to bring a recriminating suit against him, decided to beat you to the punch; and they filled the mother and child with a tissue of horrors, gave them some money, and they said and wrote down everything they were asked. After that Monsieur de Castillon, to give himself the appearance of a man who, far from picking a fight, wanted only to prevent one, duly informed your mother-in-law, and, acting in concert, had the mother and child packed off to Paris, so well paid, so full of hopes for the future and both so well prompted that, in all likelihood, they made the same accusations in Paris that were drilled into them at Aix." That is what I was told, *on*

12. The royal prosecutor in Lyons.
13. The royal prosecutor in Marseilles, who signed a warrant for Sade's arrest on July 4, 1772, perhaps a trifle prematurely, because the evidence, especially concerning the poisoning, was not yet in

that I give you my word of honor, and told me by someone who surely was in a position to know. Whatever may happen, I swear that some day I shall get his permission to reveal who he is,[14] and you shall see what an impression that will make.

Thus, in such an important matter as this, I have testifying against me a p—— who once worked for me and a child, who also was in my employ; a p—— who has everything to gain from exculpating herself at my expense, and a child who has obviously been paid off by my worst enemies. At this point, quite apart from all my own assertions, kindly let me offer the following thought: was it not visibly demonstrated, more clearly than daylight, that those people in Aix were past masters at bringing about my downfall whenever it was deemed appropriate? Since in an earlier affair in this town of Aix you had the proof of it, again clearer than daylight, why do you wish to deny those that may exist in a second affair? You will admit that this presumption is very strong, and much in my favor. Tell me, would you willingly set foot in a wood where you had been already once been robbed of your purse? and if you were robbed of your purse a second time, would you not be more than justified in thinking that they were the same thieves? If I had been in Madame de Montreuil's shoes, that alone would have sufficed to make me reject any accusations against my son-in-law emanating from that town.

Let us go on; there is still something else, and I want everything resolved. In my pocketbook three objects were found, or allegedly found, that were used against me. Let us focus on all three.

One was a prescription for delivering a pregnant woman who wanted to be rid of her fruit. That was a mistake on my part, and no doubt an imprudence to have such a thing on my person, that I admit. I most certainly never made use of it, nor did I copy it out with the intent of ever using it. In the course of my life I had occasion to see two or three women or girls—that is as much as I shall say—whom urgent reasons had forced to hide the result of their misconduct with their lover [and] had led them to commit such a crime. They confessed it to me and at the same time confided to me the very dangerous means that people in that profession used on them, means which, it seemed to me, were a threat to their lives. In Italy I heard tell of this means that they found in my pocketbook, and finding it extremely mild and not

14. The unnamed witness he swears on his word of honor to produce is in all probability a figment of his imagination.

dangerous, I noted it down out of curiosity. I believe that in the eyes of any reasonable man there is nothing here that could be upsetting and that every choirboy is well aware that savin[15] has the same effect.

The second paper was the result of an argument I had with the little doctor in Rome.[16] He maintained that the ancients poisoned iron by the means he told me and I jotted this down; and I claimed the contrary, assuring him that I thought I had read somewhere of a very different method. All that stemmed from the subject of the poisoned antique weapons we had seen together in the arsenal of San Angelo Castle. Since I wanted to include a word or two about that in my description of Rome, I wrote down his opinion, promising to send him mine as soon as I could lay my hands on it, and then, in my dissertation, to decide which of the two was more likely. In fact, I did find the opinion contradicting his, in one of the books you sent me, the fourth volume of the *History of the Celts*. 'Twas from an herb called *linveum* and, according to Pliny and Aulus Gellius, *hellebore*, which the ancients rubbed on the blades they wanted to poison. I therefore opted in favor of this opinion, contesting the one I had been given. And there is the subject of what was found in this connection. Is that still another venial sin?

But now we come to the most important point: *an entire legal opinion concerning matters very similar to those of which you stand accused.*[17] Yes, a damning piece of evidence, but it reminds me of the old story of the magpie's mess; you know that story, do you not? Well, from that story, from the one about Calas and his son, and from a good many others like them, you learn, you who imprison at the drop of a hat, that one should never judge by appearances and punish people without hearing them out, especially in a country that, through its laws and its government, thinks that it is free of all inquisitional vexations; that, in a word, there is not a single citizen whom you have the right to clap into prison without a fair trial, or who at least will not have the right, after he is out, to avenge himself in whatever manner he may choose, providing he

---

15. *Juniperus sabina,* an evergreen shrub whose shoots yield an oil used medicinally.
16. Probably Dr. Barthélmy Mesny, whom Sade visited in Florence in 1775. Dr. Mesny, however, was no "little doctor": physician to the Grand Duke of Tuscany, he was also a well-known naturalist and archaeologist.
17. Sade is citing the complaint against him; therefore the "you" refers to himself.

punish you for your injustice. Yes, whoever you may be, let this idea sink clearly into your head and listen to what I have to say on this vitally important point. This document is the confession of a poor wretch who, like myself, was seeking asylum in Italy. The idea of returning home was the furthest thing from his mind; and seeing me inclined to cross back over the Alps, he handed me his legal opinion, asking me to show it to a lawyer in France and to send him the lawyer's reaction. I promised him I would. Two days later he came to me and begged me to give him the paper back, saying that, since 'twas written in his own hand, it could serve as evidence against him; he wanted to have it transcribed but had found no one in the area who wrote French. I copied out the entire document myself, with no other thought in mind but to oblige him, and not giving a thought to the document's implications. There is another fact for which *I vouch upon my word of honor* and which I stand ready to prove beyond all shadow of doubt when the time comes.

There are all my so-called faults, together with what I have to say about them and in reply to them and what I shall prove, *I swear it,* by various proofs and other means so irrefutable that 'twill be absolutely impossible to deny the truth thereof. I am therefore guilty only of libertinage pure and simple such as it is practiced by all men, to a greater or lesser degree, depending upon the temperament or penchant that Nature happened to have bestowed upon them. Everybody has his failings; let us make no comparisons: my torturers might suffer from such a comparison.

Yes, I am a libertine, that I admit. I have conceived everything that can be conceived in that area, but I have certainly not practiced everything I have conceived and certainly never shall. I am a libertine, but I am neither a *criminal* nor a *murderer,* and since I am obliged to place my apology next to my justification, I shall therefore say that 'tis quite possible that they who condemn me so unfairly are in no position to offset their infamies by good deeds as patent as those I can raise to compare to my misdeeds. I am a libertine, but three families living in your section of the city lived for five years from my charity, and I rescued them from the depths of poverty. I am a libertine, but I saved a deserter from the military, a man abandoned by his entire regiment and by his colonel, from certain death. I am a libertine, but at Evry, with your entire family looking on, I saved at the risk of my own life a child who was about to be crushed beneath the wheels of a cart drawn by runaway horses, and I did so by throwing myself beneath that cart.

I am a libertine, but I have never compromised the health of my wife. I have never indulged in any of the other branches of libertinage so often fatal to the fortune of one's children: have I squandered mine through gambling or other expenditures that in any way deprived them, or threatened to cut into their inheritance? have I mismanaged my goods and possessions, insofar as they have been under my control? have I, in a word, given any indication as a youth that I preferred a heart capable of the heinous acts wherewith I am accused today? have I not always loved everything that was deserving of my love, and everything I ought to hold dear? did I not love my father? (alas, I still weep for him every day of my life) did I ever behave badly with my mother? and was it not when I went to be with her as she drew her last breath, and to show her the ultimate mark of my devotion, that your mother had me dragged off to this horrible prison, where she has left me to languish for the past four years? In a word, look at my life since my earliest childhood. You have in your entourage two people who followed me in that period, *Amblet* and *Madame de Saint-Germain.* From there move on to my youth, which was observed by the Marquis de Poyanne,[18] who personally watched me evolve, thence move forward until the age when I married, and look around, consult whomsoever you will, enquire whether I ever gave any signs of the ferocity I am supposed to possess and whether I ever committed any misdeeds that could have been seen as the harbinger of the crimes ascribed to me: there must be something there, for as you know, crime does not spring out of nothing. How is one to suppose, therefore, that out of such an innocent childhood and youth, I all of a sudden attained the very depths of meditated horror? No, you don't believe that. And you, who today tyrannize me so cruelly, you don't believe it either: your vengeance has clouded your mind, you have acted without thinking, but your heart understands mine, judges it better, and knows full well that it is innocent. Someday I shall have the pleasure of seeing you admit as much, but that avowal will not compensate for my torments, and I shall not have suffered any less for it . . . In a word, I want to be cleared, I shall be as soon as they let me out of here, whenever that may be. If I am a murderer, I did not commit enough murders, and if I

---

18. A friend of Sade's father and commander-in-chief of the Carabiniers, one of the most distinguished units of the royal army. He was helpful in getting the marquis a commission in the cavalry where, as we have seen, he served honorably for several years.

am not, I shall have been punished far too severely and I have every right to demand redress.

This has been an extremely long letter, has it not? But I owed it to myself, and promised myself to write it at the end of my fourth year of suffering. Those four years have now expired; here is the promised letter, written as if in the article of death, so that if death were to over-take me before I had the consolation of holding you once again in my arms, I could, as I breathed my last, refer you to the sentiments I ex-pressed in this letter, as the final thoughts addressed to you by a jeal-ous heart whose desire is to go to his grave knowing you hold him in your esteem. You will forgive the letter's disorder; it is neither studied nor witty; all you should look for in it are naturalness and truth. I crossed out a few names mentioned earlier on, so that the letter will get through, and I most earnestly beg that it be delivered to you. I do not ask you for a detailed reply, all I ask is that you let me know you have received *my grand letter:* that is how I shall call it; yes, that is how I shall call it. And when I refer you to the sentiments it contains, 'tis then you shall reread it . . . Dost thou understand me, my dear friend? Thou shalt reread it and thou shalt see that he who will love thee unto the grave was moved to sign it in his blood.[19]

DE SADE

[Attached note:]

'Tis not often that I write letters of this great length or one as im-portant when it comes to vindicating myself; and 'tis certain 'twill not happen again. Consequently, I beg those through whose hands this letter must pass to be so kind as to make sure it reaches my wife safely. I trust they will do so, and that they would not like to give me reason to believe that they detain letters of the importance of this one; in a word, letters in which I set forth my position; for were they to seize them and thus prevent them from reaching their intended party, then they would have to agree I would have every right to take legal action

---

19. In his closing sentences, Sade addresses Renée-Pélagie in the familiar "tu" form. One presumes, too, that, literally, he used his own blood in writing these final lines of his "grand letter" of explanation and justification.

one day against such methods and expose them, demonstrating the well-established interest they had in keeping me in prison, since they opposed any means I had at my disposal to vindicate myself and thus shorten my sentence.

35. To Madame de Sade

[March 4, 1781]

I don't know what you mean by the Beaumarchais prospectus. I haven't heard of it, and surely you must not have sent it, for they are always punctilious in bringing me everything you send. If the purpose of all these little acts of kindness is to give me something more to worry about, doubtless not stopping to think that in my frightful situation I have enough subjects for worry, you are simply wasting your time. For I swear to you that I have never worried about, nor shall I worry about as long as I live, the packages or prescriptions you send. All that's a lovely machine, the mechanism of which must be left to unwind in due course; in consideration of which I warn you that from now on, whenever I hear all this talk about worries or prescriptions or consignments, of what has become or not become of this thing or that, when, I say, I hear all this claptrap, I shall never respond with the least word. I shall keep asking for an object as long as it has not been sent me, I shall acknowledge its receipt as soon as I have received it. Furthermore, I have nothing to say to you upon this subject except what I have already told you three or four times over: *buy me the book, I shall be happy to have it:* this is the last time I shall mention it.

They came this morning, the 4th, to talk to me again about my walks. This may be nothing but another piece of tomfoolery, as it was the last time they came for the same thing six months back. They assure me, however, that it is not. Upon this subject, I must confess to you that sometimes when I am comfortably ensconced in my castles in Spain, putting as far from my mind as possible that revolting notion of signals, which may well be the most odious act of folly that has ever got into a prude's head since Nature first began creating prudes—I keep saying to myself: *they have kept me confined, taken away my walks, doubtless for some positive reason; I am badly off, but 'twill end sooner,* and this thought would give me some slight comfort. But no, not at all. 'Tis but one period of signals; back they come again, and, what's more, so furiously and so relentlessly that they try to convince me that the only reason I lost my walks was because some prison flunkey, the most contemptible of creatures on the face of the earth, had been paid off by the présidente de Montreuil to become insolent with me. A flunkey is insolent with me and it's I who am in the wrong! Can one cover one's scurvy little manias with pretexts as odious as those! That woman must be possessed of a fury, she must have a bottomless pit of malice, wickedness, and baseness in her soul! Yes, I repeat, I am convinced that she would have died of despair if I had not been captured and she had been deprived of distilling her venom over such a long period of years. What a veritable attack of indigestion! Good God, what an eruption! What abundance! Oh! she'd have died a thousand times over, that much is clear. And that a government exist in this world that is willing to tolerate such infamies, a government that, without examining, without inquiring, without any attempt to clarify, and only because *that's grease for the wheels of the machine*, sacrifices to such a woman a person who, if I may be so bold, is a thousand times more deserving than she of this government, which he has served and which she dishonors; what am I saying? Such horrors do exist and one does not want to go off and dwell amongst the savages! Oh! this is something I simply cannot conceive.

And so this is another signal. Wonderful. All right, you can put it away with the others, I don't understand it any better, nor shall I try to. On that I give you my word. For when all is said and done, you know it better than I, but at least I have to ask it once: how do you want me to form any kind of sound opinion out of such a tissue of nonsense, reeking as it does of the bile of that survivor of the Inquisition? I would need to know your point of departure;[1] and that is precisely what you are so fond of concealing as carefully as you can. Here are ten different starting points:

The time of my absence: this is what I refer to as the date when we were separated from each other. 1.

All the prisons and nothing else: Vincennes the first time, Aix, and Vincennes the second time. 2.

Only two Vincennes. 3.

---

1. By point of departure Sade, always on the lookout for signals, or seeing them when they do not exist, is asking the marquise for the key to the code, which of course she does not have.

The two Vincennes, plus the thirteen days' travel time being taken back there. 4.

The return alone, minus travel. 5.

And the return alone, plus travel. 6.

All that, as you see, leads to very different conclusions and absolutely rules out any possibility either of establishing anything, or, consequently, of spending any time on your conundrums. Thus you are completely defeating your purpose. And by having chosen to do too much, you have accomplished nothing. That is what always happens to those schooled in the art of mischief and wickedness. For, after all, these signals can have only two purposes: either for me to understand them or for me not to understand them. If 'tis the former, make them clearer, and give me at least one point of reference, tell me what your starting point is; if 'tis the latter, why are you sending me any signal at all? For you must be familiar enough with the liveliness of my mind to know for sure that I shall never waste an hour tarrying over anything I realize is absurd. If, when she organized all this, your mother, instead of giving full vent only to her rage, and instead of relying upon no one but valets who laugh at her behind her back as soon as they have pocketed her money, had had the common sense to have entrusted the job to a man of wit, one might have dressed it[2] in such a form that I would have worked night and day trying to solve it, and, what is worse, I would have been incapable of tearing myself away from it for a single instant. And, had I been in her shoes, this is what I would have done. Everybody knows how absorbing geometry is: the example of Archimedes, who during the siege of Syracuse was slain without lifting his eyes from his sheet of paper, is the most convincing proof. Now what about a geometry problem whose solution would include the discovery of what a man was most interested in finding out? That would, quite literally, drive him crazy. I therefore would have wrapped my riddle in all the solid trappings of a real mathematical problem. The constant truth would have been placed at the end; the only question would have been how to arrive at it; but the principles would have been solid and true; hence no danger of the whole thing ringing false, as it inevitably would in this case for anyone foolish enough to try to study it. And the fascination would become such that one would be held in its thrall. That way it would at least have been bearable, whereas what she has done is the very height of stupidity. But to do what I suggest she would have had to seek the help of some intelligent

---

2. The signal, real or imagined.

man. In any case, I am most grateful to her that she didn't, for instead of wasting the total of four months I lost during the two detentions[3] I would have spent my entire life trying to solve the riddle, and I would have been all the more sorry for all the lost time. "Oh," I know you are going to reply to me, "it's not at present you're supposed to solve the riddle, it's only after you're out, it's so one can have the pleasure of saying to you, *'What? You mean you didn't see that? You didn't guess that?'* etc." I have already had the honor of telling you, and I say it again one last time on the matter, that anyone who takes it into his head to mention these platitudes to me once I am out can either expect to receive serious abuse from me or else I shall never see that person again. 'Tis the one thing about which I declare I shall refuse to hear any banter so long as I live. Forewarned is forearmed: if you care about me at all, make sure you steer clear of any such riddles.

Moreover, I thank you most sincerely for having my walks restored; unfortunately, I am forced to linger on in this disgusting detention, 'tis better for me to enjoy this pleasure while I am here, rather than be without it. Words cannot express to you how badly I need them. I cannot write two lines without the blood rushing to my head, to a degree you cannot even conceive; and I would frighten you out of your wits, I'm sure, if you were to see me. Right now, as I write these lines to you, I'm obliged to stop after each sentence. Fresh air, and no longer making a fire, will, I hope, make me feel a little better.

The towels should not be of cotton, but of linen: they're for the razor and not for the powder; La Jeunesse knows that very well.

36. To Madame de Sade

[*Toward March 28, 1781*]

Good Lord, dear friend, how much I admire Father Massillon's[1] sermons! They lift my spirits, they enchant me, they absolutely delight me. 'Tis no bigot, this man who is speaking to you and who,

---

3. His first detention in Vincennes in 1763 as a result of the Jeanne Testard affair, and the second in the château of Saumur in 1768 following the Rose Keller scandal.

1. Jean-Baptiste Massillon (1663–1742), prominent French cleric, author, and member of the French Academy.

framing truths on all sides that the impious deny, using not the point but the flat side of his sword to make his point. 'Tis no pedant bristling with sophisms and who is trying to win you over solely by frightening you to death. 'Tis to the heart this preacher directs his maxims; 'tis the heart he seeks to win over and the heart he constantly enthralls. With each word one finds a gentle father looking out for the welfare of his children; each sentence is one that a friend might address to a friend he sees on the brink of the precipice. What purity! What moral power! and what a happy blend of strength and simplicity! At times his swift eloquence is like a stream that sweeps away all the soul's blemishes; the next moment, his tender compassion, as if frightened by the great commotion it has just produced, now covers the wounds with naught but a sweet and soothing balm, wherewith he wins over both the heart and mind. Great God! how was it possible that Louis XIV had so many millions of his subjects' throats cut in the Cévennes[2] while Massillon was saying to him, "Sire, kings are given us by the Eternal to be the salvation of their people; comfort them, you will be their father and twice over their master; be a peacemaker, Sire, the most glorious conquests are those that win over hearts." And during that period not a day went without a dozen or fifteen poor wretches being broken on the wheel in Nîmes or in Montpellier, merely because they refused to believe that one had to go to Mass. And there you have the effect of the most beautiful and the holiest truths upon the heart of the man dominated by his passions! Nothing can alter their impetuousness, and when he is forced to blush because of them, ultimately his pride, coming swiftly to the rescue, furnishes him with shameful excuses to color them with a pious zeal . . . And what an example I have before my eyes! Are we not going to see, two weeks from now, the torturer of my life draw nigh to the altars, there to receive her God, just as calmly, just as serenely, as if her soul, drunk with a desire for revenge, did not bring disgrace upon itself every day by sacrificing her daughter, her son-in-law, and her unhappy grandchildren! Yes, we shall see her approach with impunity the God she outrages, and not tremble at the sacrilege; we shall see her impious lips, those same lips that daily dare utter forth the dishonor of her entire family, receive the heavenly host which becomes at the same time the condemnation of the guilty and the comfort of the just; and, coloring her crimes with the specious sophistries of an evenhandedness whose mask she adopts only to appease her

---

2. That is, the Protestants. The Cévennes mountains in central France had long been a Protestant stronghold. But millions? Sade exaggerates.

conscience, she will dare say: *I am righteous like the Divinity, because like Him I punish.* Horrible, bane of Nature, dost thou dare carry blasphemy thus far? Wilt thou dare see in the Divinity naught but a tyrant? Wilt thou dare mold Him in thy sullied soul? And wilt thou blind thyself to the point of believing thou dost imitate His justice when thou dost but follow the infernal impressions of the enemy whom God created in order to punish people of thy ilk? Tremble! God finally grows weary of mortals' crimes, and lightning is already hovering over thy head; the thundercloud is forming even as thou art peacefully molding the instruments of thy vengeance, and heaven's revenge shall burst down upon thee even as thou dost glory in thy exultation! Look back upon thy conduct if but once: see what, over these past nine years, has become of all the mercenary minions who served thy rage; glance at this list, and see how Providence has forewarned thee of the fate in store for the likes of thee when it avenges me for thy infamies:

> *Fate of the présidente de Montreuil's minions over the nine years she has been bribing them to do me in. A word to the wise.*

Chancellor Maupeou: *completely dishonored, and lucky to get away with his head;*

The Duc de la Vrillière:[3] *dead;*

Madame Langeac: *died insane;*

Monsieur de Mende, Royal Procurator in Marseilles:[4] *removed from his position, execrated throughout his province, and today without house or home;*

The foreign monarch she implored to serve her vengeance:[5] *dead;*

---

3. A minister under Louis XV, the Duc de la Vrillière was reappointed minister by Louis XVI in 1774. It was to him the présidente turned that year to make sure the *lettre de cachet* under which Sade was imprisoned would be properly renewed.

4. As noted, Charles-Augustin de Maupeou, a famous jurist and chief adviser to Louis XV during the later years of his reign, was an archenemy of the Montreuils and largely responsible for Sade's arrest after Arceuil. He was dismissed and dishonored by Louis XVI.

5. Presumably the king of Sardinia-Piedmont, who at the instigation of the présidente issued the order, on December 8, 1773, to have Sade arrested while he was holed up in Chambéry.

The commandant of the Savoy fortress: *stripped of his post;*[6]
The turnkey: *hanged;*[7]
The only one of my relatives she won over to her cause, the only one who served her: *dead;*[8]
The police lackey she sent to arrest me: *behind bars for the rest of his life;*[9]
The man who managed my business in Provence and whom she paid to have me arrested: *dishonored in his province, thought of by one and all a rogue, a man who had lost his best clients;*[10]
The postilion who brought her to make her infamous capitulation to Maupeou at Compiègne: *crushed beneath the wheels of his carriage.*[11]

Not to mention whatever happened beyond my ken, plus what I am leaving out.

And is not all this a sign of God's grace? And is it not the hand of God gradually bearing down upon her, He who in His infinite goodness converts her to Him before He crushes her completely? O justice of the Eternal, woe unto him who shuts his eyes to You!

37. To Madame de Sade

Evening of the 1st of April [1781]

*T*hough it be the simplest thing in the world, the easiest, the least praiseworthy to fool a prisoner, though it be a most mean-spirited pastime, which necessarily proves a most mean and most vile soul, though when all is said and done this can be nothing more than the foolish and ridiculous pastime of a very old woman and of an

---

6. Monsieur de Launay, who had been commander of the Savoy fortress of Miolans at the time of Sade's arrest.
7. Name unknown: Sade tried on several occasions to bribe turnkeys while he was at Miolans.
8. Sade is referring to the abbé, his uncle.
9. Probably Inspector Goupil of the Paris police, with whom Madame de Montreuil connived.
10. Gaufridy.
11. Name unknown. The "her" Sade mentions is Madame de Montreuil.

exceedingly imbecilic creature, you have derived no glory from it, nor have I been taken in by it; it took me roughly half an hour to see through this business, I must confess.

Always an element of nobility in the tiny pleasures of the most high and all-powerful Lady de Montreuil! Lackeys and numskulls are tricked on April First, we'll fool our son-in-law, too. My God, what nobleness of character, what loftiness of spirit, what grandeur of feelings! Ah! never, never does the spring become tainted! By one feat of gallantry was a bastard of the great Turenne revealed from amongst a whole army! The purity of our origins always comes out, and the blood never betrays.

What the devil do you mean with your Montélimar fortress?[1] There has never been any fortress in Montélimar. If there were, its general staff would be mentioned in the *Military Almanac;* and under the article on *Montélimar* only the *Marquis de Chabrillant* is mentioned, and he certainly has no prison under his command. I went through my three Almanacs: in all of them Montélimar is merely mentioned, while under all the other towns where there are forts or citadels there is, next to the name of the town, the mention *such and such a fort* or *such and such a citadel.* Besides, I am familiar enough with Montélimar and the surrounding area (having spent an entire month there with the Marquis de Chabrillant, whose castle is adjacent to the city gates) to be quite certain that there has never been a fortress at Montélimar. It may have some old tower inhabited by a few bats or owls, but as for a royal keep for prisoners there is certainly nothing. I would swear to that on a stack of Bibles. Still, let us for a minute take the matter under serious consideration. Near Montélimar there is a tower for prisoners called the Crest Tower, and perhaps you misunderstand, perhaps that's the one they talked to you about and you were referring to. Going on that assumption, please be so kind as to excuse me from writing Madame de Sorans[2] this fine thank-you letter, whose style, which I am so obliged to you for mimicking for me, is absolutely what her manservant might use if she had thrown him out and he were trying to worm his way back into her service.

---

1. For some time Sade has been beseeching his wife to have him transferred out of Vincennes, at any cost. In checking other possibilities, Renée-Pélagie hit upon the possibility of Montélimar. Sade's reaction to the idea follows.
2. The Marquise de Sorans, lady-in-waiting to the king's sister Elizabeth de France, and a friend of Renée-Pélagie. It was through Madame de Sorans's influence that Madame de Sade obtained a royal decree to have her husband transferred to Montélimar.

Crest Tower is most decidedly a more frightful prison than Vincennes, and extremely unwholesome to boot; the only people they put in there are those they expect to be rid of in short order. 'Tis an abominable cloaca, where daylight is rarely seen, and it lies in the midst of pestilential swamp. If that is the place you have in mind for me, and for which favor I am supposed most humbly to thank Madame de Sorans, I shall take the liberty of declining both, and I entreat you, on the contrary, to use both her and all your own influence to request most urgently that I finish out the rest of my pain and suffering right here where I am: I am now used to this place, and I prefer to be in here than in some other prison. Believe me, we have already provided both Dauphiné and Provence with quite enough spectacles.[3] *Valence* has me in its archives next to Mandrin: *Vienne, Grenoble*, etc., have me in gold letters. Let's keep it at that. And however much your divine and witty mother delights in making public scenes, blunders, mistakes, and burlesques, do make her promise, for the sake of your children's honor, not to indulge in them so frequently. By constantly adding fuel to the fire this way it will never go out. And you may be sure that the public, which never sees the thing on the bright side, will someday make those innocent little creatures feel the full weight of their grandmother's absurd foolishness. Here again, let's keep it at that, believe me. We've already had more than enough. Did Monsieur Le Noir come up with that idea, in keeping with the practice of all police lieutenants, to give his henchmen some extra money? Propose the sum as a gift, and let them leave us alone. Offer it, pay it, I give you a free hand to do so, and will give you my power of attorney if you like. I most decidedly do not want to be transferred anywhere except to my estates, and when I go there I want to go alone, with no guard, or with you alone, but not escorted. No matter what they may offer you in this regard, propose either money, to buy ourselves out of the clutches of all these savages, or my word of honor that I prefer to pay off the debt right here. I assure you most emphatically that that is what I shall tell Monsieur Le Noir if he comes. So you can tell him the same thing.

Furthermore, you promised me that I shall see my children when I get out of here. For me not to see them will be a terrible knife-thrust. I warn you of that. Know that there is nothing in the world that could

---

3. Sade is referring to provinces where he had been escorted under police guard. The spectacle of his anticipated arrival was attended by hundreds, sometimes thousands, of spectators eager to catch a glimpse of this satanic monster.

cause me greater grief. I beseech you, whatever arrangements are made for me, to see to it that I have twenty-four hours to spend with them, wherever you like, to hold them in my arms. Otherwise, I swear that I shall conceive an undying dislike for them, and shall refuse to see them for the rest of my life. The news of Monsieur Le Noir's visit strikes me as the best thing in your letter, and yet . . . Be that as it may, if 'tis to take place, let it be as soon as possible, I beg of you, so that I may get a clear picture of all this, which makes me worry myself to death for no good reason and prevents me from spending my time in a manner which, however frivolous it may be, is still infinitely better than that of steeping me as you have been doing for four years in all your odious mother's bile and ill-temper.

Summing Up

1. I beg that I not be transferred, no matter where, and, above all, without mounted escort. I shall sacrifice up to ten thousand francs to buy myself out of any such transfer. This, I think, gives a fair idea of how much both ideas are anathema to me.

2. I consent and prefer to remain here the entire time of my punishment, however long that may be, preferring this place, dreadful though it be, to anything else that might be offered to me, even were it an entire fortress to myself, the only exception being my estate, to which I am ready to repair whenever they like, even if it were to be in exile, however painful I would find that, but in any case without escort.

3. I shall write whatever decorum calls for to Madame de Sorans when she has got me back on my lands and not into another prison, because, once again, prison for prison, I prefer this one rather than another; and to make yet another spectacle of oneself in these provinces would be an odious thing and is to be avoided at any cost.

4. You will note that, although I do indicate my preference and my conditions, I am not, however, laying down the law, knowing all too well that I am in no position to do so. But I say that I prefer Vincennes and ask that I remain here rather than anywhere else, the sole exception being my own estate.

I beg of you, to avoid upsetting me, to notify me twenty-four hours in advance when you want to come and see me with Monsieur

Le Noir. The paper[4] is very ordinary stuff, that's not at all what I asked for. No matter, 'twill do for my manuscripts. If you cannot rent Bougainville's *Voyages*,[5] buy all the volumes for me, I absolutely want to have them. Here is the shopping list which was drawn up before this latest prank. I send it to you as is; it doesn't strike me that anything needs changing.

38. To Madame de Sade

[April 11, 1781]

I earnestly beseech you, dear friend, busy as you are with all your little April Fool's Day jests, not to forget that the list of errands requested for the 14th of this month is so indispensable to me that even if I were called to fulfill my duties *as a father and a citizen* at the Montélimar barracks two weeks after the 14th, the date when I require these provisions, I'd need them all the same. My linen is quite literally lying on the floor for lack of boxes to put it in, those I have are already destined for other purposes and cannot serve to hold any linen. As for candles, I am using my last today; the same goes for the rest of my list. Therefore, do keep them coming, I beg of you, and do bear in mind that not having them will prevent me from doing any packing at all. Besides, would it really matter or do any harm if I were to leave some boxes and a few pounds of candles behind for the man who waits on me? The poor devil has in all honesty earned them. And so send, send. Do send, send, I beg of you, and especially secondary reading material, I have not a single trashy book left. You will be receiving an enormous package, which will be enclosed with the manuscript.

When I reread your last letter, I truly do believe you are mad to think that I refuse. If you had even the slightest bit of common sense and humanity, wouldn't you feel that I am here like a blind man, that I neither see anything nor hear anything, that having grown used to being deceived in everything for ten years now by a monster who

4. The writing paper Sade asked his wife to send.
5. Louis-Antoine de Bougainville (1729–1811), a French explorer and writer who spent four years circumnavigating the globe, from 1766–1769.

seems to enjoy indulging in all the most disgusting and the meanest vices, namely lying, deceit, imposture, etc., etc., etc., etc., etc., etc., etc., etc., everything puts me in a state of fear and trembling.

If what you are doing is for my own best interest, do you need to consult me or believe what I say? Does one ask a sick man for his opinion about leeching when it is indispensable to his recovery? I didn't want any journey to Aix, either. It was, so you said, necessary—although I am still not yet fully convinced it was; did that stop you from going through with it despite me and my complaints? If this move is no more advantageous, surely you will be well advised not to undertake it. But if it is—and you should know that better than I—go right ahead and pay no heed to me. Look to the future, look to your children, and do not put me in a position where I feel I have to reproach you, as I am doing today on so many subjects; nor should you put the children in a position where they will later put the blame on you. That is my last word on the matter. I put myself in your hands. Proceed as you will, and let's not discuss it any further.

Reproaches include:

Having had me arrested at the Hotel de Danemark.

Having involved yourself in your mother's twisted plots and infamies.

Having written me thirty letters in invisible ink, simply to tell me nothing but idle gossip.

Having involved and compromised the innocent hands of your children in all those infamies.

Having had me rescued at Aix for the sole and unique pleasure of having me rearrested at La Coste.

Having told me nothing during my stay there, despite the fact you had such a perfect occasion to do so through the intermediary of Chauvin, who had seen you in private for several months in a row and who also saw me tête-à-tête for several days in a row; at the very least you ought to have taken advantage of the opportunity to let me know of the length of my term, which was the one thing you knew I most desired.

Making me desire and wait here for everything I have asked from you, as though I were asking for charity, as though you were not paying for it out of my own pocket, etc.

'Tis time to make your own confession just as precisely as that. Join unto it your repentance, then promise to sin no more, and you will go straight to Paradise.

Let this serve notice that the manuscript[1] will most assuredly be awaiting you in the office on the evening of the 19th or in the morning of the 20th of this month.

39. To Monsieur Le Noir

[April 12, 1781]

*S*ir:
 Although Madame de Sade assures me most tenderly that 'tis the most useless thing in the world to lodge the slightest complaint about the infamies of which her odious mother makes me the victim, I nonetheless venture to offer on this entire matter a few reflections, which I beseech you to read and which I shall try to make as brief as possible.

When children have been as cruelly wronged as mine have been at this time, as a result of the latest dishonor into which I have been plunged yet again, and as they will be in the future because of the hatred I shall necessarily feel toward them because of my absolute conviction that I am being sacrificed through false maneuvers, the fatal consequences of which no one can foresee; when, I say, a whole host of like misfortunes are poised to overwhelm us all, should you not, Sir, use your good influence to set things right?

Would you, good Sir, harbor enough illusions or—bearing in mind that I have never done anything except to honor you as a wise magistrate—would you indeed share to some degree the unjust methods used by the monster who tyrannizes me, not to feel how odious it is to have dragged me for ten years from prison to prison, not to understand

1. In all probability his play *L'Inconstant*—*The Fickle Fellow*—a five-act comedy in alexandrines completed in late January 1781 and then reworked for several weeks, producing a clean copy on April 14, three days after this letter was written and roughly a week before he expected to have it in the marquise's hands.

that that can have no other purpose than to renew my misfortunes and let them be known to one and all throughout the four corners of France?

Who better than I has a true sense of my situation? And how deeply does it have to penetrate my being, to what degree must I dread the fifth scene[1] of frightful dishonor to which I am about to be subjected, simply because I, for one brief moment, preferred the hateful sojourn where I am to the cruel snub of this even greater misfortune?

Do have the kindness to dwell on this for a moment, Monsieur. What they are doing is setting a trap for me here. Madame de Montreuil knows full well that I shall not survive the horror of this latest infamy, this new spectacle she desires to make of me; she knows full well that I shall try to escape, which will result in the fulfillment of her most ardent desire, namely to obtain thereby the iniquitous and odious right—a right completely opposed to the laws and constitution of the government, and to which 'tis unworthy that any magistrates make themselves a party—the right, I say, to keep me under the abominable authority of a *lettre de cachet* for the rest of my life.

But she will not long enjoy her little triumph, for I tell you, Sir, that my only purpose in escaping will be to go abroad, there to end my days. Thus it is, by your having yielded to the whims of a wretched woman, who if you knew her as I do you would order to be put in chains rather than protected, thus it is, I say, that you have a man undone, robbed of his children, stripped of his worldly goods, and a family overwhelmed with both dishonor and misfortune.

Do redress all that, Sir, I beg of you, bearing in mind the two clauses in my letter that deal with what shall result therefrom.

Without question I do not have the right to make the laws, and when I say so in writing myself, 'tis useless to repeat that statement over and over again, as happened to me yesterday throughout the day, but the right to air one's grievances, to lodge a complaint, has not been denied the wretched of the earth, not even those people we dare call savages, because their king is not in the habit of spending a million to ferret out what his subjects may be doing to the country's women.[2] And this right to lodge a complaint, given the situation in which I find myself, to whom should I address myself if not to the selfsame magistrate whose task it is to make certain all citizens are assured of their equal rights? A fatal case of blind injustice? You would send to the gal-

1. Sade is referring to the fact that if he is transferred out of Vincennes to another prison, it will be the fifth such dungeon he will have known.
2. Here Sade really means "prostitutes."

lows a poor wretch who, in order to feed his father and children, had stolen a crown from a passerby, and you call that maintaining order in Paris, and without the slightest qualm or remorse you would deliver over an innocent man to his torturers, whose only goal is to dishonor him, strip him of his fortune, bring him down, debase him for the rest of his days. Yet which of the two, Sir, in your opinion is more wronged in all this, the man who has stolen a crown or I, who for ten years has been robbed of his *rightful goods and possessions, his wife, children, honor, influence, reputation, responsibilities, happiness, domestic tranquillity, etc.?* And yet what a difference in your tribunal in the fate of these two assailants! One you will send to the gallows, the other you will overwhelm with honors. No, Monsieur, no, 'tis not a misfortune, 'tis not a deprivation to be exiled forever, to lose for the rest of one's life a country one finds unworthy, a country where justice is meted out to those of its citizens who have served it with honor, those members of the military who have taken up arms in its defense. I do not deserve a torture as long as the one to which I have been subjected. I defy God Himself to prove that I deserve it. I am therefore the sole victim of the frenzied rage of a monster, and you should not put up with her.

Here is my final word on the matter, and they are not laws I am making,[3] they are prayers and opinions I am offering about what will happen if they are refused.

First clause. I ask to spend a fortnight encloseted with my wife in Paris, to consult with doctors concerning my health, which is passing poor, for not a day goes by that I don't cough up blood, and to see my children; thence to leave with my wife, and with my word as my bond, without having to incur the expense of any police escort, because 'tis not for families to pay these knaves, all of whom ought to be taken out and hanged: 'tis for the king to support such rogues and rascals in his kingdom; to leave, I say, for my estates, for as long as one wishes, whether in exile or not, I care not. For I have no desire to leave my own estates for a good long while.

In return for that clause, if 'tis granted me, I give you my word of honor, to you and whomsoever else is required to have it, duly signed and sealed with all the most authentic forms it may please you to prescribe, that I shall behave for the rest of my life in a manner that is sober, orderly, and exemplary in every possible manner, so exemplary

---

3. Sade keeps harping on this point because whenever he lodges a complaint or makes a request of his jailers, they inevitably remind him: "You, Sir, do not make the laws here."

in fact that not even an angel could behave more seemly. I further swear that I shall devote my time and energy to the happiness of my wife and my children, and to mending, insofar as 'tis in my hands to do so, both my misfortunes and the inroads made into my fortune. What is more, I shall sign whatever legal document you may require endowing Madame de Montreuil with the authority to act on behalf of my children however she sees fit, without the slightest interference from me, in consequence whereof I am ready and willing to turn over to her whatever portion of my goods and possessions she deems appropriate to that end; and I agree to approve her choice of education, profession, place of residence, marriage, etc., and to provide her with everything, even above and beyond what I have already agreed to. I also consent to wipe out the entire past, not a shred of which I shall ever mention again in the future, in short, to supplement anything I may have omitted herein by whatever it may please you add as either necessary or useful to the complete satisfaction of all concerned.

Second clause. If, instead of all the above, one decides to pursue the Montélimar project,[4] and if one is bound and determined not to renounce it once and for all, I shall go, I am ready to leave, and I say that in no uncertain terms so that you may be assured that I do not, as my wife mistakenly wrote me yesterday, find Vincennes preferable. But if that is the decision, then mark you well, I shall try to escape as soon as I possibly can, and I shall succeed, no matter what precautions may be taken to prevent me; I shall move to a foreign country; I have a prince ready to take me in, of that you may be sure, Sir, and a monarch who does not lock up his subjects over a matter of prostitutes, as he does not deliver them over into the hands of pimps;[5] and from there I shall do my level best to thwart all of Madame de Montreuil's various and sundry projects, in the cruelest way I know how; I shall publicly dishonor her by my writings, which will contain truths so well known that no one will ever be able to refute them. I shall disclose how and why honors are bestowed in France, and reveal that if I left that country it was because I did not have a hundred thousand francs per annum

---

4. Having begged his wife to get him transferred to another prison, and she having made efforts to effect a change, Sade is still terrified at being sent to a pestilential prison in or near Montélimar, as indicated earlier in his letter of March 28.
5. In the original, Sade does not spell out either term, doubtless not for fear of being censored, since the meaning is obvious, but out of deference to his correspondent, a police inspector.

wherewith to grease the palms of Themis' henchmen as did those to whom the State has sacrificed me, the same State which in my present misfortune should have acted as a father to me, since I spent my youth serving it faithfully and well, that State which repaid me only with chains and nourished me with naught but my own tears. Nor is that all I shall do. No matter what precautions they may take to prevent me, I still have one certain means to deprive my children of their birthright—at least two of them unquestionably—and I shall use it, you may be sure. I shall leave them with nothing but the breath of life they received from their mother, and the only reason I shall leave them with that is so that they may spend their lives cursing the abominable creature who was responsible for preventing them from ever having a father.

Deign to reflect upon all this, Sir. Why, when you can mold a man to your desires by using proper methods, opt to use improper ones? Is that either fair or reasonable? And is that what fate intended for us both, good Sir, I to serve as fodder for a bankrupt woman dishonored in the eyes of every thinking person, and you to offer me up to her for this purpose? My happiness is in your hands, Sir, I entrust myself to your good offices. Think of the inner satisfaction that a man as virtuous as you will feel knowing that he has dried the tears of a poor wretch of a man, knowing that he has returned that man to his duties and to his family, realizing that that entire family loves you, has you in its prayers, thinks of you as its mentor, that it revels less in the happiness it has found again on earth than in the charm of knowing 'tis owing to you and to you alone. 'Tis the personage of God Himself you will then be playing here below. Just think, Sir, think that if the Almighty has accidentally bestowed upon you some of his bounden duties, 'tis in order to be the image not of his angry thunderbolts but of his infinite goodness.

I have the honor of being, with all the sentiments due you, Sir, your most humble and most obedient servant.

DE SADE

40. To Gaufridy

[April 12, 1781]

I am told, Monsieur, that you might be so bold, so insolent, as to come and pay me a visit in Montélimar, a site to which no doubt you were involved in having me sent, the better to cheat me, the better to steal from me, and the better to entice me to subscribe to everything that you may have done against my better interests and to enhance your own. I agree that this place[1] would be most convenient for that, but I strongly advise to refrain from coming; for if I am unfortunate enough not to have a stout stick within reach—the only arm with which to receive a traitor, a rogue, and a scoundrel of your ilk—I shall excoriate you with such a round of violent invectives, in the presence of everyone within hearing—invectives I might add that are totally deserved—that I have no doubt you will greatly regret you ever had the impertinence to come and will make haste to beat a quick retreat.

41. To Monsieur Le Noir[1]

April 20, 1781

*M*onsieur,
My mind would long ago have been greatly relieved . . . Instead of the despair and pain wherewith I have for so long now been besieged, I would have felt my soul once again filled with the virtues people so greatly desire to see restored within it, had only I earlier had the meeting you honored me with the day before yesterday.

The glimmer of hope you raised within me concerning a possible remission of my sentence by means of some sort of transfer requested by Madame de Sorans and by my wife, the purpose of which is to put

1. That is, the Montélimar prison.
1. Following Sade's letter of April 12, police chief Le Noir paid Sade a visit in Vincennes six days later.

me in a better position to reestablish some order in my affairs, and the impossibility that such a transfer could be to any prisons located in the vicinity of my estates, prisons less atrocious than where I am presently being detained, such as the Tower of Crest, etc., leads me to ask most urgently that you inform the minister forthwith of the following:

1. That I have no desire whatsoever to trade one bad situation for another;

2. That no matter what castle or keep they might choose in the vicinity of my estates, it has been clearly demonstrated that there is no way I can manage my affairs from there.

The first of these articles being so obvious as to require no explanation, I shall confine myself to proving the second.

My affairs, Sir, are currently in the hands of a man[2] who takes advantage of my absence to further his affairs far more than he does mine. Since all I have to go on are the glimpses and vague notions that a rogue such as he might come and offer me in prison, where I am able to see and consult no one but him, you can well imagine how astonishingly easy it is for him to persuade me to do whatever he would like. And since 'tis only to him I have recourse, I am compelled to make up my mind, sign the necessary papers, and as a result put myself entirely in his hands for the rest of my days; a terrible disadvantage that can only result in the complete loss of all my goods and possessions and the inevitable ruin of my children. 'Tis impossible to spell out the degree to which my affairs are in a state of frightful disorder, and to what degree my presence on the spot has become an absolute necessity. 'Tis therefore for that reason, Monsieur, that I most urgently request that you be so kind as to obtain for me a place of residence that is agreeable to everyone concerned, in order to satisfy both the restrictive measures that have been imposed upon me and the kindnesses wherewith the king may choose to make them less harsh.

In Provence I have four estates: two of them, Saumane and Mazan, are situated in the Comtat; the third is a parcel of land near Arles which remains unbuilt; and the fourth, which is my normal place of residence, is called La Coste, located not far from the small city of Apt.

My presence in each of the four estates is equally essential, and I should never be able to sort out the tricks and ruses of the people who for years now have been leading me down the garden path unless I am able to listen on the spot both to the friends of these rogues and to

---

2. Gaufridy.

their enemies, in order to make up my own mind and render a new administrative decision that will be less unfavorable to my own interests. As you know better than I, Sir, that is the only manner of ferreting out the truth. But one has to be there in order for it happen. None of that is admissible if all one has to go on are the reports, made by a man who is completely unreliable, to his master in prison; in which wise, hearing only him, one is compelled to follow the route he suggests, and far from sorting things out, everything is only further confused, to such a degree that no one any longer knows which end is up.

As both *Saumane* and *Mazan* are located in the Comtat, it strikes me as neither good nor proper to request that I be allowed to live there, so long as I am under the king's orders.[3] The Arles property contains no building. That leaves La Coste, which is in a sense the chief town, the place where I have always lived, where my papers are, etc. There I can be, if one so desires, under the surveillance of whatever person the Court cares to appoint, and that for as long as the minister is of a mind to forget that he is dealing with a military officer and a man of the nobility, for whom, by both titles, nothing is more sacred than his word of honor.

I shall make no complaint whatsoever: the very glimmer of the king's bounties that you have danced before my eyes, banishing forever any bitterness my soul may have harbored, leaves room there for naught but gratitude. If, however, one is willing to spare me the shameful embarrassment of being kept under surveillance, and relieve me of that unnecessary expense, I shall commit myself to the king's order, by whatever means it shall please you to stipulate on his behalf. And I shall be so absolutely scrupulous in fulfilling the various clauses of the king's order that no one will ever have the least regret for having rendered my sentence less onerous. In which case, the gentleman Blancard, sublieutenant of the mounted constabulary, who resides in Apt, a city in the vicinity of the estate where I am asking to reside—a man of honor and probity whom the late Marquis de Muids, under whom he served, held in the highest regard—could come and check up on me as frequently as may be desired, and report back to whomsoever it pleases you as to my conduct.

As for the extent of my confinement as specified by the king's letter, here are my thoughts on the subject and the reasons that I beseech

---

3. The Comtat was not officially part of France but, since the fourteenth century, a papal territory within France. Therefore Sade is making the point that the king's authority would not obtain there.

the court to give them serious consideration. Four leagues[4] is too great a distance if one is of a mind to confine me to my château, the circumference of the estate being no more than two leagues in all, in which case two leagues would suffice. And in the event one would be willing to allow me to attend to the totality of my affairs, as I believe is absolutely essential and as I have just requested, four leagues would not be enough. Vouchsafe to hear me out for a moment, Monsieur, and use the chief town as our point of departure. There are four leagues from *La Coste* to *Saumane*, eight from *La Coste* to *Mazan*, and twelve from *La Coste* to *Arles*. Here, then, is what I suggest as the fair means to satisfy all parties: the necessity to extend the king's letter to the *Mazan* and *Saumane* dwellings and their surrounding territories seems to me indispensable, for without that, I repeat, there is absolutely no way I can administer anything but the sole estate where I shall be living. Yet twelve leagues is too much. In all my requests you will never see me trying to take advantage of anything that is offered or of slipping anything irregular into my suggestions. Surely you must remember, Monsieur, my thoughts on this matter such as I laid them out to you the other day. Anyone who takes advantage of the least act of kindness deserves not only that he be offered none in the future but that he be punished, in that, by so doing, he serves as a bad example for all those decent and wretched people who are without exception forced to bow in like manner to the severe measures the government has seen fit to impose upon them. 'Tis my view, therefore, that different restrictions be placed upon me, on the one hand regarding my three dwellings and their respective territories, which should fall into one equal category, and on the other hand my voyages to Arles, for which my presence is required once every six months at the most, and that that be clearly stipulated in the *lettre de cachet;* but also contained therein would be a special permission allowing further visits if they became necessary without any further requirement on my part, except having the honor to inform you several days in advance of such an impending visit, it also being incumbent upon me to alert the previously mentioned officer of the mounted constabulary in Apt both of my departure and my return. Which would mean, therefore, in order to spell out even more clearly my request, that I would have the right to live wherever and for whatever periods of time I deem necessary in each of my three estates upon which buildings already exist, and that I go to my Arles property only once every six months after having obtained specific permission

---

4. About twelve miles.

to do so. Concerning which, I note that the affairs of that estate being the most pressing and the most in need of my intervention, I urgently request that the first of these tacit permissions be accorded me for this coming September, and consequently that it be issued to me almost simultaneously with the king's order exiling me to my three estates.

And now, may I further ask that this entire arrangement be kept shrouded in complete silence? What need is there for the public to have news of my affairs? The officer of the mounted constabulary, or whoever might be designated as his deputy, seem to me the only persons who need to be informed, the timing being left to your discretion. It will be a simple matter to enjoin these people to silence. After all the misfortunes I have suffered in this province, is it not understandable that I greatly desire to resurface there with the appearance, if not the reality, of being a free man? From this kind of restriction of movement that will be imposed upon me there may even result some slight positive good in the eyes of the local population, who, not knowing why I am so seemingly attentive to local matters, will perhaps little by little bestow upon me once again the esteem and respect whereof my misfortunes have stripped me. When from an accident one can easily reap some positive good, why would one hesitate to do so? I leave that reflection to your extreme sagacity, Monsieur, being convinced that if you find it fair and equitable, your many kindnesses on my behalf will convince the minister to allow this plan to be implemented, especially since it seems to me to have no possible negative implications. My respect for the king's letter will be in no wise diminished, even though its contents not be known to the world at large or that I go so far as to deny its very existence, and the officer of the mounted constabulary will still be available to report upon the accuracy and promptitude of my conduct.

Allow me now if I may, Monsieur, to broach the question of my desire not to travel under guard, and as for my time of departure and the route I shall follow, that it be made a matter of my word of honor, as will my request to see my children before I leave and the urgent necessity both my wife and I feel that we repair to my estates as early as possible. Let us, if you would be so kind, take up each of these articles in the same order I have set them out for you.

First article: travel on my word of honor.

You are infinitely too fair-minded, Monsieur, not to agree that to have me taken under police escort to the very place where I myself desire to go is the most pointless thing in the world. When I broke free of my bonds, 'twas to my estates that I repaired.[5] What would be the purpose therefore of having me return there under guard? 'Twould be both a needless expense imposed on me and an overabundance of means that are quite unnecessary to the occasion.

Second article: concerning the departure and the route to be followed.

Everyone knows how many days it takes to travel from Paris to Apt in Provence. I ask that I not be forced to travel too rapidly, both because my current state of health will not allow it and because I have not traveled in some time now and have lost the habit. Let us suppose that I was allowed to travel to La Coste, near Apt, from the first to the fourteenth of June, which is allowing for four days more than the normal travel time for such a voyage, the details of which we shall shortly set forth. Monsieur de Rougemont signs me out on June 1st; if one wants to verify each one of my nightly stopovers, one can enlist whatever number of brigadiers of the mounted constabulary to do so, and then Monsieur Blancard can attest to my arrival at my estate on the fourteenth. That, it seems to me, would fulfill the letter of the law. If further security is deemed necessary, that means having me followed, as I have already said. But I must confess that I would have good reason to be deeply pained to see that, from the very start, one might suppose me capable of making so light of a tie to which I shall be bound for far longer than the mere length of the voyage itself. But on that score I shall abide by whatever you decide, as I have already said. All I am doing is making a request, in no wise laying down any conditions, and my heart is filled with only gratitude, nothing more.

Third article: to see my children.

'Tis in this article that will be found the explanation for the four extra days I have requested.

'Tis most urgently that I ask to see my children, and here is what I think would be more fair and equitable both to maintain my security and to fulfill my desire not to have the children moved too far from the place where they are being brought up, which is near Fontainebleau. Thus the site where we might meet could be either Melun, which is the post stop directly beyond Fontainebleau, or Nemours, which is the stop just before. For argument's sake, let us say Nemours. The boys'

---

5. Sade is referring to his escape, despite the presence of four armed guards, on his way back from his appeals trial in Aix on July 17, 1778. After his escape he repaired, as he notes, to La Coste.

governess will bring them there from Fontainebleau, my wife will bring her daughter from her end, and I shall arrive there from Vincennes; and the appointed day will be that same day when I am scheduled to be released, the voyage by post between Vincennes and Nemours being infinitely easy, no matter how leisurely the pace. Once there, I shall report forthwith to the brigadier of the mounted constabulary, who can vouch for my arrival and with whom, twice a day thereafter, I shall promptly check in until my departure, concerning which, when those four days I will be spending with my children will have come to an end, he can also verify that I have indeed left in the direction of Provence rather than in any other direction; moreover, since I shall be free both within our lodgings and in the city itself, my wife and I may well decide to take our children out for a breath of fresh air. For, as far as my having a police escort, I had not pondered that properly when the question was raised the other day. For first of all, if as I trust they take me at my word, there will be no more need for a guard at Nemours than there will be anywhere else along the rest of the route. For if it so happened that I were to remain for three or four days in one inn along the way, that should pose no greater a problem than if I were to stay a single extra night in the other inns along the way: 'tis absolutely one and the same. Therefore it is simply a formality, a matter of bending the rules so that the voyage is a trifle longer. The other evenings I shall report to the brigadier only once, since I shall be on my way again the following morning. But for the initial sojourn[6] I shall report in eight times,[7] since I shall be there for four days. And moreover, Monsieur, allow me if you will to address myself for a moment only to your heart. A guard . . . a third party, between a father and his children! What an obstacle! What an incredible impediment to the free flow of those delightful tears that Nature dictates in such precious moments as these! Tears which, if I may be so bold, are in themselves sufficient to reawaken in any sensitive soul both remorse for one's past misdeeds and the voice of virtue. Ah, Monsieur! do not stand in the way of those tears! they will be more persuasive than all the locks of Vincennes. Do let them flow unimpeded, let them be received in the bosom of these beloved children, with no one but their mother for witness. I shall almost forgo the divine pleasure that I keep promising myself will result from those tears if they were to be witnessed by, or

---

6. That is, the days when he will be with his children.
7. Morning and evening.

chilled by, either shackles of any kind or by the odious presence of any persons whose only talent lies in provoking them.

Fourth article: the necessity for my wife to be in my estates with me.

Let us pass now to the last article, which sets forth why my wife is needed with me in my estates.

As far as my business affairs are concerned, though she may well be less able to manage our affairs than I, for the simple reason that, hers being a decent soul quite incapable of even imagining evil, she cannot fancy that anyone would or could ever desire to act in a dishonest manner against her; yet she is more up-to-date than I, having held the rudder alone for almost ten years now: during the period both of my sentence in absentia[8] and my detention itself, she was the person in full charge of our affairs. Therefore it is quite impossible for me to undertake anything without her counsel and advice. Even to imagine that we might exchange counsel by letter at a distance of a hundred and fifty leagues[9] is excessive, both for her and me. We would have to spend entire days and nights writing back and forth, and besides, no letter is ever worth an opinion, a piece of advice, given on the spot. Such advice, such an opinion, often determines one's decision relative to some important matter, such as the offer of a lease, where a man of goodwill wants to be taken at his word and who, if asked for a delay before a reply is forthcoming, might well rescind his offer. In closing this matter, Monsieur, let no one accuse me, in what I am about to say, either of ill will or of trying to lay down the law. But if my wife does not come with me, then as far as my estates are concerned I can manage them no better there than I could were I still in Vincennes or the Tower of Crest.

May I be so bold, Monsieur—and this is only between you and me—as to set forth one other reason more important for my peace of mind, the general tranquillity of both my heart and mind, than for the immediate necessities whereof I spoke? This heart, which you have been kind enough to let me bare to you, has, over the period I have been separated from her,[10] been filled with remorse at not having recognized the full degree of tenderness, of attachment to her various duties, of love for her children, in short, of all her many virtues which I scarcely deserved and which I so sorely misjudged. And as I was in the

8. The Marseilles sentence.
9. Roughly the distance between Paris and La Coste.
10. Renée-Pélagie.

throes of this remorse, a frightful notion would sometimes seize hold of me. *What if I were to have the misfortune of losing her without ever having had the chance to make amends!* And that cruel idea straightway plunged me into the very depths of the most painful despair. The hope of this sincere return toward an object so worthy of all the feelings with which my soul is filled, the hope of making amends, so long overdue, that presently seem possible; could I refrain from confessing to you that the desire to take advantage of this opportunity is one of the fiercest I have ever felt? Ah! Monsieur, 'twould be to acknowledge but poorly all your many kindnesses toward me if I were to refrain from thus opening my heart to you in all candor, which I trust you will understand stems from my frightful situation. Yes, Monsieur, I wish to see her, to love her, to dry her tears that my misdeeds have caused her to shed, and to experience at long last that gentle and peaceful state that no man can know except through virtue, and that virtue only truly prepares him for in the sweet pleasures of Hymen.

Please forgive me, Monsieur, for so many details and so much sincerity. The day before yesterday you led me to believe that I was confiding only in a father or a friend. This comforting illusion has been the moving force behind this letter, a letter that is the work of my heart and which yours, surely, will not disavow. Yet I end it by beseeching you to do your utmost to convince everyone concerned to acquiesce completely to all my most urgent requests, and by swearing to you, as I would at the foot of an altar, that they will never have any reason to regret having done so. 'Tis with these true feelings, to which I add my most profound gratitude, that I have the honor of being, Monsieur, your most humble and most obedient servant.

DE SADE

42. To Mademoiselle de Rousset

[April 20–25, 1781]

After having spent my week working like a brute, so as not to take unfair advantage of the ten days of respite I had asked for, I flattered myself that I at least might, like the maker of heaven and earth, take Sunday as a day of rest. And I must say in all honesty that I needed that rest. Badly. And lo and behold! who should arrive *from Montélimar but a young man still wet behind the ears* to force me to write. So, my dear young lady, you can read into this letter whatever you like, for I have neither the strength to compose it nor the mind to make it coherent.

How is it possible that a person as bright and full of common sense as you . . . you who has seen with your own eyes the very properties of which I speak, how can you say, or be quoted as saying, that I can manage my affairs from Montélimar? In truth, that is an ineptitude on your part which I will find impossible to forgive, unless it turns out you are simply echoing someone else's words. But it smacks too much of the same old tune for me to be fooled or taken in by it. Everything that emanates from that source is so obvious that one can divine the contents of the letter even before one breaks the seal. *My business affairs from Montélimar!* I can manage my affairs from Montélimar to the exact same degree that I can manage them from the Vincennes dungeon. My business affairs are such that they can only be taken care of on the spot. Even were I to be exiled to my château at La Coste, but not allowed to visit all my other premises, the task would be impossible. And you well know that when the slaves of *la présidente* came looking for me to serve up the second or the fourth *of her little cannibalistic banquets*,[1] I was on my way to Saumane. You heard me say to Pépin[2] day after day: "Impossible, Monsieur, to see and make up my mind about all that except on the spot. I must go there." 'Tis not by listening to some business adviser's report, telling me as much or as little as he deems suitable, that I can properly conduct my affairs. In fact, chances are that by so doing I would harm more than help, basing any decision upon what he chooses to tell me . . . I believe him . . . I take him at his word . . . I agree, and I sign, and am therefore bound by that decision. To put some semblance of order in all that, not only must one be physically present but one must also pay the least heed to one's business adviser. In any given matter, one must speak to everyone involved, listen to what they all have to say, see both enemies and friends, then combine all that with what your adviser has to say, and come up with a decision that is both wise and equitable. Do you want an example of what I am saying, one I believe you will find incontestable, an example you witnessed with your very own eyes?

---

1. Sade is referring to the several attempts by the police, funded by Madame de Montreuil, to arrest him at La Coste.
2. One of Sade's Provençal stewards, specifically in charge of Saumane.

Let us suppose that the situation is precisely the same as it was when you came to see me at La Coste, and let us further imagine that I am at Montélimar and Gaufridy comes to see me there, in order to set forth that same matter and ask that I make my decision. Now let us see how it might go.

"Monsieur," he begins by saying, "Chauvin³ is the most honest man on the face of the earth. I cannot find a single fault in the way he manages the farm. His conduct, in short, is impeccable. When you come to La Coste, you may find there are those who speak ill of him, but you should pay them no heed, they are his enemies. In consideration for which, Monsieur, I have renewed his lease. At a slight loss, to be sure, but as a man of honor I had no other choice."

What do I do, I who see and hear only Gaufridy, I who am bound and confined to my noble prison in Montélimar, I who can see neither the lands themselves nor the peasants who dwell thereon, neither the friends nor the enemies of Chauvin? I assure Monsieur Gaufridy that he is right, that Chauvin has behaved like an angel, and as a result I sign the new lease and am bound to honor it. Then let us suppose further that I arrive at La Coste and what do I learn? I have made a completely stupid mistake, and I did so because it pleases Madame la présidente de Montreuil not to be content with ten years of vengeance and therefore, irrespective of *whether or not it leads to the ruin* of my children, her rage, which knows no bounds or reason, perforce demands even greater revenge.

Let this single example, Mademoiselle, suffice to convince you once and for all that it is absolutely impossible to manage my affairs properly other than on the premises, and further, that I need to be physically present for several successive months at each property to make sure that everything is back on track. It is therefore clear that making decisions from Montélimar will result in nothing but absurdities, and that chances are I shall in all likelihood not only make matters even worse than they were but perhaps to such a degree that they become irreparable both for me and for my children.

Either Gaufridy is an honest man or he is not. If he is, then he can very well manage without me; and if he is not, then I ought to manage without him, in which case I need to be on the premises. There: I've had my say on the matter, short and to the point, but sufficiently I trust

---

3. Sade was doubtless paranoid, but sometimes not without good reason; Chauvin was surely profiting from his absence.

to make you understand, when you are of a mind to see through your own eyes rather than through those of the villainous beast who poisons my life, that it is physically and morally impossible for me to do anything from Montélimar except the same silly songs and dances that I have been doing here. I hereby declare to you that that will be my sole occupation, and in consequence I give you my most solemn word of honor that I have no intention whatsoever of getting involved in any matters other than those that I have been attending to here. Therefore, it is perfectly useless that Gaufridy be made to come here. I declare by all that's holy that not only shall I refuse to see him but that, if I am forced to do so, I shall see him with the sole purpose of heaping upon him all the abuse at my command, and showering him with all the invectives that such a rogue deserves—for it was as a rogue, and as a traitor, knowing full well what fate had in store for me, that he came to eat at my table and drink my wine—you were there, you saw him—without warning me of the thunderbolt poised above my head, ready to strike, and in connection of which, if I may be allowed to use this expression, the villainous beggar *was preparing the sulphur.*[4] No, I shall never forgive those who betrayed me, nor shall I ever lay eyes on them as long as I live. If my affair[5] had been such that it lasted for six months, or even a year, and that that was the price I had to pay to atone for it, yes, I might have forgotten, but when it undermines both my mind and my health, when it dishonors forever both me and my children, when in a word it results—as you will see—in the most frightful problems for the future, those who in any way had a hand in it are two-faced, double-dealing liars whom I shall loathe with all my heart and soul to my dying day. The only person I shall hold exempt is my wife, who I know also betrayed me, but she has been taken in by what people told her and would otherwise never have done what she has, of that I would swear by thrusting my hand into a flame. As you can see, I am fully capable of doing her that justice. The methods they are proposing to take with me are shameful; they are odious; they are disgraceful. What

---

4. Sade has long suspected, not without reason, that Madame de Montreuil has been conniving with Gaufridy behind his back. In this instance, Sade insinuates Gaufridy's involvement in his rearrest at La Coste was not passive but active.
5. The Marseilles affair, which he blames for his by now four-plus years in prison, even though the sentence was overturned in appeal. But by "affair" he is lumping together all the so-called scandals that had landed him in Vincennes.

is the sense of making a spectacle of me by exiling me to the property of one of my cousins? It is mine that needs tending, not his. Have I not been sufficiently paraded about, have I not been sufficiently displayed throughout Provence and the neighboring provinces? Have I not been sufficiently talked about over the past ten years? Is it not time to extinguish the flames rather than fan them anew? There is but one fury, a fury escaped from hell to the detriment of my children and me, who may have a different view on all this. And moreover, shouldn't she— this unworthy woman—know that the more she focuses attention on me the more she focuses it in reverse measure upon herself and upon everything that concerns her? Our interests are too closely bound together in all this for her not to understand the importance of curbing the public's mordant curiosity about me, which can only redound to her discredit. But she is a monster, who has delivered herself over to people who are robbing her blind and laughing at her behind her back, to police lackeys, to ne'er-do-wells dragged in off the street, and a whole host of others who, if she had the slightest self-respect, she would have prevented from making any contact with even the least of her servants. Here is her advice. And Monsieur de Sartine,[6] my worst enemy on the face of the earth, the man to whom I owe my life's every misfortune, and who, at a time in my life when I ought to have turned a tiger's head—*twenty years old, newly married, having at that youthful age already fought for my country in six campaigns, leaving for Fontainebleau to meet with a minister who had just promised me a regiment of the king's men*— yes, I dare say, in a situation that would have turned the head of a tiger, caught me in this situation,[7] which he viewed as a rung on the ladder of his fortune, and brought me low, sacrificed me solely to make people say: "What an excellent police lieutenant! He plays no favorites!" And so it was that I was delivered over to him and his ilk! And so it was that I am placed in the hands of scoundrels who dispose of my honor, my fortune, and that of my children. Poor unfortunate creatures! One day you will realize how right I was. May my letters fall into your hands and teach you the truth, and may you learn therefrom both how much your father[8] loved you and how your enemies were stabbing you in the back!

---

6. Antoine de Sartine, the lieutenant-general of all Paris police, who was instrumental in getting Sade arrested and keeping him in prison.
7. The Rose Keller affair.
8. Sade, writing paternalistically, doubtless means himself.

Supplement

Finally, if Montélimar is for my own good, why hide from me the manner by which I'm to be taken there? After all the suffering I've endured, why all this difficulty explaining to me the details of my transfer? We're not dealing with an affair of State here, and yet never has Damiens[9] been more worried, more convoluted, more steeped in mystery. What? Because the words "government" and "minister" inflate that odious creature like a frog, I am obliged to spend my life as the dupe and the victim of her twisted machinations? If, I say, this Montélimar is to improve my lot, then why not come out and say so to my face? And if it is to better my situation, why take me there under guard? Who, if my lot is thereby improved, would doubt that I would go there of my own volition? But Monsieur Le Noir's toadies must be bribed, is that not so? . . . Ah, yes indeed, 'tis thus that these gentlemen put into their pockets the million the king allots to the Paris police. *They pocket it and make us pay.* How unspeakable! And they hang a poor wretch who has stolen five *sous!* One more thing, Mademoiselle: I request that I not be taken there under guard. I shall never consent to pay these official escorts, I give you my word. Let me be shadowed, if they insist, I have no objection; and if I should deviate one iota from the agreed-upon itinerary, may all the mounted police of France swoop down upon me. But why escort me under guard? Why? Absolutely convinced that all they want is to steal another six or seven thousand francs from me, when I am offering an equivalent guarantee amount that will cost me no more than fifty *louis* . . . All that is nothing more than the police being overly zealous! . . . But what good does it do me to beg and beseech? Whenever I do, Monsieur de Rougemont says *I'm trying to lay down the law!* My initial response to that remark was that I was making a request, not trying to make any law, and I would be grateful if they would forthwith cease twisting my words to suit their own purposes. There are people who are delighted to have you feed them lines, since they're completely incapable of making any up on their own. Et *beatus* . . .

P.S. You know Latin.

What do my advice and opinions matter? This morning I told Monsieur de Rougemont that I did not want to be transferred under guard, and if they absolutely insisted on doing so it would be necessary to tie

---

9. Madame de Montreuil.

me up and take me by force. And like the true gentleman he is, he replied—and I quote—*"That should pose no problem!"* So you can see, after such a remark, what does my opinion matter? They can come whenever they please, but until my dying breath I shall say and shall write unceasingly, that I never shall consent to be taken under guard, and if that should happen it will be in spite of me. Moreover, I shall always have it as proof positive that I am in no wise responsible for any payment thereof, for the very reason that I never consented to it of my own free will.

A decent fellow, you say, will escort me there. What in the devil did you have in mind when you wrote that? You know just as well as I that people who exercise that profession can hardly be called "decent." The insolent manner in which Inspector Marais conducted himself with respect to you should suffice to convince you on that score. Know, my lovely young lady, that there are no decent people who practice that profession. Those who do are riffraff straight off the streets, many of whom have barely escaped the hangman's noose, such (to cite but one example) as a knave named Muron, who was chief of a band of thieves in Lyons and who is still very active in the profession today, or at least was until very recently. He escaped just as the police were moving in to arrest his men, and he was clever enough to disguise himself and volunteer for the army as soon as he was back in Lyons. And 'twas there he was plucked to fulfill the noble post at Paris that you tell me is filled with decent and honest people. There you have a firsthand example, which I have witnessed myself, that can serve to show you in what high esteem this noble post is held in today's world. Another example: an infantry officer discharged in '48, when the war was over, as unfit for service, somehow managed, several years later at the start of the following war, to obtain a post of police inspector, in which guise he arrived one day in Strasbourg, acting as police escort for a prisoner. Unfortunately for him, his former regimental comrades-in-arms were stationed in that same city. The officers met, enticed their former, unsuspecting colleague into meeting them, whereupon they tore his uniform from his back and escorted him to the hillside fortifications at the edge of town, striking him with their canes and the flat of their swords the entire way. So you see, Mademoiselle, the high esteem in which these "decent people," who comprise the noble body of which you speak, are held. And, in truth, one should have had by now one's fill of subjecting me to such rascals. This woman[10] so haughty in her use of the words "minister" and "government," is far less so when it comes to

---

10. Madame de Montreuil.

her deeds, that is all I can say. But there is a proverb that goes: *"The shoemaker always smells of leather."*

" 'Tis in order to put you to the test that you are being sent to Montélimar; your interest and your happiness will depend on how you pass that test." Let me respond to that lovely sentence. First, I have been put to the test; there is no point in repeating it; they have seen how I behaved myself at La Coste during the time I thought myself free. Let them free me again, I shall behave in the same way, always with probity and as a man of honor and feeling, a good husband and good father, so long as I shall be free and in France. But so long as I am not free, I shall be as bad as I can be. That is an article of faith you can count on, and upon which I give you my word of honor.

Moreover, how can they judge me at Montélimar? Either I shall be free or I shall not. If I am not, how judge a man who is confined to his room? If I am, the problem will be the same, for I shall not leave the premises. As you may well imagine, since I loathe making scenes as I loathe drawing people's attention to me, I shall not exactly rush into public view, bearing the stigmata of my chains on my back. Therefore, how can anyone judge me? These so-called tests are pure sophisms, moreover, and I am going to convince you on that score with a word that will prove to you both that I am not a hypocrite and that I have no desire to impose my will, since I am going to let you in on this little secret. A man is cured or he is not: there is no in-between. If he is, he will act honorably; and if he is not he will be clever enough, knowing that everything depends on it, to curb himself for a certain period of time to make people believe he is cured. Then let the world judge him. That, Mademoiselle, is all nonsense, stupidity, protocol, I say to you, and to what end? To bribe the police lackeys, that is the sole and unique purpose.

Therefore, perish the very thought that my self-interest and happiness are dependent upon Montélimar. I tell you once again, with no ill humor intended—I can say that I feel perhaps less ill-humored today than I have at any time in my life—that my intention is to leave France no later than six months after my release: there is nothing more certain in the world than that. Remember one circumstance: I was completely free at La Coste, and convinced that I would remain so. And to what use did I put that initial period of freedom? Within a fortnight of my release had I not already taken the first step toward implementing my plan? And as you may well recall, I urgently begged you to put me in contact with a certain consul you knew in the Barbary States. Check with Chauvin and ask him whether or not I had ordered him, the very next time he was going to Marseilles, to stop by La Coste, so that he could run a very important errand for me. If I had had a trifle more time, you would have known what that errand was: *bring to La Coste the representative of one of those three countries, who is stationed in Marseilles,*[11] *so that I could work out my arrangements with him.* I was nevertheless free at that time, and unpressured, or so I thought. Yes, Mademoiselle, either there in the Barbary States or in Prussia is where the novel of my life will have its denouement. And you may be quite sure that I say it without any ill humor and without finishing the sentence with some sarcastic remark, which if I listened to my heart could quite easily, and quite naturally, be the case. So you can clearly see that everything they are doing is perfectly useless, and it would be infinitely preferable to let me profit from the few years I have left by making proper plans for my dismal old age—if indeed I have any—by granting me my freedom to tie up a few affairs essential to the welfare of my children, and then clear out as soon as possible. That would be infinitely better than making me waste my time, as they are presently doing, for if they are counting on my changing my mind, they had better know I never shall. My mind is made up whether I am free or behind bars, and I shall carry out my plans or I shall die in the effort, in which wise all that will be needed is six feet of earth: may God bring me soon to that blessèd moment! I shall be free of more than my share of grief.

Is there anything more charming in the world than your announcing to me that *"they will take precautions to make sure my presence remains a secret during my transfer?"* Well, now! What does that mean? 'Tis a lovely little mockery, that charming sentence. "Make sure my presence remains a secret during my transfer," only to arrive with great fanfare in Montélimar! That's a bit like that silly fool who, on his way to the ball at the Opera, donned his mask at the far end of the rue Saint-Honoré, only to take it off when he entered the ball. Do you realize that *Madame de Montreuil's advice sometimes contains glimmers of reason, flashes of wisdom* that are truly frightening? Take care to conceal me the entire length of the voyage, then make public my presence in Montélimar after I arrive! Good God, imagine the mind capable of concocting such a plan! How do you imagine I'll be viewed after that? And that they know 'tis me! Quite impossible!

---

11. One can only surmise what other country Sade had in mind, but the most logical would be Italy, which Sade knew and liked. (See Letter 61.)

The only way to avoid making scenes, Mademoiselle, and the only reasonable way of proceeding, is simply to send me alone to my estates, on my word of honor. If they are afraid I might digress from my route, let them have a spy follow me, with orders to summon forth the entire constabulary to track me down if I should deviate one iota. It seems to me that what I offer is more than reasonable.

Your Montélimar project is so prodigiously stupid, so unimaginative, so heavy-handed, so imbecilic, that I confess there are times when I find it impossible to cram it into my brain; at which point here is what I put in its place:

At Montélimar, the police escort will tell me he has orders to bring me to my place of abode. And in that case here is all they want: to *"escort me,"* in order to make certain that I do not stop off anywhere, especially not in Paris or in Lyons; *"escort me,"* so that an inexperienced police escort can learn once again the ways and byways to my place of abode, and thereby know the various transfer points, for such is the high-minded thinking of la présidente: corrupt the vassals, corrupt the domestics, turn them into spies. Oh! When she has done that, you see, she fancies that is all it takes, and thinks she is holding all the cards. She has had that nasty little habit ever since her dear husband, the président, began betraying her, *with his oh so minor infidelities*; she acted as if she were the jealous wife, the better to conceal her own whoring tendencies, and although she for her part never hesitated to help herself to whomsoever she fancied—the major proof of which, it is said, is that Madame de Sade is her only sure legitimate child of the twelve she has brought into this world—the better, therefore, I say, to conceal her own behavior, she corrupted the président's valets, bribed spies to follow his carriage, etc., and 'tis from there that her obsession with *spies, and police lackeys and police escorts* derived. Yes, therein lies its origin. In return for which, 'tis therefore clear as the nose on your face that the only reason for all this would be to prevent me from stopping off somewhere along the route and to bribe some scoundrel to spy on me. Let us examine the futility of both projects. What is the use of taking so many precautions to keep me from stopping off in such and such a city, since as soon as I am set free, I shall be the master of my own movements to go back wherever I please, and you may be most sure I shall do just that. And what is the point of having spies on my premises since I have no intention of remaining there any longer than it takes to make my arrangements to go abroad for the rest of my life? Were I to recognize them as such—as spies, that is—or merely suspect them—I should break both their arms. La présidente has already forced me to take such action against two or three of her rogues in Paris, as I'm sure she remembers all too well! To start in again with new scandals, perhaps new troubles of one sort or another, that's all. What! That wretched hussy won't leave me alone once and for all in my life? *She doesn't want to understand that as long as I feel the slightest chain holding me back, I'll commit one offensive act after another:* haven't I convinced her of that during the ten years it has pleased her to allow my affair to drag on? And is it for that reason she wants it to drag on even longer, so that she can accumulate further proof? No, I submit that never has a creature so dogged, so obsessed with evil as she, ever seen the light of day.

And, why, therefore, do you not want me to write my family, and what do you understand by "my family"? The only family I acknowledge are those related to my father, and nothing on the face of the earth or in the heavens above could keep me from writing to or loving them. The more they remind me of an adored being,[12] who would most surely not have allowed me to suffer as long as I have, the more they are near and dear to me, and if ever there is something I shall miss by leaving France it will be they and they alone. And I reply to you that my first effort will be to write them as soon as I can to tell them how much I love them. In short, Mademoiselle, here is the result of my reflection, broken down article by article. I place it at the end of my letter in order to make it easier to refer to whenever one so desires, all the more so since these will in all likelihood be my final reflections and final prayers.

May they be read in that spirit, and not in the sense of laying down any laws, knowing full well that in my wretched state I am in no position to do so, and assuring you that were I in a position to do so, the first law I would lay down would be to have *la présidente burned at the stake over a very slow flame.*

Summing Up

1. I am ready and willing to leave,[13] because I have no other choice and because, moreover, I have hopes to be better off than I am, in re-

---

12. Sade seems to have adored his father much more after Jean-Baptiste's death than he did before.
13. For Montélimar.

turn for which I agree to leave whenever one would like, my only request being that I be given till Thursday to wind up what I have begun.

2. I most insistently request that I not be guarded during my journey. If one absolutely insists on this score, I shall nonetheless leave, because I cannot resist force, but never shall I pay the police escort,[14] and *I shall take my revenge on those responsible for this scurrilous act by any and all means, including the worst I can dream up.*

3. I ask that I be allowed to go to my own estates and not to Montélimar, and if one insists on going through with the insipid and ridiculous project of Montélimar, I shall remain in my room throughout the voyage, without ever coming out, and as a result without ever offering anyone the sweet pleasure of judging me, and I give my word that not for one moment shall I attend to my business affairs, and I further request that Gaufridy be informed that under no circumstances should he come to see me, for if he dares do so he will be badly received.

4. If on the contrary my request is granted, that is, a fortnight in Paris in my wife's home in order to see my children, and thence to leave for my estates, whether exiled or not, then I give my most solemn word of honor that I shall do nothing that will make anyone other than completely satisfied with my conduct. And I end by swearing to you, Mademoiselle, that they who dispose of my fate will have every reason to be pleased and satisfied by granting what I desire, and every reason *to sorely regret it* if they refuse.

Were I to write twenty letters, I would say the same thing over and over again, of that I feel certain; 'tis therefore a complete waste of time to speak further about it. On Wednesday, and surely not later than Thursday, I shall send my manuscript[15] to Madame de Sade. If between now and then I think of something further, I shall include it in what I have to instruct her regarding the manuscript. If on the contrary I do not think of anything further to offer, I shall simply put at the bottom of the letter that I base my position on the contents of my letter to you, and from that moment on I shall not utter another word on the

14. Under the monarchy, aristocrats being brought to prison, or being transferred from one prison to another under police escort, had the added indignity of having to pay for their guards.
15. In all probability, his five-act comedy *L'Inconstant*, which later was retitled *Le Capricieux.*

subject. That will be proof that I have no intention of changing my mind: therefore 'twill be absolutely pointless to speak to me about it again. In which case, one can come whenever one chooses, I shall be ready; I shall leave peacefully, without so much as a word about it, *but we shall see how things proceed thereafter.* I embrace you tenderly, my dear Mademoiselle, and only hope that before I leave this most accursed of countries, I may have the pleasure of embracing you one more time other than by letters.

43. *To Madame de Sade*

[April 30, 1781]

*I*t would appear, from your sublime letter of April 26th, received the 30th, that Milli Rousset is not the only one whose mind is growing, by God! What an expenditure you have just made! At least take care, for nothing is more debilitating than those efforts; one is surprised to ramble on incoherently at the age of forty, and then upon further reflection one sees that that is where it comes from!

I shall send you the manuscript tomorrow or the day after. I wanted to send with it a short dissertation, which I am working on—for my mind, too, is growing with the springtime—a dissertation *on the dangers of solitude and the deadly effects of prisons where solitude is the order of the day.* But it will not be ready in time. 'Tis perhaps the only composition for which I did not need to consult a single reference work; *my experience alone* was sufficient, and since it is written with a great deal of moderation, and without a trace of ill humor, I have no compunction, in forwarding it to you, about submitting it to the authorities for their inspection.[1]

I have already replied concerning the paper, the various things I need, the presumed departure, etc., those that are necessary, since I am still here, the departure not yet having taken place. The same applies for the great coats, the clothing, etc., and since all that was in very simple, straightforward letters, I am sure you must have received them. Thus if you turn a deaf ear to what I request, so be it, in return for which I shall simply say that it matters little to me. If you send, I

---

1. That is, the prison censor.

shall receive; if you do not, I shall do without; you know very well what I need; that is enough, and I shall not make mention of it again.

Do you realize that you were at great risk in becoming involved in these wretched matters? I knew them like the back of my hand, and it bothered me to know you were amongst them but it was pointless to tell you; you would have responded with idle chatter."[2] Alas! I am no more than the lowest of the low, and I have never had the least inkling about how to run a state, much less a city; but since I do believe in metempsychosis, if ever I were to be reborn in the body of some municipal or state administrator, I would promulgate a law whereby men *could do whatever they so pleased with whores*, and I would also dictate that 'twas forbidden the authorities to try to ferret out dirt and thereby risk the lives of seven or eight thousand citizens, especially since I would have striking examples to back me up, including that of 1778.[3] But I repeat, that is because I am nothing more than the lowest of the low.

I have never known anything quite like the fact that you have turned a deaf ear to the copy of the letter I asked you to pass on to Monsieur Le Noir. Alas! Good Lord, if that letter was not up to snuff, then what kind of letter, I pray, must one write these days? I can make neither head nor tail of it. You seem intent on driving me to distraction. The inconsistency of what you are doing is only exceeded by its stupidity. 'Tis becoming increasingly clear that la présidente is growing old; of late her machinations no longer have the freshness, the brilliance, the ingenious force they once had! Oh! no, verily, these days her works are scarcely recognizable; they were far more sublime in earlier days! Above all, do not forget to send a large trunk full of provisions the day before I am due to be transferred, because as you recall that is precisely what she did at Pierre-Encize; we must at least make a show of staying true to our old selves.

Do you know who used to own that house across from the Luxembourg Gardens? Oh! I'm sure you know as well as I. It was the old Maillé mansion. My grandparents lived there during the reign of Louis XIII. A huge number of Maillés lived there, and today 'twould surprise me if even a tenant farmer would want to hang his hat there.

But what is the point of your seeing me once a final decision has been made regarding my fate? At that time I must leave, and you with

2. The French term Sade uses is "lanterne." Interestingly, a decade later that term took on a sinister meaning: to hang people from a lamppost.
3. Sade is referring to his arrest on August 25 of that year, when he was bound and summarily hustled out of La Coste.

me, that is absolutely essential; and if that request is denied me, what they are doing is forcing me to commit yet another stupidity, whatever it may be, for you may be sure I shall come and fetch you, even if you are in the very depths of Hell. Is that the reason you refuse to let me know where you are lodged? Oh! that does not worry me, be assured, 'twill take me no more than half an hour to search you out.

Yet 'tis passing strange that people should keep it a secret from the husband the place where his wife is living! If I were spiteful or malicious, and if I wanted to rake over the old coals one day . . . what weapons would be available to me!

I was going to return the six volumes to Mérigot. You may tell him for me that he will not receive a single one, even were I to be locked up here for another ten years, so long as he fails to send me another ten or twelve volumes for further reading. I cannot and will not read *Maintenon* in the evening; at least buy me Bougainville,[4] I've been asking you for it for a century. I've repeated to you a thousand times, 'tis unspeakable that I be reduced to begging for books. For the past fortnight I've been buying, book by book, a kind of bright candle for which they charge me one crown per book; and for the past fortnight you have been aware of it; therefore, send me a store of candles or I shall pack my trunk. I would not be taking any great risk in so doing: a month ago today *Monsieur le Commandment de Rougemont* told me that I should do so. But unfortunately, four years of experience have taught me that the truth and de Rougemont are the two most incompatible things on the face of the earth, and that he enjoys tricking the poor wretches under his command the same way others enjoy hunting or fishing. Thus his giving me notice that I should start packing was all the impetus I needed to begin making little preparations for spending the summer here, which I would not have dreamed of doing without his charitable act. *Omnis homo mendax*—the man is a complete liar. I do not believe any mortal more deserves that proverb than he. Be that as it may, I promise that next time we see each other I shall make you laugh. You are well aware of my great talent for making things up; you shall see how I made good use of it, *whenever I have fasted, after dinner,* etc.

What is this latest nonsense, which I've heard an endless number of times? *Ask to see Milli Rousset wherever I may be?* Either I shall be at my estates or I shall be here, there is no middle ground. I have gone on

---

4. Bougainville's four-year trip was documented in his multi-volume work *Voyages autour du monde (Voyage around the World)*.

about this far too long with Monsieur Le Noir; he felt so, too, and has talked to me on that subject like a judge, with what seemed to me utter honesty, wisdom, and I must say humanity. I can only commend him for it. I do believe that he is incapable of lying to me. In which wise, if I remain here, Mademoiselle Rousset knows full well that she cannot come and see me. And if I am at my estates, 'twill be up to her to request permission, *to come and try to woo me.* And I shall grant her request, but only *under certain conditions,* which are pointless to lay out, since it's of no concern to you. You have my permission to forewarn her of such.

What I see all too clearly in all this is that you will not be coming with me. In which case, my angel, we shall do our best to replace you, which is all I can say.[5] As I shall have absolutely naught to do—since without you 'tis quite impossible to even try to sort out my affairs— since I shall have nothing to do except rest, I shall sow a few little flowers on this peaceful repose with the help of Mademoiselle de Rousset *on the one hand,* and the pleasant surroundings *on the other,* and you can come whenever you please: you will find us holding our breath and in excellent spirits!

Yes, I can well imagine that the rumors about my business manager[6] may well have changed: up till now, he was thought of as no more than a plain rogue; now he must of necessity be thought of as a double-dealing crook and a traitor. And if the path upon which he has now clearly embarked is any indication, he may well be a worthy candidate for the gallows. That is how I view the matter in any event, and I embrace you.

Please request, I beg of you, that the manuscript be given to you without delay, and above all read the Author's Note before you begin the play. You can read it aloud with Mademoiselle Rousset, whom I ask to continue her efforts with the critics.[7]

I embrace you.

But I most urgently ask that you not show the play to anyone else except Mademoiselle de Rousset or to Amblet. Within a month at the

---

5. Sade is trying to make his wife jealous by implying he was, or will be, having an affair with Milli Rousset.

6. Again, Gaufridy. Sade has heard rumors that his once-trusted notary has been bought off by Madame de Montreuil.

7. Among her other devoted services, Milli Rousset was trying to see if she could interest drama critics in Sade's plays and get them performed.

very most I shall need to see a dentist. Remember, you promised you
would see to it.

44. To Madame de Sade

[May 21, 1781]

*T*here is nothing so charming as your little plan, but you reveal
therein an excess of malice: such in any case is how I view it.
Without the malice, it would be utterly delightful. Let us examine it
closely. You (or yours) are desirous of bettering my lot or of bringing
my punishment to an end; the only thing is, you're not quite sure how
this plan will turn out in the end. It may turn out well, it may not: why
then even talk to me about it? You should have left me as I was and
gone about your business. —Was your plan carried out? You should
have informed me of such at the same time you gave the news that it
was a success. Did it fail? So I remained right where I was before. The
point is, if everything you said you had done had been true—which
common sense dictates in such cases—that is certainly what you
should have done: let me know the outcome. To have done the contrary only reveals all too clearly the twisted double-dealing behind it
and shows that all this was no more than an out-and-out jibe, which
fortunately I figured out from the very start. As early as April 3 or 4, I
asked you about it, and I repeated that same request many times
thereafter, without significant variation. Yet Monsieur Le Noir's visit
was intended to produce that effect. A magistrate that you have every
reason to believe is respectable, who comes to see you, saying: *Your
punishment is over, you have paid the penalty for your misdeeds*, seems as if
he ought to be taken at his word. He betrayed me. So where does that
leave us? He demeaned himself far more than I, for between the dupe
and the rogue the difference is indeed great, and it is surely not in favor of the rogue.

And yet in all this there is one thread that runs through this entire
business. Magistrates, relatives, business associates, friends, *knaves or
the commanding officer* (which comes to the same thing), all agree to
speak as one; the instrument had but one string: it is plucked by one
and all in the same manner. Some (I refer to those whom I have un-
derlined above) like the bloated louts they are, the others slightly less

bluntly, but they all speak as one, their agreement is total: *he must be lied to, and lied to villainously.* And here is the result: I keep coming back to the letter from the Count de La Tour[1] which I came upon quite by chance in the Commandant de Miolans's quarters:

> *The intent of la présidente de Montreuil, who has obtained from the minister the proper authorization whereby she shall be in charge of all matters concerning Monsieur de Sade, is that she mislead him at every turn, from dawn till dusk; in consequence whereof, you may keep telling him that his affair will soon be over.*

It is therefore clear, given these fatal arrangements, that the plan for my punishment has been, or still is, to lie to me and mock me over a period of ten or twelve years, more or less. Well, to that I respond by asserting that there is and can only be one person responsible for that state of affairs, a hypocrite, a rogue, and an infamous scoundrel by the name of Monsieur S[artine]; only he could have counseled such a horror, only a rogue such as he could have been capable of sending more than two hundred innocent people to perish in chains or otherwise (and I shall prove it one day), only from him can such advice have emanated. The odious monster was not content to have undone me when I was in the full blush of youth;[2] no, he desires that the end of my life resemble its beginning, so that he can congratulate himself on having been, to the very end, my torturer; he who deserved to suffer the tortures of Damiens because he, through a well-known trait, thought he could topple the entire State, he who sentenced to perish on the wheel a poor wretch whom everyone knew was innocent, who could not possibly have been guilty of the crimes whereof he was charged, and whose last words before he expired were: *"I shall relate in full detail the infamy of him whose lies brought me to this pass, before the tribunal of God, who alone shall be my judge"*—remarkable words that, were I king, I would have engraved on a man's carriage, if ever he took it into his head to acquire one, and thus distinguish himself from his ancestors,

1. Governor of the Duchy of Savoy who, as noted, acting upon the request of Madame de Montreuil to the king of Sardinia-Piedmont had Sade arrested and incarcerated in the Fortress of Miolans late in 1773.
2. During his initial incarceration in Vincennes in October 1763 at the age of twenty-three because of the Jeanne Testard affair, Sade wrote the first of many letters to Sartine begging him to keep the "scandal" quiet. Sartine, whom Sade came to loathe, was indeed instrumental in both putting and keeping him in prison.

who were only too happy to earn a few meager pennies by caning the poor wretches incarcerated in the prisons of Madrid during the Inquisition. So there you have the unspeakable creature I have to deal with, the abominable character to whom we had recourse and to whom your odious mother was all the more delighted to appeal because she was well aware that he was my enemy, that he had shown himself to be many times over, and because she knew that he would give her only such advice that would indulge her revenge.

Any punishment that does not cure, that can only revolt him upon whom it is visited, is a gratuitous infamy that renders those who impose it guiltier in the eyes of humanity, of common sense, and of reason, a thousand times more than he upon whom it is inflicted. That truth is too obvious to be refuted. Well, then, what are you hoping for? And what do you dare hope to accomplish from everything you are doing, unless 'tis to make certain you rid me of every last vestige of character, render me ill-humored, turn me into a rogue, an ill-tempered wretch, and an out-and-out scoundrel like all the rest of you? For when all is said and done, whether the comparison is wholly accurate or not, you must admit 'tis essentially on the mark: but what you are doing to me is precisely what they do to dogs to make them more vicious. —*Oh! we shall always bring you to heel again, whenever we want to! all we have to do is mention setting you free, and that's what we wanted to see when we sent Monsieur Le Noir. You've been as meek as a sheep, because he came to flatter you.* That's your system, isn't it? Well then, all I have to say is, I hope you're proud of it!

In a word, there are numerous examples of my misdeeds, but there is none in the entire universe that even comes close to the vexatious means you have used against me. 'Tis iniquitous, illegal in every point, and there is no way either the king or the royal court could have ordered it, in consequence thereof I have every right to implore that I be avenged or, in case my request is turned down, to seek vengeance in my own way, following your good example.

I have no need whatsoever to ask to see Monsieur Le Noir. I still admire him enough not to want to burden his conscience with one more injustice concerning me. One day he'll thank me for it. As for you, that is a whole other matter; I have the most urgent desire to see you. Considering the length of time you've been talking about it, you must have had a thousand chances for your request to be granted or turned down. I therefore warn you in no uncertain terms that if by the feast of Pentecost I have not seen you I shall be completely convinced that this whole thing is a farce, that I am on the verge of being released, and I shall make my arrangements accordingly. Thus, you can make of this what you will on this point. Either you must come or I shall conclude that I am going to be set free; 'tis quite clear. Monsieur Le Noir has not changed, nothing has changed, and for the past ten years everything has been foreordained, stipulated, the days marked, the lies decided upon, the farces learned by heart, and the only thing that has changed is that all this has taken on more and more weight as your stupid old mother grows longer in the tooth and, abandoned by the entire universe (which never thought much of her in the first place), she sees herself slipping into the grave. To all appearances, taking as her model a slithering snake, she is bound and determined to spew out her entire allotment of venom before she expires. Get on with it, then, let her lose as little time as possible lest we become befouled by all the remaining poison wherewith her ugly entrails are filled. Let her hurry and breathe her last without further delay and render her ugly soul into the muck.

My detention, you tell me, is the object of great scandal in Provence. Ah! of that I haven't the slightest doubt; you have no need to tell me, unless 'tis to rub a bit of balm in my blood through this act of kindness. Well now, that being the case, how is it that your mother can derive such unmitigated pleasure from depriving her grandchildren of their father? And given that, why do you not want me to call her a monster unworthy of being alive? How do you fancy now that you can convince anyone in Provence that the exile from Marseilles was not tantamount to being banished from the entire province? —Oh! measures were taken, yes, measures, to keep their tongues from wagging! Oh! you would be most clever if you were ever able to figure out just what those measures were: as for myself, I swear I could not care a whit; my intentions are still the same as they always were. Once I am out, I shall soon be sheltered from my compatriots' manner of thinking, for I shall soon be far away from them.

As for what I said to you about Milli Rousset, I have nothing further to add. As long as she has been patient enough to wait for me for three years, she could just as well wait for three more, if indeed that is my term, as Monsieur Le Noir's visit would seem to indicate, for he apparently has the habit of delineating my halves. 'Tis an effort to make me believe that I shall be here for centuries, and that is unworthy of her; that is all I have to say on the matter. Nor should you come and tell me: but it's your own fault if you're not out, they offered you a transfer to Montélimar, all you had to do was agree to go there ... Your Montélimar was a fairy tale, there was never any real basis for it; and to prove it to you, I declare here and now that I accept and am ready to leave, whether under guard or not, with no strings attached. Let us see what you have to say to that, and see whether or not it's a fairy tale. And as for what I say to you, 'tis neither to feel you out nor to see what may happen next: when I again put in a request to be transferred to Montélimar I am stating an absolute truth, and I hereby declare that I prefer to go there, no matter the negative consequences, than to remain in this abominable house, where the infamies, the vileness, and the base indignities are carried to the extreme.

While on the subject, I am going to cite you three examples that are fresh in my mind. The other day I felt like eating a bit of lamb, and as you well know this is the time of year when lamb is plentiful on even the humblest of tables. I was made to pay for it out of my own pocket! What do you think of that? How mean can you get? Yesterday, hearing that green peas were on the menu and not having had the pleasure of laying eyes on any for a long while, I asked for some; what they sent me was a mishmash of dried peas from last year's crop, which I devoured as if they were fresh, so great had been my desire to have some. And as a result, twice now in the last twenty-four hours I've been sick as a dog, whereas if they had given me some fresh little green peas I would have been fine. Do you want another example, even worse? For the past three years I've been made to drink stagnant water taken from a cistern that stinks to high heaven; whereas at Monsieur de Rougemont's there is an abundance of excellent fresh spring water: but that water costs something, and were he to offer it to the prisoners 'twould mean a few crowns less per annum out of the sums this scoundrel is already stealing from them. What's more, would you believe that five or six letters,[3] and just as many conversations, have never succeeded in making that lowlife understand the following line of reason? Normal fare here consists of five courses a day, including soup, and I can tell you the devil himself would refuse to eat them, they are always detestable, the reason being that there is more for the turnkeys, who have worked out an arrangement with the cook. So I said, all right, don't give me five, give me only two courses, but spend the same amount of money for these two courses you would have paid for all five. This strikes me as only fair. If my family pays six livres a day for my food, I have every right to ask that these six livres, having deducted the amount due for my laundry, should be spent on the two

---

3. From Sade to de Rougemont.

courses, since two courses is all I take. If you refuse that request, Commandant, then one of two things has to result: if in serving me the two courses I have requested they turn out to be as bad as the five, then you yourself are stealing from me the three courses I am not taking, or you are openly admitting that your cook is conniving with your turnkeys to steal them from me; there is no middle ground there. —Well now, that line of reasoning is one that Monsieur de Rougemont has never been able to get through his thick skull. The two courses are indeed as bad as the former five, witness the green peas that almost brought me to my grave. I beseech you to lodge a most strenuous complaint on my behalf about that to Monsieur Le Noir, or if you feel my complaint is not fully justified, then I shall write a letter to this wretched little scamp de Rougemont that will make him blush with shame, assuming he still has a modicum of modesty left within him. You need most insistently to point out to Monsieur Le Noir that since I do not drink any wine nor use any candles, that I have only half as much furniture as the others and no linen at all, etc., that I expect and have every right to demand that, with the sole exception of my laundry and without anything being skimmed off into the pockets of the turnkeys, the entire sums that are expended for my food be spent on those two courses I consume, which at least ought to make them edible. For, once again, this little squirt,[4] this bastard, this nasty half-breed, this one-fourth of an Englishman, in short, this squalid excuse for a human being must know that the whole of life does not consist of playing practical jokes or having others play them for him.

True, this little joker will doubtless say: but you are the one who's forever playing practical jokes on us; so you are the one who has to pay the piper. —To which I have two things to reply: first of all, that 'tis for the présidente to pay for these practical jokes, since she is the one behind them; and secondly, I strongly suggest that she pay as little as possible for them, for they are most poorly done. First, there is one turnkey who, when he wants to perform one of his little acts of buffoonery, begins by turning to one side, since he can't bring himself to look me in the eye when he pours out his lies to me; and then there is another (this one is my favorite), who when he comes to administer the little injection his captain has ordered him to give that morning, always pokes his fellow turnkeys smartly in the ribs, to let them know he's going to tell a huge lie, and that the order to do so comes from above and that they

---

4. Sade's term is *avorton*, literally abortion.

consequently should do the same . . . The imbeciles! lie to me will they! And the poor présidente, all wrapped up in her little cocoon, convinced that everything is going exactly as planned! —As for de Rougemont, that's a whole other matter: he is considerably more subtle and a better actor. He's the only one of the band whose every performance is worth at least twenty sous; some days you could even go so high as thirty, when he arrives, having just downed a hearty meal, his tongue still awash in globules of fatty matter that stick in his craw, expresses himself more or less like this, exaggerating his *r*'s beyond belief:

Ah, no, I say! you're still not being fair to me. You are laboring under the mistaken belief that words are meant to foster understanding; dead wrong: you should not believe a single word I have the honor of saying to you, because words are absolutely meaningless

Ah no, I say . . . And with that he is overcome with a violent attack of hiccups and cannot go on. You must admit that I have the patience of Job and that I had the presence of mind to remember where I was, otherwise I would have run the knave out of room with a few well-placed kicks in the belly.

But he'll get his just desserts in due course, of that I give you my word.

In any event, allow me to conclude with the following axiom that emanates from nothing more than good common sense, and that is; 'tis not by means of vice, and the unspeakable horror that vice begets, that vice can be either punished or reformed; only virtue can accomplish that, and virtue in its purest form. 'Tis not up to the présidente de Montreuil—cousin, niece, relative, godchild and gossip monger of all the little bankrupt clan from Cadiz and Paris, 'tis not for the présidente de Montreuil, niece of a crook who was thrown out of the Invalides by none other than Monsieur de Choiseul[5] himself for thievery and financial misconduct, 'tis not up to the présidente de Montreuil, whose family includes, on her husband's side, a grandfather who was hanged to death in the Place de Grève,[6] 'tis not for the présidente de Montreuil, who has given her husband no fewer than seven or eight bastards and has acted as pimp for all her daughters, 'tis not for her to try and mortify, punish, or repress defects of character for which one is not accountable in the first place and which, moreover, have never done the slightest harm to anyone. 'Tis not up to Dom S[arti]nos, who suddenly appeared out of nowhere one fine day in Paris, without anyone know-

---

5. The Duc de Choiseul, the former secretary of state for war.
6. In Paris, the square where prisoners were executed, often in public.

ing whence he came, a bit like those poisonous mushrooms one discovers suddenly in full bloom at the edge of the woods, 'tis not up to Dom S[arti]nos who, when one checked more closely into his background, was found to have issued forth from the left side of Father Torquemada and from a Jewish woman whom the aforementioned Holy Father had seduced in the prisons of the Madrid Inquisition for which he was responsible, 'tis not up to Dom S[arti]nos, whose fortune in France was founded on his having sacrificed men as if they were cannibals, who, being in charge of the court of appeals, broke on the wheel the poor wretch to whom I have earlier referred, solely in order to enhance his own reputation and show that he was never wrong and quite incapable of misjudging anyone, 'tis not up to Dom S[arti]nos who, when he enjoyed a somewhat higher station, dreamed up all sorts of harassments and odious tyrannies relative to the public's pleasures and distractions, in order to be able to provide *lascivious lists* wherewith to enliven the late-night revels of the Parc-aux-Cerfs, which, to pay court to each successive ruling party, had some two hundred innocent people put to death either by torturing them or by clapping them in prison, and I have that figure on very good authority, namely from the very people who were directly involved; in conclusion, 'tis not up to Dom S[arti]nos, politically the greatest scoundrel and generally the most notable crook who has ever walked the face of the earth, and perhaps the first who, since outrageous behavior has become an accepted way of life, has managed to come up with the most extraordinary misuse of power, namely that of letting a prostitute consort with the prisoners—no, 'tis not up to such a frightful defender of crime to try to either censure or repress or admonish those selfsame errors that were the source of his own greatest delights in that period when he was skimming off five hundred thousand francs per annum from the million allotted him by the king to provide the court with lubricious tidbits[7] and who, at the same time, not only stole with impunity but also took unspeakable advantage of his position in order to force certain poor wretches into various vices—those same vices that today he makes a point of admonishing! —And that bit of information I have directly from the women themselves.

In a word, 'tis not for the little bastard de Rougemont, the execration of vice personified, to this dissolute villain in doublet and breeches

---

7. Sartine passed on his findings regarding the sexual misdeeds of the king's loyal subjects to the minister, who in turn would pass them on to Louis XV and Mme de Pompadour, who apparently relished them.

who, on the one hand, prostitutes his wife to augment the number of prisoners he has and, on the other hand, starves them to death in order to line his pockets with a few more crowns and pay the detestable henchmen of his debaucheries; in short, 'tis not for a knave and a rogue who, without the whims of fortune and the pleasure Lady Luck seems to take in bringing low those who are deserving of higher station and elevating those who are born only to crawl, and who, without this twist of fate, I say, would doubtless be only too happy to serve as my kitchen boy if we had both remained in the respective positions into which we were born; 'tis not for a tramp such as he to try to set himself up as censor of vices, and in fact for those same vices that he himself possesses to an even more odious degree, because, as we all know, one becomes all the more detestable and more ridiculous when one tries to cast out the mote in others' eyes when the mote in one's own eye is a thousand times greater, just as 'tis not for the lame to poke fun at those who limp any more than 'tis right that the blind lead those with only one eye.

That is all I have to say and I bid you farewell.

45. To Monsieur Le Noir

May 22, 1781

*M*onsieur,
You have done me the honor of coming to see me, of assuring me that *my errors were expiated*, of leading me to believe that my impending freedom would convince me thereof; you suggested that I pen a letter to obtain that freedom; I wrote it word for word in keeping with your good counsel; you told me that you were pleased with the contents of that letter, as indeed you were pleased with me.

Why therefore after all that, Monsieur, is that freedom to which you alluded, falsely it turns out, still but a promise? Are you trying to plant in my mind an opinion, so contrary to the decency and honesty I have always associated with you, that the only purpose of your visit was to deceive me and that you too, Monsieur, are but one more instrument of revenge of that odious creature, for human revenge is apparently the be all and end all of her existence, or who, by punishing me for her own sins, finds remorse for those with which she herself is rent? In short, could the sole reason for your visit be nothing more than to teach me a lesson, that lesson being that 'tis permitted to toy freely with those who are suffering and in pain, that these poor wretches are gullible fools when they promise to mend their ways or are tending in that direction; in short, could your visit have been naught but a lesson in vice, whereas I had every reason to expect from you a lesson in virtue? Those who compel you to take such steps debase you in the extreme by even daring to believe you capable of such acts. Therefore, kindly do me the honor of informing me, either by a letter or a personal visit, the specific reasons why a negotiation undertaken at your suggestion, and buttressed by the interest that you seemed to take in my case, has resulted in a turndown? At the same time, Monsieur, I beg you to let me know whether the moment when I shall be released is still far off.

Meanwhile, Monsieur, I most earnestly ask that I be allowed to see my wife,[1] as you have led me to believe I might, and that she be permitted to see me alone, I beg of you, Monsieur. Since the sole subject of our discussions will be our personal affairs, and since neither the State nor the government has ever been a part of these matters, however slight, I do believe that one may well dispense with that ostentatious show of harshness that should be meted out only to fools and simpletons, and that to interpose a third party between me and my wife, especially one such as Monsieur de Rougemont, would be the most pointless and most odious thing in the world.[2] Moreover, to make this *respectable* commandant waste precious moments, when *his mind* and *lovely soul* manage to find day in and day out another use of time far more worthy of him, whether devoting himself in turn to culture, improving his knowledge of science or belles-lettres, or doing his best to comfort the poor wretch whose image lies before his very eyes.

I have the honor of being, with my most distinguished sentiments, your humble and most obedient servant.

DE SADE

---

1. It has been over four years since Sade was arrested at the Hotel de Danemark, and he still has not been allowed a visit from his wife, despite all his imprecations and unstinting efforts and her entreaties as well.
2. Madame de Sade's first visit to see her husband in Vincennes came on July 13, 1781. Despite his plea, their meeting took place in the Vincennes council hall, with a guard—Sade's hated censor, Boucher—present the entire time.

46. To Madame de Sade

[Between July and October, 1781]

I cannot tell you how grateful I am, my dear friend, that you were so good as to send me the letter I requested of you, word for word. Most certainly, the letter reassured me, but the hidden horrors, the convoluted infamies that I discovered in the abominable letters your most hateful mother forced you to write—which, fortunately for me, I had initially failed to perceive—filled me once again with a new dose of sorrow and anxiety that was far stronger than the reassuring contents of your letter were able to bring me. Still in all, despite my new state of agitation, and putting aside my distress and frightful bouts of anxiety, I shall await your visit[1] in the hope that your words will have an even greater calming effect than did your letters, befouled as they were with all your mother's bile, and that the response you will give to the questions I shall ask you, and you should know that I shall be observing with an eagle eye the way you look when you respond, I hope, I say, that that response will be more meaningful to me than anything you have written. And so I wait.

'Tis therefore decided once and for all that never will you reassure me on one matter without at the same time arousing in me a state of deep concern on the other. Why do you not reply regarding my most earnest request that Boucher not accompany you when you come to see me? Can it be that someone is forcing him to come with you? Still, I am not going to comment thereon, for it seems to me that 'tis implicit in your letter that you are making every effort to make sure he doesn't come, and I shall let it go at that and not bring it up again, except to reiterate that if Boucher does accompany you, and if you are dressed in your whore's outfit as you were the time before, I swear on my word of honor that I have no intention of coming down.[2] That is the first question I shall ask when they come to fetch me: *Is Boucher down there? Is she still outfitted as she was the last time?*[3] If the answers are yes, I shall not

---

1. This refers to an impending visit; after the initial July 13 visit, Renée-Pélagie was authorized to visit her husband with relative frequency, though the authorities were quick to cancel these visits at the slightest show of independence or arrogance from the prisoner.
2. That is, coming down from his cell to the council room.
3. Sade of all people was shocked and upset at the "revealing" dress his wife wore during her first visit, and by her (to him) frivolous hairdo.

come down. If 'tis no, then perhaps they may simply be playing tricks on me; in which wise, I shall come down, but as soon as I set eyes either on Boucher or on your white dress and your hairdo, I shall straightway go back upstairs, and I swear in God's name and my word of honor that may I be considered the most cowardly man if ever I go back on my word.

DE SADE

What does this excuse mean: *you ought to see the others?* The "others'" husbands are not in prison, or if they are and these women behave in this manner, then they are all hussies who deserve naught but insults and contempt! Tell me, would you go to Easter Mass dressed up like some strolling actor or charlatan? Of course not, am I not right? Well then, the composure ought to be the same; pain and sorrow in this case ought to beget what piety and divine respect bring about in the other. No matter how outrageous the current fashion has become, you will never convince me that it applies to women of sixty. They should be your example, no matter how far removed you are from them in age. Bear in mind that my misfortune brings us closer to those who are older than we, and they—our elders—should serve as models both of behavior and dress for us. If you are decent and honorable, then you should look to please me and me alone, and the only way you may be sure of doing so is by being, in both looks and deeds, completely modest and utterly proper. In a word, I demand, if you love me (and that I shall of course be able to tell; what I ask of you cannot be refused me without unmasking you completely, by your signs and signals and by all your imbecilic and complicated turns of phrase), I therefore demand, as I said, that you come to see me wearing a dress that you women refer to as a dressing gown, and with a large, very large, bonnet as well, wherewith to cover your hair, which I would like simply to be combed out straight, with no fancy curls peeking out. Needless to say, no false curls either. A simple chignon, and no plaits. Nor should any part of your bosom be uncovered, not indecently exposed as it was the other day; as for the color of your dress, the darker the better. I swear to you on everything I hold most sacred in the world that I shall be in a state of uncontrollable rage, and there will be a most frightful scene, if you fail to follow to the letter everything I have just laid out for you. You should blush with shame for not having understood that those who decked you out the way you were the other day were making a fool of you and enjoying themselves to the hilt at your expense. Oh! just think how much fun they were having when they said to one another: *the pretty little marionette! We can make her do whatever we want!* For once in your life, be yourself. I sense that there are some things where circumstances oblige you to play their little game; but I am just as certain that there are some things asked of you that are indecent and ridiculous, perhaps even disgusting, and of those, I like to believe, you have refused to partake! As for the former, you should simply refuse, and as for the latter, you should threaten to take your own life sooner than even hear the slightest mention thereof.

The fact is, I am all too acutely aware into whose abominable hands you have fallen! For, and mark this well, I am nobody's fool, least of all yours, and I know that you are living at your mother's; I have every reason to shudder whenever I dwell on the fact that you are there! Yes, I have no hesitation in saying that I would far prefer you were living at Madame Gourdan's:[4] at least there you would know who you are dealing with and be on your guard, whereas at your mother's there's no way of telling what deceitful traps she may be setting. Do you think that I can ever forget this remark as long as I live? *I shall give fifty louis to anyone who manages to corrupt that young lady?* —No, no, that I shall never forget, and if only you would call to mind the times, the places, the situations, all my so-called misdeeds will forthwith become understandable! —My dear friend, do bear this in mind: the despair of women who have scorned virtue is the respect that is paid to virtue by those who have constantly honored it; they are like those poor wretched creatures who publicly feign not to believe in god and who call upon others to blaspheme against him even as their hearts cry out to embrace him. In like manner, embrace virtue, hold it close! 'Tis virtue that causes me to blush with shame at my indiscretions, and 'tis virtue alone that will bring me to loathe them. Man's natural inclination is to imitate; the character of a sensitive man is to try and model himself after what he loves. 'Tis the example of vices that has always been the source of my misfortunes; do not prolong them any further by providing me with proof of the most ghastly vices that could be prof-

---

4. Probably Sade's code name for Mme de Villette, Renée-Pélagie's cousin by marriage, who had invited Mme de Sade to come live with her. Married to a notorious homosexual, whom the wags of Paris dubbed *"voiture à la Villette,"* which referred to a horse-drawn carriage one enters from the rear, Mme de Villette enjoyed a dubious reputation herself. Sade claimed she was "a bit Sappho," but also told his wife that her heterosexual exploits were legion. Still, he preferred she live with the notorious Villettes than with her mother.

fered me. That would be the death of me; or, if my love of life should win out over the courage to kill myself (which I do not believe), 'twould be only to plunge me headlong into the wildest sins of the flesh, which would serve the purpose of ending my days at the soonest opportunity, one way or another. Fickleness or infidelity, they say, can serve to reawaken desire in a lover or husband; yes, in a soul that is base and vile. But never for one moment think that mine is of that ilk. I shall never pardon an offense against propriety, nor should I ever agree to see again anyone who once was mine and then ceased to be. The very notion that another person might be involved with someone I am holding in my arms has always revolted me, and I have never in my life seen again any woman whom I even suspected of having been unfaithful to me. I believe that none of this applies to you, but the fact is you have made me suspicious, and the thought is now rooted deep in my soul.[5] When they did that, what a wonderful piece of advice they gave you! I shall look into the matter most carefully, I shall verify the truth thereof: I shall find nothing (at least so I hope), but the suspicion has been planted, and in a character such as mine 'tis a slow poison, the effects of which wreak their havoc on me day in and day out, and there is absolutely nothing on the face of the earth that is capable of halting its progress. I say it once more: *when they did that what a wonderful piece of advice they gave you!* My greatest comfort was at least looking forward to the possibility of a happy old age in the bosom of a faithful friend who had never once failed me. It was, alas, my sole consolation, the only thing that dulled the pointed knives that are presently tearing me asunder. And you have had the effrontery to begrudge me that sweet hope of my declining years! I can't go on: the suspicion has been planted; the sentences are too obvious for me to blind myself to their

---

5. Sade would seem to be the last person to play the jealous husband, yet we must take him at his word. It may be that seeing Renée-Pélagie after almost four and a half years rekindled his passion. As we have seen, she did arrive outfitted coquettishly, with a low cleavage and pretty curls. Who was the presumed lover? A man named Lefèvre, a Provençal peasant whom the Abbé de Sade had taught to read and write and who, later, Mme de Sade brought to Paris as a servant. In a letter to Milli de Rousset written two weeks after Renée-Pélagie's first visit to Vincennes, she wrote: "He [Sade] is jealous. I can see you laughing from here. —And what is he jealous of you may ask? —Of Lefèvre (he does me great honor, don't you agree?) because I told him Lefèvre had bought him some books . . . Tell me if you will: where does he come up with such things?"

true meaning. Oh, my dear friend, is it true that I can no longer hold you in the highest esteem? Tell me: have you betrayed me so cruelly? If so, what a frightful future lies ahead! O great God! may my prison doors remain forever closed! I should rather die than emerge from here in order to behold my infamy, your infamy, and that of the monsters who offer you their advice! May I die rather than debase myself, rather than sink into the ultimate excesses of the most monstrous crimes, which I shall seek out with great delight in order to drown my sorrows in dissolution! I shall invent crimes so monstrous they defy imagination. —Farewell, see how calm I am and how much I need to see you alone. I beg of you, do whatever is required to see that it is arranged.

47. To Madame de Sade

[Between August and October, 1781]

*A*h! how they have just proved to me that they are making sport of my life! How they have just managed to convince me that there is not one person in the world who cares one whit about me! Ah! great God, great God! the most atrocious misfortune that I have so long dreaded has now come to pass!

You ask what is the basis for my suspicions: 'tis this.

You are the instrument of my torture. That being so, how can they fancy having you play such a role without making you extremely unhappy? If you still had the slightest feelings of friendship for me, 'twas essential they be forcibly extracted, for they were well aware that your friendship was my sole comfort, and they succeeded in that effort by giving you a lover.[1] Here then is the odious policy of your mother's most vile advisers: *encourage crime, authorize it in order to punish evil.* What a repulsive notion! What an infamous idea! and how is it possible, knowing you as I do, with all your virtue, all your decency, all your candor, that you did not sense the trap they had laid for you? How is it you were unable to avoid it? Alas! your execrable mother has now dealt me the final blow; she has stripped me of everything: possessions, honor, fortune, freedom . . . I would have endured everything, com-

---

1. Sade is assuming that if indeed Renée-Pélagie has a lover, it is all part of a master plot against him on the part of the présidente.

plained about nothing: but to steal your heart from me! . . . Oh! my dear and divine friend, oh! my former soulmate, this I shall not survive!

I have figured it out, your hateful enigma. I shall be set free on February 7 in either '82 or '84 ('tis an enormous difference, and you can see that I can discern no more than that); the detestable and imbecilic play on words is the name of today's saint, which happens to be Saint-Amand, and since one finds the word Fèvre in February,[2] you have linked the name of this rapscallion to the numbers 5 and 7. And from there your wordplay, as banal as it is stupid, indicates that my release will be at the end of five years (or 57 months), on February 7. Saint-Amand's day, Lefèvre, linked to the 7 and the 5, was your lover.[3] But do you for one moment believe that such a platitude can in the long run rid me of my suspicions? Eh! no, no! do not fool yourself: *the man has proved useful for your ideas and you have taken advantage of the man,* and 'tis upon the truth, the whole truth, of that thing that you have built the enigma, and not the enigma upon a play of words. You fear to topple your deplorable enigma by reassuring me: you are dead wrong. On the contrary, there is a time period of which I am certain and which irrevocably focuses my ideas. By your failure to reassure me, at least I know for certain the date of my release; by destroying my suspicions, everything crumbles, both the enigma and the suspicions. At which point I come to the conclusion that I had it all wrong and my mind begins to waver. Put him therefore in this same situation, since 'tis the one you most like, and reassure me about your conduct. I am full willing to ignore the date of my release, or even assume it will never happen, but I do not want to lose your heart. In a word, I most earnestly pray to see you; my life is at stake. If you refuse me that, do not prove that my life means nothing to you and therefore that I have nothing further to hope for in this world, do not prove that you no longer even pity me. I deserve at least that, for I weep for my sins, I repent of them, and the only reason I desire to remain alive and be free is to make amends for all my wrongdoings and do my best once again (if I am granted that possibility, for there is none at all if you have changed) to

---

2. French for February is *février,* which Sade links to the name of his wife's presumed lover, the rapscallion Lefèvre.
3. On August 5, Mme de Sade wrote her husband a letter, which so infuriated Sade he annotated it in obscene terms and spattered it with blood. From the date—5—and other numerical references, Sade in his fury deduces the two numbers refer to the size of Lefèvre's penis: 7 inches (length) by 5 inches (circumference).

do my best once again to make you happy. Oh! my dear friend, do not deny me that, I beg of you on bended knee! Why do you insist on driving me to despair and becoming the source of my undoing? I still hold one precious claim on you, a title that the entire universe is completely incapable of denying me: *I am the father of your children.* All right, let yourself be swayed in their name if not in mine! If you no longer like me, then I am fully prepared to die, I accept that, I shall rid you of my presence. But before I do, allow me to throw myself at your feet for a moment and weep, let me embrace your knees one last time, let me hear my judgment from your own lips, and I shall pass from this world content.

My terrible misfortune is that you have linked your visits so closely and intimately to the composition of your signals that you cannot gratify me concerning one without fearing to enlighten me about the other. But today that fear must be regarded as fantasy pure and simple, since you see that I have confessed to you the secret I discovered, and I solemnly declare to you that nothing now will ever make me change my mind. Well, now! do you want to be even surer that 'tis not my release that concerns me but solely the need, the extreme need, to see you? Go beg the minister on my behalf to grant me that favor and in return he can tack two more years of prison onto the back end of the furthest removed of my two sentences: if that is what it takes, I subscribe to it unreservedly. Do they want half my fortune? I give it in exchange for an hour with you, and you can have whoever you name to be with you during our encounter. And why in God's name did you announce that visit as just around the corner, since in truth it has to be in the dim distant future, if my release is slated for some twenty-four months hence, that is, only in '84?

Oh! ye gods, how you make me suffer! and how studied and heinous your torments! Ah! 'tis thus one makes a soul bitter and filled with despair, but that is hardly the way to bring it back to the straight and narrow! In the name of God, come pay me an hour's visit or I shall not answer for my life.

48. To Madame de Sade

[October 1781]

*Y*ou can well imagine, my dear friend, that after the moment of respite that you lodged in my soul concerning the frightful anxiety I felt about a detention as long as the one I mentioned to you recently, based on the figures you provided me, and especially after the Sainte-Aure,[1] which means 58 and which falls at that period precisely in June 1783, you can well imagine, I say, that after that I was in a terrible frame of mind. One very special thing, which I most assuredly am compelled to regard as a frightful bit of subtle cruelty on this score: not a word of consolation, not a single person offering me even the slightest hope that I was mistaken and that I was going too far. After that, you can well understand that the only conclusion I could come to was that my incarceration would be at least that, not counting the two years of exile that were destined to bring this whole affair to a close and carry my suffering to the brink of old age. Thus will your mother have been the cause of making sure my days were spent in constant torment. I shall have spent my entire life the victim of her rage and her unremitting revenge. And this woman is a devout believer, and this woman goes and takes communion . . . All it would take to turn the most pious man in the universe into an atheist is an example such as that. Oh! how I loathe her! Good God, how I detest her! And what a blessed moment 'twill be for me when I learn that this abominable creature has breathed her last! I most solemnly swear and vow by all that's most genuine to give two hundred louis to the poor the day I learn of that most blessed event, and another fifty to the servant who brings me the news or to the clerks of whatever postal service announces the event by letter. I agree and consent to whatever tortures it may please God to rain down upon me if ever I fail to comply with the terms of that oath, a written copy of which I have been carrying upon my person for more

---

1. After reassuring her husband that, largely because of his objections, she would not go to live with Mme de la Villette, she sought further to reassure him of her faithfulness and devotion by taking up lodgings in a nunnery. The one she chose was the convent of Sainte-Aure on the rue Neuve-Sainte-Geneviève. Apparently Sade sees in that choice of saints another "signal" for him to decipher.

than the past three years. I confess that I have never desired the death of anyone, with the exception of that woman! Ah! my dear friend, I beg your indulgence regarding a frivolous illusion; but as it assuages for a brief moment my sorrows, allow me to indulge for a while in such flights of fancy.

Let us assume for a moment that heaven had spared both my father and mother, as it has spared both your parents, that they had not suffered any serious setback or inconstancies to the fortune they had begun to amass, and let us further assume that the variations of that same fortune kept it from being frittered away; that both of them were still alive and in the social position that should rightfully have been theirs; and now let us suppose that 'twas you the orphan, and that you had behaved in a manner that we shall call equivocal; tell me, my dear friend, tell me, knowing the strength of character they both possessed, do you believe they would ever have treated you the way your family treats me, and can you imagine that, in the unlikely event they did, I would put up with it for one second? What is the result of that sad little dream? That I am the victim of fate and of revenge and that I have in the depths of my heart the consolation of being able to say to myself: *O my parents, never would we have allowed her to be so miserable, even were she just as guilty!*

I should never have wished such a fate for you, but if God had visited it upon you, how pleased, how delighted I would have been to rush to your defense, rally people to your cause, do everything in my power to defend you. You may be sure, my dear friend, that 'twould have been in vain that they came in search of me the day after we arrived back in Paris, my arms and my rooms would have been an asylum that no fury could ever have profaned. And I would have made them run me through with their swords a thousand times over before they were able to lay a hand on you. I would have said, with joy in my heart: she has lost everything, she has only me in the universe; I am her sole resource and her consolation. But she has sins on her conscience? So much the better. If she did not, how could she be indebted to me for coming to her defense?

The story you told me about your son is delightful.[2] Vouchsafe to take it as a lesson. It applies to you especially: he did not want them to hit his brother, and yet you allowed them to put your husband in irons.

---

2. We do not know the specifics, but can assume that Louis-Marie, the elder son, came to the defense of his younger brother, Donatien-Claude-Armand.

When you come to see me, then, kindly spare me all those base little lies: *I didn't know; somehow it just happened; I immediately sent someone to fetch a carriage, etc.*, when it comes to a project, to a scheme both vapid and stupid, a project that for a good ten years has been prearranged and planned and from which—were lightning to strike and destroy half the universe—those behind it would not deviate one iota. You know full well that I refuse to get involved in all that, that if I do nothing while you go on with your wearisome little drivel, 'tis because I want nothing to diminish or interfere with the pleasure I have in seeing you, nor do I want to give them any excuse whatsoever for suppressing your visits, but that does not mean I am any less convinced that you are lying, just as it pains me no end to see you resorting to this common defect that you see in the *food markets*, at the *cashier's desk*, or in the *anterooms*. Forsake all such affectations, I beg of you. You have no idea to what degree they end up corrupting and debasing one's soul. Duplicity leads directly to the loss of virtue. What's the point of hesitating to adopt it when one can arrive at the same end with one's mask?

Yes, I repeat to you what I said on the same score the other day: if all these foul deeds, all these petty torments of letters that are no more than warmed-over repetitions of an abomination conceived of in days of yore to be used against you, by the same hands who use it today against me, if this imprisonment, which is unduly long and infinitely too cruel, led to something beneficial to your family, efficacious for making me mend my ways, advantageous for my children, I would willingly sacrifice myself to it immediately without saying a word. But what is the result of this imprisonment, and what is the only possible result? Is your mother so blind that she completely fails to see it? Is she so deaf that she does not even suspect what people are saying? I'm quite willing to believe that people pointedly refrain from passing them on to her, but does that mean they don't exist? And you'll see when it comes time to setting up our children in life, 'tis then she will rue all her past blunders and realize that the pleasure of forever doing her sums is to buy most dearly all the self-loathing she will experience at that time, assuming of course that hell has spared her till then.

To have prolonged my prison term above and beyond that called for by the sentence of Aix-en-Provence is an infamy without example, and 'twas because she reveled in being the source of my undoing, and that of my children, for the sole pleasure of doing evil. What a monster! How I loathe her!

No matter what all the sycophants around her may say, or all those who profit from all that, she should know beyond all shadow of doubt that whenever her name comes up in public, whenever she appears at any reception, people who think either of her children or of mine are immediately reminded of my misfortunes. She ought to ponder that and see what she's gaining by prolonging my agony!

Well now! you said therefore that there was no 17³ in your last visit, nothing *especially sacred* about this number—I refer to your letter of May 17, 1777. Oh! 'twas never absent from any of your visits, and that last one was the seventeenth time I saw the commandant. I couldn't care less, 'tis the only time when I have shut my eyes to numbers. You promised to follow me, you promised me as you kissed me good-bye, you swore you would, I believed you; and had there been a thousand 17's, I know the language of your heart like I know my own, and 'twas your heart speaking when you made your promise. If you do not keep your word, you will expose me to a thousand follies when I get out of here, for I solemnly swear to you on all I hold most dear in the world that nothing will stand in my way, nothing will keep me from coming to tear you from the bowels of the earth, if 'tis there that they try to hide you to keep you out of my reach. May all of heaven's thunderbolts rain down upon me, may they swallow up my fortune with me, my children, everything I have in this world, may I not take a single step in the universe without encountering daggers or unfathomable depths if I spend eight days, once my fetters are gone, *without you.*

49. *To Madame de Sade*

[October 25, 1781]

I shall not lose a minute before responding to your letter, my dear friend. It fills me with such frightful anxiety that I cannot restrain myself for another moment. In the name of God, do not assault me with such blows, they affect me too deeply. I make threats against

---

3. Sade again is groping for meaningful signals, hoping thereby to learn the *real* date of his release.

you![1] May Heaven crush me this very instant, may I never see the light of day again if ever I have threatened you even once. Ah! ye gods, threats against the only creature I adore, she whom I hold most dear in the world! Read my last letter to your mother; she knows my heart better than anyone. I say to her, I think it and repeat it over and over again, that were I to see you holding a dagger in your hand I would cast myself at your feet and revel in your vengeance. Ah! may I be made to suffer as long as they wish, I have no quarrel with that, but let them not turn your heart against me through such unworthy reports as these. My soul will be deeply aggrieved until you tell me that you no longer believe a word of what they say. Waste not another moment in telling me so, I beg of you. And do convince Monsieur Le Noir of the same. Whoever dreamed up such dark and dreadful lies are but knaves and scoundrels. Everyone here, if they are willing to tell the truth, will attest to the fact that even when I have been in the most frightful depths of despair, never once have I uttered your name with anything but marks of affection, which I both owe you but also feel most profoundly in my heart. Come, come, visit whatever sins you care to upon me, 'twill pain me unto death, 'twill render my already wretched life even more miserable, but never fear that I would either avenge myself or even mention it to you again if it displeases you. All I ask is that you not harden your heart against me. And know beyond any shadow of doubt that my own life is less dear to me than yours, and that I should not survive for one minute were I to think that I had been the cause of your losing even so much as a single hour's sleep. My threats, and my so-called ill conduct, were aimed at the man who serves me. What does that have to do with you? In the name of God, come to see me, and meanwhile do your best to arrange for Amblet to see me as well. If you persist in believing that I have made so much as a single threat against you, I shall end my days forthwith.

---

1. Many times during his incarceration, Sade, in rage or frustration, lost his temper and swore or insulted his jailers, which inevitably resulted in his losing his walks or, worse, being put into solitary confinement. In this instance, someone reported to Renée-Pélagie that her husband had voiced threats against her.

50. To Madame de Sade

October 26, 1781

*T*he people here, whom I immediately called and questioned after my letter of yesterday evening, assured me unequivocally that they had never reported that I had ever spoken ill of you; and how could they have done so—they themselves answered, since they had never heard me make any such remark? I asked that they enlighten Monsieur de Rougemont on that score, and the preposterous response they brought back to me this morning both clarified the matter and reassured me greatly. That dear fellow is taking his revenge; that should suffice to convince you that everything he may have said is but a tissue of lies, calumnies he is concocting in retaliation for those he doubtless terms my own, and until such time as we have had a chance to see each other and to clear the matter up, I know you to be fair and equitable enough not to believe a word of it. Meanwhile I reiterate, upon my most authentic word of honor, that neither did I make any remarks or any threats, and that I love you and adore you to such a degree, my dear and unique friend, that I should rather rend myself asunder than say anything to you, or about you, that might displease you. Alas! 'tis not when my goal and my sole desire are to atone for so great a multitude of wrongdoings that I would set about trying to add to them. Did I not tell you when you came to see me that I regarded you as my only friend, and that I firmly believed you were all I had left in the world? Have I not written you twenty times over saying the same thing? You replied to my declarations, I have your letters to prove it. What then would be the point, such being my frame of mind and the state of my heart, of trying to irritate or offend you? No, my good friend, you do not believe a word of it. And I am convinced that you still have sufficient kindness in your heart, and pity for me, that you will refrain from condemning me until you have had a chance to hear me out. Till then I shall suffer the pangs of hell, but I am by now all too well acquainted with troubles and woes, and my certainty that you will judge me fairly will help me bear this further injustice, in the full knowledge that in the long run you will know I am right. Ye gods, if only you could prove your own innocence with equal force: 'tis my one and only wish, and I shall not bring it up again.[1]

---

1. Sade is still suffering—or feigning to suffer—as the jealous husband.

All that is no more than the mere annoyances, vexations, unkind cuts, and blathering of a wicked old witch who, having no greater pleasure than making herself obnoxious, expends upon that unique pastime all the talents of a weary heart and a mind that has been completely corrupted. The forces behind it are all too obvious, and all I can say is that with such baseness I should have hoped she might at least have injected a trifle more cunning into her little scheme. I see it, people are absolutely right when they say that there is no nastier beast on the face of the earth than a sanctimonious old woman. If throughout my life something has kept me as far removed as possible from piety and devoutness, 'tis canting sanctimoniousness, which I abhor, and that terrible habit the elderly have of practicing religion on the one hand and indulging in the most loathsome vices on the other.

As far as Monsieur de Rougemont is concerned, I have once again misjudged him badly. And I must confess that solely on the basis of his having served in the military, I would have thought him more candid, more honest, and above all incapable of avenging himself as he does by a long string of calumnies and an endless number of petty domestic tyrannies which, when they come to light, will surely reflect far more poorly on him than on me. One must not judge my conduct in here either by my deeds or my words. People do everything in their power to bait me, to vex me, they visit all sorts of abomination upon me, week after week they torture me beyond belief, and then they do not want me to take whatever revenge I can! They must then think I'm made of wood, and though they do their level best to render me insensate, and consequently to destroy in me the germ of all virtues, I am still not sufficiently deadened to the point of being incapable of warding off all the slings and arrows they send my way. If I had been the object of a normal judicial sentence, one could have judged both my character and my conduct, but what has been done to me has never been done to anyone else. The judgments and sentences handed down upon those guilty of the most heinous crimes committed throughout this century pale when compared to mine. Therefore, at the very least I should be allowed to lodge my complaints and take my revenge whenever and wherever I can. They give me medicines that upset my stomach, to the point where the only food I can bear is milk, and even that I have difficulty digesting, and then they are shocked when I administer a sound thrashing to the poor beggar who has chosen to exercise the vile profession of turnkey! They are sorely mistaken. So long as my blood flows in my veins I shall tolerate neither infamy nor injustice, and this latest behavior is simply atrocious. Never in my life have I put anything harmful in anyone's food, and I swear upon what I hold most sacred in the world that there was not the slightest harmful ingredient in the aniseed the girls in Marseilles ate, and the best proof is that I ate those same sweets in their presence and at the same time they did. They admitted that at the Aix hearing, as they admitted it to me personally. Thus, by that admission, that fact is proved beyond all shadow of doubt as far as I'm concerned. Whatever else I may be accused of beyond that is pure calumny, which I shall absolutely refute whenever I am given the opportunity. 'Tis therefore also proved that Monsieur de Rougemont is taking his revenge, and doing so by spreading all sorts of lies about me, doubtless because of those he claims I told about him.

I swear and solemnly declare that I have never slandered Monsieur de Rougemont. Anyone said to be a slanderer is a man who makes up lies and then spreads them to one and all in order to confuse or harm the person concerned, as he has done for example when he reports to the judge that I have made threats against you. 'Tis such a person one calls a slanderer and a knave. In my case, all I said was what I learned and what I heard other people report as gospel truth. Thus, while I have indeed spoken ill of people, 'twas not on the basis of anything I made up.

I used to have four or five friends who were also acquaintances of Monsieur de Rougemont. He is aware of that, in fact we have spoken about it together on more than one occasion. I therefore have had a chance to learn a great deal about the man from them. In earlier days, there was a period of seven or eight years when I was wont to dine twice a week at two houses on the rue Férou, one the house of Madame de——[2] and the other belonging to Chevalier de Chaponais, both of which were contiguous to that of Monsieur de Rougemont's mother. I thus had an opportunity to learn all sorts of things about him, and I committed them well to heart.

In Florence I met a man who is one of the best connected people on the face of the earth, who knows all the ins and outs of the court and the ministers, a man who proved it by revealing the truth in print, which forced him to flee his country. In any case, that gentleman spent six months with the Count du Barry, a close friend of Monsieur de Rougemont, and he told me the following: *I should greatly prefer to be*

---

2. Why Sade names one and conceals the other is unclear. One can conjecture that, his letter being scrutinized by the censor, the unnamed lady might still be subject to de Rougemont's revenge.

sentenced to the wheel than to the Vincennes dungeon, and 'tis the fear of that dungeon that has prevented me from returning to my homeland. To which I asked: *Just what do you mean by that?* And the man said to me: *Because the Count du Barry has just informed me that the warden of this dungeon is one of his former students, a man who has learned how to line his pockets by pimping for his prisoners.*

These explanation and proofs will, I trust, suffice to convince you that while I did make pointed remarks I certainly never made anything up out of whole cloth nor did I say anything that I had not heard directly from the horse's mouth. And I should add that I should never have made these remarks in the first place had I not been pushed to the brink, and if Monsieur de Rougemont is offended by them, he is a military man and knows the means whereby a man of the military deals with insults and injuries.[3] I know he is old and suffers from all sorts of infirmities, but to that I reply that he can name whomever he wishes to act on his behalf. There are plenty of stand-ins who would equalize the affair and make up for our difference in age, and whether by a pair of pistols or simple fisticuffs, I am at his orders. But let him not take his revenge by foul deeds. I shall not be in here forever, and the first thing I shall do upon regaining my freedom—and this I swear to him upon my word of honor—will be to invite him to lunch. Till then, let him treat me with the respect deserving a man who is of a mind to proffer such an invitation, and let him cease and desist from any further foul deeds or atrocities, because if he persists he will prove thereby that he is only worthy of being thrown to the dogs and of being treated in the same manner I treated his turnkey.

This Saturday morning

They are refusing to shave me or clean my room: both are nonetheless essential to the maintenance of one's health and cleanliness, and nowhere else in the world are these basic needs denied any prisoner. I shall not even mention those incarcerated in insane asylums, for there is no prison where the insane are not infinitely better treated than those here who are in full possession of their faculties. I shall mention the animals in the zoo: every week they and their cages

---

3. Sade is (half seriously) proposing a duel with the warden, one of his more unlikely fantasies.

are thoroughly cleaned. I hereby request that I not be treated any worse than they are: a bit of charm is all it takes, I suspect, and therefore I beg you to hie yourself to see Monsieur Le Noir, so that he can issue the order to have me given a proper shave and have my room swept. I hasten to have this letter sent on to you so that you can act upon it as soon as possible, for my beard is bothering me no end and my room is beginning to look like a stable. 'Tis absolutely impossible that those orders came from the king, and we all know whence they did come.[4]

As for the man whom I thrashed,[5] he need worry no more. I give my word that I shall not touch him again, and you can answer for me on that score. I embrace you with all my heart and beg you most urgently to have revised orders issued regarding all that, as well as regarding the repair of my stove.

51. *To Monsieur de Rougemont*

[November, 1781]

I have the honor of bidding good day to Monsieur de Rougemont and asking that he be so kind as to remit to Monsieur Le Noir the enclosed *Memoir.* I would also greatly appreciate if Monsieur de Rougemont would duly inform me of the results of that request. As you will see, 'tis something I sincerely need, and yet if the request is not granted I shall not commit suicide over it, in consequence whereof a yes or no answer can be communicated to me without danger. 'Tis extremely essential however that I know which it is, so that I do not lay myself open to an indiscretion such as the one I was so tactless as to have made yesterday in daring ask who it was who presided at the baptism of the precious child upon whom the gaze of the entire nation is

4. Madame de Montreuil, of course.
5. Sade's reputation left him vulnerable to snide remarks and insults on the part of the Vincennes turnkeys, to which Sade responded with like remarks and, on more than one occasion, attempted violence. Since he knew such ripostes inevitably resulted in repression of his walks or, worse, cancellation of his wife's visits, he tried as best as his hot temper allowed to control himself.

presently focused,[1] and concerning whom some beast of a prisoner had the effrontery to be interested, as if a prisoner was a human being or that a prisoner needs must remind himself that he is a citizen of France. My excuses, Sir, I apologize for my indiscretion, and assure you it will never happen again.

52. *To Mademoiselle de Rousset*

[November, 1781]

[The beginning of this letter is missing.]

*I*f Gothon left either any precise instructions in her will or if she has any surviving children, my intention is that the former be followed to the letter and that the children be taken care of.[1] If she has left any debts, I want them paid and, moreover, I want you to instruct Gaufridy on my behalf to give you one louis, the purpose of which is for a mass to be read for her at the local parish. I am going to instruct Gaufridy simply to give you that louis without providing him with any further details. 'Tis the least I can do for the memory of that poor girl and I fully intend to discharge that obligation.

Moreover, it would be prudent to ascertain whether or not she either gave, or allowed to be removed by that crowd of sycophants around her, any possessions that belong to the château, and if indeed that did happen, then every effort should be made to see to it that those possessions be recovered and returned to the château.

---

1. The birth of Louis XVI's son, the new dauphin.
1. Gothon died on October 27 of puerperal fever. A week earlier she had given birth to a boy. Sade only learned of her death the following month. His generous response is not atypical.

53. *To Madame de Sade*

[November–December, 1781]

Good deeds being engraved in my heart at least as profoundly as unworthy practices, I have doubtless been sensitive to the fact of how accommodating they were at the time of the accident to my eye[1] by allowing the man who was taking care of me to remain with me for a moment while I was taking my meals, as was allowed during my early days here. But in granting me that, they forgot one essential thing: *prescribing to me the full extent of what I am permitted to talk about and the things that I perforce must refrain from discussing.* Since the mediocrity of my genius does not allow me to perceive those limits, it was essential that I receive a *code* relative to this subject. Wrack my brain as I may to search out the most trivial and banal subjects of conversation, I still have the misfortune of drawing down upon myself rebukes that, as you well know, are wont to be paid for a trifle dearly, even bearing in mind that I swore on my word of honor to allow others to seek revenge on my behalf. But at least let them take that revenge. I thought I would be eaten alive on two previous occasions, one for having asked *the names of the new dauphin's godparents*, and again when I inquired of the surgeon *if he was expecting a large crowd for the dinner being given for the holiday.* As you can see, after that 'tis necessary for you to send me a short catalog of the things I can say, so that in the future I do not expose myself to allowing such weighty questions to slip past my lips!

Here is the crux of the matter. First of all, they gave me, and I have always said it, a most insolent man; the thick and bitter blood of that boor turns even more sour and becomes even more inflamed, over two matters: first, the obligation to remain with me, that is, to do something that is both humane and decent, two cruel conditions for a man of that ilk; the second—the cause of his despair—emanates precisely from the simplicity and sangfroid—or perhaps from the banality—of my conversation. I furnish him nothing for *the official reports;* I take not the slightest interest in who has informed upon whom; with me there is nothing juicy he can glean,[2] in consequence whereof he is absolutely

---

1. Sade uses the term "accident," but probably means "eye problems," from which he has been suffering for some time, a condition known as keratitis.
2. Then, as now, a habit of the guards was to try to entrap prisoners into saying or revealing something that could be held against them.

furious, and since he is unable to be rude about serious questions, he recriminates by whining and complaining, all of which does not make life easy for me. Moreover, please explain to me what this man means by his never-ending question: *Are you trying to worm something out of me?* I simply do not understand that, first because that is the furthest thing from my mind, and secondly because it strikes me that the man is both clumsy and thick-headed to be asking: *Are you trying to worm something out of me?* He must therefore be infested with them—I refer to the worms—since he's so afraid they may be removed from his person. And thus he suddenly is admitting, by the stupidity of his remarks, two things I had always suspected, namely on the one hand that he is party to whatever game is being played here, and on the other that there is an answer to the riddle. So you can see how subtle they are, these people in your employ![3] Yet there they are, chapter and verse. By having made such an effort to debase both of us, your mother and me, she by confining me to a jailer and me by being made the butt of a jailer's buffoons, she should at least, if there was even the slightest semblance of feeling left in her slimy soul, have had strict instructions issued to those aforesaid buffoons, by decent people who, in passing them on, would have been able to enjoin them to be courteous, decent, and honest in their dealings, both for your mother's sake and mine, to protect us from such ignominious behavior. But the responsibility for the total lack of civility on the part of this man, already exceedingly uncouth to start, lies with a rogue[4] who is even more boorish and uncouth, and these two knaves conspire together, with great outbursts of laughter, as is doubtless called for, since 'tis a kind of amusement for them, you can judge for yourself how that goes down, as you can judge what kind of a hateful and wretched creature it takes to have put someone so close to her into such a situation! I bring up these mundane matters but rarely, and even when I speak of them I do so reluctantly, but since no one is present when that man acts as he does, and since he is in a position to tell you whatever he pleases, 'tis important that I tell you from time to time my side of the story, so that you can at least judge whether things are going as planned.

For example, today I had my mattresses beaten, and in so doing they stole from me a fourth of the wool they contained. Is that a signal? If it is, give the man a tip, for not only did he do it exceedingly well, but he even went on to reassure me that *there was no longer any reason*

---

3. Again, Sade is assuming that these baitings are the work of la présidente.
4. De Rougemont, of course.

for my mattresses to be beaten or, if there was a reason, they should be done in that manner. Eternal and charming manner of reasoning! With these people, I either have to dispense with whatever I have asked for or else I pay for it very dearly, and even then it turns out to be of an extremely poor quality: there is no middle ground. In the old days, what used to be referred to as highwaymen did not hold the poor peasant for ransom with any greater impunity nor did they act in his regard any more coherently. 'Tis fair to say, the comparison is absolutely apt, and this is what they refer to as a house of correction! 'Tis surrounded by the most churlish and basest of vices that a poor wretch is supposed to learn how to cherish virtue! And 'tis for having failed to respect the ass of a whore that a father runs the risk of never knowing his children's love, because they are separated from him, of being forcibly kept from his wife's embrace, from the care of his estates and possessions, that he is robbed, ruined, dishonored, done in, that he is prevented both from guiding his children properly into the world and from improving his own lot, that he rather is made the butt and the plaything of jailers, the fodder for three or four other utter scoundrels, that he is compelled to waste his time, his money, see his health deteriorate, and that he be kept incarcerated for seven years like a madman in an iron cage! And all that, why? What causes can bring about such great effects? Has he betrayed his country? Has he plotted against his wife, his children, his sovereign? Not at all; not a single word even suggesting as much. He has the great misfortune of firmly believing that nothing is less respectable than a whore and the way in which one makes use of her should be of no greater consequence than the manner in which one passes one's stool. Most assuredly, these are misdeeds, misdeeds of such gravity they deserve to have a man brought low.

If one were to go and say to King Achem, whose harem contains no fewer than seven hundred concubines, to whom he administers three or four hundred lashes a day to any who commit the slightest infraction, and who tries out his army sword on their heads; or to the Emperor of Golconda, who never goes out for a walk except on the backs of a dozen women arranged in the form of an elephant and who immolates a dozen of them with his own hand whenever a prince of royal blood dies; if, I say, one were to go and say to these gentlemen that in Europe there is a small parcel of earth in which one dismal man retains in his employ, day in and day out, some three thousand rogues whose task it is to verify the manner in which the citizens of this little parcel of earth (people who declare themselves to be *extremely enlightened*) attach the greatest importance to spermatic matters; and that there are dungeons and prisons ready and waiting, gallows constructed, especially for those members of this *extremely enlightened people* who have not been able to understand that 'twas a major crime to loosen the floodgates to the right rather than to the left; and that the slightest overheating of the head in a moment such as this, when nature dictates that one lose it completely, but when the dismal man of whom I spoke would have us retain full control of one's senses, such a person was sentenced to death or sent to prison for twelve to fifteen years; if, I say, if one were to go and report all this to the kings I have just named, you'd have to agree that 'twould be only normal that they in turn lock up the man who bore such news . . . But that's because these people are not civilized, they do not have the great good fortune of being enlightened by the flame of Christianity, they are but slaves whereas we, on the contrary, are *very Christian, extremely civilized, and most enlightened.*

O maker of this benighted little round ball, you who with a single breath has perhaps brought into being ten billion other little worlds such as ours in the immensity of space, you for whom the loss of these ten billion worlds would cost you not even so much as a sigh of regret, how you must be amused by all these imbecilities on the part of the tiny ants wherewith it has pleased you to sprinkle your globes, how you must laugh at King Achem who whips seven hundred women, at the emperor of Golconda who turns them into post horses, as you must chuckle too at that dismal man who would have us keep our head about us when we are losing our c——! Farewell, my darling wife.

54.   To Abbé Amblet

[January, 1782]

I am more or less in agreement with Monsieur de Buffon.[1] What I like about love, and the only thing about it I deem worthy, is the climax thereof. Trying to apply metaphysics to love is, to my mind, not only extremely stupid but also monstrous, and the only exception I

---

1. Count Georges Louis Leclerc (1707–1788), who wrote under the name Buffon, was a French naturalist and the author of *Natural History*, one of the many scientific works Sade read in Vincennes.

make to that is when I am forced to intersperse a bit of it in my works, in keeping with the demands of dramatic art.

Accordingly, I desire most urgently, as soon as I am free, that the slightly less restricted display of my talents in that undertaking will have no greater success than that it has just had on the part of those who have set Monsieur Amblet's tongue a-wagging. And 'twill be with the utmost delight that, once again giving free rein to my own true nature, I shall forsake the brushes of Molière for those of Aretino.[2]

The former, as you can well see, earned me a bit of fame and notoriety in the capital of Guyana; the latter paid me six pleasant little months of minor indulgence in one of the first cities of the kingdom, and forced me to spend two months in Holland without spending a penny of my own money. What a difference!

55. To Abbé Amblet

[January, 1782]

*T*he people of this world must be more than a little annoyed to see themselves depicted in such a light. 'Tis not, it seems to me, up to him who belies so forcefully the tableau to portray them in such odious features. The world has therefore changed greatly since I left it. As I remember, in former times solace and consolation were more or less reserved for those who suffered or were wanting, and going on that assumption I thought myself deserving of more than my fair share. Without questioning you on the matter, you nonetheless offer me one considerable consolation, for if people are indeed as you portray them, then one ought to have few regrets at having violated the laws of their society: thus my soul is at peace again, and for that I thank you, for I am indebted to you. With the exception that I have little doubt, if tomorrow I were to be sent to the gallows, you would write a different

---

2. Pietro Aretino (1492–1556), satirical licentious author whose daring clearly inspired Sade. In prison, Sade had devoted much of his overt writing up till now to drama. Here he gives his old tutor fair warning that, once free, he intends to bend his talents to more scurrilous forms.

letter. I thought 'twas uniquely reserved to those lacking a soul to lend their pen to the furies of revenge, but you convince me that there is a feeling in the heart of even the most decent of men who can at times cause him to turn his back on all the others. Even Madame la présidente de Montreuil, whose sole charm is to make sure I have a falling out with everyone, and who to that purpose—the way whores do to soldiers—bends her every talent and effort, often forgets that her family tree is far more beset with unfortunate slander than mine. Let her simply go back one or two generations, no more, on either her side of the family or her husband's—I shall not elaborate further—and she will find a *poor miserable creature* who surely often cried from the depths of her heart: "*Be fair, even if you cannot bring yourself to be tolerant, and learn that one ought not to humiliate when one has reason to blush oneself; that fortune can give you the right to commiserate with misfortunes equal to your own but not the right to punish them.*"

One of my major consolations, I confess, was to receive at least once a year some proof, however passing, of your friendship. I deployed all the craftiness at my command to that end, for when it came to reciprocating, you may be assured that whatever I said or did was merely a ruse to make certain I had a word from you at year's end. I considered that my New Year's gift to myself, and I regaled myself with it much as children do their toys. But this monster, this infernal creature that no expression can ever properly depict, like a viper that blights everything it touches, wants to spew her venom even upon our long-standing friendship; she is well on her way to succeeding, 'twould seem, at least to all outward appearances, for nothing will ever erase from my heart my feelings for you. But I shall learn how to do without the pleasure of hearing from you, or of asking you for tangible proof of your feelings for me. You may inform her of her victory by showing her the most earnest request that I hereby make that you not write me further. I shall withdraw into myself, I shall dwell upon those happy days when innocence and peace formed, with flowers, the links of friendship that today they would have me break, and I shall write, with Dante:

Nussun maggior dolore
Che ricordarsi del tempo felice nella miseria.
—Dante, *Inferno*, canto 5

[*There is no greater pain than to remember,*
In our present grief, past happiness.]

56. To Mademoiselle de Rousset

From my country house, this April 17, 1782

*T*he eagle, Mademoiselle, is sometimes obliged to leave the seventh region of the air to swoop down and light upon the summit of Mount Olympus, upon the ancient pines of the Caucasus, upon the cold larch trees of the Jura, upon the snow-bedecked brow of Taurus, and even, upon occasion, near the quarries of Montmartre.

We know from history (for history is a lovely thing) that Cato, the great Cato, cultivated his field with his own hands, that Cicero himself planted trees in even rows along the beautiful avenues of Formies (I don't know whether or not they are still standing), that Diogenes was wont to sleep in a wine cask, that Abraham was known to craft statues out of clay, that the illustrious author of *Telemachus* composed some touching little verses for Madame Guyon, that Piron[1] sometimes forsook his sublime brushes of *The Metromania* in order to drink some Champagne and compose the *Ode to Priapus* (do you by any chance know this poetic trifle, so popular with today's young ladies and so truly appropriate to be integrated into any plan of education, the goal of which is to shape the mind and heart of those demoiselles destined for the fashionable world?). Haven't we seen the great Voltaire build a church to Our Lord with the same hand with which he wrote, speaking of the Holy Birth of our Redeemer:

> Joseph-the-panther and Mary-the-dark,
> Unknowingly wrought their pious work.
>
> PUCELLE

And in our own time, Mademoiselle, in our very own majestic days, have we not seen the renowned Madame de Montreuil set aside her Euclides and her Barrême[2] to come and discuss salad and olive oil with her cook?

All of which should go to prove beyond all shadow of doubt, Mademoiselle, that however hard man tries, however much he tries to raise himself to a special plane, there are two inevitable moments in

---

1. Alexis Piron, French writer and satirical dramatist whose most famous play was the one Sade mentions, *The Metromania*.
2. Probably Jean Nicolas Barrême, author of *Traité des parties doubles*, published in Paris in 1721.

the day that, despite all his efforts to the contrary, cannot fail but remind him of the unfortunate condition of all other animals save himself, which as you know, according to my way of thinking (perhaps to judge unfairly, in my opinion), according to my way of thinking, I say, bring him back closer to reality. And these two cruel moments are (excuse the expressions, Mademoiselle, they are not noble but they are nonetheless true), those two frightful moments, therefore, are: first when he *intakes* food and the second when he *expels* it. To those one could add the moment when a person learns that his inheritance is being eaten away, and again when one is told of the death of his faithful servants. Such is the situation in which I find myself, my saintly one, and that 'twill therefore be the subject of this sad epistle.

I regret the passing of Gothon. She doubtless had her faults, but she more than made up for them by her virtues and qualities; and there are many people in this world about whom one cannot say as much. Gothon loved men. But, Mademoiselle, are men not made for women, and women for men? 'Tis that not the will of nature? Gothon, as Madame de Sade has been wont to say with a show of great humor, *married because she was with child*. Well, now, Mademoiselle, a bit of philosophy here! What is the great harm in that? As for myself, I see nothing therein but virtues. In so doing, she was desirous of giving her child a father; she wanted to make sure the babe would have its daily bread; by so doing she was making an effort to see that the child might have a chance to rise above that abject class that leaves it little recourse but to descend into poverty or into crime. But she was also, on several occasions, unfaithful to her husband . . . Ah! there is where I have to draw the line! Adultery on the part of women is a subject fraught with such dire harm, the consequences thereof are so catastrophic and so deadly that I have never been able to tolerate it. Look high and low at my principles, rummage as deeply as you like into the history of my licentious affairs and you will find that rarely did I become involved in such affairs, and for every dozen virgins, or so-called virgins, that I tried to seduce you will be hard-pressed to find as many as three married women. On this point, Gothon was therefore in her wrong. Gothon was responsible for my arrest,[3] I'm aware of that, but in my eyes death effaces all her offenses, and my unhappy heart is heavy with tears, even for my greatest enemies.

Whatever wrongs one may visit upon her, Gothon was a most

---

3. Hardly. She did her best to forewarn Sade of the intruding constabulary the night of his arrest at La Coste on the night of August 26, 1778.

caring person. She was always pleasant, prompt to serve, and with a light touch; she was a good brood mare who loved her master's stables. That poor departed young woman, whose only helpmates were messieurs Pailet, Payan, Sambuc and company, would in twelve or fifteen years have become an impeccable staff. Verily, I do miss her greatly. Moreover, how can I refrain from telling you—yes, now that we have spoken of her virtues we can move on to mention her considerable qualities—Gothon, people were wont to say, Gothon had the most beautiful . . . Ah, damn it all! how can I express it? The dictionary has no synonym for that word, and decency does not allow me to write it out in so many letters, though it has only three . . . Well, verily, here 'tis then, mademoiselle: hers was the most beautiful a—— that ever managed to escape from the mountains of Switzerland in over a century . . . its reputation was second to none. Even *Monsieur le président de Montreuil,* whom business of far greater import ten years ago brought to these parts (and which, most assuredly, he performed to perfection)[4] was nonetheless unable, during one of his rare moments of leisure, not to feast his ravenous eyes upon that famous star. That momentary contemplation was what established the distinguished reputation that Gothon enjoyed for the rest of her life. And the magistrate[5] in question, all the more an expert on that part of the anatomy for the simple reason that he was known for feasting his eyes on the divine beauties of the nation's capital, was most assuredly in an excellent position to judge fairly and without prejudice the object in question. I realize that I'm forgetting here a most important proverb: *One should not speak of rope in the house of the hanged;* and that, consequently, I should refrain from focusing on these unchaste objects, the attachment whereto, or so people claim, has been the source of my misfortunes. But I was unable to refrain from indulging in this short apologia, and in a good and tender soul, whatever restrictions one may impose on oneself, the qualities of a person whose death one mourns come swarming back as soon as one dwells on her, and dictate the flow of the pen. But let us be serious once again, and for the convenience of the scribbler, let us put all that behind us, for I've always had a slight preference for vice, and have always thought that the greatest men were those who knew how to throw themselves into it completely and passionately. You see,

---

4. Visiting the magistrates and lawyers in Aix-en-Provence to assure his son-in-law's arrest.
5. The président de Montreuil had for many years been a member of the Tax Court.

there, all of a sudden, Jacques the Scribbler's a great man! He wasn't expecting it, and 'tis the first time anyone has ever labeled him that.

. . . .

[The rest of the letter is missing.]

57. *To Gaufridy*

[*April 17, 1782*]

Cursed be the city of Apt! Cursed be the city of Bonnieux! Cursed be the lawyer Gaufridy!

—What, you! you, my dear lawyer! you, the strictest observer of the laws of decency, you, the most zealous defender of Christian virginity, you have been able to endure, you have been able to tolerate within the reaches of your jurisdiction, the terrible scandal of which I have just learned! You have found it in your heart to let the chaste children of Saint-François bend their efforts at something other than leading those who go astray back onto the straight and narrow, and you have further allowed these holy keepers of the altars to come and offer the Protestants the example of perversity! *O tempora! o mores!* What is this world coming to! No, virtue has fled the face of the earth, as has decency and propriety. 'Tis there for all eyes to see: we are fast approaching that catastrophe that will plunge the world once more into the void, and thus are we come to that fearful time of desolation and abomination that the prophet Daniel foresaw and predicted. O century of candor and amenity! What have you become, you once blessed century, wherein a poor Franciscan friar finds himself sufficiently restored by a novice so that the high-mettled desires of nature are thereby assuaged within himself? To what time of infamy and horror have you yielded your place? What! 'tis young women they now need? And not content with this intolerable scandal, to boot they have to make the young ladies pregnant, who in turn give birth, and the unfortunate fruit of this unchaste behavior is available for all to see in the local hospital? And you have condoned it? and you have allowed it? So be it: I have no choice but to don sackcloth, cover myself with ashes, and walk barefoot and bare-headed to make an effort, if indeed 'tis not too late, to avert the wrath of God from falling upon my people.

Actually, lawyer, in this affair, if the truth be known, 'tis not a question of any Franciscan friar! What I'm referring to is *trees being cut down, and poachers.*[1] And what does a Franciscan friar who fathers children have to do with all that? —Ignoramuses! Don't you see that this is an explanation, and that if you had let me have my say, I was going to proceed in my own good time to let the story of the destruction flow out of the story of the construction and, through well-tempered periods, well-rounded transitions, and seamlessly narrated episodes, I was brilliantly planning on emulating the eloquence of Isocrates by a few deft strokes of my pen. What is the point of interrupting me? And how now do you expect me to pick up the thread of my tale?

All right then, let us go straight to the point, since asides and flashes of wit are clearly lost on you, there's no point in proving that one has read Demosthenes, expounded on Cicero, and learned Vadé[2] by heart! Therefore, to the point.

Trees cut down, and fruit trees to boot! Lawyer, you are going to find me a trifle harsh, but misfortune tends not to soften one's heart, on the contrary. Moreover, I am not at leisure to run on to my heart's content; I am expected for dinner, which I have every reason to believe will be exquisite, and I'm most anxious to be off. Here, therefore, in two words, is my determination: if you fail to punish, with all the vigor of the law, the rogues who committed this crime, I swear to you by all that's most holy in the world that the first thing I shall do once I am free will be to punish to the full extent of the law the former crimes committed. And further, you should know that I shall not consider them expiated, were I made to eat crow, till I have brought the entire community to its knees!

As for the poachers, I enclose a paper I ask you to pass on to the guard, and I beg of you to make certain the order contained therein is faithfully carried out, and that you help institute all the necessary legal proceedings, that you do everything in your power vigorously to prosecute the offending parties, and that you effect whatever disbursements are required to implement the said document.

That is all I had to say. You know the reasons that restrain me from bringing up matters of business; 'tis impossible for me to transgress

---

1. That is, cutting down fruit trees on Sade's land.
2. Jean Joseph Vadé (1719–1757), French poet and dramatist. One can understand Sade's attraction to Vadé, for it was he who brought into French literature and drama the language and mores of the French *halles*, Paris's colorful street markets, which, alas, were moved to the suburbs in the 1960s.

them. If you thought my silence stemmed from anything else you were sadly mistaken and you should better learn to judge my heart.

> Up, up, Rosny, they'll think I am granting you pardon.
> (Henry IV, Act 3)[3]

I am, my dear lawyer, with all the feelings you deserve, your most humble and obedient servant.

DE SADE

I ask that you pay over one louis to Mademoiselle Rousset for a special task wherewith I have entrusted her.[4]

I ask you kindly to furnish and even offer my aunts all the game they may desire and that, whether it comes from my own land or is purchased at the market, that it be given them directly; they have made their needs known. I also charge you to make certain the pension monies due them be paid precisely on time, and I further entrust you to convey to them the assurance of my most profound respects, and to do the same for my cousins.

58. To Madame de Sade

April 26, 1782

*U*pon receipt of the present letter, I would be grateful, wife Sade, my spouse, if you would, without delay and without any deductions made therefrom, see to it that payment is made from the amount duly allotted to you by the family assembly for our communal upkeep, in money of good and valid tender in the kingdom, the sum of three hundred thirteen livres and twelve sous, said payment to be turned over to Monsieur Boucher, equerry, currently employed by the state department of prisons and head clerk of the lieutenant general both of the Paris police and of other sites and places. The intention of the

---

3. It remains unclear if Sade is referring to Shakespeare (in which no Rosny appears) or a French drama involving King Henri IV.
4. To pay for the mass in Gothon's memory at the local parish.

aforesaid entire sum being to satisfy the debt to Monsieur Fonteillot, head surgeon residing at Vincennes Square, more specifically assigned to care for the prisoners whom the fair-minded minister is holding under lock and key in the forenamed prisons of the royal keep on the aforementioned square, as well as the care of the non-commissioned officers stationed therein, whose principal task is to guard and maintain the security of the said delinquents. Said payment having two aspects: first, honoring the tip customarily offered the said gentleman for his services in shaving the prisoner, under the permission and protection of the royal magistrate; second, full reimbursement for the milk regularly dispensed to me and emanating from the government's horned beasts. Drawn up with the knowledge and approval of Monsieur de Rougemont, knight of the royal and military order of Saint-Louis, lieutenant acting on the king's behalf as regards the Vincennes stronghold, and reversioner of other sites and fortresses of the monarchy. In testimony whereof, this twenty-sixth of April in the year of grace one thousand seven hundred eighty-two, it being precisely eleven in the morning and being in full possession of our health and reason, having drawn up and initialed the present document, the purpose whereof has been duly noted above.

PRISONER SADE

59. Evening Prayer

[April, 1782]

O my god, I have but one favor to ask you and you refuse to grant it to me no matter how earnest and fervent my prayers; that favor, that kindness, o my god, would be to refrain from choosing as my correctors men even more wicked than I, to keep from delivering over him who is but guilty of the most commonplace and minor offenses to scoundrels already hardened in crime, who, making a mockery of your laws, think nothing of transgressing them at every moment of the day. Put, o my god, my fate in the hands of virtue, for virtue is your image here below, and 'tis only in the hands of them who respect it that vice can hope to be reformed. O ye the highest of the high, I devoutly ask that you not choose as my masters a *monopolist*, a *thief* of the poor, a *man who has declared bankruptcy*—a *sodomite*—a *cheat* and *rogue—alguazil* of the Madrid Inquisition, a defrocked *Jesuit*, and a *female pimp*, since 'tis foreordained that I be sacrificed, o my god, since 'tis written in your great book that you have brought me into this world in order to serve as the sustenance of bitches and the swill of pigs, and that you know better than anyone that the only fruits I can cull from such a situation is to become worse than I already was, because of the excess of hate that I shall be compelled to feel toward my fellow men; at least let my example, through your holy power, redound to the benefit of my compatriots, and that the base scoundrels I have just mentioned, seeing by the total lack of success their so-called remedies have had upon me, will come to understand the impossibility of concealing their horrors any longer beneath the mask of such fanciful fair-mindedness, and will at long last dream up some other means to subjugate their fellow creatures to the outlandish and reckless excesses of their vengeance and cupidity.

AMEN
FRUCTUS BELLI

60. To Madame de Sade

[June 1782]

*N*ow here is another new plan of punishment being devised against me. Last October they wanted to see what my reaction would be to concerns about your health, and when they saw that they had touched upon the most sensitive part of my soul, they doubtless decided that 'twould be the same kind of torture they would apply the following summer, in order to correspond (as fate had willed the interval between visits) to everything that happened the summer before! I must warn you, however, that since I am completely incapable of suffering such scenes, I have firmly made up my mind to pay not the slightest attention to any kind of worry, no matter what it may be.

For the past three days they keep telling me over and over again—but their remarks are so forced and so disconnected that they thereby reveal their duplicity—about an illness that is making the rounds, from which no one is exempt. If they had not made such a point of it, and especially if they had not contradicted themselves so baldly, I might have believed it. But the person whose task it was to pass this information on is a man so utterly stupid and so utterly absurd that 'tis absolutely impossible to believe a word he says. But, one may well object at this juncture, the fact is you did believe him last year, since you paid him accordingly. That calculation is completely specious, and I maintain that not once did I take the man at his word. But I did let him run on and have his say, and I did recompense him, but only on the assumption that after so many lies a single truth might slip past his lips. But as for having believed him, I maintain and I shall prove that I did not believe him for one minute; and, verily, if you knew me, if you could fairly judge the extreme stupidity of *that Judas*, you would immediately recognize the utter impossibility of believing him.

Be that as it may, people have spoken to me about an illness that is both dangerous and widespread, and why, I ask, have they done so?[1] Within these walls, 'tis absolutely against the rules to speak of such things. Is it then determined that Monsieur de Rougemont will break the rules of the house if only to drive me to despair? 'Tis forbidden to pass on hidden notes, and if any were brought to my attention, 'twould be for the sole purpose of making me miserable. 'Tis against the rules to let the prisoners hear the latest news, and the only news they would let me hear would be those they knew would be like thrusting a knife into my breast. You can well imagine that after a time one is no longer taken in by such spiteful acts. I have just written to Monsieur de Rougemont to ask that he prevent these people from speaking to me any further, and I *hereby renew my oath that I shall kill the first one who opens his mouth*. 'Tis one of two things: either they want me to be aware of the existence of that illness and the potential effects it might have on you, or they prefer that I not know. There can be no other reason. If indeed they do want me to know, then you should write me so saying, giving me your word of honor that what you write is true, and signing your letter with the name of that mountain to which you know I

---

1. Among the methods of torturing their most infamous prisoner, the turnkeys reveled in passing on bad news to Sade, such as: "Have you heard of the terrible illness sweeping through Paris?"

must one day repair, *the name* of which no one else in the universe but you and I know; and then I shall believe it. And if they do not want me to know, what then is the point of letting drop little hints now and again or speaking in such an ambiguous manner? Anything gleaned in this way, given the utter abuse they make of this method of informing and the shameless deceit they mix into a language that should be held sacred, since 'tis the only one that can be used here, anything gleaned in this manner, I say, I take with less than a grain of salt.

If I had to sacrifice my life for you, if my blood were needed to save your life, I would believe anything and there's nothing I wouldn't do to track down the truth. But given the situation in which I find myself, what can I offer you? *My anxiety;* it serves you not one whit; completely useless if 'tis true; totally ridiculous if the news is false. Thus it does me absolutely no good to try and figure out what's what. All I can do is to beg you to let me know what is going on and to do all in your power to ease my mind when I hear it other than from your good self. There's nothing untactful in what I am suggesting there. And most surely 'twould be the person you yourself would advise me to listen to if only you could speak to me directly. So that is where I stand, quite certain in my mind that you can neither be annoyed with me about all this nor suspect that the very real and very tender feelings I have for you, and that you know I shall always have, are in any way diminished.

My motives for not being overly worried about this so-called illness:

'Tis the illness of this past winter that they are dragging out once again; but we know that illness is over. The surgeon himself told me so in April. More or less about the same time, the major told me it came from the north, and the people here assured me it came up from the south. Which ones to believe? They cannot agree; therefore they are lying. That illness carried over to the spring. Two people here, and the prisoner to whom I am closest and with whom I get along most excellently, were felled by it; I saw it and heard it. Therefore 'twas a thing of the past, not the present. Those illnesses do not last very long.

During your April visit I asked if you had come down with a cold like everyone else. You told me you had. Thus if you have already had your illness, then you have paid your dues and I can cease worrying about it anymore.

One of their more ridiculous conceits was to say that this new illness had begun on June sixteenth, because the last time I saw you was the fifteenth. And that despite all the proofs I had that that illness had run its course prior to that. In April, the surgeon said, and I quote word for word: *Now that I am finally over all those devilish colds and catarrhs,* etc. Therefore, it was over and done with. And then they went on with their ridiculous contradictions. On the morning of the eighteenth I needed something from Monsieur de Rougemont's. They said to me: *It can't be had today, he's been in Paris since this morning.* That evening he was in bed, sick as a dog; still in bed sick as a dog on the eighteenth and nineteenth, and on the twentieth the surgeon, the only person here who could take care of him, was spending the day in Paris. On the twenty-second, at five o'clock in the evening (this is even worse), the surgeon is sick in bed. At five fifteen they inform me in no uncertain terms that he is away on a visit a league from here. And so on and so forth. When I point out to the imbecile to what degree he is lying and completely contradicting himself, he flies into a terrible rage: further proof of his deceit.

No, I am being led down the garden path. Their whole point in prattling so is to make me worry. But my health no longer allows me to add any more worry to my already full plate. I tell you, I am in no state to endure any scenes, however minor. Therefore, kill me if you like, I have given you the secret of how to do it.

You have made it your business to go five months without seeing me, and since everything is comparative and because during your previous long absence, which was of four months' duration, they did their best to make me worry my head about your behavior, now they want to upset me about your health.

You have made it your business during the five months' absence, the term of which is this November, in order to come up with a neat 59 and a neat 57,[2] to write me only once a fortnight. Well then, I'm aware of that, I'm not happy about it, but I'm not going to let it plunge me into deep despair. What need is there to justify all that; who is taking their cues from you to try to pretend you are unwell? You can well accomplish the same purpose without interlarding this illness into the tale. When in writing to you I concocted some similar story, I had a reason for doing so, thus there was no meanness on my part, and what is more, you were free and could always verify whether or not 'twas true. But in your case if 'twere really the case, I have no means of finding out for myself, and therefore you have no motive. The result: I refuse to believe a word about the so-called illness as long as I have not had

---

2. More signals, whose meaning remained known only to Sade. After his release in 1790 he never mentioned them again.

proof from you and you alone, by the means I have just described. And you can neither be annoyed at me because of that stance nor doubt in the slightest my tender feelings toward you.

From this moment on until I get out of here, my philosophy—and I have managed to make it exceedingly clear on this point—will be far worse as regards everything else, and since I know all too well that the more time goes on the more you will do your best to make me worry about everything, I have amused myself by drawing up on a single chart all the different things that you might do and next to them I have listed the way I intend to react to them, without allowing my soul to linger one moment longer on each of the subjects that I shall set forth. Here then is everything you will make up, or might make up, followed by the one and only manner in which I intend to react:

Concerns about your health: they will be false, see everything I have said above.

Concerns about your behavior: you are incapable of being unfaithful. Six visits have sufficed to destroy my wild imaginings and bring me back to reality. They are insulting to you, which is reason enough why I shall never let them ever take hold of me again. I know better how to value what I love.

My children and my friends ill or deceased: 'tis patently untrue. Such news is strictly forbidden here, for the very reason of preventing such rumors from making the rounds, and that in fact is one of the most praiseworthy rules of the establishment.

My castles burned to the ground and my goods and possessions sold off: so much the better, that much less to worry about. I shall hie myself to Prussia, there to stage plays, and you shall play the guitar.[3] As for our fine family of five, we shall learn to earn our own living.

My furniture and possessions moved: fine with me, all I wanted was to have my goods and possessions closer to Paris. I no longer enjoy the notion of traveling, and Provence is very far away.

---

3. Renée-Pélagie was taking guitar lessons; Sade learned this from Milli Rousset, which made him furious. First of all (needless to say) he was insanely jealous of the guitar teacher. To which Milli Rousset wrote to reassure him: "You have no reason to be jealous of the guitar teacher. He is a proper, pious man, full of virtue, more brilliant in heart than in mind, a good friend, and amusing to boot . . . I asked him to give a few lessons, to kill time. While busy writing or doing other things, I enjoy listening to Madame practicing her scales . . ."

My books burned: fine and dandy, the only ones I shall miss are the leather-bound volumes. Most of them were printed in Holland, and are of very little value, and when I go see Villette,[4] I shall buy them all back in Geneva and have a much finer library than before.

My papers seized and burned: eh! they were only first drafts anyway; the ideas have become crystal clear in my head. I shall start all over again; this time they will be better written and much more passionate, too, and to make sure the *lady paper thief* does not steal them away, I shall bring them myself directly from my office to the printer.

They will take away your daily walks: all right, if they do I'll use the time to write verses. Whatever excuse they use to suppress my walks, whether 'tis mending my fireplace or patching up a wall, a little play in verse will instantly flow therefrom. Which reminds me, there's one already written, signed and sealed, as I previously mentioned to you; all that is holding up its departure is hearing the name *Nicolas* ring out (the name of the worker).

So then, bother me now to your heart's content, worry me to death. *Oh! that will happen as soon as your sentence is up! . . .* Eh! go take a look and see if they're coming, Jean, eh! go take a look and see if they're there, etc. *Nicolas.*

No, my pet, no, no, heavenly madame présidente, no, no, divine sequel, no. All is said. All is surfeited! All is blunted. You see that I said the strongest, and if it does not come to pass the way I proved it would, then who do you want to be the weakest? The simplest thing would therefore be to leave me in peace, and upon my word I advise it most strongly. As a result of further vexations you are certain to inflict upon me between now and the time I am destined to see you, I shall have the opportunity to dwell further upon and remember this letter often, which I am neither tempted to rewrite nor to make any longer than it already is, I therefore date it and dub it my letter of the 23rd.

I begin my two hundred tenth week here.[5]

I return the fourth [volume] of *Conjurations.*

---

4. Charles de Villette, Renée-Pélagie's cousin, into whose home she had contemplated moving a year earlier till Sade's jealousy made her change her mind.
5. It is difficult to tell what Sade is using as his starting date, and therefore difficult to discern the date of this letter. If he's using as his starting date his rearrest at La Coste on August 26, 1778, then the letter would have to have been written in early September, 1782. The French edition indicates variously the months of June and July, 1782, as the date for this letter.

61. *To Madame de Sade*

[1782]

I don't know what they plan for me when I leave here. I told you, and I persist in saying, that what I desire is to go home with you. Still, I am not loath to spending two or three days in Paris before that, wanting absolutely to see my daughter, on whom I've never laid eyes; and they would be hard-pressed to keep me from satisfying my o'erwhelming desire to see her. You ask what my plans are: I have made none, and I swear to you that I have refrained from building any castles in Spain; I've been misled far too often. I want to leave here an entirely free man, with no strings attached. The time of exile is far behind us. That would have been acceptable at the time my sentence was handed down; it would have been welcome; it would have been a punishment to fit the crime; it would have spared me the indignity of completely ruining my reputation in my native province, a shame that can only have been concocted by my cruelest enemies working in concert. Now I must leave here free. If that happens, my plan is to go spend a year on my estates in order to set things right there, and thence to take up my abode there, where I shall spend the remainder of my days. I shall have lived sufficiently for the piddling pleasures of others; 'twill be time to live for myself. But where will that be? Ah! you should know it well, if you remember all our earlier conversations. If they set me free on the condition of exiling me, even were it to my own estates, then let them keep a close watch on me day and night, for I shall not remain there, I shall abscond to Florence or Naples. If 'tis exile, doubtless there will be a guard in attendance: in which case I state categorically that having had my fill of paying the police and their henchmen, I shall most assuredly not pay them any more than I paid the lackey in Aix-en-Provence, and I hereby give my word of honor that I shall not pay a penny to anyone. I have written it before, I have written it since, and I shall repeat it to my dying day. May I be looked upon as the lowest of men if ever I pay a penny for that purpose. Is it possible that these gentlemen do not have, in the entire length and breadth of Paris, other fools, other pigeons than me, that they have had me and only me for the past ten years to ante up and pay off their *alguazils?* You do not know who the triumvirate[1] consists of—someone I

---

1. He is referring to the three-judge panel in Provence that passed sentence on him, which, he is maintaining, was heavily prejudiced against him.

know has been exceedingly remiss in that case: the triumvirate consists of three white-wigged gentlemen, one of whom is in fact quite handsome and in his day enjoyed a certain reputation in Paris. This past summer there was on this score a rather charming story upon the occasion of a certain *powdering episode* that took place during the month of July, at a slight remove from the earth. It was reported that this bewigged one's valet had tried to leave his master, because after the powdering exercise his master became so swelled up with pride that he had to add six extra plaits to his wig. His valet, having already fashioned no fewer than fourteen on each side, said to him: *"Monseigneur, I fear I must leave your employ,"* and without further ado he up and left. How stupid the people of Provence are, to tell stories that are as dull as they are *blasphemous!* In any event, to come back to the triumvirate, here's one to top all others: since I point all of them out to you only in order to remind you of my reasons for challenging their testimony against me, reasons that your mother should ponder a bit more profoundly, to avoid having the wool pulled over her eyes, I shall cite, next to each one, just what the reason is. Regarding the first-named, the reason is so overwhelming that I cannot find any way to tone it down sufficiently so that the censors will let it pass. All I ask is that you remember that 'tis infinitely overpowering and of such a nature as to nullify completely anything and everything he may testify against me. I swear 'tis so, and shall prove it. The second character of the triumvirate held some position in the province to which I was posted in June 1764.[2] I did not go and pay him an official visit, and when that was brought to my attention, I replied that, *firmly believing I held a much higher position than he, I should not be the one to call upon him first.* This remark was passed on to him. A certain Malhiver, a captain of dragoons with whom you may recall I later became involved on the rue Neuve-Luxembourg, told me that he had personally heard from a most reliable source that this captain *had been piqued by my remark and stated that he would never forgive me.* I replied to Malhiver, who was not a close friend, that I didn't give a f——. Alas! in those days I was not aware that, like the Romans, we would go and seek out our dictators behind a plow: the bewigged one has since risen in life, I have fallen, and only the remark I made has remained unchanged. What further proof does one need that, when a man's freedom

---

2. Sade is doubtless referring to his trip that month to Dijon, where on June 26 he made his acceptance address to the High Court of Burgundy upon the occasion of formally assuming the position of lieutenant-general of the king for the provinces of Bresse, Bugey, Valromey, and Gex.

is at stake, a judge such as he, who swears that he will never forget the slight he has suffered, must be deemed untrustworthy? Madame de Montreuil will back me up on that. As for the third personage of the triumvirate, whom I compare to Lepidus, his reason for keeping me in prison is quite obvious. I know from Marais—for you know that I always quote my sources—that the prisons of *Paris, Vincennes, the Bastille,* and *Charenton* bring him in no less than twenty-five thousand livres per annum in revenues. Given that figure, 'tis simple enough to figure out that the gentleman in question wants to keep these prisons as full as possible. At this point, 'tis to my mother-in-law I direct my remark, she who is fair-minded, equitable, she whom I have heard say a thousand times over: *I know all too well the horrors of these prisons; they make you pay when they put you in, they make you pay when they release you; 'tis a complex network of horrors.* So the question I raise to her is whether she should listen to the advice of man-number-one, whose motives for keeping me in I shall not go into, etc., of a second who has sworn that he will never forgive me for a remark I made, and of a third who grows rich at my expense? Let us have her response! Let her not forget that she is a mother, that I am perhaps the most obedient and the most loving of all her children.[3] In any case, enough of all that. You asked me to tell you what the triumvirate was; I told you. My letter must be let through.[4] If what I say is false, they should laugh and let it pass. If they stop it, then 'tis proof positive that my complaints are justified. With what weapons they are then arming me when, having made all these allegations, I might just as well add: *And when I lodged my complaints on this score, when I shed tears of blood in the bosom of my wife, they intercepted my letters and would not let them through, in the fear that such disastrous truths might come to light.*

What in the world does this sentence mean? Do you remember our butterflies at La Coste? That sentence is extremely peculiar: I am in fact dumbfounded by it. They are two different ways to interpret it. Did you really mean to put butterflies? If it is butterflies, you know that butterflies are something special we have between us, something only the two of us can do together. You offer to find me some, which therefore is tantamount to saying you are ready and willing to come to terms with me. If 'tis that, yes; and that's the way I understand it, and that's the way I want to understand it. If on the contrary you used the

---

3. Though an in-law, Sade is suddenly including himself among the hated Mme de Montreuil's offspring.
4. By the censors.

term butterflies generically, by which you meant or implied snails or vipers, which the meaning of the sentence seems to indicate, then no, no, no, my dear friend, my feelings for you are such that I cannot even hear such language as that. But whichever way you meant it, since 'tis nonetheless passing strange, I beg you to send me which of the two meanings you intended; I am more curious than I can say. . . . .
. . . .
[The balance of the letter is missing.]

62. To Madame de Sade

[October 21, 1782]

I have, my dear friend, but one favor to ask of you, no more, and I still hope that your former friendship for me, or if you prefer your pity, will not let you say nay. That favor is to have me transferred from here to anywhere else, even were it shackled hand and foot to the cage of Mont-Saint-Michel. I would prefer it and mercifully ask that you cause it to happen. Yes, I prefer it a thousand times more than being constantly exposed to the odious attempts by that scoundrel de Rougemont to have me poisoned, he who doubtless has come to some arrangement with your mother to finish me off. For the past six weeks that rogue has been doing everything in his power to give me drugs that are having a serious negative effect upon my health and are causing me pain and anguish more violent than any criminal could ever endure on the wheel. And the proof that this rogue de Rougemont has sold me down the river is that they now keep me confined to my room and serve my food through a trapdoor, the way they do with the insane. They carry their outrageous behavior to the point of not letting the surgeon visit me, proof positive that my life is no longer worth a penny. Farewell, that is my last word to you. May heaven make you happy without me, since they fancy that my death is necessary for your happiness. If that is true, then I leave you without remorse, and I swear and solemnly declare that if I have but one regret, 'tis that in leaving this world I am unable to take along with me the odious scoundrel who stooped not only to fatten his own purse but then to use the monies he is raking in at the price of my life to indulge in his own unworthy pleasures. Have me transferred where you will and under whatever conditions, I beg of you on bended knee, if you still have an ounce of pity left for me in your heart. If you do not, I shall have to believe that you yourself are an accomplice to my death.

63.   *To Monsieur Le Noir*

October 22, 1782

*D*espite the fact that I am quite certain none of my letters has ever been delivered to you, and that you have unjustly, if I may be so bold, abandoned the most important role wherewith your situation endows you, namely that of doing me justice and enlightening me concerning the results of the rage of those who continue to harry me relentlessly, despite that, I say, I owe it to myself to inform you personally of my complaints relating to the most recent horrors that have been visited upon me, which I shall set forth as truthfully and briefly as possible.

From September 3 to October 20 inclusive, Monsieur de Rougemont, doubtless paid off by my wife's family, has upon thirteen different occasions had the villainy to mix in with the normal foods allotted me here a drug that has the effect of making me painfully ill to my stomach, so much so in fact that had they fed me poisons the reaction would have been no less violent. As soon as I had detected what they were doing, I asked to be given only soft-boiled eggs, on the assumption that they would be impossible to tamper with: on the second or third day my request was denied. I lodged a complaint about the pain I was suffering. They laughed in my face. I appealed to the surgeon into whose hands I have been entrusted to cure the ills that had been foisted upon me. I asked that he speak to Monsieur de Rougemont on the matter. All I was able to elicit from him by way of response were some cock and bull stories. At which point I said that, since they were refusing to deal with me according to the law, if it happened again I would take matters into my own hands. And they did it again. I took my revenge on whomever I could, Sir, and in that I was guided by this axiom of the law of nature, which shall be my guiding principle throughout my life: *whenever justice has been denied me, respond by taking matters into my own hands*. Whereupon Monsieur de Rougemont has taken it upon himself, doubtless to cover up his little sport, to withdraw the few pleasures necessary to my health that had hitherto been granted me, as a result of which, Monsieur, either I must allow myself to be poisoned or if I object to it, then I am punished.

No, Monsieur, no, they are not and cannot be the orders of the king. 'Tis impossible they be such, and I beseech you therefore in the name of fair-mindedness that I be treated in strict accordance with those orders. You may be sure, Sir, that one day I shall lodge a most serious and vigorous complaint in connection with an infamy of that sort. I shall state that I first brought this complaint to your attention. Would you be pleased, therefore, if 'twas said that you refused to see that justice was done me? I most earnestly ask of you that I not be punished because others are in their wrong; I ask you most urgently that this kind of misdeed not be repeated and that they enjoin this infamous scoundrel who within these walls trafficks with the lives of the poor wretches through whom and by whom he has been allowed to earn his sad and somber living, that he be enjoined, I say, from any longer poisoning the already poor nutrition that he gives me, and that I at least be allowed to remain alive, which is not the case at present, since my refusal to go along with his double-dealing compels me to restrict my diet to milk. There in a nutshell, Monsieur, is the essence of my complaint to you and concerning which I have the right to expect, both by your position and your person, justice that will be both prompt and swift. When a prisoner brings such serious complaints as these to your attention, Monsieur, 'tis quite impossible that you refuse to see him yourself or send someone in your place, and that is all I ask of you.

Now then! what in the world can be the reasons behind such perfidy? Is it the destruction of my life? If so, there's no need to let me linger all this long. No, I categorically reject that idea, and do not despise my wife's parents sufficiently to suspect them of such behavior. But one idiotic and frightful notion does come to mind here. *His misdeeds*—for such is the way they will probably put it—*are the fruit of an overheated imagination; break down his constitution in order to annihilate his imagination.* What an absurd line of reasoning, Sir! 'Tis not from an overheated imagination that so-called misdeeds derive, 'tis from a constitution that has been too beaten and battered. To try to destroy it further would therefore only have the effect of nurturing the cause of the disorder, not curing it. A child of twelve could easily have fathomed that. But what about his rage and his thirst for revenge, they reason? In a word, are they reprisals? They are unjust, Monsieur. I have never even once in my life mixed any drugs into any matter whatsoever, certainly nothing that could have negatively affected the health of a human being, and certainly without that person's knowing it, and if my Marseilles trial has not rendered that principal charge null and void to the extent I would have wished, 'tis the fault of those who manipulated the trial from start to finish, and I can now see the reason why I have been treated thus. Aside from that, I defy anyone on the face of the earth to prove to me, or be able to prove to himself, that I have ever done anything of the sort. Vouchsafe therefore to see that justice is rendered me, Monsieur, and since despite all the promises you have made to me and the flattering hopes you falsely raised in my heart when you came to see me, I am still reduced to vegetate here in this horrible hell, I beg of you at the very least not to keep me any longer in suspense, as they are doing day in and day out, between the few pleasures that one is able to procure and the most abominable humiliations one is made to endure, and vouchsafe to keep me out of harm's way.

In the hope of the swiftest justice, I have the honor of being, Sir, your most humble and most obedient servant.

DE SADE

64. *To Madame de Sade*

[1782]

*Y*our *merits*, Madame Marquise, and your little persiflage, which to my thinking is lacking in wit, will have no effect whatsoever upon me: 'tis to that point I wish to address myself in this response. An idea cannot be compared to a work that springs from one's mind. 'Tis easy enough to be mistaken when one is alone in judging a work of this sort; 'tis far more difficult when it comes to an idea, and, unless one hasn't a brain in one's head, 'tis impossible not to know whether an idea is excellent or whether it's not. Now then, I assert and affirm that the idea of my project is excellent: never fear of ever hearing me say the same of any of my written works. I know enough about architecture, and I have sufficiently studied all the beautiful examples of that art in Italy, where I spent all my time with people involved in that profession, to know when an idea is good or bad, and I say to you again that my idea is superb, so sublime in fact that there is not the slightest chance it will ever be realized. There is no country in Europe, nor any sovereign rich enough, to bring it to fruition.[1] Thus, either your designer never said what you told me he said or he is a dolt or total ass to request that he be hired to carry it out, knowing full well that 'twas quite impossible. 'Tis therefore no more than a lovely pipe dream—but one I love and intend to have on display in my office one day. Here is a minor supplement that you should pass on to him, which is essential if the construction were to be done properly. *Baste!*

I firmly refuse to respond to Milli Rousset's tedious small talk. How is it possible that she can focus her mind on such claptrap? I can understand, and even find amusing, that one consciously wastes one's mind on matters of some piquancy ('tis why *Le Portier des Chartreux* never astonished or surprised me), but I cannot conceive anyone spending one's time discussing pots and pans or other kitchen utensils or the poor wretch who has syphilis or all the other stupidities contained in the plan it doubtless took Madame de Montreuil a good six weeks to concoct and fully as long for poor Rousset to transcribe, she whose talents lie a hundred leagues in the opposite direction. Thus her divine letter number 223 is going to fall into complete oblivion. I shall lower myself to deal with all these base details once I am on the premises: till then I don't want to give them so much as a single thought. Please remember that I do not want a concierge in her employ: I fail to understand how she ever got that idea into her head in the first place and how you could for a moment have supported it. Please be kind enough to refute that as loudly and expeditiously as possible.

Of all the books you sent me, there are only two that bear a second reading, and 'tis books like those two that I need and want. Kindly fill out the enclosed catalogue; I repeat that I want it done most urgently. The *Iliad* bears but a single reading. The *Italian Anecdotes* do not even bear that; they are books that have a value for their chronol-

---

1. In the course of this year, Sade's fervid mind was elaborating a wild, ambitious architectural project: a monumental "House of the Arts," a circular building some 260 feet in diameter, surrounded by a dozen footpaths each leading to a building housing a different art. That project may well have been Sade's response to the king's architect, who that year had been commissioned to build a new theater for the Comédie Italienne. As Sade notes, doubtless in response to his wife's pooh-poohing the project, he had seriously studied architecture, especially during his Italian sojourn, and took pride in his project, knowing full well it was too ambitious and costly ever to see the light of day.

ogy, works you keep on your table to refer to but would never read anymore than you would a dictionary. Therefore, fill out my list, I beg of you.[2]

Enclosed please find a little note for Amblet, which I ask you to forward to him; and when the manuscript comes back to you, be so good as to incorporate the minor corrections contained in this note.

Since the story of the Medicis is not complete, make sure not to break off relations with the doctor but, on the contrary, humor him. —Eh! As a friend, wouldn't it have been better to have me go away and spend my days locked up in the doctor's office in Florence, where I could have worked on that story, which most assuredly would one day have enhanced my reputation, rather than having me sent here to try to make some sense out of the imbecilic regurgitations of Madame la présidente de Montreuil? . . . I shall make a very special bet with you and your whole crew: I'll wager that keeping me here for a period of ten years will end up costing a good hundred thousand francs, all for the purpose of making me a hundred times worse than I ever was before and for harming not only my honor and reputation but those of my children by a solid hundred degrees. You will have to admit that 'tis paying a pretty penny indeed for the pleasure of such ridiculous spitefulness and insipid numbers.

In former times, the doctor took me on as a paying guest. A manservant and I under his roof, including room and board, cost 800 livres, and one was well lodged, you may be sure; add an additional 1,200 for living expenses, etc., and now calculate how far ahead we would have been at the end of ten years. I would have emerged from the doctor's hospital with a hundred thousand francs more in my pocket, a fine work to offer to the public, and my head filled with good ideas and thoughts. Now look at the other side of the coin and see what will result from what you are doing. But what was called for was silence and closure? Ah, no sooner said than done. At Florence there

---

2. One might be astonished at the apparent freedom to read in Vincennes—or any other prison—in pre-revolutionary France. In fact, Malesherbes, who became minister of the royal household only two years before Sade's imprisonment, did much to improve conditions in his majesty's prisons. In 1775 he issued the following to the warden of Vincennes: "No prisoner is to be denied material to read and write." Under Louis XVI, further liberalizations continued, including allowing prisoners to have their own personal libraries. Sade, always acutely aware of his rights and privileges, took full advantage of this Malesherban order throughout his prison stay.

was a French ambassador who was a trifle better than Monsieur de Rougemont in my view. I am the first to admit that he would certainly not have played exactly the same role (members of the military as vile as he do not grow on trees). But Barbantane, who is my cousin and has wit, would have vouchsafed for me, would have had in his pocket an appropriate order under the king's private seal in case it might have occurred to me to leave the confines of Florence, in which wise I would have found myself back in Vincennes in a week's time; he would have been entrusted with my correspondence back and forth, with managing my money, etc.; I would have taken an assumed name; and in the eyes of that entire troop of rogues and knaves whose sole desire in life is to see that I am kept under lock and key, they could have been informed that I was visiting the grand duke and they would have had no reason not to believe it, so long as I was out of sight and they no longer heard mention of me. These are the measures one takes when one has a spark of intelligence, as opposed to how you act when you are imbeciles pure and simple, and prefer being protected by subalterns and lowlife rather than being concerned about the well-being and happiness of your kith and kin.

You wanted a letter for my children? Here it is. With me, your wishes are my desires, and as you see I do your every bidding and do it without delay. 'Tis the goodness of my heart and my longing to please you that will it, and not, you may be sure, any self-interest, for I am not looking for any response to it. I prefer a hundred times over not to write letters than to be the recipient of heavy and incredibly stupid sentences o'erflowing with philosophical blather and reeking of the bilious black venom of my unworthy tormentor. Remember, I want no reply to that letter; let them write it if they are so moved, but if they do, refrain from sending it on to me.

This letter is the expression of my feelings about my children. They will have the letter, they will read it over and over, and they will remember what it says . . . Do you for a moment believe that I would be so hostile both to them and to myself, that I would ever oppose these principles? If ever I were, they would despise me, and they would be perfectly right to do so. Let this remind you of the little descriptive note I sent you this past winter, and may it persuade you how far removed I am from trying to instill in them any harmful principles. Oh, no! perish the thought: if I had to choose between having them put to death or corrupting their hearts I would not hesitate for a minute, and would even go so far as to say the former was by far the lesser evil.

Nor should you think for a moment what I write in that letter to the children has been in any way influenced by my stay in prison; 'twould be quite the contrary, in fact, for my time here has had only negative effects upon me. I have thought this way my entire life, and you know it as well as I do. To make my profession of faith to you here and now, all you need do is ponder how I have always striven to assure both *your own* well-being and that of *the children;* the happiness of all four of you is and will always be my constant and sole concern. As long as you have known me you have always heard me say the same thing. That is my plan of action when my misfortunes will have come to an end.

But as for me, for myself *personally,* I make you no promises. The beast is too old. Believe me, cease and desist from trying to educate him. Julie failed in her attempt to do the same with M. de Wolmar,[3] and yet Julie was much beloved by the man. There are certain systems that are so governed by one's existence, especially when they go back to one's weaning, that 'tis quite impossible to give them up. The same holds true for one's habits: when they are so prodigiously linked to one's physical being, ten thousand years of prison and five hundred pounds of chains will only serve to strengthen them further. It will doubtless come as a great surprise to you if I tell you that *all these things* and the memory thereof [are] always what I call to mind when I want to block from my mind my present situation. Morals are not dependent upon ourselves, they are part and parcel of our basic makeup. What does depend upon us is the choice not to spread our own personal poison abroad to others, and to make sure that those around us not only are protected from pain and suffering but, even more, that they are not even aware of its existence. Acting impeccably when it comes to one's children, and doing the same with one's wife, so much so that 'tis impossible for her, even when she compares her fate with that of other women, to have the slightest suspicion about her husband's morals: these are the kinds of things we can control, the kind of things a good and decent man ought to do, for nothing says that, just because a man's morals are a tad different from those of others, he is therefore a scoundrel. Keep such things private, especially keep them from your children, and make certain your wife is spared them as well; and may your duties toward her be faithfully carried out *in all areas*. There in a nutshell is what I believe and what I promise.

---

3. Sade is referring to Jean-Jacques Rousseau's *Julie, ou la nouvelle Héloïse,* published in 1761.

Virtues are not something you can simply don or shed, *and in such matters* one is not any longer free to adopt this or that taste of the time any more than one is free to stand straight when one is born a hunchback; nor is one capable of forcing one's natural inclinations into this or that prevailing opinion any more than one is free to be a brunette when one is born a redhead. This is and always has been my philosophy, and never will I deviate from it. —Still in all, in 1777 I was still fairly young; my overwhelming misfortune could have laid the foundation; my soul had not yet become hardened, as you have since so assiduously made sure 'twould be made invulnerable to any decent feelings. A completely different plan on your part could have wrought different results of a very major kind: you opted not to implement it. For that I am infinitely grateful to you; I greatly prefer clearing my mind of your figures[4] than to have to banish from it an infinite number of things and details, quite delightful in my view, that serve so well to ease my misfortunes when I let my imagination run wild.[5] You were ill advised, without question; but in all honesty I much prefer that things turned out as they did.

You will tell Gaufridy all manner of things, but I shall no longer write to him, any more than I shall write directly to the Saint—to whom, this autumn, in the course of the evenings I find so endless and so sad, I shall perhaps take it upon myself to pen a few wanton thoughts: except for that, nothing.

If you let me know what my children's reaction to my letter was, what they said to you about it, I would be most pleased, but no reply. The New Year's visit will be soon enough.

[P.S.] Try to find a copy of [Buffon's] *Natural History;* I have asked for it before and I most urgently renew that request.

When you fail to pander to my more respectable tastes, all the more reason to indulge in the others. And 'tis thus as always that the accursed base spirit wherewith you completely surround yourself serves me so admirably well without your being aware of it, and for want of happiness to point out the routes of goodness I fall deeper into the excesses of evil.

---

4. That is, the presumed signals in her letters.
5. Sade is doubtless thinking of the obvious pleasure he has been deriving from his writing: that year—1782—he had not only completed his *Dialogue Between a Priest and a Dying Man* but had also been delighting in his scandalous work of revenge: *The 120 Days of Sodom.*

65.   To Madame de Sade

February 4, 1783

My infirmity prevents me from taking care of myself. I beg you to send me a manservant,[1] and try to get it into your head that when I had the honor of marrying you 'twas not in order to diminish either my material wealth nor my situation; but on the contrary to increase them. If ever you were so unfortunate as to be in my place, I would see to it that you were not obliged to serve yourself.

I beg you to send me an oculist, and the *best one in Paris*, please.[2]

I further ask that you have them grant me permission to leave my door open when the room is full of smoke (except at night). 'Tis absolutely necessary that I take a little exercise, and since I can neither read nor write any longer, at least I should be able to take walks, unless you prefer that I become completely giddy before the week is out.

I also request that you obtain permission for me to take my walks in the garden. I should truly like to know what kind of positive results you might fancy could possible result from the doltish cruelty of allowing me to take three or four walks every day, then forbidding me from taking any for years on end? Is it the inmates of the insane asylum you take on to implement your plans? Air is as essential to me as life itself, I've repeated that to you twenty thousand times over, and I can no more do without it than I can do without dinner.

And because you see me so gentle and polite when I see you, you then go off and have the gall to redouble your tortures ever more ferociously. And after that you say: *he's a good little animal, you can make him do whatever you want.* I warn you: beware. As far as my being a perfect gentleman during your visits, you'll see in the future how I behave, for by acting thus all I'm doing is leaving myself open to being considered weak.

Adieu, and do remember that 'tis exceedingly dangerous to make yourself detested by those with whom you will later have to deal in person, as you should remember that there are some things that are completely unforgivable; and remember, too, that you should always beware of a former enemy.

---

1. Often, imprisoned aristocrats were allowed to have their own valets serving them, a privilege de Rougemont denied Sade.
2. The doctors sent, the Grandjean brothers, were Louis XVI's own oculists.

Yes, do bear all that in mind, 'tis the last heartfelt thought I intend to pass on to you.

For six weeks now I have been out of candles, beef marrow, and preserves. Please be good enough to send me some without delay.

66. To Madame de Sade

[Sometime after February 4, 1783]

My last short letter was dated the 4th, and since then I have completely lost the use of my eye and suffered the pangs of hell. I renew the requests I made in that letter and especially ask that you make arrangements to send me an oculist. If I do fall ill, and there's no doubt I shall, I most urgently request that I not be guarded by a soldier. I am not made for that, and I shall not suffer the man to come near me.

I have near me at present a man who, seeing me suffer like the poorest of wretches, and in such a state that I am unable to bestir myself, tells me over and over that 'tis nothing, that I've never been better, all of which is intended to make sure I do not dispense with his charming services. Send me a manservant, I cannot do without one. I prefer to die than to go on as I am. I cannot read your letters or anything else. I embrace you and suffer greatly.

67. To the Stupid Scoundrels Who Are Tormenting Me[1]

[About February 10, 1783]

*B*ase satellites of the *tuna mongers of Aix-en-Provence*, vile and odious valets of my torturers, invent therefore, to torment me, tor-

---

1. Whether this letter, presumably meant for Madame de Sade, was ever sent—or, if sent, passed the censor—remains unclear. But Renée-Pélagie was meticulous about preserving her husband's letters, so either it got through or was among the papers culled from his cell after the storming of the Bastille.

tures that will at least result in some good. What benefit can derive from the idleness to which your spiritual blindness binds me, except to make me curse and mentally tear to shreds the unworthy procuress who has in such cowardly manner sold me into your hands? Since I am now no longer able either to read or write, here is the hundred-eleventh torture I have dreamed up for her.[2] This morning, in the midst of my suffering, I saw her skinned alive, dragged over thistles, and then tossed into a vat of vinegar. And I said to her:

Execrable creature, this is what you deserve for having sold your son-in-law to unfeeling brutes!

This is what you deserve for having acted as pimp for both your daughters!

This is what you deserve for having dishonored your son-in-law!

This is what you get for having forced him into a position where he hates the children to whom you have sacrificed him!

This is what you deserve for having caused him to lose the best years of his life, when after his sentence he counted upon you to save him!

Here is what you deserve for having preferred your daughter's vile and detestable little offspring to him!

This is what you deserve for all the evil you have visited upon him for thirteen years in order to make him pay for you own follies!

And as I increased her own torments I insulted her in her pain and forgot my own.

My pen falls from my fingers. 'Tis time for me to suffer. Farewell, my torturers, 'tis time for me to call down every curse upon you.

68. *To Madame de Sade*

[February 13, 1783]

*M*y eye is just as bad as ever, and here all they do is burn it and dry it *and do all in their power to make me lose it completely.* I beg of you to send me an oculist. For over a fortnight now I have been asking you to, and you must have faint kindness in your soul to let me go on asking such a thing all this time. What's more, I need

---

2. Madame de Montreuil.

someone to wait on me. I am absolutely incapable of taking care of my-self. Half the time I find myself without things I sorely need. I floun-der about, break everything I own, mutilate myself from dawn to dusk. The manservant here does everything he can—I can only compliment him on his efforts—but he cannot do everything. I have need of some-one who will be with me from nine in the morning till noon, and again from six till eleven in the evening. Please, I beg of you, see to it that you find such a person. So long as I was well, I never asked you for any-thing extraordinary. Now 'tis no longer my fault, and I cannot do with-out what I ask of you. If you have any plans for coming to see me, obtain permission to visit me in my room, for I shall most certainly not come down to the council room. 'Twould be well beyond my strength to do so.

Send me:

Two lampshades, of the kind that circle the candles completely, and the best rosewater, the most delicate and expensive, which can be found at Cadet's shop.

It tires me terribly to write this, and I beg you on bended knee not to force me to ask for these same things twenty times over. I embrace you with all my heart.

My suffering is beyond description.

69. To Monsieur Grandjean

February 20, 1783

*T*he person that Monsieur Grandjean[1] came to see at Vincennes has taken the utmost care to wash out his eye daily with the sea-water eyewash that had been prescribed to him, as well as follow as-siduously the injections of iris powder. The only problem is, he sees no

---

1. The Grandjean brothers were the most famous oculists of the time. The el-der, Henri, was, as noted, the king's oculist. Among the treatments prescribed for Sade's corneal opacity were: bleeding, the application of leeches, com-presses of well-cooked chervil, iris powder, seawater eyewash, and elder blos-som eyewash. It was a wonder Sade didn't go blind.

real change in the status of the eye in question; the opacity remains constantly and absolutely the same, and although the surgeon assures him that he sees an improvement there, the patient perceives none whatsoever. Since this condition greatly fatigues the other eye, and since the patient is beginning to notice a similar weakening of that eye as well ever since it has had to work all by itself, he begs Monsieur Grandjean to prescribe another remedy that will act more rapidly. Moreover, the patient fears that these constant eye washes on so delicate a part of the body may in the long run cut into the eye and give rise to a fistula. He has raised that possibility with the house surgeon, whose response did nothing to reassure him about this fear. The patient would therefore be extremely obliged if Monsieur Grandjean would be kind enough to prescribe a remedy that would effect a cure more efficiently and more promptly, and at the same time cause the patient no discomfort.

70. *To Madame de Sade*

March 18, 1783

*T*he milk bowl is fine both in color and type, but I need one that is much larger, the size that will hold a pint and a half.

The man[1] who serves me has just been forbidden to deliver any more sponge cake to me. Thus when you send any further packets of these, 'tis Monsieur de Rougemont's servants who should send you a note of thanks, for they will be enjoying them. I do not want any more sent me, in whatever shape or form you might choose to send them, and this I state categorically.

Two dozen meringues and two dozen lemon cakes from the Palais Royal pastry shop.

The architectural plans for the new Italian Opera in Paris, and the name of the play they plan to open with.

Two sponges, the finest available. Six pounds of candles and two large nightlights.

---

1. A prison guard, not a personal manservant.

A dark-green jacket, with a silk fringe, with or without silver, the size being the same as the one the tailor sent me a fortnight ago.

What is generally called a pitcher or a jug. It's a little earthen pot, dark brown in color, which is used to heat or boil milk or coffee. It should be large enough to hold a bit more than a pint; actually, get the one that holds a pint and a half.

Some chocolate.

And a little dog, preferably a pup, so that I may have the pleasure of raising it, either a spaniel or a setter; I want only one of those two, no other breed will do.[2] If they tell you that animals are not allowed in here, your answer should be to laugh in their face. In this enlightened century, people are too smart to still believe in a prejudice of such overwhelming stupidity. And if they persist, and if they say to you: *No, Madame, 'tis strictly forbidden for Monsieur de Sade to see any animals, then your response should be: in that case, Sir, then set him free.*

I am most pleased at the great progress the young gentlemen your sons have made; to be talented is a great gift, and 'twill surely serve them both in good stead![3]

I kindly ask that you acknowledge at your earliest convenience receipt of my manuscript. Although I have already noticed a goodly number of errors since I packed it off to you, such as words and rhymes that are too oft repeated, and having promised that I would refrain from saddling you with pages of corrections, I shall keep to my word, and La Jeunesse can do the job of inserting them. That will keep him occupied and he's as competent as anyone to make the insertions. Nonetheless, since this is a necessary distraction, I am repairing it so that the title page to which it clearly applies does not have to be scribbled in. Since I was working on the final draft of two works simul-

---

2. Sade was a dog lover. At La Coste, he had two setters that accompanied him everywhere on his walks.

3. Exactly how Sade felt about his sons remains unclear. In one of his letters he refers to them as "terrible brats"; also, he did allow rather too easily the hated présidente to take charge of their upbringing and education. Still, there is considerable evidence of paternal affection in his letters. At the end of his fourth year in prison, he asked Renée-Pélagie for their portraits as a New Year's present; several times he asked for samples of their handwriting. In his requests for a prison transfer, he asks to spend time alone with his wife and children. And in a 1779 letter to his wife, he confesses to dreaming about them every night.

taneously, I made a mistake with the *epigraph*, using the epigraph intended for the novel on the play, and the one meant for the play on the novel. That is an error that will be misconstrued if not corrected. Here is the proper epigraph for the comedy I sent you:

They were charged with overseeing public mores and they corrupted them; they were thought to be the guardians of virtue and they became the devotees and models of vice.

M. PC, pages 231 and 232[4]

Do be good enough to make this slight change.

The oculists have sent a wonder-working powder that will, they say, produce miraculous results. You have to blow the powder into the eye, which presumably results in what is commonly known as *dust in your eyes;* in other words, claptrap.

Most assuredly, you do me great honor. If you keep on this way, you're going to give me a very swelled head. I had never thought myself either sufficiently attractive or seductive to throw dust into anyone's eyes, in other words, blind anyone to the facts. Apparently I was mistaken; clearly a lack of self respect!

Forthwith, I picked up my *mirror* and I made up a *riddle* and said: Oh! how right they are: *I am one good-looking fellow, and smart as a whip to boot!* I'm no longer surprised that I have blown powder in peoples' eyes. Oh! the poor eyes! Oh! how heavy the eyes of those I have blinded!

I send you fond greetings, Marie.[5]

In the "Country Library" there is a volume—I cannot tell you which—that ends with a very short story whose title, I believe, is "An Extraordinary Adventure" or "A Very Peculiar Adventure," something of the sort. I desperately need that volume; ask La Jeunesse to try and find it, and when he does kindly send it on to me immediately. All he need do is leaf through the various volumes until he finds the one that ends this way. I cannot tell you how impatient I am to have it. Which probably means that it will be a good while coming, no? The book entitled ——— is on its way to you and I'm also sending the others.

---

4. One suspects the "M" refers to either Molière or Montaigne, two writers Sade greatly admired. But the exact attribution remains elusive.
5. *Je vous salue, Marie* in the French, which could also be translated: *Hail, Mary,* linking Mme de Sade to the Virgin.

71. To Madame de Sade

[March 26, 1783]

Still one more worry, my dear friend, still one more persecution, *one more manuscript.*[1] But bear in mind that I am not insisting that you read it; all I ask is that you place it cheek by jowl with the other works of mine that you have already been kind enough to store away in a safe place. If however you had in mind to reread this tragedy to recover a bit from the boredom of a second reading, I did add a short play[2] at the end that you may make you laugh now and then—not too often, however, for if you laugh too much I'll find it no laughing matter at all.

I believe you will find the tragedy somewhat improved. I corrected all the errors I could find in it, the chief of which was the unpardonable inconsistency of the assault launched by Charles upon a city into which he had sent a negotiator without ever knowing whether or not the negotiations had succeeded. In the new version he sets a deadline: he announces that if at the end of that deadline his officers have not reported back, then he will launch his attack. The appointed time arrives without there being any possibility of his learning what has happened with the negotiations, and one sees why. The attack begins; nothing is more simple, whereas in the earlier version it was not.

What's more, I reiterate that I had no intention of putting either anything allusory [*sic*] or allegorical in these plays, and that I have no problem changing anything that might shock or displease. Each play contains a hundred more verses than the rules call for; thus you can see that there's plenty of room to trim and pare as much as you like.

As far as the little play is concerned, I have but one word to say to whoever finds fault with it:

First: 'tis in no wise necessary that in the end vice be punished and virtue rewarded. 'Tis a timeworn mistake, that, and I can prove it by harking back to Aristotle, to Horace, to Boileau, and by quoting some twenty comedies of Molière, who is the model for all of us.

Second: that the depraved person is a woman, and that most assuredly if I had punished that woman, my play would be detestable.

---

1. The tragedy *Jeanne Laisné.*
2. Together with the full-length play, Sade sent a curtain raiser, *A Foolish Test,* or *The Credulous Husband.*

But though she goes unpunished, who would like to emulate her? That is what art is all about. In comedy it does not consist of punishing vice but of portraying it in such a way that no one would dream of emulating it; and that being so, one has no need to punish it. The condemnation of vice takes place *sotto voce* in the souls of all the spectators.

If they take me to task *on the matter of morals*, I shall cite in my defense some fifteen of Molière's comedies, *Georges Dandin* first and foremost; among the moderns, *Happily* and *Figaro*, plays in which manners and morals are not respected as they are in my play.

In the second couplet of Sevigné, there is a criticism of *the societies of sensible women* that you will be so kind as to view—you and those around you—as no more than idle banter, signifying nothing. Read this couplet over a second time and see whether it contains anything more than *words* and *lovely rhymes*.

But what it does is cast a tinge of ridicule and self-conceit on this role, and that's all I was looking for; 'tis foppish jargon, nothing more.

Besides, I've no word that you even received the manuscript; such amenities are doubtless no longer in vogue. I fear dull and equally stupid knock-about scenes are all people require today.

Please don't forget the various requests I made and the legal actions I asked you to take on my behalf concerning the theft of my manuscript of *The Unfaithful*.[3] You would greatly oblige me if you would not let that matter lie.

To change the subject, tell me now, if you don't mind, whether you don't think I ought to be as surprised as I am bitter and deeply affected both to see that even the outside dates you had presumably set for my release had come and gone, and to see that, in order to console me for the despair into which that perforce dost plunge me, that you choose these moments of pain both to deprive me of your visits and to prevent me from having a bit of fresh air, and to have me, in a word, at all times and in all places, treated in the most harsh and shameful manner imaginable. Do you really believe that any other like example of tyranny and boorish imbecility exists anywhere in the annals of the entire world? Personally, I doubt it. And what is the purpose of all that? And what could the purpose possibly be? That is the question I cannot help asking over and over again. And that is what, in France, they call justice! A gentleman is shamefully sacrificed to that so-called justice, a gentleman who has served his country honorably and who, I dare say,

---

3. A manuscript Sade sent, as he sent all his works for safekeeping, to his wife, which apparently was lost—or more likely confiscated.

is possessed of a fair number of virtues, is offered up as a sacrifice—to whom?—to whores! The blood boils, the pen falls from my hand when I dwell upon such infamies. I confess that such foul deeds are beyond my grasp and that my mind is not strong enough even to understand them. But these refinements of barbarism, these deprivations of everything at the very moment when my pain and sorrow are at their worst, when I am most in need of comfort and solace, and when what would serve me most would be to alleviate my situation, this conspiracy, this formal desire to harden my heart, to vex me and destroy in me all virtue! Yes! I say it openly and without fear, whoever is the prime mover behind this punishment can only be an arrant scoundrel, a brainless scoundrel, and the greatest enemy I can ever have on the face of the earth! . . .

I wish you good evening, beg you to write me, to come and see me, and above all to arrange for me to be able to breathe some fresh air. You know that 'tis a season when that becomes even more essential to me than life itself. 'Tis impossible to describe for you how great my suffering is.

I embrace you with all my heart.

You can if you like receive my manuscript at present: 'tis completely aright, and I feel no need to fiddle with it any further. Please be so kind as to let me send it on.

72. *To Madame de Sade*

[April 20, 1783]

𝓦hat you have reported to me in your last letter is false, and Monsieur de Rougemont sent me word this morning that there was no question of my walks being restored anytime in the near future. The unworthy education of tub-thumping double-dealers wherewith you were inculcated must have been so deeply rooted within you that you are completely incapable of rectifying your odious lies. It seems that this bare and vile defect of backstairs gossip is so deeply ingrained in you that 'tis easier to render your soul than to forge the art of lying so foully and so basely. And what do you think you will gain from all that? What do you think will result from what you are doing? Ah! You shall see! I warn you in advance and swear to you most solemnly that when we are all together again not a word of truth will issue forth from my lips, and I shall so refine the art of lying that 'twill be precisely at the moment when you think it in my best interest to tell the truth that I shall tell the most blatant lie.

How your lies and duplicity—and I refer not only to you but to your tro——op of a mother—are so clearly visible in everything you do and say! The latest *stupidity* consists of two points: *the door to my room remaining closed, and the deprivation of fresh air.*

After four and a half months to be exact, they give me back one-half of what they have taken away. Which leads me to believe that 'twill be four and a half months hence that the rest will be restored to me: not a word. All that was naught but a tissue of lies, an effort to pull the wool over my eyes, an emulation of the lackeys and fraudulent ancestors who adorned your family tree, since you are doing precisely what they did.

At least tell me when I shall have them back. What difference does it make whether or not I am told? Will it inform me when I am to be released? Haven't you already committed that same stupid blunder six or seven times, without it resulting in anything positive for me? *"But if you are informed, you will spend all you time adding and subtracting."*

Eh! what bast——ly beasts you are: what does it matter whether or not I do my figuring before or after? You can see that your fears on that score are both vapid and clumsy beyond compare, since heretofore any calculations I made were for naught. I presume that in a month give or take I shall be allowed to take a walk. I ask you now, pray tell me if whether, being made aware of that fact today and therefore figuring when that date might be, or doing the same thing a month hence, makes the slightest difference? Would you like to be further reassured? May the devil take me here and now, as I pen these words, if I have any real desire to make such calculations, and if I request that my walks be restored for any other reason than that I simply can no longer exist without some fresh air, that I no more sleep at night than I can digest the foul food here. And may lightning strike me dead and reduce me this minute to dust if I ask you when these amenities will be restored to me for any other reason than to have a decent night's sleep for the duration of my calvary here, and not, as you assume, in order to have the certainty and the consolation of knowing when my suffering will come to an end. But as for my release, if I ponder, and if I draw therefrom no conclusion, may I be blinded on the spot.

I should very much like to know what purpose it might serve, or will have served, to thus forbid my walks, to take them away then restore them, and so on? The only reasonable thing you might possibly adduce is that, calculating the total time of my detention, you figure a certain period of it when I shall be deprived of fresh air, and you have divided up that totality in such wise that *if I am not allowed my walks presently,* or on the contrary *if I am,* then I shall somehow be able to figure out how outrageously long the rest of my detention will be. But my response to that is: all you needed to do was have my walks forbidden during the four winter months; you could have arranged for that, and I would not have been deprived during the spring and summer of something as necessary to me as life itself. But did you have to resort to numbers? Ah! numbers! 'Twill be a matter of some debate, you'll see. From what tribunal does that sowlike wench, to whom I am linked only because I had the *great misfortune* of marrying her daughter, believe she has the right to torment me with her numbers? But she is getting her revenge! Oh, in that case, you're implying the minister[1] allows people to take their revenge? Well then, if he allows her to act thus, by what right would he prevent me by taking mine? And that I fully intend to do, and *'twill be swift and sure.*

Good night, go munch your little God-on-High and assassinate your parents. As for myself, I'm off to b—— o——,[2] and I have not the slightest doubt, I assure you, that when the act is over I shall have done less ill than you.

73.   *To Mademoiselle de Rousset*

April 26, 1783

*I*t saddens me greatly to see from your last letter, my dear Miss,[1] that your ideas of fair and unfair are completely muddled in your head, and that that head, in other aspects rather amusingly well organized, nonetheless lends to prejudice what it ought to accord to reason.

---

1. Sade is referring to the government minister who supervises the prison system.
2. In French, *b. le v.*—*branle le vit*—masturbate, or "beat off." What other recourse was there for an oversexed, isolated prisoner.
1. In English in the letter.

'Tis with the intention of setting your ideas a bit aright, of rendering them more mature, through a slight infusion of philosophy, that I am going to clarify, and without further ado pass on to you, a short discourse on the matter of laws, wherein what was only sketched out in my January letter will appear here in some greater detail. You will find therein, in considerably greater abundance, various examples of the futility of our vices and virtues culled from other peoples of the earth. From which you will more easily be able to calculate what the intrinsic value of the sum total is, and to what extent 'tis unfortunately all too true that here below all is naught but system and opinion. Haven't you been struck by the assertions culled from the reality of these examples, wherein we are so greatly at odds with so many of our brethren? If not, I would be greatly surprised. 'Tis nonetheless from this treasure trove that our most famous writers—our Helvitiuses, our Montesquieus, our Rousseaus, etc., have drawn their most triumphant premises, because a premise is always considerably stronger when it is backed up by a proof. In which case, it is hard to refute.

Oh! my dear Fanny,[2] let those who are supposed to be exemplary show us that they truly are, and we shall have no further need of laws; let those whom chance or luck have caused to rise to positions of prominence behave irreproachably, and they shall have every right to demand the same from us.

'Tis the manifold misuse of authority on the part of the government that multiplies the vices of individuals. With what face do those who are at the head of government dare punish vice, dare demand virtue, when they themselves provide the example of every depravity on the face of the earth?

By what right does this crowd of leeches who slake their thirst on the misfortunes of the people, who, through their despicable monopolies plunge this hapless and unhappy class—whose only wrong is to be weak and poor—into the cruel necessity of losing either their honor or their life, in the latter instance allowing the poor wretches no other choice but to perish either out of poverty or on the gallows; by what right, I say, do such monsters claim to require virtue from others? What! when in order to satisfy their cupidity, their avarice, their ambition, their pride, their rapacity, their lust, I see them remorselessly sacrifice millions of their king's subjects, why should not I, if it so pleases, sacrifice others just as they do? By what means do they make amends for the universe of their crimes? By what means do they atone for their

---

2. Another nickname for Milli de Rousset.

foul deeds? Who, I ask, who gives them the right to do whatsoever they please, and to punish me, if I take it upon myself simply to do as they do?

O centuries of barbarity, O savage centuries, when the vanquished enemy served as fodder to the victor, an adornment to his triumph, no, you do not even come close to an atrocity such as this! Wretched were those who were defeated in battle, but at least you had weapons with which to defend yourselves! Today, all we have left is our tears, and we deal with them bravely.

At least these tyrants should learn how to choose their victims more fairly. They should learn not to vent their spleen upon those who know them intimately, upon those whose penetrating gaze will reach down even unto their most secret thoughts. Such hands, as soon as they have freed themselves from their chains, will tear away the blindfold of illusion, and by so doing will leave the idol on its pedestal completely exposed, so that the newly enlightened multitude can see with its own eyes the raw and disgusting matter wherewith 'tis composed.

Fanny, my dear Fanny, you no longer ask me for news of everything that is happening. You, my dear Miss, are losing interest regarding the concerns of your *Lovelace*. Yet how amused you would be if only you could see *Lady Mazan*[3] during the visits she makes to her husband, if only you could see her casting a sidelong glance as long as she can at her dense *Submer*,[4] trying to make him understand that she is going to betray him; and he, who can see no farther than the end of his nose, having failed to see the glance, asks what she means by that, by that stupid outburst, which reminds me ever so much of those fat turkeys that are forced to swallow chestnuts . . . Ah! Fanny, Fanny, the mere act of recounting the story makes me laugh all over again! Lies and deception are greatly to be admired, especially when practiced by a dolt. Such a person seems to grow fatter and fatter by virtue of all the efforts made to become subtle, just as 'tis true as ever that nature and lies work poorly together.

Adieu, tomorrow I shall be dining at *Milady Folleville's*.[5] I trust you can join us there. We shall discuss politics, and sip a bit of punch. We

---

3. Madame de Sade. The Marquis de Mazan was a pseudonym Sade used during more than one of his flights abroad.
4. The epithet, which Sade underlines, remains intriguingly elusive, though Sade is clearly referring to himself.
5. Literally, Lady *Crazycity*. Sade's view of Parisian high society is increasingly caustic.

shall keep to ourselves, drink sparingly, listen to no one, and share a few spiteful words.

74.   *To Mademoiselle de Rousset*

[May, 1783?]

To Mademoiselle
Mademoiselle de Rousset
Wherever she may be.

Mademoiselle:

I was on the verge of responding to your letter, and you would most surely been pleased with the objects that . . . all the more so because . . . what? No, I was saying . . . you would truly have been most touched when, all of a sudden, just as I was just taking pen to hand, an accursed carillon,* the sole instrument of misfortune that I can still hear within these walls, began to chime, making an infernal racket. Since a prisoner is always completely self-centered and lives in the firm belief that whatever takes place is done with him and him alone in mind, that every word uttered has a purpose—what did I do but take it into my mind that this accursed bell-ringing was speaking directly to me and was saying, very distinctly:

> *I pity you—I pity you,*
> *You're doomed to be, you must*
> *End up as dust, as dust.*

I rose to my feet in a state of indescribable fury, and all I wanted to do was rush over and beat the bell-ringer's brains out, but then I saw to my great regret and sorrow that the *door to revenge* was not yet open. So I sat back down, took pen again in hand, and decided that what I really ought to do was respond to this knave the bell-ringer in the same spirit and tone, since I had no other choice,

So I said:

---

* The carillon was from a nearby church. You either have to sing these couplets to the tune of the carillon or toss them into the fire, for they are not made to be read. (*Sade's note.*)

From pleasure, from joy
You must depart
My heart, my heart.

Friar, friar
Be pleased to meet
A hand that b——s, that b——s.[1]

But here—with naught but worry
My hand remains, may god be
praised,
My own best friend.

So come—do come
And with thy c——
Provide release for all that's pent.

Half of me, half of me
Is made to be, pitilessly,
Tantalus, Tantalus.

O what a fate! o what a fate,
'Tis simply more than I can take.
'Tis killing me, 'tis killing me.

Grain untended, dies forlorn
Come fetch at least
The seeds, the seeds.

Martyr I am, martyr will be
Suffering's my fate, that I see,
Without surcease, without surcease.

At this point I stopped, I counted, and I saw that all I had written was to the tune of a dirge. Ye gods, my friend, I cried out to myself, your mind's as bad as that of madame la présidente; and at least as puffed up with pride as when that lady departs after a session with Madame Gourdan. I immediately set about polishing this masterpiece, which I am having sent on to you so that you can see with your own

---

1. In the French, Sade, as he often does, elides: "qui b . . . , qui b . . . " the full word intended being *branle*, masturbate.

eyes, Mademoiselle, how I am coming along and how my wit is increasing by leaps and bounds.

By the by, Mademoiselle, send me some of those wonderful little Provençal green peas; this year 'tis impossible for me to eat any, Dom Sebastien de Quipuscoa[2] has placed an embargo on little green peas—ergo either I have to forgo eating any at all or eat those served the cartmen and carriers—last year it was cherries that were forbidden, but he didn't profit in the slightest from that little game because I was paying for it; he put in a special request with madame la présidente for permission this year to make a *slight profit* on what is served me—oh! the poor beggar doesn't miss a trick, of that you may be sure—and when one lodges a complaint, his response is that 'tis too *trifling* for him to bother with.

If you should run into anyone in Provence to whom I owe an annual pension or who asks you for some wheat, tell them point-blank that 'tis too *trifling to bother with*.

Adieu, my angel, do think of me from time to time when you are between the sheets, your thighs widespread and your right hand busily . . . looking for fleas. At such times, remind yourself that the other hand should be busy as well. Otherwise the pleasure is only half what it could be.

One hand should be . . . thus occupied, and the other the way madame la présidente does her sums.

75. *To Madame de Sade*

[Between July 3 and 11, 1783]

*W*hat in the world is this accident at the dungeon[1] you keep talking about? There's been no accident here. On July 2 they were

---

2. One of Sade's many derogatory titles for Monsieur de Rougemont.
1. That is, Vincennes. On July 2, a lightning rod had been set up on one of the towers to test its efficiency. The very next day lightning struck, leading some of the neighboring populace to report to the authorities that there had been a catastrophe at the dungeon. Word got back to Madame de Sade. Worried, she wrote her husband to keep away from this infernal new invention, lest he be killed. Sade's tragicomic reaction is typical.

setting up a lightning rod on the roof; there was a thunderstorm, in the course of which lightning struck the rod, as it happens in such cases. Is that what you're referring to? If so, 'tis not an accident, 'tis an experiment, nothing more. I'm nonetheless no less touched by what you write me on that subject; but verily, if that were the cause of my death, 'twould be, of all the possible accidents, among the least terrible. In fact, as far as I'm concerned I should prefer it above all others because of all deaths 'tis over in an instant and one does not suffer. Perhaps 'tis for that reason that of all the scourges of life, being struck by lightning is the one that I feared the least, since even during the fiercest thunderstorms it didn't occur to me even to close the windows, nor did lightning ever produce in me that natural emotion it does in animals. And as for yourself, another accident voided: there you are living on a grand scale, ensconced in the sweet pleasures of your widowhood; and there, too, *is your son, the young count himself,* ready willing and full able to come into his fortune. *Young, handsome, and rich,* with no longer a father around to *embarrass* him . . . What a marriage! what an institution! . . . A princess, at the very least . . . Upon my word, keep up what you've been doing! Yes, word of honor, if la présidente has in her possession one of these lightning rods, let her aim it at me—and if all works out well that's the best thing that could happen to make you all happy. What's more, the only one amongst you who might mourn my passing would perhaps be the young knight, because he would benefit in no wise from my death, and also because he's a fine and sensitive young man . . . But he doesn't really know me. How old was he? *Four years old* at most when I left him; his mourning could not conceivably be very profound; he must scarce remember me.

Do you realize that you should soon think of sending the young count to Provence, so that the people who dwell on his lands get to know him. He really ought to learn something about his estates . . . In short, one never knows what may happen, and 'tis always good for a lord to be known personally by those under his jurisdiction. In what army corps does he intend to enlist? Will you be so kind as to supply me with that information?

If your lofty occupations, madame marquise, allow you the time to think of him to whom you owe the existence of these offspring, about whom you seem presently besotted and for whose benefit you sacrifice even your own husband, would you be so good as to recall that for a full year now I have been deprived of fresh air, which causes me to suffer horribly, that I can absolutely no longer sleep at night, I mean not a wink, and that in a word, amongst all the various ways of assassinating a man that the scoundrels your mother has surrounded herself with may have advised, I beg of her to choose one that is shorter, for the excessive heat waves make it impossible for me to endure her present method, namely to keep me here any longer. Moreover, I beg of you to ask Monsieur Le Noir to send an oculist to see me; I am in urgent need of one. I wrote him expressly about that, and I have also spoken to Monsieur de Rougemont about it. Thus I ask that you make sure 'tis done as promptly as possible.

Tell Hugues Aubriot* (Monsieur Le Noir) that he's pulling your leg when he tells you you can't come until after the dungeon repairs are completed. When the lightning rod is struck by lightning, no damage is done, and at present the only repairs being made to the dungeon are those being made by Monsieur de Rougemont's gardeners, who are enlarging and beautifying a garden into which the said Mustapha prohibits anyone from entering for fear that someone might eat some of his fruit.

Send me some fresh linen; I cannot do without it in this heat; I am completely out of fresh linen.

Tomorrow we may have a much more lively scene than that of the lightning rod. The little hired brute, the one who blinded me, is supposed to come to shave me, and for the past two years people have been egging him on to play the role of *Harlequin the paralyzed barber,* in order to legitimize the gash in the face he is supposed to inflict upon me. Let him beware! Whenever he shaves me I am always holding in my hand a pair of very sharp scissors, and I swear to you upon all that is most holy in the world that if ever he tries to implement any of his foul deeds, as he has done with my eye, I shall drive the scissors deep into his heart.

I am returning a stupid novel (*Betzi*).

You must have ten volumes of Velly;[1] you will have the two following volumes only in a few days, because I'm making a slight pause, because of my eyes, every time I've finished ten volumes.

To carry it out. 'Tis one of your phrases. Oh, how your style smacks of the knaves you see! That is precisely the same expression used by the police lackeys, the informers and spies, the Hugues Aubriots, the

---

* The leader of the Parisians who under Charles VI rose in revolt, and provost marshal of the Paris shopkeepers, thereby in control of the police in the capital. (*Sade's note*)
1. Paul-François Velly, the author of the very influential *Histoire générale de France.*

Albarets of this world, and all the other vile riffraff that befoul France, and all of whom, from first to last, I would have burned to death at the stake were it in my power to do so. Therefore—rid yourself of such trite expressions, for by resorting to that kind of jargon you will seem like a policeman's wife; no one will want to come near you. Leave such language to madame la présidente; pricks are made for swine.

Make sure, I beg you, to respond without exception to the last list I sent you.

76. *To Madame de Sade*

[July, 1783]

*B*e so good as to tell me which of the two it is, Goodie *Cordier*[1] or *Gaffer* Fouloiseau,[2] who is against my having any shirts. You can deny clean linen to the inmates of a hospital, but I do not intend to go without it. How your meanness, that of your origin and that of your parents, shines forth in your every act! My dove, the day I so far forgot what I was as to be willing to sell you what I am may have been to get you under the covers—but it wasn't to go uncovered. You and your crew, keep what I say there well in mind until I have the chance to bring it out in print.

If I go through as much linen as I do, blame it on the laundress who every day either loses or tears to shreds everything of mine she can get her hands on, and rather than remonstrate with me, enjoin his lordship the warden to issue orders remedying this state of affairs. Not a month passes but all this costs me eight or ten francs. Should such things be allowed?

At any rate, I declare to you that if inside the next two weeks the linen I request is not forthcoming I shall interpret this as proof positive that I am on the eve of deliverance, and shall pack my baggage; only my imminent release can possibly justify your stupid refusal to send me something to put on my back. Let them but remove the madmen from this establishment and one will be less loath to use what the

---

1. Monsieur de Montreuil. The full family name was Cordier de Montreuil.
2. One of Madame de Montreuil's henchmen.

house provides, one could then forgo asking to have things sent all the time from home. This place was not intended for the insane; Charenton is where they are to be put, not here, and the disgraceful greed that led to keeping them locked away there seems now to have been set aside by the police, the result being that those who are not mad risk becoming so by contagion. But the police are tolerant, tolerant of everything except discourtesy toward whores. You may render yourself guilty of every possible abuse and infamy so long as you respect the backsides of whores: that's essential, and the explanation is not far to seek: whores pay, whereas we do not. Once I am out of here I too must contrive to put myself a little under the protection of the police: like a whore I too have an ass and I'd be well pleased to have it shown respect. I will have *M. Fouloiseau* take a look at it—even kiss it if he'd like to, and I am very sure that *moved* by such a prospect he will straightway record my name in the book of protégés.

The story was told to me that upon arriving in Paris (when you had me arrested) it was thus you went about having yourself *certified.* Before anything else the question was one of determining whether the said ass had or had not been outraged—because my good mother-in-law claimed I was *an outrager of asses.* Consequently she wanted *an examination by an expert.* There she was, as I understand it, telling him: *You see, gentlemen, you see, he's a little devil, full of vices; he might even . . . perhaps . . . who knows? There's so much libertinage in that head of his! . . .* And, as I understand it, there you were, lifting your petticoats. Magistrate Le Noir adjusts his spectacles, Albaret is holding the lamp, Le Noir's *alguazils* have got pen and paper. And a report upon the state of the premises was writ out in these terms:

"*Item,* having betaken ourselves to the said Hotel de Danemark at the requisition of *Dame Montreuil* née *Cordier, Marie-Magdeleine,* we did uncover the said *Pélagie du Chauffour,*[3] daughter to the aforementioned, and having with care made proper and thorough examination we proclaim the said *du Chauffour* well and duly provided with a set of two very fair buttocks, excellently formed and intact within and without. We did ourselves approach and have our assistants as nearly approach the said member. They, at their risk and peril, did pry, spread, sniff, and probe, and having like ourselves observed naught but health in these parts, we have delivered these presents, whereof usage may be

---

3. The reference is to the Montreuil country residence, the château d'Echaffour.

made in conformance to the law; and do furthermore, upon the basis of the exhibition described above, grant the said *Pélagie du Chauffour* access to the Tribunal and in the future our powerful protection.

"*Signed:* Jean-Baptiste Le Noir, trifler extraordinary in Paris and born protector of the brothels in the capital and surroundings."

Well? Is that how it went? Come, be a friend, tell me about it . . . *In addition* or, if you prefer, *in spite of it all,* you have not sent me a quarter of the things I need.

To begin with, I need linen, most decidedly I must have linen, otherwise I make ready my departure; then four dozen meringues; two dozen sponge cakes (large); four dozen chocolate pastille candies, vanillaed, and not that infamous rubbish you sent me in the way of sweets last time.

What, will you tell me, are these twelve quarter-quires of paper? I asked for no quires of anything; I asked you for a copybook to replace the one containing the comedy I had conveyed to you. Send me that copybook and don't prattle so, it's very tiresome. So acknowledge receipt of my manuscript. It is not at all of the sort I'd like to have go astray. It belongs safely in a drawer for the time being; later, when it goes to the printer, it can be corrected. Until then it need not get lost. With manuscripts you delete, you amend, you tinker, they are meant for that; but they are never meant to be stolen.

For God's own sake! when will you finally be tired of truckling? Had you ever noticed one of your servilities meet with success, I'd let it pass; but after close to seven years of this, where has it brought you? Come, speak up. You aim at my undoing? you would unsettle my brain? If so, you are going to be wonderfully rewarded for your efforts, for by everything that is most holy to me I swear to pay every one of your farces back, and with good measure; I assure you I shall grasp their spirit with an artfulness that will stun you, and shall compel you all to recognize for the rest of your days what colossal imbeciles you have been. I confess I was a long while believing your Le Noir had no hand in these abominations, but since he continues to suffer them, that alone proves he has his part in them and convinces me that he is no less a damned fool than the others.

Do not forget the nightcap, the spectacles, the six cakes of wax, Jean-Jacques' *Confessions* and the coat M. de Rougemont claims that you have. I am returning a boring novel and vols. 4 and 6 of Velly. With these I send a hearty screw in the buttocks and am, devil take me, going to give myself a flick of the wrist in their honor! Now don't run off and tell the présidente so, for being a good Jansenist, she's against wives being *molinized*.[4] She maintains that M. Cordier has never *discharged anywhere* but in her *vessel of propagation* and that whomsoever steers any other course is doomed to roast in hell. And I who had a Jesuit upbringing, I who learned from Father Sanchez that one must avoid *plunging in over one's depth*, and look hard lest one *swim in a vacuum*, because, as we learn from Descartes, *nature abhors a vacuum*, I cannot agree with *Mama Cordier*. But you're a philosopher, you have a most charming misconstruction, a way of moving and a narrowness in that misconstruction and heat in *the rectum*, which is why I am able to get on with you so well.

I am yours indeed, in truth your own.

Directly this letter reaches you, will you please go in person to the shop of M. Grandjean, oculist, rue Galande by Place Maubert, and tell him to send straight to M. de Rougemont the drugs and instruments he promised to furnish the prisoner he visited in Vincennes; and while you are about it, go see *your protector Le Noir* and tell him to arrange to let me have a little fresh air. He enjoys plenty of it, does Le Noir, although a wickeder man than I by far: I've paddled a few asses, yes, I don't deny it, and he has brought a million souls to the brink of starvation. The king is just: let his majesty decide between Le Noir and me and have the guiltier broken on the wheel, I make the proposal with full confidence. In addition to the neglected errands and to those requested above, attend, if you please, to procuring for me one pint of eau de Cologne, a head-ribbon, and a half-pint of orange water.

77. *To Madame de Sade*

[July 1783]

*M*y amiable queen, there is truly nothing more entertaining than the insolence of your lackeys. Were one less than certain that your numbers are riddles (squaring nicely, by the way, with my manner of thinking), your errand boys would be in line for a sound

---

4. From Luis Molina, a sixteenth-century Jesuit, much disliked by the Jansenists because of his doctrine of grace, which they staunchly opposed.

caning one of these days. Ah! would you hear the latest? They are giving me their estimates upon how much longer I am to remain here!
What a farce! 'Tis for you, charming princess, 'tis for you who are on
your way to sup in intimate elegance with Madame Turnkey (at the
hospital today), I say 'tis for you, my cunning one, to take the temperature of my captors, for you to divine just when it is going to suit them
to unkennel me, for you to learn their pleasure of my lordships Martin,[1] Albaret, Fouloiseau, and the other knaves of that breed whom you
will deign to permit me, for my part, to consider so many cab horses fit
for whipping or to serve the public convenience at whatever hour and
in any kind of weather.

To refuse me Jean-Jacques's *Confessions*, now there's an excellent
thing, especially after having sent me Lucretius and the dialogues of
Voltaire; that demonstrates great judgment, profound discernment on
the part of your spiritual guides. Alas, they do me much honor in reck-
oning that the writings of a deist can be dangerous reading for me;
would that I were still at that stage. You are not sublime in your methods of doctoring, my worthy healers of the soul! Learn that it is the
point to which the disease has advanced that determines whether a
specific remedy be good or bad for the patient, not the remedy in itself. They cure Russian peasants of fever with arsenic; to that treatment, however, a pretty woman's stomach does not well respond.
Therein lies the proof that everything is relative. Let that be your
starting point, gentlemen, and have enough common sense to realize,
when you send me the book I ask for, that while Rousseau may repre-
sent a threat for dull-witted bigots like yourselves, he is a salutary author for me. Jean-Jacques is to me what *The Imitation of Christ* is for you.
Rousseau's ethics and religion are strict and severe to me, I read them
when I feel the need to improve myself. If you would not have me become better than I am, why, 'tis high time you told me so! For me,
good is a state both uncomfortable and disagreeable, and I ask no more
than to be left to wallow in my slough; I like it there. Gentlemen, you
imagine your *pons asinorum* must be used and must succeed with
everybody; and you are mistaken, I'll prove it to you. There are a thousand instances in which one is obliged to tolerate evil in order to destroy vice. For example, you fancied you were sure to work wonders,
I'll wager, by reducing me to an atrocious abstinence in the article of
carnal sin. Well, you were wrong: you have produced a ferment in my

---

1. A police sheriff.

brain, owing to you phantoms have arisen in me which I shall have to render real. That was beginning to happen, you have done naught but reinforce and accelerate developments. When one builds up the fire too high under the pot, you know full well that it must boil over.

Had I been given *Monsieur le Six*[2] to cure, I'd have proceeded very differently, for instead of locking him up amongst cannibals, I would have cloistered him for a while with some whores, I would have supplied him whores in such numbers that damn me if after these seven years there'd be a drop of fuel now left in his lamp! When you have a steed too fiery to bridle, you gallop him over rough terrain, you don't shut him up in the stable. Thereby might you have guided *Monsieur le Six* into the *right path*, into what they call the *path of honor.* You'd have brought to an end these *philosophical subterfuges*, these devious practices Nature disavows (as though Nature had anything to do with all this), these *dangerous* flights of an all too ardent imagination which, ever in hot pursuit of happiness and never able to find it anywhere, finishes by substituting illusions for reality and *indecent detours* for lawful pleasure . . . Yes, in the middle of a harem *Monsieur le Six* would have become *the friend of women;* he would have discovered and *felt* that there is nothing so beautiful, nothing so *great* as her sex, and that outside of her sex there is no salvation. Occupied solely in serving ladies and in satisfying their delicate desires, *Monsieur le Six* would have sacrificed all of his. Indulging in none but seemly practices, decency would have become a habit with him, and that habit would have accustomed his mind to quelling penchants that had hitherto prevented him from pleasing. The whole treatment would have ended with our sufferer appeased and at peace; and lo! see how out of the depths of vice I would have enticed him back to virtue. For, once again, to a very vicious heart, virtue is but a lesser vice. Think not that 'tis child's play to retrieve a man from the abyss; your mere proposal to rescue him will cause him to cling tight to where he is. Content yourself with having him conceive a liking for things milder in their form but in substance the same as those in which he is wont to delight. Little by little you will lift him up out of the cloaca. But if you hurry him along, jostle him, if you attempt to snatch everything away from him all at once, you will only irritate him further. Only by slow degrees is a stomach accustomed to a diet; you destroy it if you suddenly deprive it of food. True,

---

2. That is, himself. Having been incarcerated in cell number 6 in Vincennes, he took to referring to himself as *Monsieur le Six*, the gentleman in 6.

there are certain spirits (and of these I have known only one or two) so heavily mired in evil, and who unfortunately find therein such charm, that however slight it were, any reform would be painful for them; 'twould seem they are at home in evil, that they have their abode there, that for them evil is like a natural state whence no effort to extricate them might avail: for that some kind of divine intervention would be required and, unhappily, heaven, to whom good or evil in men is a matter of great indifference, never performs miracles on their behalf. And, strangest of all, profoundly wicked spirits are not sorry for their plight; all the inquietudes, all the nuisances, all the cares vice brings in its train, these, far from becoming torments to them, are rather delights, similar, so to speak, to the rigors of a mistress one loves dearly, and for whose sake one would be aggrieved not to have to suffer upon occasion. Yes, my fairest of the fair, by God's own truth, well do I know a few spirits of this kind. Oh! and how dangerous they are! May the Eternal spare us, thou and me, ever from resembling them, and to obtain His mercy let us both before we lay ourselves in our beds kneel down and recite a *Paternoster* and an *Ave Maria* with an *Oremus* or two in honor of Mr. *Saint* [real name excised in letter[3]]. ('Tis a signal.)

With a great kiss for each of your buttocks.

I would remind you that you have sent me beef marrow in the past when the weather was just as warm as it is at present, and that I have none left; I beseech you to send me some without fail by the 15th of the month. Also, two night-ribbons, so as not to have to wait when one needs replacing: the widest and darkest you are able to find.

Herewith the exact measurements for a case I would be obliged if you would have made for me, generally similar to the other you sent me but with these dimensions, to be observed to the sixteenth of an inch and with a top that screws on three inches from the end. No loops, no ivory clasps like the last time, because they don't hold. This case (since your confessors must have an explanation for everything) is to store rolled-up plans, prints, and several little landscapes I've done in red ink. And I believe indeed [one or two words obliterated] were it for a nun, ought to put [several words obliterated]. Kindly attend to this errand as soon as possible; my plans and drawings are floating loose everywhere about, I don't know where to put them.

---

3. Not by Sade. Some sensitive soul, perhaps Renée-Pélagie, carefully cut the name out of the letter.

Those who tell you I have enough linen are wrong. I am down to four wearable shirts and am completely without handkerchiefs and towels. So send me what I have requested, will you please, and put a stop to your silly joking upon this subject. Send me linen, plenty of linen . . . Bah! never fear, I've plenty of time ahead of me to wear it out.

78. *A Certificate*

August 31, 1783

I the undersigned do hereby acknowledge that the farce of August 31, 1783—save on the point of it being a trifle monotonous, for there have been some eighteen others that resemble this latest to a tee—but save on that one point, I say, I certify that the said farce was performed to utter perfection. The said guard was most insolent, he said, and I quote accurately, *that he could no longer lend any more of his money, that he had a wife and children to feed; that when one wanted to incur an expense one ought to have the means to pay for it, and that one should not be expected to be treated any differently than the others when one was not in a position to ask any favors; that he no longer desired to provide any further monetary advances, all the gentleman needed to do was have his money sent sooner, etc., all of which was performed with zeal, vigor, and character.* He flushed crimson. His leprosy (for 'tis worth your knowing that they choose to have me waited upon here by a leper and that, however much I protest, 'tis a complete waste of breath on this score; one day I shall inquire whether 'tis the intention of the king to have the prisoners served by lepers), his leprosy, I say, turned bright purple; and I further certify that Lekain[1] in his mightiest rages had never been more handsome in his life.

In witness whereof I have delivered over to him the present certificate, so that his full gratuities may be paid him punctually and rigorously.

DE SADE

---

1. Henri Louis Cain (a.k.a. Lekain) (1729–1778), a famous French actor of the era, most famous for his roles in Voltaire's works.

79. *To Madame de Montreuil*

September 2, 1783

I importune you but very rarely, Madame, and you must perforce believe that when I do 'tis solely because I have a most urgent and pressing need to do so. Of all the many blows you have visited upon me since I have been here, none has affected me more deeply than the one wherewith you have torn my heart asunder. You are involved in a concerted effort to make me believe that my wife is bringing dishonor upon her name. Is it possible, great God, is there a mother anywhere who either tolerates these infamies or does her best to try to persuade her son-in-law that they are true! Your scheme is ghastly, but what lies behind it is easily brought to light, Madame. You would like to see me separate from my wife, and once I am out of here, make sure I would make no effort to take up with her again. How badly you have mis-judged how I feel about her if you could even have thought that any-thing in the world might have produced such an effect. Were you to depict her to me holding a dagger in her hand, trying to thrust it into my heart, I would throw myself at her feet and say to her: Strike, I have well deserved it. No, Madame, nothing, nothing in the universe will ever be capable of distancing me from her, and I shall continue to wor-ship her no matter what revenge she may seek to take. I have too much to atone for, great God, I have too many misdeeds to rectify! Do not al-low me to die in a hopeless state without being able to make her forget the errors of my ways. Love, esteem, tenderness, gratitude, respect, all the feelings a soul can muster, are united in me for her, and 'tis in the name of all these, I must confess, Madame, rather than any cry of con-science, that I beseech you to give her back to me as soon as I am out of here. Do you think for a moment that having been imprisoned as long as I have has not provided me with a great deal of food for thought? Do you truly believe that my detention has not caused me to be smitten with remorse? I ask only one favor of you, Madame, and that is to let me prove it. I have no desire whatsoever that you take my word for it. I want to be put to the test. Let us be allowed back to-gether again, under whatever surveillance and in whatever country you may choose. There let us be kept under surveillance from morn-ing till night, for as many years as you like, and at the first sign of any misconduct on my part, however slight, let her be taken from me and may I never be allowed to set eyes upon her again, and let me one last time be deprived of my freedom or, if one prefers, let them take my life; I am ready to agree to anything. Need I say more, Madame? Can I open my heart to you any more fully? Pray have a modicum of pity for my situation, I beseech you! It is atrocious. I know that by so saying I am offering you the chance to gloat, but I care not one whit. I have, unfortunately, too greatly troubled your tranquillity, Madame, to have the slightest regret about giving you the chance to gloat at my expense. If your goal was to see me groveling in mortification, in the depths of humiliation, in a state of despair and wretchedness as profound as any man can suffer, then revel to your heart's content, Madame, enjoy your triumph, for you have reached your goal; I defy anyone to say that there is any creature in the world whose life is more precious than hers is to me. May heaven be my witness when I say that if I am to keep her 'tis only for the purpose of trying to put my life to rights again, 'tis only in an effort to make amends to the virtuous and sensitive soul of your adorable daughter to whom, in the frightful delirium of my wild aberrations, I caused great pain and anguish. Ah! great God above, how deep is my despair and how I rue having made her suffer! Also, Madame, religion and Nature both keep you from pursuing your revenge unto the grave; they forbid you from turning your back on my repentance, and from spurning my heartfelt desires to make amends. To that ardent prayer I add another, Madame, and that is to beseech you most earnestly not to have me released from prison if you have no intention of seeing me reunited with my wife. Do not, I beg of you, toss me into a new abyss of misfortunes; do not have me released only to have me rearrested the next day. For that is what would happen, I warn you, Madame. I cannot for a moment see myself a free man unless 'tis flying into her arms. Were you to swallow her up somewhere in the entrails of the earth, I should go and seek her out and spirit her away. The minute I am free I shall go see Monsieur Le Noir and ask him again for my wife. If he turns me down, I shall rush to the minister, and if that effort fails, or any other I might undertake, I shall cast myself at the feet of the king and ask him to restore to me what heaven has given me and that no man can put asunder. Were they to place all sorts of obstacles in my way, were they to toss me back into prison, well then, I'd prefer that, I'd prefer that a thousand times more than living free without her. At least in irons my conscience is at peace; it takes comfort in the knowledge that 'tis impossible for me to make amends to her. If and when I am free, my movements will be unrestricted, and 'tis an absolute necessity then that I either make it up to her or lose my life. Do not thrust me back once again into new calamities, I beseech you, Madame, and do not have me released from here unless I am to be reunited with her, and if I am not, then leave me where I am. Have the kindness to let me see her as soon as possible, and I entreat you to make sure we can be alone. I have some very interesting and very special things to tell her, that you would be well advised be kept from third parties, no matter whether or not you believe they are completely trustworthy. Allow me to say, Madame, that as I finish this letter—which I swear will be the last letter I shall write to whomever, no matter how long my suffering may be—allow me to say that I throw myself at your feet and ask your forgiveness for everything that might have been able to wrench me from the horror of my fate. Do not take this letter as the despair of a man who has lost his mind, but view it rather as reflecting the true feelings of my heart. I hopefully await the results of your commiseration, Madame; I implore it without shame, and with you I blush for naught but my misdeeds.

I am respectfully, Madame, your most humble and most obedient servant.

DE SADE

80. To Madame de Sade

[Early September 1783]

I beseech you to write me. I am worried about your health. You have never let as much time go by without my hearing from you. To try to destroy a husband's interest in his wife is one of the most sublime policies that has ever existed; there's something truly angelic about it, an act I can only term inspired. By great acts are great men known! I am convinced that the man who described the state of my suffering by saying:

And his wife let eight or ten months go by without writing to him,

oh, yes, I am convinced that the knave who dreamed up a phrase such as that would consider himself greater than *Alexander* and more profound than *Lycurgus*. 'Tis very much in the same vein as the homily they din into my head day in and day out. They wrote:

And because they had not added faith to the formidable mysteries of Christ's religion, they dinned a homily into his head every day for six months; and thus you will see that that made him believe that God and bread are one and the same.

'Tis more or less in that same manner they converted the anti-papists in the Cevennes mountains. Since that took place not even eighty years ago, each of us remembers how well it worked.

Oh, no, no! I swear upon all that's most holy that I shall never believe the lessons of a god who believes that 'tis right and good to treat his creature in a most scurrilous manner in order to honor the creator. Construct your ungodly chapels, adore your idols, O detestable pagans! But so long as you transgress the sacred laws of Nature, mark you well that by so doing you oblige me to hate you and despise you.

Be that as it may, do let me hear from you, I beg of you. If 'tis part of your practical joke not to write me, then send a brief word to the officers of the establishment; they will pass it on to me, and that semi-proof of your existence and your good health will give me some slight reassurance.

You have an excuse for writing, I gave it to you on purpose two months ago. I have a large package all wrapped up and ready to be given to you; send someone to fetch it, and when you do include a word from you.

This package contains six pieces of raw leather that require bleaching, all of which I shall need in the next two months. What am I going to do if you don't have them done, as you always have every year in the past? 'Twill put me in a pretty pickle. The pieces of leather are to wrap round my latest work, which I'm also most anxious to send you, so that La Jeunesse can make a fair copy of it[1] and also so that I can turn my attention to something else, which I find impossible to do as long as the old work is here next to me. And I have a great desire to work; I have an overall plan that keeps running through my mind, which I very much want to bring to fruition. I absolutely must make up for lost time. They wake me up every day at *five o'clock* in the morning; I can use my eyes to good advantage only till four in the afternoon. So I must therefore profit from that time period. If you still are the least bit interested in what is happening to me, I would tell you that from four in the afternoon till midnight my poor wretched eyes continue to

---

1. As noted, La Jeunesse through the years dutifully copied Sade's prison manuscripts and drafts.

be horribly painful. But what does such a minor item mean to the daughter of a woman who has been so bold as to deprive me of the sense I hold most dear? But be patient: if men refuse me their justice, I shall still find means to take justice into my own hands. Justice too has eyes. And I shall also have *some powder.*[2] All I need is some money to track down these no-good knaves; and that I shall find, and that I shall use.

81. To Madame de Sade

September 19 and 22, 1783

*T*his morning I received a fat letter from you that seemed endless. Please, I beg of you, don't go on at such length: do you believe that I have nothing better to do than to read your endless repetitions? In truth, you must have an enormous amount of time on your hands to write letters of that length, and you must also assume I have all the time in the world to reply. Still in all, since the present letter is one of great consequence, I beseech you to read it with a clear mind and complete composure.

I have just found three signals of most uncommon beauty. There's no way in the world I can keep them from you. They are so sublime that I'm convinced that, in reading them, you will, despite all your efforts to the contrary, applaud the extent of my genius and the wealth of my knowledge. One might say of your clique what Piron said of the French Academy: you who number forty here have the mind of four.[1] Your sequel is the same thing: your six there have the mind of two. Well, then, with all your collective genius, and although you have being working on *your masterpiece* for only twelve years, I am going to give you two-to-one odds,* if you like, that my three signals are worth more than everything you have done to date . . . Hold it, I'm mistaken, upon my word there are four . . . Well, then! 'tis three or four, and as you know three-quarters is a strong number.

---

2. Presumably gunpowder, to back up his threats.
1. The French Academy was made up of forty "immortals."
* What! two-to-one: not bad, that, eh? Don't you wish you had thought of that? (*Sade's note*)

First signal I made up: Christopher[2] de Sade

From the first clipping you cut out or tore out to bring to my attention, you must cut off the b——s of Cadet de Basoche[3] (Albaret) and send them to me in a box. I shall open the box, I shall cry out in admiration, and then I shall say: Oh, good God! what the blazes can that be? —Jacques the prompter, who will be there, somewhere behind me, will answer: *'Tis nothing, Sir; can't you see that it's the number 19?* —No! I say, I can't make that out. —With all due respect, do you have any as good as that?

Second signal, same author:

Whenever you want to indicate *the number 2, the double, a duplicate copy, your own double, paying something twice,* etc.,[4] here's how you should go about it: you must place in my room a handsome creature in some theatrical pose (the sex doesn't matter to me; to some extent I take after your own family, I'm not overly choosy in that respect; and besides, since we're dealing with a *mad dog,* etc.), as I was saying, you must have a handsome creature in a pose not unlike that of the Callipygian Venus[5] there, in all its splendor. I have nothing against that part of the body; like your father the magistrate, I am of the opinion that 'tis plumper than the rest and as a result, for anyone who has a strong predilection for the flesh, 'tis always better than what is *close-cropped* . . . As I enter the room, I shall say (for the sake of appearances) to the prompter, or whoever is there: What in the name of all that's holy is that disgraceful object? And the prompter will say: Monsieur, 'tis only a copy.

Third signal, still from the same source:

When you want to act as a major intermediary for someone, as you did this summer with the thunder and lightning rod (which I found so hilarious I almost died laughing), you should set fire to the powder keg

---

2. Probably Sade himself; he sees Christ's tribulations as similar to his.
3. One of Sade's many nicknames for Albaret.
4. Lely suggests that the "doubling" refers to heterosexual sodomy.
5. The famous statue, renowned for its beauty and especially that of its shapely buttocks, is in the Farnese collection in Naples, which Sade visited the year before his Vincennes imprisonment.

(which is standing right next to the bed I sleep in): the effect will be sublime.[6]

Oh! Here is the most beautiful, don't you agree?
Finally, the fourth:

Whenever you have in mind to make a nine-sided 16 (listen to me carefully), you must take two skulls[7] (two, do you hear? I could have said six, but even though I served in the king's dragoons, I'm a modest enough fellow), and while I'm outside taking a walk in the garden you'll put them in my room, so that I can find them already there when I return. Or else you can let me know that a package has been received for me from Provence; I shall hasten to open it . . . and there 'twill be— and I shall be overcome with fear (for I'm extremely timid by nature, as I've proved once or twice in my life).

Ah, good people, good and decent souls! Believe me when I say you should cease and desist from trying to invent things that are so ordinary, so insipid, and so easy to fathom, *'tis not worth the time* and effort you put into them. There are plenty of other things you can do than devising and contriving, and when one is not predisposed to inventing one would be far better off making shoes or nozzles rather than inventing *awkwardly, clumsily,* and *stupidly*.

The 19th, but mailed the 22nd

By the way, send on my linen; and tell those who *think* that I should learn to take care of myself that they should *think* again, because Monsieur de Rougemont, who is a far better *judge* than they, has just determined that my stove is in dire need of serious repair, and he is having it taken care of. Thus for once in our lives why don't we all try and pull together in the same direction, if that were possible, for even though you're all a lowdown scurvy lot, we should nonetheless

---

6. As mentioned, there were frequent thunderstorms in Paris that summer, which frightened Mme de Sade. She was also concerned that the newly installed lightning rods on the roof of Vincennes were attracting lightning. She could, Sade suggests, simulate the thunder by setting fire to one of the fortresses' powder kegs—which was not by his bed—and blow up the place.
7. He is probably alluding to the skull apparently used during the theatricals at La Coste during the winter of 1774–75.

make an honest effort not to have some pulling to the left while the other is pulling to the right. Pull the way Monsieur de Rougemont does; 'tis a man of good common sense, who always pulls in the right direction . . . or lets himself by pulled when he doesn't pull himself. —My valet sends his greetings to you and asks you to remind madame la présidente kindly not to forget that she had promised him, when the time came, to have his son promoted to the rank of sergeant.

82. *To Madame de Sade*

[November 4, 1783]

*E*nclosed, my dear friend, a small sample of the work[1] I mentioned to you earlier. I collected almost two hundred similar character traits, all of which I portrayed and arranged like the one I'm sending for you to judge. I made a point of keeping strictly to the facts; all I did was add a bit of local color in the details. I was afraid that the work you just sent me, *French Anecdotes*, might have caused the pen to drop from my hand, as they say. But that work is totally different from mine, 'tis a simple, boring chronology, which belongs on the desk of any working man. These little character traits of mine, arranged as you see, will, I dare hope, have both the ring of truth about them and yet retain all the flair of a novel. Besides, you will judge for yourself, and 'tis not a crime to talk for once about belles-lettres and literature, I should like your opinion about whether you think a fair copy of the work should be made. In the event you do, kindly send me—I haven't the time to make an exact count—a notebook the size of a quire, that is twenty-five pages, of the same size as the ones I used for my comedies, with the margins already marked as they are on this sample enclosed. The Griffin stationers will mark the pages up for you. I shall be ready to begin on the 18th of this month. If by then I haven't received the notebook, I'll assume that you didn't like the piece. And I shall not pursue it further. To finish the work I need a great deal of encouragement, for as this kind of compilation is not in the least up my alley, I would push

---

1. Probably not extant, this work conceived by Sade was different from anything else he wrote—apparently a kind of catalogue of people and their characteristics that he doubtless drew upon in writing his novels and plays.

ahead with it only out of boredom and for want of anything better to do. I have neither the slightest taste nor the least inclination for it. And if I do not receive the notebook I shall take comfort in the knowledge that I shall then be free to undertake something much more to my taste and considerably more enjoyable. You be the judge.

I wish you a very happy and joyous birthday,[2] and I am sending you this bauble as a bouquet, believing that both because you are personally familiar with the country and because I seem to recall that one of your forebears came from there, I thought it might interest you. If I am wrong, forgive me, but know that the gesture was well intentioned. Leave it at that, and know that in my heart of hearts all I want is to convince you most sincerely that I love you and that I shall always love you as long as I live, despite everything they might inveigle you into doing, and of which I am quite sure you are completely ignorant.

I have received everything, but since I have my usual share of grumbling and harping, and perhaps even a number of crazy recriminations, I prefer not to defile a letter and a shipment whose sole purpose is to celebrate your birthday and to let you know how profoundly and sincerely I would have preferred to celebrate it in a completely different manner.

In any event, stack this little notebook in with my comedies, for I have no other copy, and the draft I have kept is quite illegible.

83. To Madame de Sade

[Beginning of November, 1783]

Good God! how right he is when M. Duclos tells us on page 101 of his *Confessions*[1] that *the witticisms of barristers always stink of the backstairs.* Allow me to go him one better and say that *they smell of the out-*

2. Renée-Pélagie's birthday is actually in December, not November. Had Sade forgot? Unlikely. Perhaps he assumed the letter might take a month to pass the censor and reach its destination. Or, perhaps the true date of the letter, which was undated, was December 2, 1783.
1. *Les Confessions du comte de ****, published in 1742, is less a novel than a gallery of portraits and a collection of anecdotes.

room, of the outhouse: the brainless platitudes your mother and her *Keeper of the Tables* invent are of an odor not to be suffered in any proper salon. And so you never weary of their drivel and their pranks! and so we are to have buffoonery and lawyers to the bitter end! Well, my chit, feed on that stuff to your heart's content, gorge yourself on it, drink yourself high with it. I am wrong to try to teach you proper manners, quite as wrong as he who would attempt to prove to a pig *that a vanilla cream pasty is better than a t——*. But if you give me examples of obstinacy, at least refrain from criticizing me for mine. You cleave to your principles, eh? And so do I to mine. But the great difference between us two is that my systems are founded upon reason while yours are merely the fruit of imbecility.

My manner of thinking, so you say, cannot be approved. Do you suppose I care? A poor fool indeed is he who adopts a manner of thinking to suit other people! My manner of thinking stems straight from my considered reflections; it holds with my existence, with the way I am made. It is not in my power to alter it; and if it were, I'd not do so. This manner of thinking you find fault with is my sole consolation in life; it alleviates all my sufferings in prison, it composes all my pleasures in the world outside, it is dearer to me than life itself. Not my manner of thinking but the manner of thinking of others has been the source of my unhappiness. The reasoning man who scorns the prejudices of simpletons necessarily becomes the enemy of simpletons; he must expect as much, and laugh at the inevitable. A traveler journeys along a fine road. It has been strewn with traps. He falls into one. Do you say it is the traveler's fault, or that of the scoundrel who lays the traps? If then, as you tell me, they are willing to restore my liberty if I am willing to pay for it by the sacrifice of my principles or my tastes, we may bid one another an eternal adieu, for rather than part with those, I would sacrifice a thousand lives and a thousand liberties, if I had them. These principles and these tastes, I am their fanatic adherent; and fanaticism in me is the product of the persecutions I have endured from my tyrants. The longer they continue their vexations, the deeper they root the principles in my heart, and I openly declare that no one need ever talk to me of liberty if it is offered to me only in return for their destruction. I say that to you. I shall say it to M. Le Noir. I shall say it to the entire earth. Were I brought to the foot of the scaffold, I'd not change my tune. If my principles and my tastes cannot consort with the laws of this land, I don't for a moment insist upon remaining in France. In Europe there are wise governments that do not dishonor people because of their tastes and do not cast them into jail because of their opinions. I shall go elsewhere to live, and I shall live there happily.

The opinions or the vices of private individuals do no harm to the State; only the morals of public figures exert any influence upon the general administration. Whether a private person believes or does not believe in God, whether he admires and venerates a harlot or treats her with kicks and curses, neither this form of behavior nor that will maintain or shake the constitution of a State. But let the magistrate whose duty it is to see a given town be provided with food double the price of commodities because the purveyors make it worth his while; let the treasurer entrusted with public funds leave hirelings unpaid because he prefers to turn those pennies to his own account; let the steward of a royal household in all its numbers leave luckless troops, whom the king has allowed into his palace, go unfed because that officer would have a hearty meal at home the Thursday before *Shrove Tuesday*—and from one end of the country to the other the effects of this malversation will be felt; everything goes to pieces. And nonetheless the extortioner triumphs while the honest man rots in a dungeon. *A State approaches its ruin*, spake Chancellor Olivier[2] at the Bed of Justice held in Henry II's reign, *when only the weak are punished, and the rich felon gets his impunity from his gold.*

Let the king first correct what is blatantly amiss in the government, let him do away with its abuses, let him send to the gallows those ministers who deceive or rob him, before he sets about repressing his subjects' opinions or tastes! Once again: those tastes and opinions will not undermine his throne, but the unworthy behavior of those near the throne will topple it sooner or later.

Your parents, you tell me, dear friend, your parents are taking measures to prevent me from ever being in a position to claim anything from them. This extraordinary sentence is all the more so for demonstrating that either they or I must be knaves. If they think me capable of asking them for anything beyond your dowry, I am the knave (but I am not; knavery has never made any inroads into my principles, it's too base a vice); and if, on the contrary, they are taking measures to prevent my receiving that upon which my children must naturally count, then they are the knaves. Kindly decide which it is to be, the one or the other, for your sentence leaves no middle ground. You point your finger at them? I am

---

2. François Olivier (1493–1560), chancellor of France under François I and Henri II.

not surprised. Neither am I surprised at the trouble they encountered marrying you off, or at the remark one of your suitors made: *The daughter, I'm nothing loath; but spare me the parents!* My surprise shall cease at the fact they have been paying me your dowry in vouchers that lose two-thirds on the market; no more shall I marvel that those who were concerned for my interests always used to warn me: *Have a care there, you've no idea whom you are dealing with.* One should not be the least bit surprised at people who take measures not to pay the dowry promised to their daughter; and I have long suspected that the honor of having sired three children upon you was going to be my ruin. 'Tis doubtless to secure it that your mother has so often had my house entered and my *papers* filched. It will cost her but a few louis to have some documents disappear now out of the notaries' files, to have some notes to Albaret falsified: and when at last I emerge from here I shall still be quite able to beg in the streets. —Well, faced with that, what recourse do I have? To me three things will always remain as consolation for everything: the pleasure of informing the public, which is not fond of the foul tricks lawyers play upon noblemen; the hope of advising the king by going and casting myself at his feet if need be, to ask restitution for all your parents' little escapades; and, should all that fail, the satisfaction, to me very sweet, of possessing you *for your own sake,* my dear friend, and of devoting the little that shall still be mine to your needs, to your desires, to the very special charm that will fill my heart seeing you are once more dependent on me.

DE SADE

84.   To Madame de Sade

[November 23–24, 1783]

*C*harming creature, you want my soiled linen, my old linen? Were you aware that 'tis the epitome of refinement? You see how I can separate the wheat from the chaff. Listen, my angel, I would like nothing better than to satisfy you on this score, for you know full well that I respect peoples' tastes and their fantasies; no matter how seemingly strange or odd they might be, I find them all respectable, both because we are not their masters and because when you take a really close look at even the most peculiar and the most bizarre of them, they always emanate from some principle of sensitivity. I shall be only too happy to prove it whenever you like: you know that no one analyzes things the way I do. Therefore, *my turtle dove*, I would like nothing better than to gratify your request; this said, I have to believe that 'twould be mean and stingy not to give my old linen to the man who waits on me. I have therefore done so, and I shall always do so; but you can speak to him about it; I've already mentioned it to him, only hinting, you may be sure. He understood me, and he promised to see what he could find. Thus, *my pet*, please do speak to him about it, and I'm sure he'll be only too happy to comply. —Ah! heavens above! if by so short and sweet a route I might procure *all sorts of things from you*, soon devoured, if I could only hold them, what I wouldn't do! I would steal them if I could! would pay their weight in gold! I would say: Hand them over, good Sir, give them to me this minute, for they once belonged to her whom I adore! I will breathe in the aromas of her life; they will inflame the fluid that flows in my nerves; they will bring into the bosom of my existence something from her, and verily I shall believe I have found happiness! All this said, my darling, can you find it in your heart to send me some fresh linen, given the urgent need I have for it?

You ask me, *my fine feathered friend*, how I would like the notebook containing 300 sheets, that is, 600 pages: well now, *my dove*, to that I shall answer that what I need is a notebook like the one that contains the *Inconstant One.*[1]

For the love of *Mohammed*, you say that the case I asked you for caused you all sorts of trouble.[2] I can easily understand that were it al-

---

1. This five-act play was started New Year's Eve 1780, completed January 24, 1781, and corrected between late January and April. Later the author changed the title to *L'Homme inégal—The Man of Many Moods*, and finally settled on *Le Capricieux—The Fickle Fellow*. Sade kept reworking the play almost till the end of his life, the final version bearing the note: "Read and corrected for the last time June 6 and 11, 1811."

2. Renée-Pélagie's devotion to her husband knew no bounds. The "case" [*etui*] to which Sade refers was intended for his only sexual outlet, masturbation, or simulated sodomy. Sade gave the precise dimensions of these wooden cases, which were rounded and oblong, presumably with a lid that could be opened and closed and which, he pretended, could be used to hold papers or small objects. Sade's use of them was of course quite different. He also had her buy *flacons*—flasks—for him, which were intended for the same purpose. To satisfy his demands, Madame de Sade had personally to approach master carpenters on the Faubourg Saint-Antoine to place her orders, all of whom

ready made it might well be a source of trouble, but when 'tis only a matter of having it made, I have more than a little difficulty getting into the restricted capacity of my cerebellum that the very act of placing the order can have a negative effect on the nerves within you that, acting upon the soul, trigger the sensation of pain. They take you for a madwoman, you tell me; now that I fail to understand; and I find it impossible to allow that the request for a large case by a small woman can cause the slightest disorder in the pineal gland, where we atheist philosophers are prone to locate the seat of reason. You will explain all this to me in due course, and meanwhile kindly place the order for the case and send it to me because I need it most urgently and because, without it, I am forced to resort to a makeshift cover which, though the same size as my drawings, tends to tear them.

You have sent me the handsome young lad,[3] *darling turtle dove.* The handsome young lad: how sweet these words fall upon my ear, which is slightly Italian! *Un' bel giavanetto, signor,* they would say to me if I were at Naples, and I would say: *Si, si, signor, mandaleto lo voglio bene.* You have treated me like a cardinal, *my darling pie . . .* but unfortunately 'tis only in a painting . . . My case, I say, at least my case, since you are reducing me to illusions!

Ducky darling, on this subject let me regale you for a moment with a story that took place in Rome while I was there. For there are times when one has to pause and enjoy a moment of merriment: if you doubt it, ask about *Lieutenant Charles,* who came to enjoy a moment of fun and games with me only a week or so ago, announcing that he was the *king's special envoy.*

Anyway, in Rome there is a cardinal whom, out of discretion, I shall not name, one of whose maxims was that the fluid of one's nerves, activated each morning by the corpuscles emanating from the charms of a pretty young girl, had a distinctly positive effect on a man by making him studious, cheerful, and healthy. Accordingly, a matron, who had been favored with this fascinating detail by his Grace, takes it

---

were quite aware, whatever her claims to the contrary, what the "flasks" or "cases" were for. Worse, she reported to him, the carpenters "take me for a madwoman and laugh in my face . . . Please get someone else to do this errand for you." But Sade was so insistent, and so demanding, she continued to run this hated errand for him, despite the enormous embarrassment it caused her. Sade had other erotic code names: *prestiges* for dildo, *vanille* for aphrodisiacs, and *manille* for his preferred kind of masturbation.

3. Renée-Pélagie had sent him a portrait of a handsome young lad.

upon herself to send into the private chambers of His Eminence each morning a pretty little virgin. There she is received by a gentleman of the cloth, who examines her and introduces her to the cardinal. One day, Signora Clementina (for that was her name), being ignorant of this ceremony and knowing that the prelate, full of respect for a vestal, would never commit any outrage to Nature and confine himself to making a few cursory examinations that could, at the very most, verify in his eyes what both sexes have in common, Signora Clementina, I say, one day being at a loss to find the daily female divinity, takes it into her head to replace her by a *handsome boy* dressed up as a girl. Having ushered him in, the signora withdraws and the gentleman proceeds to his examination. "Oh! Your Holiness, what treachery do I behold," he cries out. "Signora Clementina deserves to be . . . ! We should do the same to her!" The cardinal draws nigh, puts on his glasses, verifies what he has just been told, then, smiling with kindness and ushering the child into his chambers, says: "Peace be unto you, my friend, peace be unto you. We may have been duped, but turnabout is fair play: *she'll simply think I made a mistake!*"

October 23rd.

While we're on that subject, *dear little pig of my heart,* * I shall mention to you that I have made an attempt to make you a drawing of the cushion I need,[4] owing to the fact that my backside is in a sorry state. I should like you not only to see it but to feel it with your finger, and accordingly I have cut out with all the artistry at my command a sheet of paper on which I have traced an exact replica of the cushion I have in mind; the sheet of paper is precisely what the cushion should be; kindly have it stuffed with feathers and horsehair (which is an excellent combination), and have it covered with a sturdy fabric the same on all sides. The sheet of paper is the size I want, but if there is a choice it should be larger rather than smaller, soft but well padded. If you are

---

* No offense intended: 'tis only that pork is one of my favorite meats, and I have scant opportunity to eat it in here. (*Sade's note*)
4. Suffering increasingly from hemorrhoids, Sade compounded the problem by spending as many as ten or eleven hours a day writing. A donut-shaped cushion enabled him to sit for long periods without undue pain.

sending me this cushion, *sweet enamel of my eyes*, then no need to send the padded napkin; if you are not, then I must have it.

The model of the stocking and the little case are already on their way to you, *blood vessels of my heart*, and here is the model for the rug: 42 inches long, 30 inches wide, made of good quality green wool bordered on all sides by a silk ribbon.

Be they good or bad (the bad ones are as useful to me as the good), I beseech you, *star of Venus*, to send me all the new plays that have been performed in one theater or the other in the course of 1783, together with the new yearly almanacs, which is to say at the end of next month or the beginning of January.

You may be quite sure, *soul of my soul*, that the purchases I shall make once I am out of here, and my initial act as a free man—after I have kissed you on both eyes, both tits, and both buttocks—will be to purchase forthwith at whatever cost:

The Best Elements of Physics, Natural History by Monsieur de Buffon, in quarto, illustrated; the complete works of Montaigne, Delille, Arnaud, Saint-Lambert, Dorat, Voltaire, Jean-Jacques Rousseau, with the sequel to the *Voyager*; the histories of France and of the Byzantine Empire, all the works that either I do not have in my library, or have only partially. Considering how much I would truly like to have these books, and given that I shall most surely buy all of them one day, please do check and see, *mirror of beauty*, how many of them your current financial resources allow you to send me in the interim, for I am no longer interested in renting any from the lending libraries.

'Tis uncommonly witty, *my darling nerve-pricker*, to criticize and poke fun at books, and 'tis on that head that Monsieur Duclos is actually wrong when he says, as I mentioned to you the other day, that the pastimes of barristers stink of the backstairs: for what could be more fulfilling, what more noble, than poking fun at the title of a book? No French writer, either in the century of Louis XIV nor that of Louis XV, has ever reached such a sublime pinnacle of genius. I ask you only one thing, and that is to try to make sure that the contents of the book live up to the mockery of the title—which till now you have not managed to do, for I find it impossible to read the recently published novels you've sent me, although they do create the most beautiful numerical figures in the world: *the number 59 evolving into 84 from the number 45*, in a word, things that are truly luminous. Would it not be possible, *O image of divinity*, to somehow work it out so that all these numbers and all these major character traits conjoin in good books? Above all, do not buy anything by Monsieur Rétif,[5] in the name of God! He is a Pont-Neuf author, fit only for the *bibliotheque bleu*, and I find it most extraordinary that it could even enter your mind to send me anything by him. In short, do send me more new novels, but be more discriminating in your choices.

'Tis absolutely impossible for me to enjoy the rebuttal of *The System of Nature* if you do not send me a copy of the book: do go and make a good case for that on my behalf, *violet of the garden of Eden*, and tell them that they should in no wise stand in the way either of my rehabilitation or my recovery *of high principles*. I own that the operation will be difficult, and those principles that I have adopted over thirty years, which are rock-solid, will not easily be made to topple: but still, they should not do anything that might stand in the way of the possibility of success.

O seventeenth planet of space, you should not make light or joke about the head-ribbons. First of all, a woman ought never to make her husband's head the subject of idle banter; and secondly, *O quintesse of virginity*, these ribbons are a bonus pure and simple, they will not become part of any memoir, they are a gift from you, nothing more. And you would have me believe, *O source of all that is angelic*, that this refusal is an act of meanness? I am well aware that *Lieutenant Charles*, about whose head one could make much sport, had his own personal witticism regarding head ribbons; but now, *O symbol of modesty*, that *Lieutenant Charles* has earned his six livres, it seems to me that nothing further is standing in your way of sending me the head-ribbons. I leave to you the quantity and the quality. *O miracle of Nature*, I have asked you to send me a handsome pair of buttocks, whenever a duplicate set might become available, and instead of that who do you send but *Lieutenant Charles*, who informs me that he is of the king's service! *Dove of Venus*, that is what I call mistaking the cause and the effect.

O rose escaped from the bosom of the Graces, the only thing further I have to ask is why you refused to send me the peach wine? Explain to me if you will what the analogy is between the State constitutions and the fibers of my stomach? Is it possible, *my pretty one*, that one or two

---

5. Rétif de la Bretonne, also known as Réstif. Nicolas Rétif (1734–1806) was the author of some 250 works focusing on peasant life and lower-class women, the most famous of which was *Le Paysan perverti ou les dangers de ville*. Known also as the "Rousseau of the Gutter," Rétif was thoroughly detested by Sade, who knew him and who thought his teasingly erotic work was detestable. One might add that Rétif returned the compliment.

bottles of peach wine could in some way break the Salix Law or strike a serious blow at the Justinian Code? *O favorite of Minerva*, 'tis to a drunkard that such a refusal makes sense, but I who am intoxicated by naught but your charms, of which I shall never be satiated, *O ambrosia of Olympus*, do not, I beseech you, deny me my peach wine! *O delight of my eyes*, I thank you for the lovely print of Rousseau that you sent me. *Flame of my life*, when O when will thy alabaster fingers come and re-place Lieutenant Charles's chains for the roses of your bosom? Adieu, I plant a kiss on that bosom and so to bed.

This 24th, at one o'clock in the morning.

85.   To Madame de Sade

[Late November, 1783]

God be praised, here at long last is the letter with the three ques-tions; 'tis some nine months now I've been waiting for it, and I've been growing most impatient. My case should be made to follow the model exactly, without the slightest modification, and I need it as soon as possible. All the books I asked you for have already been published, and 'tis only to torment me pure and simple that you choose not to send them to me, and verily, 'tis most stupid, and most banal, to play games with me regarding these books. Of all the many crass blunders committed by your guides and counselors, that is the most outrageous.

As far as the case is concerned, I can make neither head nor tail of why it should be an apparently endless problem; all the shopkeepers who deal in this sort of merchandise make cases to order, and to have one made to the specifications I sent you presupposes a certain width at most. But as for the *folie*, not a word. If you aren't sure, ask your cousin Villette.

You need to tell your shopkeeper that the case is meant to hold *culs—culs de lampes*, that is[1]—yes, lamp bases and some other little

---

1. Sade is clearly punning here as well as trying to circumvent the censor. *Cul* literally means "ass"; *culs de lampes* are rounded architectural ornaments gen-erally used on ceilings that resemble the bottoms of church lamps.

drawings I have made in red ink, and so I beseech you to send it to me, because without it I am obliged to resort to some stopgap measures, which have the defect of wrinkling and tearing my papers and *culs* . . . I mean lamp bases, which is most disagreeable. 'Tis out of pure modesty and so as not to frighten you that I asked you to have the case made eight and a half inches on all sides, for if worst came to worst it could have been nine inches square, using the size of my lamp bases as a basic measure. But I told myself, nine inches square is going to frighten these people who are already afraid of their own shadow, so I settled for eight and a half.

How do you expect me to appreciate the rebuttal of *The System of Nature* if you refuse to send me the rebuttal at the same time you send *the book being refuted?* 'Tis as if you asked a judge to render his verdict without having seen the evidence of both parties. You have to admit that that is quite impossible, despite the fact that the *System* is verily and indubitably the basis of my philosophy, and I am and shall remain a faithful disciple of that philosophy even at the cost of my life, if it came to that. Still, since 'tis a good seven years since I last read it, there is no way I can remember it in sufficient detail to follow and appreciate the rebuttal. I would very much like to do my best to see if I have been mistaken, but at least provide me with the means to do so. Kindly ask Villette to lend me the book for a week, no more, and let there be no equivocation on that score, 'twould be utterly stupid to deny me a book that I recommended to the Pope himself, a golden book in a word, a book that ought to be in every library and whose tenets should be in the heads of everyone, a book that undermines and destroys forever the most dangerous and most odious of all fantasies, the one that has caused more bloodshed here on earth than any other, one against which the entire universe should rise up and destroy once and for all, if the people who make up this universe had the slightest idea of what constitutes their true happiness and tranquillity. Personally, I cannot even conceive that there are people who still believe in religion, and I can only conclude that if they do 'tis only a sham. For in that case, either they are imbeciles, people who find it beyond them to think things through, however superficially, or who cannot or will not make the slightest effort to get to the heart of the matter. For beyond any shadow of doubt, theism cannot for a moment stand up to the slightest scrutiny, and one would have to be completely ignorant of the workings of Nature not to recognize that it operates on its own and without any primary cause, and that so-called primary cause, which explains nothing and which on the contrary requires explanation, is naught but the *nec plus ulta* of ignorance.

Well now, here's a letter that, I have no doubt, will *prolong* my stay within these walls, don't you agree? You should tell my *prolongers* that their prolongation is a waste of time, for were they to leave me here for another ten years they would not see one whit of improvement when they do release me, of that you may be sure—either kill me or accept me as I am, for may hell freeze over if I ever change—I have told you before and I tell you again, the beast is too old—there is no longer any hope he will change—the most honest, the most candid, the most sensitive of men, the most compassionate, the most charitable, a man who idolizes his children, for whose happiness he would walk through fire, meticulous to a flaw in his desire to make certain he will neither have the slightest negative influence on their morals nor damage their minds in any wise nor have them adopt any of his own beliefs, a man who adores his relatives (by which I mean blood relatives), the few friends he still has in this world, and above all his wife, whose happiness means everything to him and to whom more than anything in the world he desires to make amends for the many youthful indiscretions—because the fact is, *by her nature his wife is not made for that*, 'tis a truth that I sensed and expressed to her a good six months before I landed here; she can attest to that. So much for my virtues. As for my vices, much given to uncontrollable anger, extreme in everything, a profligate imagination when it comes to morals the likes of which the world has never seen, atheist to the point of fanaticism, in two words let me say it once again: either kill me or take me as I am, for I shall never change.

86.   To Madame de Sade

[First days of January, 1784]

I beseech you to think most seriously about what you have written me on the subject of my son. This morning I have solemnly sworn the same thing to Monsieur de Rougemont, and if 'tis necessary I shall swear to all of Europe. No reason in the world will make me consent to my son's becoming a sub-lieutenant in the infantry, and that he shall never be. If you were to allow him to join the infantry against my wishes, I give you my word of honor that I shall force him to leave that branch of service, and there is no means to which I would not resort to attain that end.[1] Ponder well what I say, and see for yourself the full run of misfortunes that such stubbornness on the part of your mother will necessarily entail. Even were your son to join the infantry with the promise of a regiment in his pocket, I would still resist it with all my might. I absolutely do not want him to serve in any other branch but the cavalry. From the moment he first opened his eyes, that was what I had planned for him, and I shall most assuredly not change my mind. If it takes 20,000, nay, 40,000 francs to bring that about, I am prepared to provide it. I have always refused you full power of attorney as I did the right to act by proxy, and that you know well. Well, then, as far as this matter is concerned I am ready and willing to sell, pledge, borrow, deprive myself of whatever it may take, no matter what, if that is necessary; I am bound and determined that he enter the cavalry. By the same token, there is nothing I wouldn't do to make certain he does not spend one minute in the infantry. I have been told that you were going to come and visit me shortly, and I was greatly pleased to hear it. If 'tis true, then you can bring along with you, my dear friend, a power of attorney and a notary; I am fully prepared to make whatever commitment you like, provided 'tis to have my son enter the cavalry. But most assuredly, he will not serve in any other branch, that I swear to you once again.

DE SADE

I kindly ask that you forbid him to write me again till he has sworn to obey my wishes. Enclosed my letter to him. The errands I asked you to run for me are now six weeks' stale, which is perfectly ridiculous. 'Tis impossible to use the ointment you sent me. What I asked for was not ointment, but a salve, a salve of the consistency of wax, one that will stick to the part affected and not wipe off the way this one does.

Kindly send it immediately, for I am suffering greatly. And the ointment the surgeon gives me has the same problem as yours; thus I effectively have none at all.

---

1. Louis-Marie de Sade, now seventeen, was preparing to join Rohan Soubise's recently formed infantry regiment. Sade, who had always wanted his son to be in the cavalry, was furious.

You sent me six useless volumes by Koch. All I wanted was the seventh, and that is not part of the set and is sold separately. Always so much money thrown out the window, and always for simply not having thought things through!

Send me therefore, I beg of you, the works of Saint-Lambert of Delille and whatever new comedies may have appeared; that and the succeeding volumes of the *History of France*, the *Later Byzantine Empire*, and the *Voyager.* Those are what I basically need and want as far as books are concerned, and I beg you to send them to with all due speed.

I am absolutely out of stockings, and have been for a long time now. So add that item to your package as well. Enclosed please find the rest of my list, all of which I know will meet with your approval; in the future I shall entrust this task to a third party, since I am weary of spending my life drawing up lists.

I can see by how the wind is blowing that the conditions for my release are being made more and more difficult, and I sense that to attain it I shall be forced to make some sort of major commitment. I shall agree and consent to any conditions that strike me as reasonable. As for all ridiculous conditions, the sole result of Madame de Montreuil's whims and fancies, which will go against the laws *of Nature, the rights of a father or of a citizen*, I hereby swear that I shall agree to them as well, because I want to leave here, but I have not the slightest intention of keeping to them.

I am returning with this letter your lovely ointment.

87. *To Louis-Marie de Sade*

[Early January, 1784]

I have no son capable of joining a regiment of which I do not approve. He may be the son of Madame de Montreuil, but he is not mine; and from you, Sir, all I expect to receive is a letter wherein you will give me your word of honor that you will accept no other branch of service than the one I shall obtain for you. Till then, I kindly request that you not write me again.

88. To Louis-Marie de Sade

[About January 10, 1784]

*I*t has just come to my attention, Monsieur, that your mother's parents have made the decision that you should accept a sub-lieutenancy in one of the worst infantry regiments in France. I forbid you, Sir, to accept that appointment; you are not made for a sub-lieutenancy of infantry, and I cannot and will not allow you to join that branch. Either you will not serve at all or you will under the command of Monsieur de Chabrillant, a relative of yours, in the cavalry.

If in defiance of my express order that you not accept such a post, Sir, I were to learn that you had been so weak as to obey your relatives who, as long as your father is alive, have no right or authority over you, then you may bid me eternal farewell, for I shall never lay eyes upon you for the rest of my life.

Those who encourage you to disobey that order from me will be held responsible, in their souls and their consciences, for whatever misfortunes your disobedience will bring down upon your head, and I shall call down curses upon it if, within two months from now, I have not received written confirmation from you that you have carried out my wishes.[1]

COUNT DE SADE, YOUR FATHER[2]

---

1. Despite all his blustering, Sade was in no position to carry out his threat. A short while later, Louis-Marie became, indeed, a sub-lieutenant in the hated infantry, stationed at Port-Louis.
2. As Lely notes, there was "utter confusion" on the matter of titles. "In the army and in the letters of Ministers of the Crown about the Arceuil affair, Sade's imprisonment in Savoy, and so forth, he appears as *Count*, but in his marriage contract, the arrest warrant of October 29th 1763 and the proceedings at both Arceuil and Marseilles and elsewhere he is described as *Marquis*" (Lely, p. 257).

89. *To Madame de Sade*

[After January 10, 1784]

I trust, Madame, that you will have passed on to your parents the results of our most recent conversation concerning the ridiculous appointment intended for your son. Be so kind as to remit the enclosed letter to him, so that he can see for himself what my express intentions are as far as he is concerned, and I will hold you responsible for informing me if he intends to disobey them. I most urgently beg your mother to refrain from involving herself in my children's affairs. I have no need whatsoever either of her little twists and turns, nor of the considerable influence her younger son from Normandy may have in helping place my son in military service. All I do need is my freedom. Were I to be master of my own actions today, tomorrow your son would be placed in the service for which he was destined and where 'tis appropriate he be. I had, moreover, written and told you a thousand times over that none of my children will ever leave their school or your house until I have spent a full year with them. Nothing in the entire universe will make me change that opinion. Nor shall either of my two sons join any branch of service whatsoever until they have learned how to ride properly and until I have personally chosen a servant to accompany them. Ponder well these three points, in the full knowledge that no reason whatsoever could ever make me alter my views thereon. If one acts against my express desires, as is most likely, since I am in prison and unable to prevent it from happening, mark my words that the first thing I shall do once I am free will be to force him to leave that branch of service. That I swear on my most sacred and most authentic word of honor. On that point have no doubts, Madame. Do not try to turn me against my children. Some people seem to be doing everything in their power to do so, and I dare say 'tis not very clever of them. You, the king, and the judiciary, the entire legal code of the kingdom, no matter what precautions one may take under previous or current laws, will not prevent me from reducing the four estates I own in Provence to a *hundred pistoles of income*, and that without selling off so much as a single inch of land. That is the secret that you never fathomed, and never will, and that I most assuredly will put into effect if you permit my son to disobey me. What is more, Madame, I shall do my best to inspire in him the same kind of feelings for you that you are trying to instill in him about me.

Since madame your mother's head is inclined to plan well ahead, when she dreamed up this fine position for your son she doubtless also had in mind some plan or other for an equally excellent marriage a few years down the road. In order to avoid having to bring up these same subjects over and over again, I have the honor of hereby declaring to you, and attesting thereto by this same letter, Madame, and under the same seal as my word of honor, that I most assuredly will not give my approval to any such marriage before he is twenty-five years of age, and not a day sooner. It is my express desire that he be married nowhere but in *Lyons* or *Avignon*, and under no circumstances would I allow either he or you, or therefore myself, to take up residence in Paris. I have told you time and time again, Madame, that once all this is over my intention is to repair to and live in my own province. I have no doubt that my children will follow me there, and just as certainly 'tis there they shall marry and take up residence.

'Tis in vain that you make Baron de Breteuil your spokesmen in all such matters. My present situation, and the extremely high regard in which I hold this minister, a man full worthy of respect for a thousand different reasons,[1] oblige me to agree to whatever he requests; but once I am free, I shall take the liberty of reminding him that a *pater familias* is the master of his children, and that 'tis quite impossible for anyone to deprive him of those rights. You must see by the style of this letter that 'tis written with all the self-control at my command. It contains the same things I have been repeating to you for seven years now, and you may be quite sure that I shall never change my opinion. I finish by giving you, and signing, my most genuine and sacred word of honor.

DE SADE

Moreover, Madame, now that your elder son has become a man in his own right in the world, I must warn you that I intend to follow the well-established family custom, wherein the head of the family assumes the title of count and names his eldest son the marquis. As for

---

1. Baron de Breteuil, the newly named minister of the royal household for Paris, was much more humane than his predecessor and took steps to improve conditions in the prison system. As a result, Sade was allowed to receive more frequent visits from his wife.

myself, I shall doubtless do the king's bidding, whatever that may be, since I do not have a single letter patent that stipulates either my responsibility nor my duties, not a single letter, from either the princes or the ministers, that addresses me by this title. I tell you this so that you may familiarize the public which, having become accustomed to a different title, will subsequently have trouble changing its ideas. As for my own ideas, you may rest assured that they will never change.

90. To Madame de Sade

[End of January, 1784]

*G*iven the impossibility of having the frank and open exchange we could have if you were here on one of your visits, and lest you mistake the tone I am obliged to use in my letters as a lack of spine on my part, or even acquiescence, when it comes to the subject of my son, I say once again and do solemnly swear that on the matter in question my feelings will never change; that I am absolutely against his joining the regiment in which you wish to place him against my wishes; and that in the event you persist and place him there despite what I say to you, then the first thing I shall do once I am free is to oblige him to leave that regiment immediately, and in order to convince you that 'tis not for the base reason that you dared ascribe to me yesterday for so doing, a reason that you should blush even to dare let enter your mind, in order to convince you, I say, that far from standing in the way of his advancement as your unworthy parents dared prompt you to tell me, I am fully prepared if 'tis what it takes, to sacrifice half of my fortune, nay, two-thirds if necessary, to make sure he obtains even the lowliest post in the carabiniers. To that end, I am ready and willing to sign whatever paper, make whatever pledge, might be required. All you need do is bring along a notary and I shall sign whatever you like. But as for serving in Soubise's infantry regiment, that he will not do under any circumstances, and on that I swear to you on everything I hold most sacred in the world. There is nothing more ridiculous than hearing you say what you did yesterday on that score: *The king*, you said, wants him to *join the infantry!* Verily, you do me the honor, you and those around you, of believing that because I am confined to a single room I have therefore become an imbecile. Do you for a moment believe that

I do not know the constitution as well as you? Are we in Turkey, or have we been born serfs under the authority of some despot who holds the power of life and death over his slaves? No, no, Madame, the king's authority does not go so far as to remove a son from his father's control; the authority of paternal rights takes precedence over that of a monarch, of that you may be quite sure.

Leave it to your mother, all puffed up with pride as she is from having succeeded in paying off three or four police puppets, to hold to the little bourgeois notion that the king can do no wrong, just because the police informers, her faithful disciples, tell her that 'tis a sin to question the king's word. —Yes, leave her that fathead Marais; she is made for him, but not you, and mark you well that in spite of all that odious woman's servile stupidities, the only two people who have the final say about your children are you and me, that I do not want your son to serve under Soubise, and that your friendship for me and duty to me oblige you to yield to my desires, especially when they are founded on such firm reasons as those I shall cite at the appropriate time.

Meanwhile, keep in mind the genuine oath that I have sworn to you, namely that nothing on the face of the earth will persuade me to leave him where you seem bound to place him, and that no later than six weeks following my release I shall at long last seek proper redress under the law to undo all the infamies that your odious parents have inflicted on me day in and day out.

DE SADE

91. To Gaufridy

[February 3, 1784]

I have just learned from Madame de Sade, Monsieur, that I have had the misfortune to lose one of my aunts.[1]

---

1. Sade's paternal grandfather, Gaspard François de Sade, had five daughters, only one of whom married. The other four all became nuns, two at the convent of Saint-Laurent in Avignon, two at different convents in Avignon. The cloistered sisters saw little of their errant nephew, but rumors of his deeds and misdeeds reached them nonetheless, doubtless from their brother the Abbé

My intention is that the annuity that aunt received be shared between my two surviving aunts (I refer to the two nuns). Please be so kind as to inform them of this, Monsieur, and the new situation should take effect from the day of my aunt's death, in such wise that there be no hiatus in this modest income, not even a single moment, and that from the time it ceased to be given over into the hands of Madame La Coste[2] it pass in equal shares to these two ladies of Saint-Benoit and Saint-Bernard. I would also be grateful if you would, in carrying out my orders most promptly on this matter, at the same time also inform them, while offering them a thousand pardons on my behalf, that because of my many hardships and the mediocrity of my fortune, I am not in a position to offer a more concrete proof of my affection and respect, and one more commensurate with the dictates of my heart.

In the event I were to suffer a second loss such as this, I commend you to act in the same manner as you have here with regard to my remaining aunt, so that the final surviving aunt will be the recipient of her sisters' annuities. As soon as this has been done, please be good enough to inform Madame de Sade of it, so that she may then pass the information on to me. At the same time, please tell my aunts that I would have taken care of this matter much sooner if only I had been informed of it sooner.

I have the honor of being, Monsieur, your most humble and obedient servant.

COUNT DE SADE

---

de Sade. Despite the disturbing echoes, all four seemed never to give up on the marquis. Hence his gratitude, which one has to believe was sincere.
2. Marguerite-Félicité de Sade, also known as Madame La Coste, was an ordinary nun in the convent of Saint-Bernard in Cavaillon. Since it was she who died, Sade is confused when he asks that her share be divided between the two surviving sisters at Saint-Bernard and Saint-Benoit. His other surviving aunt, Anne-Marie Lucrèce, was in Avignon.

92.   To Madame de Sade

[End of February, 1784]

*H*owever great my desire to see you, my dear friend, I ask you most sincerely and most urgently not to run the risk of coming to visit me in such frightful weather. There are a thousand dangers you risk if you do try to come, all of which worry me to death when I think of you thus exposed. This weather cannot long endure. Thus the few days I shall be kept waiting will cause me less suffering than the mortal anguish wherewith I shall be overcome the minute you leave me in such weather as this; because, after you leave, I shall have no way of knowing what has become of you, and that drives me to distraction. Your mother must be either dead drunk or completely mad in thus risking her daughter's life, in order to form a 19 and a 4, or a 16 and 9, and not be weary of this little numbers game she has been playing for twelve years now. Oh! what an indigestion that horrible woman had suffered from all the numbers she has ingested! I am convinced that if she had died before the eruption, and if they opened her up, a million numbers would have come tumbling from her entrails. You have no idea how much I loathe all these numbers and convoluted intricacies. I am told that using numbers is the language of negotiators. Well, then! I shall never negotiate for the rest of my life, for considering all the insuperable horror you have given me over all that gibberish, I believe that if the king were to give me the top-ranking ambassadorship in his kingdom, I would refuse it.[1]

But I am wrong in saying *I believe*. Nothing is more certain. Believe me, do not head off in the wrong direction. I can see what's going through your mind, but I declare and solemnly swear to you on all that I hold most sacred in the world, that were the king to offer me [the ambassadorship] to a monarchy, I would not take it. You have instilled in me too great a loathing for chains: I would turn my back on them even were they covered with flowers.

---

1. Somehow Sade had got it into his head—probably misreading a sentence or thought expressed in one of his wife's letters—that the king was about to offer him an ambassadorship, at the request or urging of la présidente, if only to get him out of France. Nothing could have been further from the truth: Madame de Montreuil, and doubtless the king's ministers, wanted him right where he was.

To go live in whatever part of the world I choose and there, together with my wife and children, to devote myself wholly to science and the arts, that in a nutshell is what I most desire. And I most solemnly declare and swear to you that anything that might in any way divert or distract me from that goal, or restrict me to any degree, I shall firmly and resolutely refuse. Therefore, mark my words, do not undertake any such efforts on my behalf, nor should you pursue the matter of Soubise's infantry regiment on behalf of your son. For I say to you once again, it simply will not work. I have told you this many times over. And despite everything I say, you plow right ahead; in all fairness, you're the one who will bear the consequences. You know that when you go to the ministers and request a favor for someone who actually does not want that favor, they look upon it askance; therefore, there's no point taking that risk.

Do not, I repeat, take such a risk, for I swear to God and upon my own life that I want nothing and will accept nothing. Nor should you allow your son to join the Soubise infantry, and if you do so against my express wishes, as soon as I am free my first act will be to remove him from same.

'Tis because of all these lovely projects no doubt that you tease me in a thousand different ways about my literary works. Another sure way to bind me to such endeavors and throw myself headlong into them to the point of madness. If I had written a decent play, no matter what the genre, I would have stopped at that, and I solemnly declare to you that I would never have gone any further. But since I am not fortunate enough to have succeeded, I want to devote myself to writing day and night, to the absolute exclusion of everything else. That is my character, as you well know, and yet you never want to admit it. 'Tis you who will have to bear the consequences for not taking me at my word.

Believe me that what I am about to tell you is deeply and indelibly engraved in my mind and heart. You know my faults, as you know how much they are near and dear to me. Now then, I swear upon my word of honor that if someone—someone whose word I trusted—were to come to me and say: *What you are doing poses no problem whatsoever, Sir; you may rest assured that you are quite free to go on as you have, no one will any longer stand in your way.* Yes, I declare that if I were told that by someone in authority I would immediately take such a violent dislike to my shortcomings that I would never again indulge in them as long as I lived. But 'twas for them I was clapped in prison, and for that reason alone I shall treasure them all my life. I have kept no secrets from you and those around you; I have revealed my character, made no bones about what makes me tick, for some twenty years now, and you have chosen not to take advantage of it; rather you have preferred to take me the wrong way. That being so, when I leave this place behind, there's no point in having my possessions removed, for 'twill not be long before I am carted back to this same room.

I await your thoughts about the scene I described to you during your last visit, and the answer—yes or no—about the project in question. If you *tease* and *procrastinate*, I shall forthwith start working on my tragedy about *François I,* the full outline of which I have already prepared; and which, if I dare say so myself, will be sublime.

I embrace you with all my heart, and I beseech you not to expose yourself to this foul weather. At least let that naughty white bosom of yours be well protected or I shall fly into a terrible rage against you. And in God's name, bring me some stockings!

For I am sorely lacking IN STOCKINGS, SADE.[2]

And do follow up to make sure they are sent, etc.

---

2. Sade is making a pun impossible to translate. Having asked several times for cotton stockings (*bas*), he notes that he is "bien mal en bas," which means "sorely lacking in stockings," but also, by signing his name thereafter, could mean "a very poor ambassador" (*bien mal ambassade*).

Part
Two

Letters from
the Bastille

In the first weeks of 1784 a decision was made to shut down the Vincennes dungeon, partly the result of pressure from the increasingly restive populace, partly because Sade was one of only three prisoners remaining in Vincennes. On February 29, with no warning, Sade and the two other prisoners, both aristocrats, were unceremoniously taken from their cells and brought to the even more forbidding Bastille.

The Bastille, in the heart of what is today Paris's fourth arrondissement (or district), at the Porte Saint-Antoine, was built from 1370 to 1382. Originally constructed to house the military, it was soon turned into a state prison. It contained eight towers, each of which was given a name. Upon his arrival there on February 19, 1784, Sade was lodged in Liberty Three on the third floor of Liberty Tower, one of two towers—the other was called Bertaudière— that comprised the Saint-Antoine cell block. There was only one cell per floor, an octagonal room about fifteen feet in diameter. The cells all had high ceilings—some as much as twenty feet; the walls were whitewashed and the floors were of brick. There was one window in each cell secured by three sets of bars, which filtered out most of the light. Still, Sade's window was higher than the prison walls, and he could at least catch a glimpse of the city beyond.

When he was spirited away from Vincennes without warning, most of his belongings—his books, his manuscripts, his wall hangings, his paintings and family portrait, his clothing, his bed linen, his "rump cushion," without which he could not work—were left behind. It was not until two months later, on April 29, that he was delivered all his Vincennes possessions.

If at Vincennes he disdained and reviled the warden, de Rougemont, at the Bastille he encountered an even more formidable foe, Monsieur de Launay, the commandant, who took an immediate dislike to his new ward who, he complained to his superior, the lieutenant general of police, was "violent and extremely difficult."

For the next five years, there would be a running battle between de Launay and Sade, one all-powerful and vindictive, the other powerless except to provoke, by voice and pen, and to remonstrate against the constant injustices to which he was subjected.

Sade was far from the only famous prisoner sequestered in the Bastille. Some of the most celebrated names of French history and literature had earlier been lodged within its storied walls: Jacques d'Armagnac, Bernard Palissy, Fouquet, and Voltaire, to name but a few.

93. *To Madame de Sade*

March 8, 1784

*T*hirty-four months after having formally refused a transfer to a dungeon at the doorstep of my own lands,[1] where I was promised I would have complete freedom, and then having asked the favor of allowing me to remain in peace where I was, no matter how poorly off I was, for whatever length of time it pleased your mother to sacrifice me to her vengeance, thirty-four months, I say, after that event, to find myself whisked away by force, completely unexpectedly, without the slightest warning, the whole thing wrapped in mystery and surrounded by all sorts of burlesque secrecy, the entire event steeped in an enthusiasm and fervor that would scarcely have been excusable in the initial turmoil of an affair of the first magnitude, and now, after a dozen years of misfortunes, as dull as it is ridiculous! And to have me taken where? To a prison where I am a thousand times worse off and a thousand times more oppressed than the wretched place whence I came. Such methods, Madame, no matter how much one tries to disguise or gloss over this atrocious deed with hateful lies, such methods, you must confess, has to be the last straw as regards all the hate that I have sworn against your family most foul. And I truly believe that you would be the first to underestimate me sorely if the episodes of my revenge did not one day equal in all their ferocity those they have heaped on me. Do not worry, and you may rest assured that neither you nor the world at large will have the slightest reproach to make me on that score. But I shall have neither the merit of dreaming up, or *in cold fury* of seeking to invent, whatever may cause the venom I intend to use all the more poisonous. The deep well within me will furnish whatever I need, I shall harden my heart, let all the mechanisms of revenge do their worst, and you may be sure the venom I shall spew forth will be fully worthy of that unleashed against me.

But let us get down to the details. In such cases, actions speak louder than words, and so long as one's arms are tied, silence is golden. These are the lessons in lying I have been forced to learn: I shall learn from them, yes, I shall indeed learn from them, and one day, Madame, I shall be as double-dealing as you.

---

1. That is, Montélimar.

For twenty years now, Madame, you have known that 'tis absolutely impossible for me to live in a room heated by a stove, and yet (thanks to the loving care of those who were involved in this transfer) here I am locked up in just such a room. These past few days I was so indisposed that I stopped lighting a fire; and no matter what the weather may become, I still shall not light one. Fortunately, summer is nigh; but if I am still here next winter, I beg you to take whatever steps are necessary to see that I have a room with a fireplace.

You know, too, that exercise is even more necessary to me than food itself. And yet I am in a room that is scarcely half the size of the one that I had, in which 'tis impossible to take as much as even a few steps, and when I am allowed out, which is rare, 'tis only for a few minutes, into a little courtyard, where all one breathes is the stench of the warders and the kitchen. Worse, one is taken there by guards who prod me with a ramrod affixed to the end of their guns, as if I had tried to dethrone Louis XVI himself! Oh! how one learns to loathe major things when one attaches such importance to minor ones!

You are also well aware that my dizzy spells and my frequent nosebleeds, both of which I have when I'm not lying down with my head perched extremely high, had obliged me to have an oversized pillow. When I tried to take this wretched pillow with me, you would have thought I was trying to steal the list of those who had conspired against the State; barbarically, they tore it from my hands and declared that matters of such magnitude had never been tolerated. And indeed I realized that some secret rule or regulation of government doubtless stipulated that a prisoner's head should be kept lowered, for when to remedy that situation owing to the fact that my oversized pillow had been denied me I humbly requested four planks of wood, they took me for a madman. A swarm of commissioners descended upon me, who, having verified that I was indeed most uncomfortable in bed, in their infinite wisdom concluded *that the rules were the rules* and 'twas impossible to change them. Verily I say unto you that you have to see it to believe it, and were we to learn that such things were taking place in China, our tender and compassionate Frenchmen would waste not a moment shouting to the high heavens: *Oh! those barbarians!*

What is more, I am told that I must make my bed and sweep up my room. As for the former, so much the better, for they made it up most poorly and I enjoy making my own bed. But as for the second, 'tis unfortunately a hopeless case; my parents are at fault in this, because they never included sweeping up in their articles of education. There was no way they could ever foresee . . . *many things*. If ever they had, there'd not be a servant in any public house in the country who could hold a candle to me in the sweeping department. Meanwhile, I beg of you to have someone give me a few lessons. I suggest that the man who serves me here sweep my room only once a week for the next four or five years: I shall watch his every move, and you shall see, after that learning period I shall do just as fine a job of sweeping as he.

For seven long years at Vincennes I was allowed the use of knives and scissors, without there ever being the slightest problem. I haven't improved any over the course of those seven years, that I admit, but I haven't grown any worse, either. Would you be so good as to point that out to them, and accordingly have them restore my right to use these two objects?

I am stripped naked, thank God, and before long I shall be as naked as the day I was born. I was not allowed to take anything along with me, no matter what: a shirt, a nightcap made the lackey burst into invective, de Rougemont to shout himself hoarse, in consequence thereof I left everything behind, and I most insistently urge you to bring me during your very first visit two shirts, two handkerchiefs, six napkins, three pairs of slippers, four pairs of cotton stockings, two cotton caps, two hairnets, a cap of black taffeta, two muslin cravats, a dressing gown, four small pieces of linen five inches square that I need to bathe my eyes, and several of the books that are on my previous list. And that list assumes that within a fortnight I shall be receiving my cases and equipment from Vincennes, for if there is any delay in their arrival, then I kindly ask that you double or triple the quantities requested, depending on how long you deem it will be before my baggage arrives.

I would also be greatly indebted if you would make sure I receive the following items, which have nothing to do with my cases; that is, I still need them whether or not my belongings arrive sooner or later. (The most pressing objects: the cushion for my rear, left behind at Vincennes, and my fur-lined slippers, both my mattresses, and my pillow.)

Half a dozen jars of jam, half a dozen pounds of candles, several packages of small candles, the kind that contain fifteen to a package; a pint of Cologne water of better quality than the last you sent, which was worthless, a pint of rosewater for my eyes, to which kindly add a sixth portion of eau-de-vie; that is, the pint of rosewater should contain five parts rosewater and one part eau-de-vie; and the sequels to those books that I have been asking for such a long time now, as well as the remaining comedies above and beyond those already received from the catalogue I sent you.

May there be a swift reply to the objects requested in this letter, if 'tis not too far beyond your earthly powers, so that at least for once I can say that you served some useful purpose to me during my detention, and above all the two mattresses from my bed and the oversized pillow. I leave the rest to your good judgment.

If the oculists tell you that seawater and the powder in question [are] still necessary for my eye, which is still in as bad shape as ever, have those items, left behind at Vincennes, forwarded to me as soon as possible.

Please see to it that my baggage is sent on to me with all due speed.

Well now, my dearly beloved, most amiable, and above all extremely straightforward spouse, you tricked me good and proper when you promised me, each time you paid me a visit, that 'twould be you who would come to fetch me, that I would be free and would see my children! Were it possible to be more despicably, more shamefully deceitful and untruthful? And do tell me now whether you still believe that those who so villainously betray your husband are working in your best interest, in the hope of making you happy? . . . My dear friend, if that is what they tell you, they are deceiving you: tell them that you have it directly from me.

Since I was brought back to Vincennes, after all the horrors that preceded it and that I at least have not forgotten,[2] but since I was returned there, only two further thrusts of the dagger were available to you and yours: to have me transferred to a different prison, and to have my son enrolled in a branch of service in which I absolutely do not want him to serve, and that without my laying eyes on him to tell him so. Now you have struck both those blows. I shall remember to show my gratitude, that I swear to you by all I hold most sacred in the world.

I salute you most humbly, Madame, and beseech you to devote a bit of your attention to my letter, to my requests and my errands, all the more so because it is my firm intention in this new environment to send you lists, lists, and more lists. Whereupon I declare that this will be my first and my last letter.

[P.S.] I believe you would be well advised to reward the man in charge of services here, about whom I hear only good things, and especially because I can already most cruelly sense the difference. Kindly see to it.

---

2. Sade is referring to his rearrest in August 1778 when police invaded the La Coste château at four in the morning.

94. To Abbé Amblet

[April (?) 1784]

*Y*es, my good and dear friend, yes, whatever you may say to the contrary, your critical remarks are more indulgent than they are truthful.[1] You have drawn your colors from a palette sprinkled with venom: how then could the tints be other than harsh? Perhaps I should have preferred more truth and less condescendence on your part. But I am wretched, my enemies triumphant: one must be sacrificed to their sins.

However little importance I ascribe to my own misery, I do ascribe great importance to your remarks, in which wise I trust you will not judge it inopportune if I say a word or two about your remarks. I am going to follow you word for word, not about the corrections you have made—for those I can but thank you most graciously—but about those that I have not been able to bring myself to make, because I seemed to detect therein naught but bitterness and condescension toward those people that my kind of work drives to despair and, if only for that reason, links me to them for the rest of my life, so strong is my desire to please them.

In referring to Pierre the Hermit, I cannot say: *the most remarkable character in the play.* He is not the most remarkable character in Jerusalem; Renaud and Armide are most certainly as special as he; therefore I am obliged to put what I did: *one of the most remarkable characters of Tasso.*

The language of painting is used everyday in poetry; the muses are sisters; these are intimately interlinked. Homer and Michelangelo have both been called painters of Nature. 'Tis rendered by one in beautiful verses, the other by the adroit mixture of his colors, but Nature is the rule for both, therefore both can have the same language.

All operas are doubtless composed of several lyric scenes that form the various acts: 'tis nonetheless true that convention calls for us to apply this same term to a short drama, be it in prose or in verse, where the dialogue, spoken rather than sung, is punctuated by ritornellos. These works are also called *melo*-dramas, which (as you know

---

1. Sade is doubtless referring to his former tutor's critical reading of his play *Tancrède*, which was drawn from Tasso and which Sade completed in January 1784. The play has been lost.

better than I) being a literal translation from the Greek, means simply a drama with music.

'Tis Monsieur de La Harpe[2] who is greatly opposed to this new genre, and 'tis from one of his most recent works, wherein he bitterly attacks it, that I borrowed the words *perverse* and *monstrous*, terms that he uses to denigrate the genre, and I quoted those terms in italics simply to demonstrate how ridiculous they are. But considering the proposed intent of the poem, I saw no reason to cite him as my source.

I know that both *Esther* and *Athalie* are performed without music, but I also know that the lyrical scenes of Rousseau's *Pygmalion* are performed to very lovely and excellent music, and my little work is supposed to be in this same vein and, so I trust, will one day be set to music.

Only truth is beauty, truth alone is kind and good.

Could it be Madame de M[ontreuil] by any chance has brought your attention to that maxim? If so, then I say to you that she is in complete contradiction with herself.

I do not have a copy of Tasso to hand, but I believe I am correct in saying that I followed the position Tasso describes word by word, and that the body is laid to rest very close to Tancrede. Moreover, that is merely a theatrical situation that can easily be changed: all one need do is put Chlorinda on the grassy bank and Tancrede in his tent. Everything is in place, and that would not necessitate any change whatsoever in my scene.

All the reproaches that Tancrede makes, *that he is the most criminal of men, that he is the disgrace of all Nature*, etc., are word for word from Tasso; I did not add a single one, of that I am quite sure. Do verify that, if you would be so good, by referring to Chant XII. In other words, I have not eliminated a single one of them.

Shamefully faithless is bad, I agree with you, but you should know that before I settled on that phrase I tried no fewer than 15 different variants in that one verse, and I came to the conclusion that was the only possible choice, if you agree with me that from the time *of Jean de Meung down to Monsieur de La Harpe* there are no fewer than thirty or forty million verses made solely for rhyming; if, I say, you would be so indulgent as to ponder that thought, you might pardon my most detestable *shamefully faithless*, which I offer because 'tis so devilishly difficult to find a better phrase. I cannot, however, let your condemnation of Tancrede's monologue pass without rebuttal, and I find that:

---

2. A theater critic of the day.

> *Ah! you enrapture me, O fatal illusion*
> *But the better to punish me by your impression.*
> *'Tis to torment me with even greater fury*
> *That you seem to ascribe it to my idolatry,*
> *And you vanish whene'er a joy e'en fairer*
> *Arises for a moment from your somber error,*

are and remain fine verses, verses that are in no wise prosaic.
You also take issue with these:

> *Death, by blackening a beauty so pure,*
> *Would have feared to flout the laws of Nature.*

I have the misfortune of believing that they are among the least poor thoughts that have ever escaped my hand.

The first law of Nature was to give birth to beauty, and that law was so strong, and so necessary, that even Death, the great destroyer who respects nothing, cannot triumph over her: *Death, by blackening a beauty so pure, would have feared, would not have dared, to flout the laws of Nature.*

And that thought is not beautiful! O horse of Pegasus, you next to whom I am but a wretched dropping, inspire me always to other verses of equal force, and I shall not give up the fond hope of one day perching on a comfortable chair, bewigged in-folio, directly beside the *divine La Harpe* and company!

I had thought that *rigidity* was a synonym of *rigor*, and I had also thought I was well versed when it came to words of this kind, for I have for so long associated them with words of art. Since you tell me 'tis not so, then I stand corrected, my dear friend, I believe you and I have substituted *severity* in its place. Do you approve?

You do not approve of *dark* and *gentle*. Nothing more gentle however, and nothing darker, than a beautiful summer's night. Thus, since I wanted to make that sublime comparison, which comes directly from Tasso, I thought I could do so by using the epithets *dark* and *gentle*. You do not accept them: I substituted *pure* for *gentle*, but it makes for a repetition; and yet I find no other word.

You find fault with the following portrait, and yet I find it quite good:

> *Nothing can alter my adorable lover,*
> *And the masculine pride of this soul so bright,*
> *On this radiant brow where worth burns bright*
> *Still mingle the traits of a languishing look.*

I see nothing contradictory in that, and the gentle and pure, or dark, that precedes it, marries well with the following quatrain, it seems to me. You have to bear in mind the context in which those lines occur: a lover always flatters, and, since he is exaggerating, he can be inconsistent. I know from my own experience that a woman such as she did exist, and because I was blinded by love I sang her praises; but today, seeing her for what she really is, I swear I would be unable to so much as pay her a lowly compliment. Nothing cools one's ardor more than the fulfillment of one's desires—nothing, that is, except residence in the Bastille.

There are verses, you say, which do not scan properly. Oh! my dear friend, do not tell me that. I do not claim that my ability to scan impeccably stems from my innate talent but from the fact that I am extremely well organized; so I take no credit therefrom! But I would be physically incapable either of uttering, or hearing, a verse that did not scan properly. Which being so, judge for yourself whether or not I am capable of writing such a verse. Would you like to make me a little wager? You give me one crown for every properly scanned verse I write, and I shall give you a thousand crowns for each verse that is false. Is that a deal? Here is the only verse we might quibble about:

Will you come and join me in your eternal delights?

I do not have my principles of versification in front of me, but I believe I am correct in saying that everyone agrees that *joie* [the French for, in this case, "delights"] and its various rhyming words—*voie* [see], *croie* [believe], *Troie* [Troy], etc., are only two syllables when they occur at the end of a line, but always one syllable when they occur in the body of the verse. This said, I may be mistaken. If people here were not in the habit, every six months or so, of stealing first my books, then my personal papers, I would not make such mistakes, and I would at least profit from being able to consult necessary sources. But 'tis much more fun to drive me to the point of exhaustion and despair, to keep me perpetually in a state of idleness, to make me waste my time.

Nor can I bring myself to agree with you that my verses are prosaic, and I dare say that, from start to finish, the fact of always being alone is a great source of strength.

Moreover, my dear friend, it is impossible for me to turn my back on my muse; it sweeps me along, forces me to write despite myself and, no matter what people may do to try to stop me, there is no way they will ever succeed. I already have stashed away in my portfolio more plays than the most highly regarded contemporary authors do, and the canvasses have been stretched for more than twice what I have actually written. If I had been left to my own devices, I would have had some fifteen plays ready to be performed when I get out of prison. But they have preferred to trick me and torment me to death.

Only the future will tell whether my tormentors were right or wrong. In any event, 'twould be an immense pleasure for me to see my works performed in Paris, and if they were well received, my reputation as a man of wit might possibly make people forget my youthful transgressions and would, in a sense, rehabilitate me. I would devote myself heart and soul to my work, to the exclusion of absolutely everything else. I shall even go so far as to say that is my sole recourse, and the reason is physical: to combat a powerful force one has to be at full strength oneself. But la présidente does not see things that way, for the simple reason that she makes a profession of seeing everything through a false lens. She lives in constant fear that I shall portray her in one of my plays; let me set her mind at rest: I shall leave the *Calibans* of this world to Shakespeare; for whatever reason, they don't go over well in our theater. No matter; she's afraid, and therefore she'll do everything in her power to convince me my talent is nil. In that she is doomed to failure; she will only succeed in making me cherish that talent all the more, simply because she's against it. If in the future circumstances should take me away from Paris—as I wish to God they might—there are four other royal courts in Europe where my works will be greeted with open arms. I shall doubtless establish residence in one of those four countries and there peacefully live out my remaining days, happy in the knowledge that I am no longer breathing the same air as *my life's tormentor*.

You advise me to take up writing history? I have tried: they have thwarted me in that effort,[3] and besides, I don't really have the taste or talent for history. What's more, even the best-written books of history have trouble finding more than two hundred readers, whereas even the least talented comedies manage to attain an audience of three or four thousand souls.

---

3. Because, Sade implies, to write history he would need all sorts of reference works constantly available, and, despite the extent of his personal library, obtaining many tomes he needed or wanted was like pulling teeth.

Please forgive me for such a long letter; but I write you so rarely that when I do I more than make up for it. I embrace you with all my heart. A thousand greetings to Madame de Saint-Germain.

95. *To Madame de Sade*

June 8, 1784

So now the real reason why you have been so terribly overheated, why you have been in such a frightful state each time you have come to see me, is at long last revealed:[1] 'tis because you have come on foot, like some shopkeeper, like some *streetwalking prostitute* . . . And your parents allow that, and your knavish servants make no effort to prevent it! How low can they stoop! What unspeakable conduct on their part! . . . Listen, I have made a vow to myself not to lose my temper, I promised to write this letter with as cool a head as I can . . . Thus I have only one word to say to you, and that is, if ever again you arrive in such a state, I swear to you on all that I hold most sacred in the world that I shall refuse to see you, that I shall return immediately to my room and I shall never again come back downstairs to see you as long as I live. And what is the reason for you to act in such an inexcusable manner? If you truly cared for me at all, would you not make every effort to take care of yourself, would you not sense that my only happiness, my only hope, is to find you in good health when I get out of here? Why do you want to disappoint that sole and dear hope to which I hold so strongly, by so exposing yourself to bodily harm the way you do, by risking your very life? A woman alone, on foot, in the streets? Think of the dangers . . . a drunken man . . . a stone thrown by some street urchin . . . a tile that falls from some roof onto the street . . . the shaft of some carriage that tears loose . . . some other problem I can't foresee . . . Even assuming that none of those dangers actually come to pass: the fact is, you arrive bathed in perspiration in a damp room, you remain there for a good two hours without changing clothes, and then you head home the same way you came. Verily, you must be out of

---

1. Madame de Sade had paid her husband a visit at the Bastille the day before, June 7.

your mind, I mean mad beyond all description, to put yourself thus at risk . . . And have you thought for one moment of the distress it causes me? Isn't my situation difficult enough without your making it even worse by the worry that such foolishness causes me? If you persist in behaving this way, I swear I shall refuse to see you for the rest of my life. Nor do I want to hear you claim that you are doing it *in order to get a bit of exercise.* When a woman such as you needs to get some exercise, all she has to do is go for a stroll in the park: there are enough parks in Paris specifically made for that purpose; and she does not come on foot to pay visits. I shall return the book for which you paid twelve livres; I do not want it bruited about that I am ready and willing to pay twelve livres for books while my wife deprives herself of even the most basic necessities of life. Doubtless that was what you had in mind all along; to raise your esteem in people's eyes, at my expense; 'twas to make people say: *Monsieur spares himself no expense, while Madame is forced to travel about on foot,* and thereby make me look even more ludicrous than I already am. Thank you for that latest kindness; 'tis most touching; I really can't thank you enough. —Ah! there's really no point trying to overcome, by whatever means I can find, the humiliation into which the horror of my fate has forced me, while at the same time, by your own meannesses and odious methods, all you are trying to do is thrust me a hundred times deeper into that state of utter embarrassment. But what precisely do you do with my income, after all? I suppose I cost you roughly two thousand crowns a year: that leaves you with an annual income of twenty-eight thousand livres. What *do* you do with it? Debts have to be dealt with. That I take to mean: *paying off debts according to the rules of Paris,* which translates into, *thirty thousand livres over a period of fifteen years* paid into the hands of *managers, bailiffs, administrators, tutors,* and other rogues and scoundrels of the same ilk, in order to liquidate *sixty thousand* in debts . . . Oh! I know all your mother's little tricks of the trade, as well as those of all the crooks she uses to eat up our nest egg! And that is why madame goes about on foot, so that *Comrade Albaret* can save two or three thousand francs, which fit nicely into her own pocket, thank you. Patience, patience . . . You had better have your accounting books strictly in order, *Ladies* or Gentlemen of the administration, that is my advice to you, for they will have to deal with someone who will be casting an eagle eye upon them. Odious stepmother, mother unworthy to bear that name, to think that you would allow your own daughter to go out and about on foot in weather such as this, expose her to the danger of an inflammation of the lungs simply so that she can further bribe the band of scoundrels who surround and advise her! And you expect me to keep that to myself! You think that I shall not let it be known far and wide as soon as I am in a position to do so! May the prison locks that presently keep me from crying out how urgently these atrocities need to be made known, may they be opened only to let me tell all of Europe how odious her conduct is, and may I be allowed to remain alive so that I may depict her, in the eyes of the entire universe, as *vile* and as *base* as she deserves to be portrayed! To have a hundred thousand crowns of income and allow her daughter to go about on foot! Yes, 'tis to risk her daughter's life; 'tis known and proven that not a day goes by without someone having an accident in the streets of Paris. Who is to say that you will not be the next person to whom such misfortune will befall? In short, I do not want you to come any longer by foot. First and foremost, I forbid you to do so by the prerogatives that are mine as your husband, my tender feelings for you, and *the misfortunes that are mine*. Is that not enough? Well then, I throw myself at your feet in the name of everything you hold most dear in the world and beseech you not to inflict this further sorrow upon me! If it happens again, know both that I shall find out about it, be obliged to disown you, no matter how long and difficult it may be for me to adjust to that situation, and you may be sure that I shall never see you again as long as I live. No excuses, no procrastinations, by saying: Oh! but I live only a stone's throw from here. I couldn't care a fig! Even if you lived literally in the shadow of the Bastille, I would forbid you to come and see me on foot. If 'tis the expenses I'm incurring that bother you, and if we are both obliged to cut all our expense to the bone in order to pay off *the scoundrels in your mother's entourage*, then so be it. Do let me know, and I shall take *upon myself* whatever steps are required, assume whatever hardships are necessary, I shall do without everything, I shall eat only bread and sleep upon the bare floor, providing you lack for nothing. The next time you come, I forbid you to bring me anything. And 'tis not only when you're paying me a visit that you come by foot, since you mentioned that one day you ran into *Aldonze*.[2] That proves you go out frequently. Mark thee well, I strictly forbid you to do that ever

2. Probably a code name. *Aldonze*, or *Aldonse*, is an old Provençal name that the Count de Sade had wanted as the second name for his son. However, the parish priest at Saint-Sulpice in Paris, unfamiliar with the Provençal name, wrote Alphonse on the birth certificate.

again, and bear in mind that there is no way you can wound me more than to repeat those same despicable acts and stupidities such as the one you have just made.

Please give the enclosed letter to Agatha.[3]

I beseech you, please reassure me and put my mind at ease; do let me know that you swear you will never again come on foot.

[Letter enclosed]

To Madame Le Faure,

I was much reassured to learn, Mademoiselle, that you were in my wife's service, and I flattered myself that since you had long been attached to her there was no danger she would do anything stupid or imprudent so long as you were there. But what I have learned revolts me, and I hope and trust you are thoroughly aware that I shall never forgive you for having allowed her to go [through Paris] on foot. Whenever she has need to go out, and her mother is so *vile* and so *loathsome* as to not provide her forthwith with her best horse-drawn carriage available, I ask that you order La Jeunesse to go out and fetch for her the best and the handiest he can find on such short notice, even though she might need it for only an hour; and starting today, June 8, the date of this request, if I learn that you have failed to comply with this request, I give you my word of honor that as soon as I am able to, my first concern will be to put my wife into the hands of someone who knows better how to take of her than you obviously do.

I send you my greetings.

---

3. Madame Le Faure for many years had been in Madame de Sade's service.

96. *To Madame de Sade*

THE SUBLIME REASONING OF MADAME CORDIER, WIFE OF THE PRESIDING JUDGE OF THE SAME NAME

September 4, 1784

'*T*is a good six months now that they have been driving my son-in-law to distraction with mere trifles: *they've blinded him in one eye, they've lied to him, they've only rarely let him out for walks in the fresh air.* All of that is nothing; I'm reaping no enjoyment from it, my belly is bloated, I have trouble digesting my food, I toss and turn all night. Enough, O ye torturer! Draw nigh, and do a better job of tormenting my son-in-law, I beg of you.

THE TORTURER
OR THE FORMER BODYGUARD DE LOSME

But Madame, he is behaving like an angel. What the devil do you want us to do to him?

MADAME CORDIER

You rascal, you! What do you think I'm paying you for, to sing his praises? What do I care whether he's behaving properly or improperly? If you cannot focus on his faults or shortcomings, then punish him for his virtues. Are you completely ignorant of the art of making scenes, of settings traps? Isn't that what I'm paying you for? My son-in-law's sentiments are tainted with a streak of nobility? then treat him impudently, and he'll respond to the bait by telling you to go f——off: when he does, they'll confine him to his room; consequently, no more walks. And then, think of him as having a *noble streak in him,* with me who is nothing but *noble!* —My son-in-law is extremely well organized; he doesn't like to throw money out of the window. Make him pay 28 livres, seventeen sous for an object that is really worth six livres. I shall split the profit with you. He'll protest, he'll claim that he's being made to pay far more for what he buys than what the article is worth: at which point, inform him that *his right to buy* has been suspended, to teach him not to be so profligate. Thus, you can see, you imbecile, since you can't seem to focus on his faults, now he'll be punished for his virtues! And I shall sleep more peacefully, shit better, etc.

And yet that is the way your atrocious mother so basely reasons! And that is the way for the past twelve years that abominable creature has been leading me down the garden path and sticking her nose in every aspect of my life! And you truly believe that I shall not take my revenge? And you fancy for a moment that the word *free* will make me forget everything that's been done to me? If that were ever to happen, you may judge me the most cowardly and most unworthy of men.

At this season of the year the two foods I need for survival are fresh air and fruit: I see very little difference between slitting my throat or being deprived of those two necessities. The food here is horrible. So long as I had the means to supplement the normal prison fare, I said nothing. But when it reaches a point where I can no longer survive, 'tis time to lodge a complaint. Although asking you about my needs or talking to a stone is more or less the same thing, I nonetheless beg you to make a case for the fact that I cannot live without these two things, and let them shift their harassments to something else if that is possible, because they ought not to focus on a person's basic needs, and for me those two really are. If only you could see the *stinking and absolutely abominable so-called meat* they serve here, you would easily understand that someone who is used to refined food needs to supplement it out of his own money. They can no longer use the pretense that my complaints are based upon the fact that I *steadfastly maintain they are stealing from me,* for I have given a sworn statement to the contrary. Thus if they refuse to let me purchase supplementary food 'tis only because of their own anger and ill temper, especially when you are as prompt to pay as I trust you are. Meanwhile, please be so kind as to take care of the following list:

The list of errands, which if one wishes may be detached from the enclosed letter, that I kindly request my wife to send me without delay.

A basket of fruit containing the following:

peaches	12
nectarines	12
pears	12
bunches of grapes	12

half of which should be ripe and ready to eat, the other half less ripe, in a state to last three or four days;

Two jars of jam;

A dozen Palais-Royal biscuits, six of which souffléd with orange flowers, and two pounds of sugar;

Three packages of night candles.

Please do expedite these shipments; and so that my wife not fall back on the pretense that she has no money to pay for them, I enclose a money order herewith.

I ask the Presiding Judge de Montreuil to pay over to Madame de Sade, his daughter, the sum of two hundred livres, said sum to be deducted from the arrears of her dowry, which I shall settle at the time we make a complete and proper accounting as soon as I am in a position to do so. Done at Paris this fourth of September seventeen hundred and eighty-four.

DE SADE

97. *To Madame de Sade*

[*Late 1784*]

I know full well that *vanille* causes overheating and that one should use *manille*[1] in moderation. But what do you expect? When that is all one has—when one is reduced to these two items for one's source of pleasure! The only thing better I could do would be to deprive myself of everything out of the ordinary. One good hour in the morning for *five manilles*, artistically graduated from 6 to 9, a good half hour in the evening for three more, these last being smaller—no cause for alarm there, I should think; that seems more than reasonable; besides, when that is what you are used to, no one is any the worse the wear for it—and verily it gets the job done. I challenge someone to come up

---

1. As noted, Sade and his wife collaborated to thwart the censors with a private code in their letters. The terms *vanille, manilles* and *prestiges* have been defined earlier, and if this letter is to be believed, Sade often indulged in *manille* several times a day, with the help of the cases (*étuis*) and flasks (*flacons*) that his faithful, ever-adoring wife provided him.

with anything better—and furthermore, I defy anyone to tell me that I haven't learned something from being in Vincennes. What's more, I must say to you that whatever you lose in one area you more than make up for in another, 'tis like the person who is burning down the right side of his house and building it up on the left. For on the side that is not burning—'tis a truly exemplary piece of wisdom, this— sometimes three months in truth, nor is it because the bow is not taut—oh, don't worry, on that score it is everything you could hope for as far as rigidity goes—but the arrow refuses to leave the bow and that is the most exasperating part[2]—because one wants it to leave— lacking an object, one goes slightly crazy—and that doesn't help matters in the least—and 'tis for this reason I tell you that prison is bad, because solitude gives added strength only to ideas, and the disturbance that results therefrom becomes all the greater and ever more urgent.

But I've already made up my mind about the stubborn refusal of this arrow to leave the bow, all the more so because when, ultimately, it does cleave the air—'tis veritably an attack of epilepsy—and no matter what precautions I may take I am quite certain that these convulsions and spasms, not to mention the physical pain, can be heard as far as the Faubourg St. Antoine—you had some inkling of this at La Coste—well, I can tell you 'tis now twice as bad, so you can judge for yourself. In consequence thereof, when you take everything into consideration, there is more ill than good, so I'll stick with my *manille*, which is mild and has none of the above painful side effects. —I wanted to analyze the cause of this fainting spell, and believe that 'tis because of the *extreme thickness*—as if one tried to force cream out of the very narrow neck of a bottle or flask. That *thickness* inflates the vessels and tears them. That being so, the common wisdom is—the arrow ought to leave the bow more often—to which I agree most whole- heartedly—the only problem being, it simply doesn't want to—and to try to hold it back when it doesn't want to leave literally gives me such vapors that I think I'm dying. If I had the means—that is, means other than the *manille* (for the *manille* does not send the arrow flying, either), but if I had those other means which I utilize when I am free, the

---

2. More code words, though easily decipherable: the "arrow" is sperm, the "bow" his penis. Sade is suffering from a sexual dysfunction—and has for many years, according to this letter—where ejaculation is extremely difficult, often resulting in a kind of epileptic fit. It is entirely possible that his wild sexual fantasies are directly related to this dysfunction.

arrow being less recalcitrant and flying more frequently, the crisis of its departure would be neither as violent nor as dangerous—for its danger can be explained by the difficulty of departure. When one wants to enter some place, if the door opens easily you make little effort when you push it; but if the door sticks, the force you must use to open it becomes all the greater, because of the door's resistance. Here, 'tis the same thing: if the arrow were to fly more frequently, 'twould be *more fluid;* and consequently there would be fewer [violent] episodes; and in the reverse situation, *terrible episodes, violent efforts* if the arrow, filled to overflowing because of its excessive long lack of use, is obliged to tear open its quiver as it departs. —Imagine in your mind a rifle, and in its firing chamber is a bullet, the nature of which is that the longer it remains in the gun the larger it grows; if you fire the rifle within a couple of days, the explosion will be relatively light; but if you leave the bullet there for some time, then it will burst the barrel as it exits.

If you have a doctor you trust completely, explain to him everything I have just told you, for I am quite convinced that there is no one on the face of the earth who experiences a crisis such as I do in this situation; in consequence thereof, as soon as I am free I have every intention of consulting a doctor and explaining the whole problem to him—for 'tis quite certain that I am suffering from a physical or congenital defect that other men do not have, a defect that was less apparent when I was younger but which, as I grow older, is going to manifest itself more and more forcefully, and that idea drives me to despair. As soon as I am able to, I absolutely want to straighten this out, and as a result I shall rigorously follow whatever regime the doctor prescribes. Please don't contradict me, saying that 'tis not only a physical problem but a moral one as well, for to that I reply that in here I have tried every possible test—forcing myself to be in total self control as long as I possibly can, and yet when the arrow leaves the bow, I not only lose my head completely but it remains in that state for an even greater length of time because the crisis itself is so long and drawn out, and my convulsions are of a violence that are simply beyond description. Not that I get myself all worked up about all this before it happens; on the contrary, the more my mind is in a state of frenzy the less likely it is that the arrow will leave—and that is something you've seen and witnessed yourself, and surely remember all too well. And the longer the arrow remains unsheathed, the more worked up one becomes—in consequence thereof all the problems of which you're aware. If the arrow refuses to fly, and you try to force it, *horrible vapors;* if you succeed—*a frightful crisis*—and if you don't succeed, one's head is in *a hellish state*. You be the judge of whether I need to consult a doctor and whether or not I am in dire need of taking baths which, I am quite sure, would help alleviate, if not solve, the problem. —Please reply and let me know if you can tell me what you think about all that, and be assured that you have all my most tender feelings.

98.   *To the Author of the News*[1]

July 31, 1785

$\mathcal{S}$ir:
    The public, overwhelmingly in favor of your latest column concerning an article from the Bastille relative to the adventures of the Count de S., would apparently like you to write more about this famous prisoner, and speaking for myself, since I once had the honor of making the gentleman's acquaintance, I would be most appreciative if you could furnish me with further anecdotes regarding his detention. I am sending you by the very next post the details you inquired about, and meanwhile I have the honor of being, Sir, etc.

REPLY

    In response to your request, Monsieur, I shall try to comply by relating to you a rather amusing anecdote that closely parallels the one I alluded to in my last column.
    You have doubtless heard of what is referred to in the Inquisition of Madrid or in our own dungeons of Chatelet as the *prison stool pigeon*. He's a kind of well-paid spy, who is locked up in a cell with some poor wretch the authorities are out to get, and from whom they want to elicit some kind of confession or other. This so-called companion of misfortune insinuates himself into his neighbor's confidence; he sympathizes with him, fills him with some cock and bull story about his

---

1. Although ostensibly addressed to a newspaper columnist, one can presume it was sent to Mme de Sade.

own background, offers him a ray of hope, gains his trust, and since the poor wretch wears his heart on his sleeve, the stool pigeon soon entices him to make the confession he was after. After which, the stool pigeon disappears and the poor wretch is hanged.

That Themis, the goddess of law and justice, is so stupid and barbaric as to stoop to such atrocious measures in order to multiply her victims or entice her lackeys into indulging in such dark and dubious pleasures, is a kind of horror that one can only add to all those others wherewith she constantly and continually befouls both herself and her miserable henchmen; but to add one more repulsive tactic to all the others is scarcely enough to raise an eyebrow: blood is drawn, Themis gulps it down, all methods are good and *valid* providing they do the trick.

But in a royal prison, under the safeguard and protection of the monarch, amongst people who have dedicated their lives to his service, that the snakes of that odious goddess succeed in sending forth their venom as freely as they are wont to do in the filthy nooks and crannies of their own abominable lairs, that is what doubtless strikes one as most surprising, and that indeed is precisely what happened yesterday to the prisoner who was the subject of my most recent article, which I gather you found interesting.

To come to the point, I must first admit that I have a *weakness* for our hero . . . Yes, Monsieur, a weakness! Who after all does not have a weakness? The world is molded out of *weaknesses*, and as our contemporary philosophers are wont to say, 'tis through the world's *weaknesses* that the machine whose job it is to do away with virtue accomplishes its task. There can be no equilibrium without weakness, as we all know. Without Nicolas Cordier,[2] who had the *weakness* to go borrow fifteen thousand francs, his pistol at one's throat; without Guillaume Partiet, who had the *weakness* to steal from the infirm and disabled; without Nicodem d'Evry, who *had the weakness* to have someone shit in his mouth; without Claude de Montreuil, who out of *weakness* slept with his sister and three daughters, the entire universe, which sustains itself only through *weaknesses,* suddenly dragged off into the vast deserts of space, would perhaps be hundreds of millions of miles farther from the sun than it is today.

Be that as it may, the *weakness* of our dear count is not nearly as great. It consists merely of his absolute loathing to have to account to

---

2. Sade is enumerating the weaknesses, or serious shortcomings, of his wife's family.

anyone, and as you can well imagine his torturers have seized upon *that weakness* to further vex and mortify their unhappy patient. But guess to whom they made him accountable? . . . *The prison stool pigeon!* That's right, good Sir, *the stoolie!* As a result, yesterday the count was questioned, sympathized with, comforted, filled with hope, but most of all questioned by his presumed companion-in-misfortune, but since it appears that you know the man, I shall cut my story short and leave it to your imagination to figure out how he behaved and how he responded to that provocation.

Are you not utterly amazed, Monsieur, as am I, that such tactics are used with a man of good common sense? Such shopworn tricks of the trade, such base and vile methods, completely despicable and so unworthy of decent people? But verily, Sir, 'tis not with decent or honorable people we are dealing here but with a troop of out-and-out scoundrels, who have the misfortune of thinking that the count is as stupid as they.

I have the honor of being, Sir, etc.

More to follow.

99. To Commander Sade[1]

[October, 1786]

*M*onsieur de Sade, having found that all the reasons that have been presented to him regarding the preservation of his goods and possessions make all sorts of sense, and having felt, in complete agreement with his uncle, how essential it is that someone be put in charge of this stewardship, hereby declares that no one is more com-

---

1. The marquis's paternal uncle, Richard-Jean-Louis de Sade. A year younger than Sade's father and two years older than the Abbé de Sade, he was a humorless pedant whose holier-than-thou attitude impressed Madame de Montreuil greatly but few others. In 1787 he was appointed Grand Prince of Toulouse. Despite Sade's refusal, the Sade family attained a writ from the Châtelet of Paris granting the commander and the Sade family the right to control the marquis's estates and his children's education.

petent to fulfill this function than the Count de Sade[2] himself, and that the reasons he is being kept in prison are no more compelling than those that render his detention both harmful and hurtful to him, to his wife, and to his children. As a result, he kindly requests that the Commander de Sade set forth in his written report to the minister all the details he included in his requisition explaining both how urgent it is for him to be physically present on his estates and how essential it is that the king's order be lifted, this after so long a detention and because of reasons so compelling, the minister is too fair-minded to refuse Commander de Sade's request. This reply is the last one he will make on this subject. There is no point asking any further for a power of attorney,[3] which he will not grant so long as he remains in prison.

100. To Madame de Sade

November 16, 1786

One cannot refrain from being convinced of Madame de Sade's innate predilection for throwing her money out the window. One had thought her thrifty, but it now becomes apparent that one was wrong, for extreme thriftiness does not consist of depriving oneself of the basics (that is called avarice): it consists of obtaining produce of whatever kind and paying for it at the lowest possible price. That is the only reasonable means of being thrifty; and 'tis most assuredly not that of a woman who simply sends a footman to purchase a bit of Indian ink diluted in charcoal at Dulac's, for which she pays the sum of six livres for a purchase that is worth no more than ten sous. True thriftiness consists of going to buy such things oneself, trying them out on the spot, and buying them only when they have proven to be of top quality. To spare her the problem of going herself, Madame de Sade

---

2. Sade means himself.
3. Earlier that month, two notaries, at the behest of his family, visited Sade in prison and tried to convince him to sign a power of attorney relinquishing his rights to handle his affairs. Sade refused. Sade's letter to his uncle is the result of that demand.

would be so kind as to send her footman to pick up the purchase, return it to Dulac, or ask that he exchange it; in any event, we do not want what you bought. Madame de Sade is thus excused from having to run an errand which nonetheless, this being *female merchandise*, should concern only a lady, and despite her lack of thriftiness and her inferior India ink, her husband embraces her.[1]

A true copy.

101.   To Madame de Sade

November 25, 1786

*T*he Spanish and Portuguese replies are becoming most pressing.[1] It seems to me the simplest thing would be to find and send for a teacher whose native languages they are, ask him those questions, and have him write out the answers, in return for which you should pay him a crown, which is more than he would receive for a lesson that would take him a lot more time and effort. Please, I beg of you, send on those written answers as soon as possible.

102.   To the Staff Officers of the Bastille

[1787 (?)]

*M*onsieur de Sade hereby declares to the staff officers of the Bastille that the governor of this establishment is com-

---

1. In the original letter, the last word is followed by six "bayonets," which are presumably six kisses.
1. Sade was writing his novel *Aline and Valcour*, part of which was set in those two countries. To finish it, he needed answers concerning the geography and mores of both places.

pelling the undersigned to drink a wine that is so adulterated that his stomach is upset by it every day. The undersigned is convinced that 'tis not the king's intention that the governor be allowed to adversely affect the health of those he is in charge of feeding and keeping, and that for the purpose of lining the pockets of either Monsieur de Launay[1] himself or of his underlings.

In consequence, the undersigned kindly asks that the staff officers, whom he knows to be both equitable and honest, step in and mediate on his behalf so that justice may be served in this matter.

103.   *To Madame de Sade*

August 24, 1787

*T*here are some things that give such pleasure one simply cannot find words to express them. One's soul is too moved, too touched; one needs to withdraw into oneself for a moment in order to savor and appreciate fully what one is feeling, which would be lost without that inner contemplation. 'Tis the tale of him who thanks you from the bottom of his heart for the delightful present you have just given him . . .[1] a divine and beloved present that gives rise to feelings which, as they grow and multiply over time, will, despite all those who wish him ill, till he breathes his last sow a thousand flowers, forever budding and blooming anew, on the thorny path of his life.

He embraces you and will thank you far more fully when he has the opportunity of holding you in his arms.

P.S. The portrait, the tortoise-shell frame, everything is lovely, everything appreciated, everything affords an incredible pleasure; and you may rest assured that I would sooner forfeit my life than ever forgo a possession that will remain with me till my dying day

---

1. Commandant of the Bastille.
1. Four days before, Madame de Sade had spent a two-and-a-half-hour visit with her husband, during which she had given him a present of her portrait in a tortoise-shell frame.

104. To Monsieur du Puget, Knight of the Kingdom[1]

[Early October, 1787]

*A*ll things considered, Sir, a letter to Monsieur de Launay such as you have advised me, after everything that that police official takes the liberty of inflicting upon me, strikes me as ill-considered; it would seem to be either an act of submission toward him or a kind of fence-mending vis-à-vis the soldier Miray. The fact is, I flatter myself that you know me well enough to realize that that is the furthest thing from my mind. Truth to tell, 'twould be duplicitous on my part to take that step, and duplicity is a vice I loathe: to implore his forgiveness and feign to be repentant would be devious and hypocritical, when my mind and heart are entirely focused on the best and surest means to avenge myself for all the daily insults these three rogues[2] have visited upon me during my detention here, and to broadcast their infamies the length and breadth of France. I shall succeed in that effort, I hope, and that notion consoles me for everything else. Once again, all this is but one more scene staged by my family, a scene for which that lowlife de Losme was contemptible enough to assume the role of stage director. 'Tis the hundredth such scene, with more to follow before we're through . . . But when we do reach the end, as the proverb has it, he who laughs last laughs best. My fortune and my life, and this I swear to you, will be as nothing to me, except insofar as they enable me to wreak revenge on my torturers and expose them for what they are to the entire country.

Therefore, to have my walks restored, 'tis to Baron de Breteuil, and to you, Sir, that I shall address myself, beseeching you most earnestly to support with all your might my urgent need to get some fresh air, and to see to it that my eyes, which are in dire straits, are taken care of, for if I am deprived of the ability to breathe there is no question but that I shall soon go blind.

---

1. The king's lieutenant-general at the Bastille, Du Puget, liked Sade, and had in fact attended a prison reading of Sade's *Jeanne Laisné or The Siege of Beauvais*, staged in the council hall of the Bastille in the fall of 1787.
2. Monsieur de Launay, Major de Losme–Salbray, and a soldier named Miray who was an aide to the warden were all detested by Sade. Less than two years later, Sade got his revenge. When the Bastille was stormed on July 14, 1789, all three men were dragged out by the mob to the Place de Grève and killed.

I would not presume, Monsieur, to ask you to burden yourself personally with my letter to the minister; I limit myself to asking that you support my request for my walks to be restored.

Together with the enclosed I add another essential request relative to my health, which I most earnestly ask that you support in like manner. During the more than four years that I have been confined here, I have not yet had the opportunity to see a doctor. The condition of my eyes, and the lack of satisfactory care I have had from oculists, absolutely demands that I consult other specialists, and I ask to see a doctor.

Also enclosed is a letter for my wife, which I take the liberty of commending to your care; and in thanking you for the care and attention you have bestowed upon me, and that I deserve only to the degree that my feelings toward you are both warm and heartfelt, in sending you, I say, my most sincere esteem, I dare tell myself that I am infinitely closer to you, kind sir, than your most humble and obedient servant.

DE SADE

This morning you said to me *that I should take but scant notice of people's roots, of where they came from.* That is true, but only when people's virtues blind you to their birth; in which wise, they should even be esteemed far more than those of noble birth, whose lives are useless or completely wasted, who, waving the parchment of their patrimony before the eyes of society, only reveal how great is the difference between themselves and their illustrious forebears. But when the son of a gardener from Vitry (Losme), the son of a ferryman from Avignon (Miray), the son of an overseer of galley slaves (Jourdan), having only recently crawled up out of their muck and dissolution, bring to the positions in which their baseness has placed them naught but the shameless vices of their origins, everything combines to thrust them back down once again—without their so much as being aware of it—into the stinking quagmire which is their native habitat; and their noses, which they have barely managed to raise above the ground, make them look, in my opinion, like some dirty and disgusting toad that is making a momentary effort to emerge from its mire, only to sink down again and merge back into the soil.

O Launay, Losme, and Miray, unworthy comrades of the most amiable, most witty, and most decent of men, look at yourself, all three of you, in this picture and tell me whether in all of Paris there is a mirror that portrays you more true to life.

105. To Madame de Sade

1787

I have an overwhelming desire to scold you: the way in which you ramble on endlessly without making the slightest sense is frightful and, verily, beyond all comprehension. With you, one never knows what to believe, and that is absolutely atrocious. The more I think about it, however, I see 'tis really not astonishing: since we have no longer been together, my pet, you have really come into your own. And yet, I confess, I fail to see what lies behind your behavior, and you are the strangest of women. Do you for a moment fancy that I shall forgive you for all that? You have to know that I am completely embittered because of your behavior. Farewell. This evening I am trying to write, like some animal, like an ass, like some Spanish stallion: thus I bid you good-bye. Do come and see me, I beseech you. Come whenever you like, I shall always be pleased and honored by your visits, and you may be sure that, in spite of all the pain and anguish you cause me, you will be the object of my close embrace, yes, I shall embrace you with all my heart and soul.

106. To Monsieur du Puget, Knight of the Kingdom

1787

*T*omorrow during your visit they have been most kind as to allow this tragedy of Beauvais, which we talked about briefly the other day, to be performed. Will Sir du Puget decline to offer his opinion? The author would be most grateful to have it, but the request is ill-timed, we know . . . To give up an entertaining day for something you know will be boring! I can't conceive how such things come to pass, and I remember clearly that when I was part of the social whirl I used to look upon these invitations as traps, or ambushes . . . to which I asked my doctor to respond and make my excuses.

107. *To Madame de Sade*

[*October, 1788*]

I am greatly disturbed, my dear friend, to be costing you so much money, especially at a time when you are ill; but when I committed to that expenditure I was quite unaware that you were not feeling well: if I had known, I most assuredly would never have made it.

I was sorely mistaken about the cost of my move.[1] The expenditures are considerably more than I had thought; not that I spent any more than was absolutely necessary, and the only item that might be thought of as extravagant cost but one louis; everything else was of basic necessity, and is limited to an old wall hanging, an army cot, and some paper: that is strictly all there is in my room, and yet I am still twenty louis short. Please, my dear friend, do me the favor of seeing to it that they will be ready for me without fail at the end of the month, for everything is virtually finished, 'tis not the time to hold back. If you are at all concerned about my well-being in the context of the wretched situation in which I find myself, have no regrets, for at least I shall be as well off as one can possibly be in prison, and reasonably healthy to boot, which is the most important. I embrace you and beg of you to take care of yourself. You have no idea how much the knowledge that you're not feeling well upsets me, and how much I am distressed to know that, at this very moment, I am the cause of so much trouble and expense.

You must without fail acknowledge receipt of this letter within the next few days, failing which I shall be obliged to ask the officers to inform you of its contents. Adieu. News of your health, I beg of you.

---

1. In September Sade had requested transfer to another cell, number 6 in the same tower, a request that was granted. But any costs involved in the move had to be borne by the prisoner. In addition, because of his obesity and continuing eye problems, he was granted a disabled man of the prison staff to attend to his needs when he was ill and run errands for him, which was an added expense, however modest.

Epilogue

For the eight months between October 1788 and mid-June 1789, Madame de Sade was allowed to visit her husband at the Bastille virtually every week or ten days. Thus there are few if any letters between them during this period. They met in the council room of the prison, always under the watchful eye of a guard, which continued to irritate Sade no end, but he generally managed to control himself, knowing any temper tantrum would curtail or end the visits. Throughout the spring Renée-Pélagie brought him news of the increasing unrest of the city, where worsening food shortages and the seeming indifference of both court and clergy to the people's plight had brought them closer and closer to open rebellion.

On the second day of summer Madame de Sade, bedridden and unable to make her planned visit to the Bastille that day, wrote Gaufridy that she had heard of a meeting held at the Jeu de Paume, during which an "infuriated populace" had demanded that "the damn priests be taken out to the gallows and strung up," adding that some of the local bishops had also been insulted. She doubtless would not have reported the incident to her husband had she been able, for his views of the clergy had not changed, but hers had. Still lodged at the convent of Sainte-Aure, she was increasingly under the influence of her father confessor, who kept reminding her that, approaching fifty as she was, she should soon make peace with God. Her indefatigable mother was working on her just as assiduously, and the combined effort was having its effect. She even hoped, it turned out, that she might convince her husband that he too should make peace with the deity, the priests having assured her that it was never too late, even for one gone so far astray as the marquis. Thus her grave concern about the treatment of the clergy at the hands of the populace was all the more understandable.

In the course of the following week, Madame de Sade was able to inform her husband about the growing unrest in the streets, but inside the fortress he had already noted the heightened preparations: gunpowder had been placed on the tower platforms, the cannons had been loaded, and additional troops had hurriedly been brought in. In the late morning of July 2, as Sade was waiting for a guard to escort him from his cell to his daily exercise walk on the towers, a disabled war veteran named Lossinotte, who roughly a year before had been assigned to help Sade in his housekeeping, arrived to announce that his walk had been canceled. Furious, Sade ordered the man, whom he had described to Major de Losme-Salbray, the second in command at the Bastille, as the "stupidest and most insolent valet I have ever seen," to go back to de Launay, the commandant, and ask him to reverse the decision. When Lossinotte reported back that his request had been denied, Sade seized what some have described a *stovepipe and others as a funnel used for emptying the contents of chamber pots into the moat below, and thrust it through his window bars. With the help of this makeshift megaphone, he began to shout to the people in the street that the prisoners' throats were being slit and urged them to come and save them. At which point guards rushed him, wrestled the "megaphone" from him, and subdued him. The Bastille prison logbook for July 2 duly noted the incident, and de Launay, made understandably nervous by the unrest in the neighborhood, sent a runner to Versailles, armed with a letter to Monsieur de Villedeuil,[1] minister of state, requesting the immediate transfer of Sade. Relating the details of the incident, de Launay wrote:*

> *I have the honor of informing you that, having yesterday been obliged, because of the current circumstances, to revoke the walk that you were kind enough to permit Monsieur de Sade on the towers, at noon he went to his window and began to shout at the top of his lungs—which was heard by everybody who lives in the area as well as by passers by—that the Bastille prisoners' throats were being slit, that they were being assassinated, and that the people should come to their aid. He kept repeating his shouts and loud complaints. This is a time when it seems extremely dangerous to keep this man here, where he will be disruptive to the maintenance of order. I therefore feel bound to recommend, My Lord, that this Prisoner be transferred to Charenton or some similar establishment where he cannot disrupt the order, as he constantly does here. This would be a propitious moment to relieve ourselves of this person, who cannot be controlled and over whom none of the officers has any influence or authority. It is impossible to allow him to exercise on the towers, since the cannons are loaded and to do so would be extremely dangerous. The entire officer corps would be infinitely obliged if you would be kind enough to have Monsieur de Sade promptly transferred.*
>
> DE LAUNAY[2]

For once, French bureaucracy was swift and sure.

That same day, Monsieur de Villedeuil responded, not to de Launay but to Lieutenant Crosne of the Paris police:[3]

---

1. Whose name, perhaps prophetically, literally means "mourning city."
2. Gilbert Lely, *Vie du Marquis de Sade*, rev. ed. (Paris: Au Cercle du Livre Précieux, 1966), Book V, p. 190.
3. Roughly two weeks later, Crosne resigned his post and fled to England. He returned to Paris under the Terror and was arrested, incarcerated at Picpus, and executed on April 28, 1794.

Versailles, July 3, 1789

Enclosed please find the orders of the king. Given the circumstances described in the enclosed letter from M. de Launay, I felt obliged to suggest to his majesty that the Count de Sade be transferred from the Bastille to Charenton. I ask that you be kind enough to expedite this move as quickly and secretly as possible, unless you find a more efficacious manner of remedying this problem, which you are authorized herewith to put into effect immediately.

Please be kind enough to send M. de Launay's letter back to me, indicating what action you have taken in this matter.

DE VILLEDEUIL[4]

At one in the morning of July 4, six men entered Sade's cell, tore him from his bed "naked as a worm" as the prisoner himself described it, hustled him downstairs, and threw him into a waiting carriage. With Inspector Quidor of the Paris police holding a pistol to his throat, he was driven through the dark streets of Paris to Charenton, an insane asylum run by the order of friars known as the Petits Pères, or Brothers of Charity.[5] The Charenton logbook for July 4 reads as follows:

BROTHERS OF CHARITY CHARENTON ASYLUM—*His lordship the Count de Sade (Louis, Aldonce, Donatien). Order of July 3, 1789. Period— without limit. Deprived of his liberty since 1777, at the request of his family, following a criminal trial on a charge of poisoning and sodomy, of which crimes he was subsequently found innocent, and further because of his extreme immorality, indulging in a great deal of debauchery coupled with periods of insanity, which make his family fearful that in one of his attacks he may disgrace them.*

Though originally an asylum for the mentally ill, Charenton had over the previous century allowed itself to become as well a veritable prison for perfectly sane people held under lettres de cachet. One of Sade's contemporaries was quick to deplore that subtle but meaningful evolution, praising the order's care but adding that he was most upset to see the Brothers of Charity's hospitals turned into "little Bastilles."

---

4. Lely, *op. cit.*, p. 192.
5. Founded under Louis XIV through the benevolence of one of the king's advisers, Sébastien Leblanc, who bequeathed most of his fortune to the order in 1670 on the condition it be used to care for the indigent ill.

Sade himself was more harsh. He described the place as "a dark building buried in the earth up to its roof, a horrid place so arranged that air can never reach the interior, and the sobs and screams of the prisoners cannot be heard by any except for seven or eight jailers." And, he added, as for the Brothers of Charity, here were the grounds for becoming one: laziness, baseness, a taste for the dissolute, lust, gluttony, or the need to flee a world in which one had dishonored oneself.[6]

But Sade had more immediate concerns than the dismal nature of his new surroundings. The day of his departure from the Bastille, his cell there had been sealed by order of Monsieur Chenon, commissaire of the Chatelet district. Sade desperately needed to regain his possessions, especially his precious manuscripts, "fifteen volumes in all ready for the printer," the fruit of his past ten years' efforts. He signed a power of attorney to his wife giving her the authority to break the seals, in the presence of Commissaire Chenon, and reclaim his manuscripts, books, furniture, and portraits. There is some question as to the date he signed that power of attorney: Lely has it July 9, but a document recently discovered by the historian Robert Darnton, which is Monsieur Le Noir's account, places it at the 13th. The difference may seem slight but in fact is crucial, for Sade accused his wife of gross negligence in not acting more swiftly, which might be justifiable if she had received the document on the 9th. If it was the 13th, however, she actually would have acted quite expeditiously, for promptly on the morning of the 14th she went to see Commissaire Chenon, their plan being to proceed forthwith to the Bastille. But fortunately for both, an insurrection broke out in Chenon's part of town and he was compelled to remain at his post throughout the day. Had they gone to the fortress earlier, they might have been caught there by the storming masses, who sacked and pillaged Sade's cell.[7]

Five days later, doubtless realizing that whatever extenuating circumstances there might be, she would be blamed for the irreparable loss by her irascible husband, the marquise wrote Chenon disclaiming any further responsibility in the matter and asking him to recoup and dispose of the cell's contents however he saw fit, asking however that he do his best to make sure the papers and effects were not seen by all and sundry, since, she said, "I have personal reasons for wishing not to be burdened with them."

Foremost among the papers was the manuscript of The 120 Days of Sodom, which Sade had composed, on the basis of some earlier sketches, over

---

6. From the Sade family archives. Cited in Maurice Lever, A Biography, p. 351.
7. Actually, Chenon was assaulted the following day in the gardens of the Palais Royal by a roving group of men and women on the lookout for any prey. They tried to hang him from a nearby tree but finally let him go.

a roughly five-week period commencing October 22, 1785. Fully aware of the dangerous and inflammatory nature of the work, Sade made care to work on it only in the evening, from 7 to 10 P.M., when there was the least chance of a guard's interruption. For further security, he wrote the work on very thin pieces of paper, each less than five inches wide, in a minuscule hand. As soon as he had completed one sheet, he pasted it to another, until at the end of twenty days he had completed one side, which was over thirty-nine feet long. At that point he turned it over and wrote the balance on the other side, finishing the work on November 28. The virtue of the format was that it could be rolled into a tight scroll, which he could easily conceal between the stones of his cell. And now it was gone. Lely rightly suggests that it was doubtless especially over this lost manuscript that Sade shed "tears of blood," as he later described it.

In a sense, Justine, Juliette, Philosophy in the Bedroom, *and* La Nouvelle Justine *were Sade's efforts during his early post-prison years to reconstitute* The 120 Days of Sodom, *which he assumed lost forever. But miraculously it was not. As we noted in our introduction to that work's first English-language publication well over thirty years ago:*

> *Though Sade would never know it, the precious roll had not been destroyed. It was found, in the same cell of the Bastille where Sade had been kept prisoner, by one Arnoux de Saint-Maximin, and thence came into the possession of the Villeneuve-Trans family, in whose care it remained for three generations. At the turn of the present century, it was sold to a German collector, and in 1904 it was published by the German psychiatrist, Dr. Iwan Bloch, under the pseudonym of Eugène Dühren. Bloch justified his publishing the work by its "scientific importance . . . to doctors, jurists, and anthropologists," pointing out in his notes the "amazing analogies" between cases cited by Sade and those recorded a century later by Krafft-Ebing. Bloch's text, however, as Lely notes, is replete with "thousands of errors" which hopelessly denature and distort it.*
>
> *After Bloch's death, the manuscript remained in Germany until 1929, when Maurice Heine, at the behest of the Viscount Charles de***, went to Berlin to acquire it. From 1931 to 1935, Heine's masterful and authoritative text of the work appeared in three quarto volumes, in what must be considered the original edition of the work.*[8]

---

8. Marquis de Sade, *The 120 Days of Sodom and Other Writings*, compiled and translated by Austryn Wainhouse and Richard Seaver (New York: Grove Press, 1966), p. 186.

In those early days at Charenton, Sade must have sorely regretted his impetuous act of July 2, for in all likelihood he would have been freed when the Bastille was stormed twelve days later. Still, he could take some solace from the news that Bastille commandant de Launay, as well as Major de Losme-Salbray and the aide Miray—all of whom Sade loathed—had been hauled from the fortress to the Place de Grève and there slaughtered. That did not, however, make up for the loss of his papers. And meanwhile, there he was, still imprisoned under a lettre de cachet, *for an indeterminate period.*

But the hated lettres de cachet *were under fire, especially the so-called familial ones, whereby people could have family members incarcerated, often on personal grounds. Days before the revolution, on June 23, 1789, the king himself had come out against them—a trifle late, to be sure, but heads of state throughout history are often painfully slow to act or react to the urgent realities around them. It wasn't until March 16, 1790, that the National Assembly formally abolished the* lettres de cachet, *which the king ratified on March 26. Those imprisoned under such letters, the decree proclaimed, were free to go wherever they pleased.*

A week before, on March 18, Sade's two sons, who had not seen their father for fifteen years, went to Charenton to inform him personally of the decree; exceptionally, the three were allowed to walk freely about the grounds and have dinner together unsupervised. When they informed their grandmother of the visit, she responded, perhaps sincerely, that she hoped he would be happy but doubted he had the capacity for happiness. To her confidant Gaufridy, however, to whom she passed on the news five days later that his favorite client might soon be free, she mused whether there might be a loophole in the decree, whether families might still take it unto themselves to keep their loved ones imprisoned by some sort of personal lettre de cachet. *Opting for caution in those troubled times, however, Madame de Montreuil decided to remain neutral. That way, she figured, if events turned sour (read: if Sade decided to avenge himself), it would be difficult for anyone to blame her. "Whatever happens," she wrote, "one would have nothing to explain."*

Exactly ten days later, on April 2, a Good Friday, Sade left Charenton a free man, after thirteen long years of impossible incarceration. He left, as he describes it, "with only one louis in my pocket," wearing a waistcoat and no breeches—breeches being the mark of aristocracy. He first went to Sainte-Aure and asked to see his wife, but was coldly rebuffed. As for former friends, most had fled Paris if not the country. He then decided to try Monsieur de Milly, a procurator at the Chatelet court, who was now retired but had formerly handled Sade's affairs in Paris. Monsieur de Milly received him warmly, offered him temporary room and board, and lent him six louis, enough to keep him for a week or so. Four days later, Sade moved to the Hotel du Bouloir, a stone's throw from de Milly's house and hard by the Place des Victoires, the spot where all his trouble had begun, for it was there, exactly twenty-two years before, he had propositioned Rose Keller on April 3, Easter Sunday.

But Rose Keller was the farthest thing from Sade's mind at that point. Money was foremost in his thoughts, and for the moment the only place he could get it was, ironically, from la présidente. On April 12, Sade boldly approached her, and doubtless to his surprise she lent him a few louis, with the admonition however that he write Gaufridy immediately and obtain money to pay her back and have the wherewithal to fend for himself. It was made clear that he should not try her again. But Sade had already written Gaufridy the fourth day after his release, while he was still at Monsieur de Milly's, asking for money and also informing the lawyer that he had petitioned the Paris court to restore him his civil rights. Since the petition was bound to be granted, Sade informed Gaufridy in that same letter that from now on, "I and I alone am now in charge of administering my affairs, I alone will decide how they are to be managed. Therefore, from now on you will deal only with me."

Having not heard back for a week, on April 12 he urgently wrote again:

108. To Monsieur Gaufridy

April 12, 1790

I came out of Charenton (to which I had been transferred from the Bastille) on Good Friday. The better the day the better the deed! Yes, my good friend, 'twas that day I regained my freedom; as a result, I have decided to celebrate it as a holiday for the rest of my life, and instead of those concerts, those frivolous walking parades that custom has irreligiously sanctified at that time of year when we ought to be moaning and weeping, instead, I say, of all those mundane vanities, whenever the forty-fifth day after Ash Wednesday brings us to another Good Friday, you shall see me get down on my knees, pray, resolve to mend my ways, and keep to those resolutions.

Now to the facts, my dear lawyer, for I can see that you are about to echo what everybody is telling me: *'tis not talk we want, sir, but facts*— to the facts then: the facts are that I landed in the middle of Paris with only one louis in my pocket, not knowing where to go, where to lodge, where to dine, where to find myself any money. Monsieur de Milly, procurator at the Châtelet, who has been looking after my interests in this part of the country for twenty-six years, was kind enough to offer me his bed, some board, and six louis. Not wanting to overstay my welcome or become a burden, I had set forth after four days at M. de Milly's with only three louis left of the original six to fend for myself, to find an inn in which to stay, a domestic, a tailor, my meals, etc., all that with three louis.

Given my circumstances, I asked la présidente de Montreuil to ask her notary to advance me three louis, on condition that I write you immediately in order to reimburse the borrowed sum and second to remain alive—a request that the lady graciously accorded. Therefore, my good lawyer, I beseech you to dispatch to me without any delay whatsoever the preliminary sum of 1,000 crowns, the same sum I asked you for the other day, and whereof my need is no less extreme than the promptitude of your response is essential.

Letter 109.   To Monsieur Gaufridy

[Early May, 1790]

I have just this moment received your letter of the fourteenth: since it arrives too soon to be in answer to mine, I shall overcome my disappointment at not encountering here one of those charming notes which by far outvalue love letters, and with which one obtains money immediately.

You must not doubt that if I did not write to you during my detention, 'twas because I was deprived of the means to do so; I truly cannot forgive you for assuming my silence was due to anything else. I would not have bothered you about business details; in my position what would have been the point? But I would have inquired after your news, I would have given you my own; upon the chains that weighed so heavily upon me we might have dropped a flower or two. But my captors would not allow it; I did venture a letter to you in that vein, it was returned to me, *thrown* back at me, after that I wrote no more. Therefore, my dear lawyer, I repeat it, I cannot forgive you for having doubted my feelings in your regard. We have known one another since childhood, I need not remind you of it; a long-standing friendship made it natural that it be you in whom I placed my trust when long ago I asked you to take on the management of my affairs; what motive could I have had for changing my attitude?[9] It is not your fault I was arrested at La Coste, but mine, I believed I was in safety there and I had no idea what an abominable family I had to contend with. I assume you will understand, that when I speak here of family I am referring only to the Montreuils; you cannot have the faintest idea of the *infernal* and *anthropophagous* manner in which these people have behaved with me. Had I been the last and lowliest of the living, nobody would have dared treat me with the barbarity I have suffered thanks to them; in a word, my eyesight is gone and my chest ruined; for lack of exercise I have become enormously fat, so much so I can scarcely move about; all of my feelings and sensations are extinguished; I have no more taste for anything, no taste for love; the society I so madly missed looks so boring to me today . . . so forlorn and . . . so sad! There are moments when I am moved by a wish to join the Trappists, and I cannot guarantee that I may not go off some fine day and vanish altogether, without anyone ever knowing what has become of me. Never have I been such a misanthrope as since I have returned into the midst of men, if in their eyes I have the look of a stranger, they may be quite sure that they have the same effect upon me.

I have kept myself busy during my detention; consider, my dear lawyer, I had fifteen volumes ready for the printer,[10] now that I am at large, hardly a quarter of those manuscripts remains to me. Through unpardonable thoughtlessness, Madame de Sade allowed some of them to be lost, let others be seized, and lo and behold thirteen years of toil gone for naught! Three-quarters of these writings had remained behind in my room at the Bastille; on the fourth of July, I was removed from there to Charenton; on the fourteenth the Bastille was stormed, overrun, and my manuscripts, six hundred books I owned, two thousand livres' worth of furniture, precious portraits, the lot is lacerated, burned, carried off, pillaged, without my being able to recover so much as a straw; and all that owing to the sheer negligence of Madame de Sade. She had had ten whole days[11] to retrieve my possessions; she had to know that the

---

9. Sade is wheedling, conveniently forgetting his prison fulminations against Gaufridy, whom he rightly suspected was conniving with Mme de Montreuil. Now, however, he has to be nice; Gaufridy is his sole hope for obtaining money from his estates.
10. Sade is referring to his *Catalogue raisonné des oeuvres de l'auteur,* which he had drawn up in the Bastille on October 1, 1788.
11. As noted, Sade is exaggerating. Obviously her hands were tied until she had his power of attorney on the thirteenth.

Bastille, which over that entire ten-day period they had been cramming with guns, powder, soldiers, was being prepared either for an *attack* or for a *defense*. Why then did she not move quickly to get my possessions out of harm's way? my manuscripts? . . . my manuscripts? . . . my manuscripts over whose loss I am shedding tears of blood! . . . Other beds, tables, chests of drawers can be found, but not ideas. . . . No, my friend, no, I shall never be able to describe to you my despair at their loss, for me it is irreparable. Since then, the sensitive and delicate Madame de Sade refuses to see me. Anyone else would have said: "He is unhappy, we must dry his tears away"; this logic of feelings has not been hers. I have not lost enough, she wishes to ruin me, she is asking for a separation. Through this inconceivable proceeding she is going to justify all the calumnies that have been spewed out against me; she is going to leave her children and me destitute and despised, and all that in order to live, or rather to *vegetate deliciously*, as she puts it, in a convent[12] where some *confessor* is doubtless consoling her, making her see where the path of crime, with all its attendant horror and indignity, is going to take us all. When 'tis my most mortal enemy who has her ear,[13] the advice my wife is receiving could not possibly be worse, nor more disastrous.

You can easily understand, my dear lawyer, that since I shall now have to provide out of my assets for the sums drawn from my wife's dowry (one hundred sixty thousand livres), this separation will be the ruin of me, which is what these monsters are after. Alas, great God! I would have thought that seventeen miserable years, thirteen of them in horrible dungeons, would expiate a few rash follies committed in my youth. You can see how wrong I was, my friend. The rage of Spaniards is never appeased, and this execrable family is Spanish.[14] Thus could Voltaire write in *Alzire: What? You have a Spaniard's look— and you have the capacity to forgive?*

Sade also began to renew old acquaintances, and despite the exodus of many he found several friends and relatives who greeted him warmly: the Countess de Saumane, a couple he had known earlier named Clermont-Tonnerres.[15] He

---

12. Sainte-Aure, where their daughter, Madeleine-Laure, also resides.
13. Madame de Montreuil.
14. That is, the Montreuils.
15. Count Stanislaus de Clermont-Tonnerres (1747–1792) and his wife. The countess was a cousin of Sade's on his mother's side. The count was a moderate reformer in the manner of the English school and one of the founders of the Anti-Jacobin Society. In August of 1792 he became a victim of the Terror.

also decided to mend some family fences, and three weeks after his release he wrote to his aunt, Gabriella-Eléonore de Sade, the abbess of Saint-Benoit in Cavaillon, a town about 15 miles from La Coste.

110. To Gabriella-Eléonore de Sade

April 22, 1790

My dear Aunt:
[...] I would be lacking in my most cherished and sacred duties if I failed to inform you that I have just regained my freedom; all I need for my cup of happiness to be full is to come and embrace you, which I would doubtless do if I were not retained here by urgent business.

'Tis only in your embrace, my dear and amiable aunt, that I can pour forth the frightful sorrows to which I am prey at all hours of the day and night at the hands of the Montreuil family; had they allied themselves to a carter's son they would not have treated him in such a terrible and humiliating fashion. I have wronged them, true, but seventeen years of misfortune, thirteen of which were consecutive, spent in the two most horrible prisons in the realm . . . prisons where I was made to suffer all the torments imaginable; did not this assemblage of tortures and wrongs more than make up for my faults . . . faults of which they are far more culpable than I . . . I assure you that these people are monsters, my dear aunt, and the greatest misfortune of my life is to have become involved with them; in marrying into that family I acquired a whole host of bankrupt cousins, a smattering of twopenny tradesmen, a couple of relations sent to the gallows, and all that without any protection, without a friend, not to mention an honest soul; now that they cannot keep me in prison, these scoundrels are working together to bring about my ruin—they are doing their level best to separate my wife from me, and since in the early days of my marriage they encouraged me to draw on her dowry, I shall now have to pay it back, which will be my ruin.[16] I shall scarcely have enough to live on and I,

---

16. The amount Sade would be made to repay came to over 160,000 livres. Later on, Madame de Sade made an arrangement, ratified by the count, to allow her ex-husband to pay her only the interest on that sum annually.

who married only to have the assurance that my house would be filled in my old age, here I am bereft, abandoned, and isolated, reduced to the same sad fate that befell my father in his declining years, the very situation that I always feared the most.

Not one of those scurvy rogues—except for my children, about whom I have nothing but good to say—not a single one, I say, has extended a helping hand. When I left prison I found myself in the middle of Paris with only one louis in my pocket, without knowing where I could turn to find room or board, much less someone to lend me a crown when my louis was gone; and when I implored these unspeakable people for help, all I got in return were rebukes and backhanded compliments; the door slammed in my face everywhere, especially by my wife, which is the height of horror; no, no, my dear aunt, never has anyone been treated so shabbily, I say it once again, never has any such thing even been imagined.

I had some furniture, some linen, a great many books, and more than fifteen volumes of my own manuscripts, the fruit of my solitary labor; out of negligence, or rather out of an incomprehensible spitefulness, these frightful people allowed all that to be lost at the time the Bastille was stormed; more, fearing at that time that I might be set free they arranged to have me transferred to another prison; they never wanted me to take my possessions with me; they had my old cell sealed; eight days later the place was stormed, my cell broken into, and I lost everything . . . from the fruit of my fifteen years labor I was able to salvage nothing . . . and all that because of those miserable scoundrels upon whom I trust God will one day take revenge for me.

My dear, good aunt, you whom I have never ceased to adore, a thousand and one pardons for having bored you at such length about my problems, but my heart is so filled with sorrow that 'tis impossible not to confide in someone so good and kind hearted as yourself. I beseech you to write me, to bring me up to date about your health, to let me know that you still have a bit of love for me left in your heart. And I trust you are convinced that there is no one in the world who is as tenderly and respectfully attached to you as I am.

I also ask that you send my fond wishes to all my aunts and cousins who are still with us, and also to Madame de Raousset;[17] if she

---

17. A Provençal relative of Sade's with whom he had quarreled.

still holds any grudge against me I would be grateful if you would do your best to mend relations.

I assure you, my dear aunt, of my most profound respect.

DE SADE

Sade's obvious pleasure at being free was clearly tempered by his wife's refusal to see him and subsequent suit for separation with all the attendant financial stress that move imposed on him. But it was also negatively affected by the strange world into which he emerged.

111. To Monsieur Reinaud

May 19, 1790

[. . .] Essential business to be finished here, and the fear of being strung up on a *democratic* gallows, will keep me here till next spring. Then, that is to say the first days of March, I count on going with my children to Provence. Such are my plans, Monsieur, which I plan to carry out if God and the enemies of the nobility let me live. Apropos of which, do not take me for a fanatic. I assure you that I am completely impartial, angry at seeing my sovereign in irons, overwhelmed by what you gentlemen in the provinces cannot understand, namely that it is impossible for good to be done so long as the monarch's sanctions are constrained by thirty thousand armed bystanders and some twenty cannons, though I have to add I have few regrets about the old regime; obviously it caused me too much grief for me to shed any tears over it. There you have my profession of faith, which I make without fear.

You ask me about the news here; on the one hand, the most important item is that the Assembly today refused to allow the king to have anything to do with war and peace.[18] On the other hand, 'tis the provinces that are causing us the greatest concern; Valence, Montauban, Marseilles are the scenes of horror, where cannibals daily en-

---

18. This letter, begun on May 19, had to have been finished four days later, the Assembly's decree further eroding the king's powers having been signed only on May 22.

act plays in the English manner that make our hair stand on end . . .
Ah! I have been saying for a long time that, speaking for myself, this
gentle and loving *nation*, which had feasted on Marshal Ancre's grilled
buttocks, was only biding its time to be galvanized into action and
show that, forever balanced between savagery and fanaticism, it would
revert to its natural mode at the first opportunity.

But enough of this; we must be prudent in our letters; never has
despotism pried so avidly into private lives as does freedom.

*Renée-Pélagie did sue for divorce, which was granted automatically, since
Sade wisely decided not to contest it. Over the next decade, Sade did his best
to accommodate to this puzzling, dangerous, and fast-evolving post-
revolutionary world into which he had emerged. Despite his protestations of
patriotism, however, and despite a number of fiery pamphlets he penned for his
revolutionary section, Citizen Sade's heart was simply not in it. In the early
1790s, money was becoming only a fraction of face value, so even when
Gaufridy performed, Sade often went to bed without any supper. Worse, his estates in Provence—La Coste, Saumane, and Mazan—the source of his spo-
radic income, were sacked and pillaged by the local populace, bringing Sade,
as he expressed it to Gaufridy, "to the brink of suicide." It was little consolation to him to learn that the other mansions and châteaux of the region were
also being ransacked.*

*Though Renée-Pélagie's door at Saint-Aure remained steadfastly closed
to him, Sade did see his children. He was proud and fond of the boys and even
of his daughter, now nineteen, though he had to admit the young lady's future
doubtless lay best in the convent where she was currently lodged with her
mother. In a letter of August 18, 1790, to Gaufridy, Sade notes without em-
bellishment:*

> *I assure you that mademoiselle my daughter is as ugly as I painted her
> to you. I have seen her three or four times; I have examined her very
> carefully, and I can assure you that both in mind and body she is little
> more than a plump country lass. She is staying with her mother who, I
> can assure you, imparts neither manners nor wit to her. As far as that
> goes, she is very well-off where she is, seeing what her situation is: in any
> case, what else can be done about it?*[19]

---

19. In his letter of January 15, 1779, from Vincennes to Mlle de Rousset, Sade
had admitted that the young lady, then only seven, was downright ugly.
Clearly the years had not improved her looks.

A week later, Sade took up with a young actress in her late twenties, Marie-Constance Renelle, whose husband, Balthazar Quesnet, had deserted her, leaving her alone with a small child. In November, Sade rented a little house at 20, rue Neuve des Mathurins. Two months later, Marie-Constance, who was nominally if not actually his housekeeper, moved in. Upon learning of Sade's latest adventure with an actress, the lawyer Reinaud, writing from Aix, twitted him about his penchant for actresses, slyly reminding him of La Beauvoisin. Sade was quick to correct him, both about ladies of the theater and about his relations with Marie-Constance:

> *Me, beware of actresses? You may rest assured I shall! All it takes is to know that breed first hand to despise it as it should be despised. Oh! no, no, we are far from the stage here, and nothing is more virtuous than my little setup! First, there is not a mention of love; she is, purely and simply, a kindly, decent bourgoise, sweet and good, with a fair measure of wit. Estranged from her husband, who is in some kind of business in America, she has agreed to take charge of my little home. She lives on the meager pension her husband has left her; I give her room and board. As of now, that is all she gets out of the arrangement.[20]*

For the next twenty-four years, Marie-Constance Quesnet remained Sade's devoted companion—his "angel sent from heaven" as he described her—and he became as devoted to her as she was to him. It would seem that the uncontrollable fire that had once burned inside him all the years had now indeed been, if not extinguished, at least banked. In Marie-Constance, to whom Sade gave the name Sensible*—"Sensitivity"—he seems to have found the person who, at long last, gave him the inner stability he had always lacked.*

If there was stability within, the world outside was increasingly problematic, especially for one of the old aristocracy such as Sade. Robespierre and the Committee for Public Safety were hard at work cleansing the new republic of unwanted souls, often on the flimsiest of charges. Sade trod gingerly through this parlous period, keeping as low a profile as possible, registering himself as a "man of letters," churning out revolutionary pamphlets and letters to cover his tracks, and doggedly pursuing the dream he had had since his days in Vincennes: to see his plays performed. On that front, his success seemed always just around the corner: plays were rejected, others accepted then never performed. On October 22, 1791, one of his plays, Count Oxtiern, *had its premiere at the Molière Theater, which the author proudly reported to Gaufridy a few days*

---

20. Paul Bourdin, *op. cit.*, p. 228–29, cited in Lely, Book V, p. 303.

later. But during that first performance there was a disturbance in the audience—often the case in those newly democratic days—and subsequent performances were canceled.

There were some triumphs, however, notably the publication of his novel, Justine, or The Misfortunes of Virtue,[21] *which appeared in the summer of 1791 through the auspices of the daring, entrepreneurial publisher Girouard. Taking advantage of the new freedom of the press that, as so often happens, flowers in the immediate wake of a revolution then dies aborning,[22] Girouard rightly sensed there was a ready public for such a revolutionary work and not only agreed to publish it but asked the author "to spice it up," which Sade was only too happy to do.[23]*

One of the strangest ironies of Sade's post-prison life occurred two years later. Despite his lukewarm feelings for the revolution in general, and his profound disgust for its excesses, Sade was above all a pragmatist, painfully aware of how precarious his situation was. Registered as a "man of letters," Sade offered his services to his local revolutionary office, the Section des Piques (formerly Vendôme), which welcomed his talents, literacy not being one of the peoples' strong points. His pamphlets were read and applauded publicly, not only in his own section, but often throughout Paris. In April 1793, he was appointed by his section to a special jury investigating the alleged counterfeiting of paper money, an assignment he gleefully reported to Gaufridy:

> *You'll never guess in a hundred years! . . . I'm a* judge! *. . . a prosecuting judge! Who would ever have predicted that, lawyer, who fifteen years ago would ever have predicted that? As you can see, my head is maturing, and I'm becoming wise in my old age . . . So congratulations are in order, and above all make sure to send* the judge *some money, failing which I'll have* you *sentenced to death! Spread the good word about in your part of the world, so that people at long last recognize me as a good patriot, for that, I swear to you, is what I am, heart and soul.[24]*

---

21. Two octavo volumes, bound in leather.
22. Despite that presumed freedom, Girouard prudently decided to put the place of publication as Holland.
23. Girouard paid for his daring three years later when he was executed under the Terror.
24. Lely, *op. cit.*, Book VI, p. 367.

In that same letter Sade imparted to his lawyer an even more startling piece of news. Who had come to see him in his Piques office but the président de Montreuil, begging for help, for the Committees of Surveillance were on the prowl to ferret out recalcitrant aristocrats and dispatch them to the Revolutionary Tribunal. The two men had not seen each other in fifteen years, and one can only imagine the temptation for the ex-prisoner to vent his wrath at his in-laws, especially knowing that the doddering old gentleman before him—Montreuil was then seventy-seven—had been sent by his wife, she doubtless deciding that any help her son-in-law might grant would be more likely if she remained out of sight.

Surprisingly—or was it?—Sade received the président kindly and sat with him for a full hour, chatting and presumably assessing the Montreuils' increasingly precarious position. A word from Sade and the Montreuils, whom Sade characterized to Gaufridy later that year as "my greatest enemies . . . known scoundrels, criminals . . ." would have been arrested and, doubtless, executed. What did this man of so many contradictions do? "I take pity on them," he wrote Gaufridy. "I repay them, for all the harm they have done me, with contempt and indifference." On August 2, Sade placed both their names on a "purification list," thus saving their lives. "That," he informed Gaufridy, "is how I avenge myself."

Later that year Sade, trying constantly to sail with the oft-changing wind, made a major political blunder. The anticlerical wind was blowing strong in the fall of 1793, and Citizen Sade was called again by the Section des Piques not only to draft its petition renouncing all religions save that of liberty, but to read it before the Convention, which he did to considerable applause. A week later, however, Robespierre decreed that the anti-Christian campaign should end, saying that while unpatriotic priests should indeed be punished, that did not mean the suppression of priests or the priesthood.

Whether it was that political gaffe, the new law against relatives of émigrés—which meant Sade, because both his sons fell into that category—or the latest accusation—on December 8, 1793, Sade was arrested, this time the charge being that he had attempted, two years before, to enlist in the Royal Constitutional Guards, on offense punishable by death. Only by bureaucratic chance did he escape the guillotine. After almost a year under prison conditions far worse than those he had suffered at the hands of the monarchy, he was once again set free in October of the following year.

In August 1795, again in the relatively liberal climate following the execution of Robespierre on July 28, 1794, Sade's Aline and Valcour *appeared, and two years later, in late 1797 and early 1798, Sade's huge* The New Justine, or the Misfortunes of Virtue, *followed by the* Story of Juliette, Her

Sister, *was also published. But any pleasure he may have felt at seeing this major segment of his prison writings in print was short lived.*[25] *On March 6, 1801 (5th Vantôse year IX) while Sade was at his new printer, a man named Nicolas Massé, the police arrived and whisked both men off to the local police precinct. Napoleon was now enthroned, and had brought high morality back into power with him. These scandalous works of Sade were, to his mind (he whose campaigns had left hundreds of thousands dead), "outrageous."*

Massé, either to save his own skin or because he had been involved in the police raid to start, denounced the author and was released twenty-four hours later. Ironically, the prison to which Sade was remanded was named Sainte-Pélagie, originally a convent but converted to a prison during the revolution. The following year, on March 14, he was transferred to the Bicêtre Prison. We have a first-hand description of the now almost sixty-two-year-old prisoner by Charles Nodier, who saw him early the morning of his transfer. Commenting on his "enormous obesity, which hindered him from walking," he also noted in the man "vestiges of grace and charm in his manner and language. His tired eyes nonetheless still retained a measure of brilliance and delicacy that glowed from time to time like the last spark of a dying ember."[26]

Roughly a month later, Sade's family convinced the prefect of police to have Sade transferred from the frightful Bicêtre to Charenton, where he would be much more comfortable. The Brothers of Charity no longer administered the asylum, which had become empty in 1795. In 1797 the Directory had ordered it reopened and put Monsieur de Coulmier in charge. The new director, a man of taste and intelligence, was assured in a letter from his new patient that, once there, he would be "deserving of the director's approval . . . and would do his best to convince him that all the low opinions he may have heard about him were groundless."

Shortly, Marie-Constance sought and received permission to join Sade at Charenton. She, as well as Sade himself, petitioned the authorities a dozen times over the next few years, asking that he be set free, to no avail.

Sade found some solace in his last years, convincing Monsieur de Coulmier of the therapeutic value of drama for the inmates. Thus he became a kind of Charenton theater director, rehearsing and putting on plays, including (proudly) some of his own, giving elocution and acting lessons, and sometimes performing. Hearing of which, the authorities once again tried to suppress this curious liberal therapy, but Monsieur de Coulmier argued on its behalf, and prevailed.

---

25. Not bearing his name, however; that would have been far too dangerous.
26. Lely, *op. cit.*, Book VII, p. 543.

As for his nemesis, the woman he had most loathed and detested, on whom he had promised in dozens of his prison letters to take revenge the minute he was free, he not only never did but, as noted, saved her life and that of her husband under the Terror—at great risk to his own, one might add. There is no record that Sade and la présidente ever met after 1790. Monsieur de Montreuil died on January 15, 1795, two years after his visit to his son-in-law at the Section des Piques. The présidente survived him by six years. If Sade took note of her passing, there is no record of it.

Renée-Pélagie, blind for several years and like her husband exceedingly obese, died on July 7, 1810, at the age of 69, and was buried in the village cemetery at the family home, the Château d'Echaffour in Normandy, without ever having laid eyes on her husband again. A year earlier, Lieutenant Louis-Marie de Sade, who had distinguished himself in the emperor's army, was killed in Italy. Sade's younger son, Claude-Armand, a mirthless, timorous man who, like his maternal grandmother, was deathly afraid of scandal, turned several of his father's manuscripts over to the authorities, knowing they would be burned. As for Madeleine-Laure, she lived to the age of seventy-three. When she died on January 8, 1844, she was buried next to her mother at the Château d'Echaffour. On their gravestone is inscribed: "Both as virtuous as they were benevolent."

Sade himself remained incarcerated at Charenton until his death on the night of November 11, 1814, attended only by the medical student, L. J. Ramon. Of his seventy-four long and tortured years, this "freest of men" spent more than half his adult life—over thirty years—behind bars.